Python for Data Analysis

Data Wrangling with pandas,
NumPy, and Jupyter

Wes McKinney

Beijing · Boston · Farnham · Sebastopol · Tokyo

Python for Data Analysis

by Wes McKinney

Published by O'Reilly Media, Inc., 1005 Gravenstein Highway North, Sebastopol, CA 95472.

O'Reilly books may be purchased for educational, business, or sales promotional use. Online editions are also available for most titles (*http://oreilly.com*). For more information, contact our corporate/institutional sales department: 800-998-9938 or *corporate@oreilly.com*.

Acquisitions Editor: Jessica Haberman	**Indexer:** Sue Klefstad
Development Editor: Angela Rufino	**Interior Designer:** David Futato
Production Editor: Christopher Faucher	**Cover Designer:** Karen Montgomery
Copyeditor: Sonia Saruba	**Illustrator:** Kate Dullea
Proofreader: Piper Editorial Consulting, LLC	

October 2012:	First Edition
October 2017:	Second Edition
August 2022:	Third Edition

Revision History for the Third Edition

2022-08-12: First Release

See *https://www.oreilly.com/catalog/errata.csp?isbn=0636920519829* for release details.

978-1-098-10403-0

[LSI]

Table of Contents

Preface

The first edition of this book was published in 2012, during a time when open source data analysis libraries for Python, especially pandas, were very new and developing rapidly. When the time came to write the second edition in 2016 and 2017, I needed to update the book not only for Python 3.6 (the first edition used Python 2.7) but also for the many changes in pandas that had occurred over the previous five years. Now in 2022, there are fewer Python language changes (we are now at Python 3.10, with 3.11 coming out at the end of 2022), but pandas has continued to evolve.

In this third edition, my goal is to bring the content up to date with current versions of Python, NumPy, pandas, and other projects, while also remaining relatively conservative about discussing newer Python projects that have appeared in the last few years. Since this book has become an important resource for many university courses and working professionals, I will try to avoid topics that are at risk of falling out of date within a year or two. That way paper copies won't be too difficult to follow in 2023 or 2024 or beyond.

A new feature of the third edition is the open access online version hosted on my website at *https://wesmckinney.com/book*, to serve as a resource and convenience for owners of the print and digital editions. I intend to keep the content reasonably up to date there, so if you own the paper book and run into something that doesn't work properly, you should check there for the latest content changes.

Conventions Used in This Book

The following typographical conventions are used in this book:

Italic
> Indicates new terms, URLs, email addresses, filenames, and file extensions.

Constant width

> Used for program listings, as well as within paragraphs to refer to program elements such as variable or function names, databases, data types, environment variables, statements, and keywords.

Constant width bold

> Shows commands or other text that should be typed literally by the user.

Constant width italic

> Shows text that should be replaced with user-supplied values or by values determined by context.

 This element signifies a tip or suggestion.

 This element signifies a general note.

 This element indicates a warning or caution.

Using Code Examples

You can find data files and related material for each chapter in this book's GitHub repository at *https://github.com/wesm/pydata-book*, which is mirrored to Gitee (for those who cannot access GitHub) at *https://gitee.com/wesmckinn/pydata-book*.

This book is here to help you get your job done. In general, if example code is offered with this book, you may use it in your programs and documentation. You do not need to contact us for permission unless you're reproducing a significant portion of the code. For example, writing a program that uses several chunks of code from this book does not require permission. Selling or distributing examples from O'Reilly books does require permission. Answering a question by citing this book and quoting example code does not require permission. Incorporating a significant amount of example code from this book into your product's documentation does require permission.

We appreciate, but do not require, attribution. An attribution usually includes the title, author, publisher, and ISBN. For example: "*Python for Data Analysis* by Wes McKinney (O'Reilly). Copyright 2022 Wes McKinney, 978-1-098-10403-0."

If you feel your use of code examples falls outside fair use or the permission given above, feel free to contact us at *permissions@oreilly.com*.

O'Reilly Online Learning

 For more than 40 years, O'Reilly Media has provided technology and business training, knowledge, and insight to help companies succeed.

Our unique network of experts and innovators share their knowledge and expertise through books, articles, and our online learning platform. O'Reilly's online learning platform gives you on-demand access to live training courses, in-depth learning paths, interactive coding environments, and a vast collection of text and video from O'Reilly and 200+ other publishers. For more information, visit *http://oreilly.com*.

How to Contact Us

Please address comments and questions concerning this book to the publisher:

O'Reilly Media, Inc.
1005 Gravenstein Highway North
Sebastopol, CA 95472
800-998-9938 (in the United States or Canada)
707-829-0515 (international or local)
707-829-0104 (fax)

We have a web page for this book, where we list errata, examples, and any additional information. You can access this page at *https://oreil.ly/python-data-analysis-3e*.

Email *bookquestions@oreilly.com* to comment or ask technical questions about this book.

For news and information about our books and courses, visit *http://oreilly.com*.

Find us on LinkedIn: *https://linkedin.com/company/oreilly-media*.

Follow us on Twitter: *http://twitter.com/oreillymedia*.

Watch us on YouTube: *http://youtube.com/oreillymedia*.

Acknowledgments

This work is the product of many years of fruitful discussions and collaborations with, and assistance from many people around the world. I'd like to thank a few of them.

In Memoriam: John D. Hunter (1968–2012)

Our dear friend and colleague John D. Hunter passed away after a battle with colon cancer on August 28, 2012. This was only a short time after I'd completed the final manuscript for this book's first edition.

John's impact and legacy in the Python scientific and data communities would be hard to overstate. In addition to developing matplotlib in the early 2000s (a time when Python was not nearly so popular), he helped shape the culture of a critical generation of open source developers who've become pillars of the Python ecosystem that we now often take for granted.

I was lucky enough to connect with John early in my open source career in January 2010, just after releasing pandas 0.1. His inspiration and mentorship helped me push forward, even in the darkest of times, with my vision for pandas and Python as a first-class data analysis language.

John was very close with Fernando Pérez and Brian Granger, pioneers of IPython, Jupyter, and many other initiatives in the Python community. We had hoped to work on a book together, the four of us, but I ended up being the one with the most free time. I am sure he would be proud of what we've accomplished, as individuals and as a community, over the last nine years.

Acknowledgments for the Third Edition (2022)

It has more than a decade since I started writing the first edition of this book and more than 15 years since I originally started my journey as a Python prorammer. A lot has changed since then! Python has evolved from a relatively niche language for data analysis to the most popular and most widely used language powering the plurality (if not the majority!) of data science, machine learning, and artificial intelligence work.

I have not been an active contributor to the pandas open source project since 2013, but its worldwide developer community has continued to thrive, serving as a model of community-centric open source software development. Many "next-generation" Python projects that deal with tabular data are modeling their user interfaces directly after pandas, so the project has proved to have an enduring influence on the future trajectory of the Python data science ecosystem.

I hope that this book continues to serve as a valuable resource for students and individuals who want to learn about working with data in Python.

I'm especially thankful to O'Reilly for allowing me to publish an "open access" version of this book on my website at *https://wesmckinney.com/book*, where I hope it will reach even more people and help expand opportunity in the world of data analysis. J.J. Allaire was a lifesaver in making this possible by helping me "port" the book from Docbook XML to Quarto (*https://quarto.org*), a wonderful new scientific and technical publishing system for print and web.

Special thanks to my technical reviewers Paul Barry, Jean-Christophe Leyder, Abdullah Karasan, and William Jamir, whose thorough feedback has greatly improved the readability, clarity, and understandability of the content.

Acknowledgments for the Second Edition (2017)

It has been five years almost to the day since I completed the manuscript for this book's first edition in July 2012. A lot has changed. The Python community has grown immensely, and the ecosystem of open source software around it has flourished.

This new edition of the book would not exist if not for the tireless efforts of the pandas core developers, who have grown the project and its user community into one of the cornerstones of the Python data science ecosystem. These include, but are not limited to, Tom Augspurger, Joris van den Bossche, Chris Bartak, Phillip Cloud, gfyoung, Andy Hayden, Masaaki Horikoshi, Stephan Hoyer, Adam Klein, Wouter Overmeire, Jeff Reback, Chang She, Skipper Seabold, Jeff Tratner, and y-p.

On the actual writing of this second edition, I would like to thank the O'Reilly staff who helped me patiently with the writing process. This includes Marie Beaugureau, Ben Lorica, and Colleen Toporek. I again had outstanding technical reviewers with Tom Augspurger, Paul Barry, Hugh Brown, Jonathan Coe, and Andreas Müller contributing. Thank you.

This book's first edition has been translated into many foreign languages, including Chinese, French, German, Japanese, Korean, and Russian. Translating all this content and making it available to a broader audience is a huge and often thankless effort. Thank you for helping more people in the world learn how to program and use data analysis tools.

I am also lucky to have had support for my continued open source development efforts from Cloudera and Two Sigma Investments over the last few years. With open source software projects more thinly resourced than ever relative to the size of user bases, it is becoming increasingly important for businesses to provide support for development of key open source projects. It's the right thing to do.

Acknowledgments for the First Edition (2012)

It would have been difficult for me to write this book without the support of a large number of people.

On the O'Reilly staff, I'm very grateful for my editors, Meghan Blanchette and Julie Steele, who guided me through the process. Mike Loukides also worked with me in the proposal stages and helped make the book a reality.

I received a wealth of technical review from a large cast of characters. In particular, Martin Blais and Hugh Brown were incredibly helpful in improving the book's examples, clarity, and organization from cover to cover. James Long, Drew Conway, Fernando Pérez, Brian Granger, Thomas Kluyver, Adam Klein, Josh Klein, Chang She, and Stéfan van der Walt each reviewed one or more chapters, providing pointed feedback from many different perspectives.

I got many great ideas for examples and datasets from friends and colleagues in the data community, among them: Mike Dewar, Jeff Hammerbacher, James Johndrow, Kristian Lum, Adam Klein, Hilary Mason, Chang She, and Ashley Williams.

I am of course indebted to the many leaders in the open source scientific Python community who've built the foundation for my development work and gave encouragement while I was writing this book: the IPython core team (Fernando Pérez, Brian Granger, Min Ragan-Kelly, Thomas Kluyver, and others), John Hunter, Skipper Seabold, Travis Oliphant, Peter Wang, Eric Jones, Robert Kern, Josef Perktold, Francesc Alted, Chris Fonnesbeck, and too many others to mention. Several other people provided a great deal of support, ideas, and encouragement along the way: Drew Conway, Sean Taylor, Giuseppe Paleologo, Jared Lander, David Epstein, John Krowas, Joshua Bloom, Den Pilsworth, John Myles-White, and many others I've forgotten.

I'd also like to thank a number of people from my formative years. First, my former AQR colleagues who've cheered me on in my pandas work over the years: Alex Reyfman, Michael Wong, Tim Sargen, Oktay Kurbanov, Matthew Tschantz, Roni Israelov, Michael Katz, Ari Levine, Chris Uga, Prasad Ramanan, Ted Square, and Hoon Kim. Lastly, my academic advisors Haynes Miller (MIT) and Mike West (Duke).

I received significant help from Phillip Cloud and Joris van den Bossche in 2014 to update the book's code examples and fix some other inaccuracies due to changes in pandas.

On the personal side, Casey provided invaluable day-to-day support during the writing process, tolerating my highs and lows as I hacked together the final draft on top of an already overcommitted schedule. Lastly, my parents, Bill and Kim, taught me to always follow my dreams and to never settle for less.

## CHAPTER 1

Preliminaries

1.1 What Is This Book About?

This book is concerned with the nuts and bolts of manipulating, processing, cleaning, and crunching data in Python. My goal is to offer a guide to the parts of the Python programming language and its data-oriented library ecosystem and tools that will equip you to become an effective data analyst. While "data analysis" is in the title of the book, the focus is specifically on Python programming, libraries, and tools as opposed to data analysis methodology. This is the Python programming you need *for* data analysis.

Sometime after I originally published this book in 2012, people started using the term *data science* as an umbrella description for everything from simple descriptive statistics to more advanced statistical analysis and machine learning. The Python open source ecosystem for doing data analysis (or data science) has also expanded significantly since then. There are now many other books which focus specifically on these more advanced methodologies. My hope is that this book serves as adequate preparation to enable you to move on to a more domain-specific resource.

Some might characterize much of the content of the book as "data manipulation" as opposed to "data analysis." We also use the terms *wrangling* or *munging* to refer to data manipulation.

What Kinds of Data?

When I say "data," what am I referring to exactly? The primary focus is on *structured data*, a deliberately vague term that encompasses many different common forms of data, such as:

- Tabular or spreadsheet-like data in which each column may be a different type (string, numeric, date, or otherwise). This includes most kinds of data commonly stored in relational databases or tab- or comma-delimited text files.

- Multidimensional arrays (matrices).

- Multiple tables of data interrelated by key columns (what would be primary or foreign keys for a SQL user).

- Evenly or unevenly spaced time series.

This is by no means a complete list. Even though it may not always be obvious, a large percentage of datasets can be transformed into a structured form that is more suitable for analysis and modeling. If not, it may be possible to extract features from a dataset into a structured form. As an example, a collection of news articles could be processed into a word frequency table, which could then be used to perform sentiment analysis.

Most users of spreadsheet programs like Microsoft Excel, perhaps the most widely used data analysis tool in the world, will not be strangers to these kinds of data.

1.2 Why Python for Data Analysis?

For many people, the Python programming language has strong appeal. Since its first appearance in 1991, Python has become one of the most popular interpreted programming languages, along with Perl, Ruby, and others. Python and Ruby have become especially popular since 2005 or so for building websites using their numerous web frameworks, like Rails (Ruby) and Django (Python). Such languages are often called *scripting* languages, as they can be used to quickly write small programs, or *scripts* to automate other tasks. I don't like the term "scripting languages," as it carries a connotation that they cannot be used for building serious software. Among interpreted languages, for various historical and cultural reasons, Python has developed a large and active scientific computing and data analysis community. In the last 20 years, Python has gone from a bleeding-edge or "at your own risk" scientific computing language to one of the most important languages for data science, machine learning, and general software development in academia and industry.

For data analysis and interactive computing and data visualization, Python will inevitably draw comparisons with other open source and commercial programming languages and tools in wide use, such as R, MATLAB, SAS, Stata, and others. In recent years, Python's improved open source libraries (such as pandas and scikit-learn) have made it a popular choice for data analysis tasks. Combined with Python's overall strength for general-purpose software engineering, it is an excellent option as a primary language for building data applications.

Python as Glue

Part of Python's success in scientific computing is the ease of integrating C, C++, and FORTRAN code. Most modern computing environments share a similar set of legacy FORTRAN and C libraries for doing linear algebra, optimization, integration, fast Fourier transforms, and other such algorithms. The same story has held true for many companies and national labs that have used Python to glue together decades' worth of legacy software.

Many programs consist of small portions of code where most of the time is spent, with large amounts of "glue code" that doesn't run often. In many cases, the execution time of the glue code is insignificant; effort is most fruitfully invested in optimizing the computational bottlenecks, sometimes by moving the code to a lower-level language like C.

Solving the "Two-Language" Problem

In many organizations, it is common to research, prototype, and test new ideas using a more specialized computing language like SAS or R and then later port those ideas to be part of a larger production system written in, say, Java, C#, or C++. What people are increasingly finding is that Python is a suitable language not only for doing research and prototyping but also for building the production systems. Why maintain two development environments when one will suffice? I believe that more and more companies will go down this path, as there are often significant organizational benefits to having both researchers and software engineers using the same set of programming tools.

Over the last decade some new approaches to solving the "two-language" problem have appeared, such as the Julia programming language. Getting the most out of Python in many cases *will* require programming in a low-level language like C or C++ and creating Python bindings to that code. That said, "just-in-time" (JIT) compiler technology provided by libraries like Numba have provided a way to achieve excellent performance in many computational algorithms without having to leave the Python programming environment.

Why Not Python?

While Python is an excellent environment for building many kinds of analytical applications and general-purpose systems, there are a number of uses for which Python may be less suitable.

As Python is an interpreted programming language, in general most Python code will run substantially slower than code written in a compiled language like Java or C++. As *programmer time* is often more valuable than *CPU time*, many are happy to make this trade-off. However, in an application with very low latency or demanding resource utilization requirements (e.g., a high-frequency trading system), the time spent programming in a lower-level (but also lower-productivity) language like C++ to achieve the maximum possible performance might be time well spent.

Python can be a challenging language for building highly concurrent, multithreaded applications, particularly applications with many CPU-bound threads. The reason for this is that it has what is known as the *global interpreter lock* (GIL), a mechanism that prevents the interpreter from executing more than one Python instruction at a time. The technical reasons for why the GIL exists are beyond the scope of this book. While it is true that in many big data processing applications, a cluster of computers may be required to process a dataset in a reasonable amount of time, there are still situations where a single-process, multithreaded system is desirable.

This is not to say that Python cannot execute truly multithreaded, parallel code. Python C extensions that use native multithreading (in C or C++) can run code in parallel without being impacted by the GIL, as long as they do not need to regularly interact with Python objects.

1.3 Essential Python Libraries

For those who are less familiar with the Python data ecosystem and the libraries used throughout the book, I will give a brief overview of some of them.

NumPy

NumPy (*https://numpy.org*), short for Numerical Python, has long been a cornerstone of numerical computing in Python. It provides the data structures, algorithms, and library glue needed for most scientific applications involving numerical data in Python. NumPy contains, among other things:

- A fast and efficient multidimensional array object *ndarray*
- Functions for performing element-wise computations with arrays or mathematical operations between arrays
- Tools for reading and writing array-based datasets to disk
- Linear algebra operations, Fourier transform, and random number generation
- A mature C API to enable Python extensions and native C or C++ code to access NumPy's data structures and computational facilities

Beyond the fast array-processing capabilities that NumPy adds to Python, one of its primary uses in data analysis is as a container for data to be passed between algorithms and libraries. For numerical data, NumPy arrays are more efficient for storing and manipulating data than the other built-in Python data structures. Also, libraries written in a lower-level language, such as C or FORTRAN, can operate on the data stored in a NumPy array without copying data into some other memory representation. Thus, many numerical computing tools for Python either assume NumPy arrays as a primary data structure or else target interoperability with NumPy.

pandas

pandas (*https://pandas.pydata.org*) provides high-level data structures and functions designed to make working with structured or tabular data intuitive and flexible. Since its emergence in 2010, it has helped enable Python to be a powerful and productive data analysis environment. The primary objects in pandas that will be used in this book are the DataFrame, a tabular, column-oriented data structure with both row and column labels, and the Series, a one-dimensional labeled array object.

pandas blends the array-computing ideas of NumPy with the kinds of data manipulation capabilities found in spreadsheets and relational databases (such as SQL). It provides convenient indexing functionality to enable you to reshape, slice and dice, perform aggregations, and select subsets of data. Since data manipulation, preparation, and cleaning are such important skills in data analysis, pandas is one of the primary focuses of this book.

As a bit of background, I started building pandas in early 2008 during my tenure at AQR Capital Management, a quantitative investment management firm. At the time, I had a distinct set of requirements that were not well addressed by any single tool at my disposal:

- Data structures with labeled axes supporting automatic or explicit data alignment—this prevents common errors resulting from misaligned data and working with differently indexed data coming from different sources
- Integrated time series functionality
- The same data structures handle both time series data and non-time series data
- Arithmetic operations and reductions that preserve metadata
- Flexible handling of missing data
- Merge and other relational operations found in popular databases (SQL-based, for example)

I wanted to be able to do all of these things in one place, preferably in a language well suited to general-purpose software development. Python was a good candidate language for this, but at that time an integrated set of data structures and tools providing this functionality did not exist. As a result of having been built initially to solve finance and business analytics problems, pandas features especially deep time series functionality and tools well suited for working with time-indexed data generated by business processes.

I spent a large part of 2011 and 2012 expanding pandas's capabilities with some of my former AQR colleagues, Adam Klein and Chang She. In 2013, I stopped being as involved in day-to-day project development, and pandas has since become a fully community-owned and community-maintained project with well over two thousand unique contributors around the world.

For users of the R language for statistical computing, the DataFrame name will be familiar, as the object was named after the similar R `data.frame` object. Unlike Python, data frames are built into the R programming language and its standard library. As a result, many features found in pandas are typically either part of the R core implementation or provided by add-on packages.

The pandas name itself is derived from *panel data*, an econometrics term for multidimensional structured datasets, and a play on the phrase *Python data analysis*.

matplotlib

matplotlib (*https://matplotlib.org*) is the most popular Python library for producing plots and other two-dimensional data visualizations. It was originally created by John D. Hunter and is now maintained by a large team of developers. It is designed for creating plots suitable for publication. While there are other visualization libraries available to Python programmers, matplotlib is still widely used and integrates reasonably well with the rest of the ecosystem. I think it is a safe choice as a default visualization tool.

IPython and Jupyter

The IPython project (*https://ipython.org*) began in 2001 as Fernando Pérez's side project to make a better interactive Python interpreter. Over the subsequent 20 years it has become one of the most important tools in the modern Python data stack. While it does not provide any computational or data analytical tools by itself, IPython is designed for both interactive computing and software development work. It encourages an *execute-explore* workflow instead of the typical *edit-compile-run* workflow of many other programming languages. It also provides integrated access to your operating system's shell and filesystem; this reduces the need to switch between a terminal window and a Python session in many cases. Since much of data analysis coding involves exploration, trial and error, and iteration, IPython can help you get the job done faster.

In 2014, Fernando and the IPython team announced the Jupyter project (*https://jupyter.org*), a broader initiative to design language-agnostic interactive computing tools. The IPython web notebook became the Jupyter notebook, with support now for over 40 programming languages. The IPython system can now be used as a *kernel* (a programming language mode) for using Python with Jupyter.

IPython itself has become a component of the much broader Jupyter open source project, which provides a productive environment for interactive and exploratory computing. Its oldest and simplest "mode" is as an enhanced Python shell designed to accelerate the writing, testing, and debugging of Python code. You can also use the IPython system through the Jupyter notebook.

The Jupyter notebook system also allows you to author content in Markdown and HTML, providing you a means to create rich documents with code and text.

I personally use IPython and Jupyter regularly in my Python work, whether running, debugging, or testing code.

In the accompanying book materials on GitHub (*https://github.com/wesm/pydata-book*), you will find Jupyter notebooks containing all the code examples from each chapter. If you cannot access GitHub where you are, you can try the mirror on Gitee (*https://gitee.com/wesmckinn/pydata-book*).

SciPy

SciPy (*https://scipy.org*) is a collection of packages addressing a number of foundational problems in scientific computing. Here are some of the tools it contains in its various modules:

`scipy.integrate`
Numerical integration routines and differential equation solvers

`scipy.linalg`
Linear algebra routines and matrix decompositions extending beyond those provided in `numpy.linalg`

`scipy.optimize`
Function optimizers (minimizers) and root finding algorithms

`scipy.signal`
Signal processing tools

`scipy.sparse`
Sparse matrices and sparse linear system solvers

`scipy.special`
Wrapper around SPECFUN, a FORTRAN library implementing many common mathematical functions, such as the `gamma` function

`scipy.stats`
Standard continuous and discrete probability distributions (density functions, samplers, continuous distribution functions), various statistical tests, and more descriptive statistics

Together, NumPy and SciPy form a reasonably complete and mature computational foundation for many traditional scientific computing applications.

scikit-learn

Since the project's inception in 2007, scikit-learn (*https://scikit-learn.org*) has become the premier general-purpose machine learning toolkit for Python programmers. As of this writing, more than two thousand different individuals have contributed code to the project. It includes submodules for such models as:

- Classification: SVM, nearest neighbors, random forest, logistic regression, etc.
- Regression: Lasso, ridge regression, etc.
- Clustering: *k*-means, spectral clustering, etc.
- Dimensionality reduction: PCA, feature selection, matrix factorization, etc.
- Model selection: Grid search, cross-validation, metrics
- Preprocessing: Feature extraction, normalization

Along with pandas, statsmodels, and IPython, scikit-learn has been critical for enabling Python to be a productive data science programming language. While I won't be able to include a comprehensive guide to scikit-learn in this book, I will give a brief introduction to some of its models and how to use them with the other tools presented in the book.

statsmodels

statsmodels (*https://statsmodels.org*) is a statistical analysis package that was seeded by work from Stanford University statistics professor Jonathan Taylor, who implemented a number of regression analysis models popular in the R programming language. Skipper Seabold and Josef Perktold formally created the new statsmodels project in 2010 and since then have grown the project to a critical mass of engaged users and contributors. Nathaniel Smith developed the Patsy project, which provides a formula or model specification framework for statsmodels inspired by R's formula system.

Compared with scikit-learn, statsmodels contains algorithms for classical (primarily frequentist) statistics and econometrics. This includes such submodules as:

- Regression models: linear regression, generalized linear models, robust linear models, linear mixed effects models, etc.
- Analysis of variance (ANOVA)
- Time series analysis: AR, ARMA, ARIMA, VAR, and other models
- Nonparametric methods: Kernel density estimation, kernel regression

- Visualization of statistical model results

statsmodels is more focused on statistical inference, providing uncertainty estimates and p-values for parameters. scikit-learn, by contrast, is more prediction focused.

As with scikit-learn, I will give a brief introduction to statsmodels and how to use it with NumPy and pandas.

Other Packages

In 2022, there are many other Python libraries which might be discussed in a book about data science. This includes some newer projects like TensorFlow or PyTorch, which have become popular for machine learning or artificial intelligence work. Now that there are other books out there that focus more specifically on those projects, I would recommend using this book to build a foundation in general-purpose Python data wrangling. Then, you should be well prepared to move on to a more advanced resource that may assume a certain level of expertise.

1.4 Installation and Setup

Since everyone uses Python for different applications, there is no single solution for setting up Python and obtaining the necessary add-on packages. Many readers will not have a complete Python development environment suitable for following along with this book, so here I will give detailed instructions to get set up on each operating system. I will be using Miniconda, a minimal installation of the conda package manager, along with conda-forge (*https://conda-forge.org*), a community-maintained software distribution based on conda. This book uses Python 3.10 throughout, but if you're reading in the future, you are welcome to install a newer version of Python.

If for some reason these instructions become out-of-date by the time you are reading this, you can check out my website for the book (*https://wesmckinney.com/book*) which I will endeavor to keep up to date with the latest installation instructions.

Miniconda on Windows

To get started on Windows, download the Miniconda installer for the latest Python version available (currently 3.9) from *https://conda.io*. I recommend following the installation instructions for Windows available on the conda website, which may have changed between the time this book was published and when you are reading this. Most people will want the 64-bit version, but if that doesn't run on your Windows machine, you can install the 32-bit version instead.

When prompted whether to install for just yourself or for all users on your system, choose the option that's most appropriate for you. Installing just for yourself will be sufficient to follow along with the book. It will also ask you whether you want to add Miniconda to the system PATH environment variable. If you select this (I usually do), then this Miniconda installation may override other versions of Python you have installed. If you do not, then you will need to use the Window Start menu shortcut that's installed to be able to use this Miniconda. This Start menu entry may be called "Anaconda3 (64-bit)."

I'll assume that you haven't added Miniconda to your system PATH. To verify that things are configured correctly, open the "Anaconda Prompt (Miniconda3)" entry under "Anaconda3 (64-bit)" in the Start menu. Then try launching the Python interpreter by typing **python**. You should see a message like this:

```
(base) C:\Users\Wes>python
Python 3.9 [MSC v.1916 64 bit (AMD64)] :: Anaconda, Inc. on win32
Type "help", "copyright", "credits" or "license" for more information.
>>>
```

To exit the Python shell, type **exit()** and press Enter.

GNU/Linux

Linux details will vary a bit depending on your Linux distribution type, but here I give details for such distributions as Debian, Ubuntu, CentOS, and Fedora. Setup is similar to macOS with the exception of how Miniconda is installed. Most readers will want to download the default 64-bit installer file, which is for x86 architecture (but it's possible in the future more users will have aarch64-based Linux machines). The installer is a shell script that must be executed in the terminal. You will then have a file named something similar to *Miniconda3-latest-Linux-x86_64.sh*. To install it, execute this script with `bash`:

```
$ bash Miniconda3-latest-Linux-x86_64.sh
```

 Some Linux distributions have all the required Python packages (although outdated versions, in some cases) in their package managers and can be installed using a tool like apt. The setup described here uses Miniconda, as it's both easily reproducible across distributions and simpler to upgrade packages to their latest versions.

You will have a choice of where to put the Miniconda files. I recommend installing the files in the default location in your home directory; for example, */home/$USER/ miniconda* (with your username, naturally).

The installer will ask if you wish to modify your shell scripts to automatically activate Miniconda. I recommend doing this (select "yes") as a matter of convenience.

After completing the installation, start a new terminal process and verify that you are picking up the new Miniconda installation:

```
(base) $ python
Python 3.9 | (main) [GCC 10.3.0] on linux
Type "help", "copyright", "credits" or "license" for more information.
>>>
```

To exit the Python shell, type **exit()** and press Enter or press Ctrl-D.

Miniconda on macOS

Download the macOS Miniconda installer, which should be named something like *Miniconda3-latest-MacOSX-arm64.sh* for Apple Silicon-based macOS computers released from 2020 onward, or *Miniconda3-latest-MacOSX-x86_64.sh* for Intel-based Macs released before 2020. Open the Terminal application in macOS, and install by executing the installer (most likely in your Downloads directory) with bash:

```
$ bash $HOME/Downloads/Miniconda3-latest-MacOSX-arm64.sh
```

When the installer runs, by default it automatically configures Miniconda in your default shell environment in your default shell profile. This is probably located at */Users/$USER/.zshrc*. I recommend letting it do this; if you do not want to allow the installer to modify your default shell environment, you will need to consult the Miniconda documentation to be able to proceed.

To verify everything is working, try launching Python in the system shell (open the Terminal application to get a command prompt):

```
$ python
Python 3.9 (main) [Clang 12.0.1 ] on darwin
Type "help", "copyright", "credits" or "license" for more information.
>>>
```

To exit the shell, press Ctrl-D or type **exit()** and press Enter.

Installing Necessary Packages

Now that we have set up Miniconda on your system, it's time to install the main packages we will be using in this book. The first step is to configure conda-forge as your default package channel by running the following commands in a shell:

```
(base) $ conda config --add channels conda-forge
(base) $ conda config --set channel_priority strict
```

Now, we will create a new conda "environment" with the conda create command using Python 3.10:

```
(base) $ conda create -y -n pydata-book python=3.10
```

After the installation completes, activate the environment with conda activate:

```
(base) $ conda activate pydata-book
(pydata-book) $
```

It is necessary to use `conda activate` to activate your environment each time you open a new terminal. You can see information about the active conda environment at any time from the terminal by running `conda info`.

Now, we will install the essential packages used throughout the book (along with their dependencies) with `conda install`:

```
(pydata-book) $ conda install -y pandas jupyter matplotlib
```

We will be using some other packages, too, but these can be installed later once they are needed. There are two ways to install packages: with `conda install` and with `pip install`. `conda install` should always be preferred when using Miniconda, but some packages are not available through conda, so if `conda install $package_name` fails, try `pip install $package_name`.

If you want to install all of the packages used in the rest of the book, you can do that now by running:

```
conda install lxml beautifulsoup4 html5lib openpyxl \
              requests sqlalchemy seaborn scipy statsmodels \
              patsy scikit-learn pyarrow pytables numba
```

On Windows, substitute a carat ^ for the line continuation \ used on Linux and macOS.

You can update packages by using the `conda update` command:

```
conda update package_name
```

pip also supports upgrades using the `--upgrade` flag:

```
pip install --upgrade package_name
```

You will have several opportunities to try out these commands throughout the book.

While you can use both conda and pip to install packages, you should avoid updating packages originally installed with conda using pip (and vice versa), as doing so can lead to environment problems. I recommend sticking to conda if you can and falling back on pip only for packages that are unavailable with `conda install`.

Integrated Development Environments and Text Editors

When asked about my standard development environment, I almost always say "IPython plus a text editor." I typically write a program and iteratively test and debug each piece of it in IPython or Jupyter notebooks. It is also useful to be able to play around with data interactively and visually verify that a particular set of data manipulations is doing the right thing. Libraries like pandas and NumPy are designed to be productive to use in the shell.

When building software, however, some users may prefer to use a more richly featured integrated development environment (IDE) and rather than an editor like Emacs or Vim which provide a more minimal environment out of the box. Here are some that you can explore:

- PyDev (free), an IDE built on the Eclipse platform
- PyCharm from JetBrains (subscription-based for commercial users, free for open source developers)
- Python Tools for Visual Studio (for Windows users)
- Spyder (free), an IDE currently shipped with Anaconda
- Komodo IDE (commercial)

Due to the popularity of Python, most text editors, like VS Code and Sublime Text 2, have excellent Python support.

1.5 Community and Conferences

Outside of an internet search, the various scientific and data-related Python mailing lists are generally helpful and responsive to questions. Some to take a look at include:

- pydata: A Google Group list for questions related to Python for data analysis and pandas
- pystatsmodels: For statsmodels or pandas-related questions
- Mailing list for scikit-learn (*scikit-learn@python.org*) and machine learning in Python, generally
- numpy-discussion: For NumPy-related questions
- scipy-user: For general SciPy or scientific Python questions

I deliberately did not post URLs for these in case they change. They can be easily located via an internet search.

Each year many conferences are held all over the world for Python programmers. If you would like to connect with other Python programmers who share your interests, I encourage you to explore attending one, if possible. Many conferences have financial support available for those who cannot afford admission or travel to the conference. Here are some to consider:

- PyCon and EuroPython: The two main general Python conferences in North America and Europe, respectively

- SciPy and EuroSciPy: Scientific-computing-oriented conferences in North America and Europe, respectively

- PyData: A worldwide series of regional conferences targeted at data science and data analysis use cases

- International and regional PyCon conferences (see *https://pycon.org* for a complete listing)

1.6 Navigating This Book

If you have never programmed in Python before, you will want to spend some time in Chapters 2 and 3, where I have placed a condensed tutorial on Python language features and the IPython shell and Jupyter notebooks. These things are prerequisite knowledge for the remainder of the book. If you have Python experience already, you may instead choose to skim or skip these chapters.

Next, I give a short introduction to the key features of NumPy, leaving more advanced NumPy use for Appendix A. Then, I introduce pandas and devote the rest of the book to data analysis topics applying pandas, NumPy, and matplotlib (for visualization). I have structured the material in an incremental fashion, though there is occasionally some minor crossover between chapters, with a few cases where concepts are used that haven't been introduced yet.

While readers may have many different end goals for their work, the tasks required generally fall into a number of different broad groups:

Interacting with the outside world
Reading and writing with a variety of file formats and data stores

Preparation
Cleaning, munging, combining, normalizing, reshaping, slicing and dicing, and transforming data for analysis

Transformation
Applying mathematical and statistical operations to groups of datasets to derive new datasets (e.g., aggregating a large table by group variables)

Modeling and computation
Connecting your data to statistical models, machine learning algorithms, or other computational tools

Presentation
Creating interactive or static graphical visualizations or textual summaries

Code Examples

Most of the code examples in the book are shown with input and output as it would appear executed in the IPython shell or in Jupyter notebooks:

```
In [5]: CODE EXAMPLE
Out[5]: OUTPUT
```

When you see a code example like this, the intent is for you to type the example code in the In block in your coding environment and execute it by pressing the Enter key (or Shift-Enter in Jupyter). You should see output similar to what is shown in the Out block.

I changed the default console output settings in NumPy and pandas to improve readability and brevity throughout the book. For example, you may see more digits of precision printed in numeric data. To exactly match the output shown in the book, you can execute the following Python code before running the code examples:

```
import numpy as np
import pandas as pd
pd.options.display.max_columns = 20
pd.options.display.max_rows = 20
pd.options.display.max_colwidth = 80
np.set_printoptions(precision=4, suppress=True)
```

Data for Examples

Datasets for the examples in each chapter are hosted in a GitHub repository (*https://github.com/wesm/pydata-book*) (or in a mirror on Gitee (*https://gitee.com/wesmckinn/pydata-book*) if you cannot access GitHub). You can download this data either by using the Git version control system on the command line or by downloading a zip file of the repository from the website. If you run into problems, navigate to the book website (*https://wesmckinney.com/book*) for up-to-date instructions about obtaining the book materials.

If you download a zip file containing the example datasets, you must then fully extract the contents of the zip file to a directory and navigate to that directory from the terminal before proceeding with running the book's code examples:

```
$ pwd
/home/wesm/book-materials

$ ls
appa.ipynb  ch05.ipynb  ch09.ipynb  ch13.ipynb  README.md
ch02.ipynb  ch06.ipynb  ch10.ipynb  COPYING     requirements.txt
ch03.ipynb  ch07.ipynb  ch11.ipynb  datasets
ch04.ipynb  ch08.ipynb  ch12.ipynb  examples
```

I have made every effort to ensure that the GitHub repository contains everything necessary to reproduce the examples, but I may have made some mistakes or omissions. If so, please send me an email: *book@wesmckinney.com*. The best way to report errors in the book is on the errata page on the O'Reilly website (*https://oreil.ly/kmhmQ*).

Import Conventions

The Python community has adopted a number of naming conventions for commonly used modules:

```python
import numpy as np
import matplotlib.pyplot as plt
import pandas as pd
import seaborn as sns
import statsmodels as sm
```

This means that when you see `np.arange`, this is a reference to the `arange` function in NumPy. This is done because it's considered bad practice in Python software development to import everything (`from numpy import *`) from a large package like NumPy.

## CHAPTER 2

Python Language Basics, IPython, and Jupyter Notebooks

When I wrote the first edition of this book in 2011 and 2012, there were fewer resources available for learning about doing data analysis in Python. This was partially a chicken-and-egg problem; many libraries that we now take for granted, like pandas, scikit-learn, and statsmodels, were comparatively immature back then. Now in 2022, there is now a growing literature on data science, data analysis, and machine learning, supplementing the prior works on general-purpose scientific computing geared toward computational scientists, physicists, and professionals in other research fields. There are also excellent books about learning the Python programming language itself and becoming an effective software engineer.

As this book is intended as an introductory text in working with data in Python, I feel it is valuable to have a self-contained overview of some of the most important features of Python's built-in data structures and libraries from the perspective of data manipulation. So, I will only present roughly enough information in this chapter and Chapter 3 to enable you to follow along with the rest of the book.

Much of this book focuses on table-based analytics and data preparation tools for working with datasets that are small enough to fit on your personal computer. To use these tools you must sometimes do some wrangling to arrange messy data into a more nicely tabular (or *structured*) form. Fortunately, Python is an ideal language for doing this. The greater your facility with the Python language and its built-in data types, the easier it will be for you to prepare new datasets for analysis.

Some of the tools in this book are best explored from a live IPython or Jupyter session. Once you learn how to start up IPython and Jupyter, I recommend that you follow along with the examples so you can experiment and try different things. As with any keyboard-driven console-like environment, developing familiarity with the common commands is also part of the learning curve.

 There are introductory Python concepts that this chapter does not cover, like classes and object-oriented programming, which you may find useful in your foray into data analysis in Python.

To deepen your Python language knowledge, I recommend that you supplement this chapter with the official Python tutorial (*http://docs.python.org*) and potentially one of the many excellent books on general-purpose Python programming. Some recommendations to get you started include:

- *Python Cookbook*, Third Edition, by David Beazley and Brian K. Jones (O'Reilly)
- *Fluent Python* by Luciano Ramalho (O'Reilly)
- *Effective Python*, Second Edition, by Brett Slatkin (Addison-Wesley)

2.1 The Python Interpreter

Python is an *interpreted* language. The Python interpreter runs a program by executing one statement at a time. The standard interactive Python interpreter can be invoked on the command line with the `python` command:

```
$ python
Python 3.10.4 | packaged by conda-forge | (main, Mar 24 2022, 17:38:57)
[GCC 10.3.0] on linux
Type "help", "copyright", "credits" or "license" for more information.
>>> a = 5
>>> print(a)
5
```

The `>>>` you see is the *prompt* after which you'll type code expressions. To exit the Python interpreter, you can either type **exit()** or press Ctrl-D (works on Linux and macOS only).

Running Python programs is as simple as calling `python` with a *.py* file as its first argument. Suppose we had created *hello_world.py* with these contents:

```
print("Hello world")
```

You can run it by executing the following command (the *hello_world.py* file must be in your current working terminal directory):

```
$ python hello_world.py
Hello world
```

While some Python programmers execute all of their Python code in this way, those doing data analysis or scientific computing make use of IPython, an enhanced Python interpreter, or Jupyter notebooks, web-based code notebooks originally created within the IPython project. I give an introduction to using IPython and Jupyter in this chapter and have included a deeper look at IPython functionality in Appendix A. When you use the `%run` command, IPython executes the code in the specified file in the same process, enabling you to explore the results interactively when it's done:

```
$ ipython
Python 3.10.4 | packaged by conda-forge | (main, Mar 24 2022, 17:38:57)
Type 'copyright', 'credits' or 'license' for more information
IPython 7.31.1 -- An enhanced Interactive Python. Type '?' for help.

In [1]: %run hello_world.py
Hello world

In [2]:
```

The default IPython prompt adopts the numbered In [2]: style, compared with the standard >>> prompt.

2.2 IPython Basics

In this section, I'll get you up and running with the IPython shell and Jupyter notebook, and introduce you to some of the essential concepts.

Running the IPython Shell

You can launch the IPython shell on the command line just like launching the regular Python interpreter except with the `ipython` command:

```
$ ipython
Python 3.10.4 | packaged by conda-forge | (main, Mar 24 2022, 17:38:57)
Type 'copyright', 'credits' or 'license' for more information
IPython 7.31.1 -- An enhanced Interactive Python. Type '?' for help.

In [1]: a = 5

In [2]: a
Out[2]: 5
```

You can execute arbitrary Python statements by typing them and pressing Return (or Enter). When you type just a variable into IPython, it renders a string representation of the object:

```
In [5]: import numpy as np

In [6]: data = [np.random.standard_normal() for i in range(7)]
```

```
In [7]: data
Out[7]:
[-0.20470765948471295,
 0.47894333805754824,
 -0.5194387150567381,
 -0.55573030434749,
 1.9657805725027142,
 1.3934058329729904,
 0.09290787674371767]
```

The first two lines are Python code statements; the second statement creates a variable named data that refers to a newly created Python dictionary. The last line prints the value of data in the console.

Many kinds of Python objects are formatted to be more readable, or *pretty-printed*, which is distinct from normal printing with print. If you printed the above data variable in the standard Python interpreter, it would be much less readable:

```
>>> import numpy as np
>>> data = [np.random.standard_normal() for i in range(7)]
>>> print(data)
>>> data
[-0.5767699931966723, -0.1010317773535111, -1.7841005313329152,
 -1.524392126408841, 0.22191374220117385, -1.9835710588082562,
 -1.6081963964963528]
```

IPython also provides facilities to execute arbitrary blocks of code (via a somewhat glorified copy-and-paste approach) and whole Python scripts. You can also use the Jupyter notebook to work with larger blocks of code, as we will soon see.

Running the Jupyter Notebook

One of the major components of the Jupyter project is the *notebook*, a type of interactive document for code, text (including Markdown), data visualizations, and other output. The Jupyter notebook interacts with *kernels*, which are implementations of the Jupyter interactive computing protocol specific to different programming languages. The Python Jupyter kernel uses the IPython system for its underlying behavior.

To start up Jupyter, run the command jupyter notebook in a terminal:

```
$ jupyter notebook
[I 15:20:52.739 NotebookApp] Serving notebooks from local directory:
/home/wesm/code/pydata-book
[I 15:20:52.739 NotebookApp] 0 active kernels
[I 15:20:52.739 NotebookApp] The Jupyter Notebook is running at:
http://localhost:8888/?token=0a77b52fefe52ab83e3c35dff8de121e4bb443a63f2d...
[I 15:20:52.740 NotebookApp] Use Control-C to stop this server and shut down
all kernels (twice to skip confirmation).
Created new window in existing browser session.
```

```
To access the notebook, open this file in a browser:
    file:///home/wesm/.local/share/jupyter/runtime/nbserver-185259-open.html
Or copy and paste one of these URLs:
    http://localhost:8888/?token=0a77b52fefe52ab83e3c35dff8de121e4...
 or http://127.0.0.1:8888/?token=0a77b52fefe52ab83e3c35dff8de121e4...
```

On many platforms, Jupyter will automatically open in your default web browser
(unless you start it with `--no-browser`). Otherwise, you can navigate to the HTTP
address printed when you started the notebook, here `http://localhost:8888/?`
`token=0a77b52fefe52ab83e3c35dff8de121e4bb443a63f2d3055`. See Figure 2-1 for
what this looks like in Google Chrome.

Many people use Jupyter as a local computing environment, but
it can also be deployed on servers and accessed remotely. I won't
cover those details here, but I encourage you to explore this topic
on the internet if it's relevant to your needs.

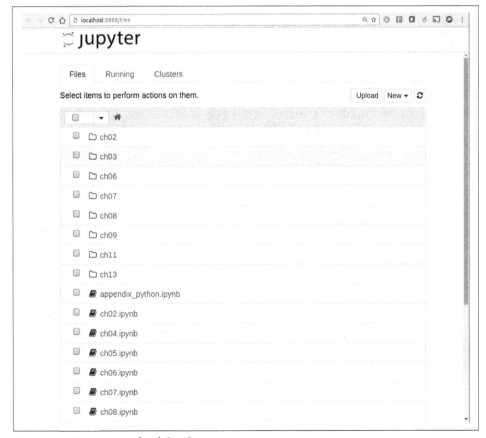

Figure 2-1. Jupyter notebook landing page

To create a new notebook, click the New button and select the "Python 3" option. You should see something like Figure 2-2. If this is your first time, try clicking on the empty code "cell" and entering a line of Python code. Then press Shift-Enter to execute it.

Figure 2-2. Jupyter new notebook view

When you save the notebook (see "Save and Checkpoint" under the notebook File menu), it creates a file with the extension *.ipynb*. This is a self-contained file format that contains all of the content (including any evaluated code output) currently in the notebook. These can be loaded and edited by other Jupyter users.

To rename an open notebook, click on the notebook title at the top of the page and type the new title, pressing Enter when you are finished.

To load an existing notebook, put the file in the same directory where you started the notebook process (or in a subfolder within it), then click the name from the landing page. You can try it out with the notebooks from my *wesm/pydata-book* repository on GitHub. See Figure 2-3.

When you want to close a notebook, click the File menu and select "Close and Halt." If you simply close the browser tab, the Python process associated with the notebook will keep running in the background.

While the Jupyter notebook may feel like a distinct experience from the IPython shell, nearly all of the commands and tools in this chapter can be used in either environment.

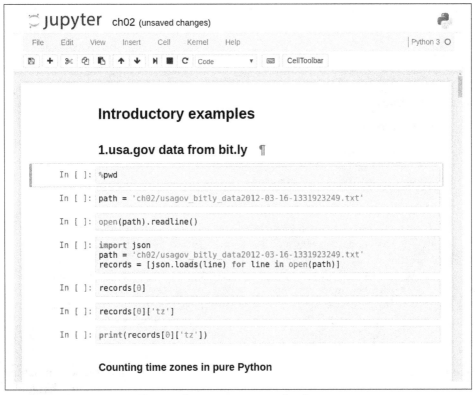

Figure 2-3. Jupyter example view for an existing notebook

Tab Completion

On the surface, the IPython shell looks like a cosmetically different version of the standard terminal Python interpreter (invoked with `python`). One of the major improvements over the standard Python shell is *tab completion*, found in many IDEs or other interactive computing analysis environments. While entering expressions in the shell, pressing the Tab key will search the namespace for any variables (objects, functions, etc.) matching the characters you have typed so far and show the results in a convenient drop-down menu:

```
In [1]: an_apple = 27

In [2]: an_example = 42

In [3]: an<Tab>
an_apple    an_example    any
```

In this example, note that IPython displayed both of the two variables I defined, as well as the built-in function `any`. Also, you can also complete methods and attributes on any object after typing a period:

```
In [3]: b = [1, 2, 3]

In [4]: b.<Tab>
append()  count()   insert()  reverse()
clear()   extend()  pop()     sort()
copy()    index()   remove()
```

The same is true for modules:

```
In [1]: import datetime

In [2]: datetime.<Tab>
date          MAXYEAR      timedelta
datetime      MINYEAR      timezone
datetime_CAPI time         tzinfo
```

 Note that IPython by default hides methods and attributes starting with underscores, such as magic methods and internal "private" methods and attributes, in order to avoid cluttering the display (and confusing novice users!). These, too, can be tab-completed, but you must first type an underscore to see them. If you prefer to always see such methods in tab completion, you can change this setting in the IPython configuration. See the IPython documentation (*https://ipython.readthedocs.io*) to find out how to do this.

Tab completion works in many contexts outside of searching the interactive name-space and completing object or module attributes. When typing anything that looks like a file path (even in a Python string), pressing the Tab key will complete anything on your computer's filesystem matching what you've typed.

Combined with the %run command (see "The %run Command" on page 512), this functionality can save you many keystrokes.

Another area where tab completion saves time is in the completion of function keyword arguments (including the = sign!). See Figure 2-4.

```
In [12]: def func_with_keywords(abra=1, abbra=2, abbbra=3):
             return abra, abbra, abbbra

In [ ]: func_with_keywords ab
                            abbbra=
                            abbra=
                            abra=
                            abs
```

Figure 2-4. Autocomplete function keywords in a Jupyter notebook

We'll have a closer look at functions in a little bit.

Introspection

Using a question mark (?) before or after a variable will display some general information about the object:

```
In [1]: b = [1, 2, 3]

In [2]: b?
Type:        list
String form: [1, 2, 3]
Length:      3
Docstring:
Built-in mutable sequence.

If no argument is given, the constructor creates a new empty list.
The argument must be an iterable if specified.

In [3]: print?
Docstring:
print(value, ..., sep=' ', end='\n', file=sys.stdout, flush=False)

Prints the values to a stream, or to sys.stdout by default.
Optional keyword arguments:
file:  a file-like object (stream); defaults to the current sys.stdout.
sep:   string inserted between values, default a space.
end:   string appended after the last value, default a newline.
flush: whether to forcibly flush the stream.
Type:       builtin_function_or_method
```

This is referred to as *object introspection*. If the object is a function or instance method, the docstring, if defined, will also be shown. Suppose we'd written the following function (which you can reproduce in IPython or Jupyter):

```
def add_numbers(a, b):
    """
    Add two numbers together

    Returns
    -------
    the_sum : type of arguments
    """
    return a + b
```

Then using ? shows us the docstring:

```
In [6]: add_numbers?
Signature: add_numbers(a, b)
Docstring:
Add two numbers together
Returns
-------
the_sum : type of arguments
```

```
File:       <ipython-input-9-6a548a216e27>
Type:       function
```

? has a final usage, which is for searching the IPython namespace in a manner similar to the standard Unix or Windows command line. A number of characters combined with the wildcard (*) will show all names matching the wildcard expression. For example, we could get a list of all functions in the top-level NumPy namespace containing load:

```
In [9]: import numpy as np

In [10]: np.*load*?
np.__loader__
np.load
np.loads
np.loadtxt
```

2.3 Python Language Basics

In this section, I will give you an overview of essential Python programming concepts and language mechanics. In the next chapter, I will go into more detail about Python data structures, functions, and other built-in tools.

Language Semantics

The Python language design is distinguished by its emphasis on readability, simplicity, and explicitness. Some people go so far as to liken it to "executable pseudocode."

Indentation, not braces

Python uses whitespace (tabs or spaces) to structure code instead of using braces as in many other languages like R, C++, Java, and Perl. Consider a for loop from a sorting algorithm:

```
for x in array:
    if x < pivot:
        less.append(x)
    else:
        greater.append(x)
```

A colon denotes the start of an indented code block after which all of the code must be indented by the same amount until the end of the block.

Love it or hate it, significant whitespace is a fact of life for Python programmers. While it may seem foreign at first, you will hopefully grow accustomed to it in time.

I strongly recommend using *four spaces* as your default indentation and replacing tabs with four spaces. Many text editors have a setting that will replace tab stops with spaces automatically (do this!). IPython and Jupyter notebooks will automatically insert four spaces on new lines following a colon and replace tabs by four spaces.

As you can see by now, Python statements also do not need to be terminated by semicolons. Semicolons can be used, however, to separate multiple statements on a single line:

```
a = 5; b = 6; c = 7
```

Putting multiple statements on one line is generally discouraged in Python as it can make code less readable.

Everything is an object

An important characteristic of the Python language is the consistency of its *object model*. Every number, string, data structure, function, class, module, and so on exists in the Python interpreter in its own "box," which is referred to as a *Python object*. Each object has an associated *type* (e.g., *integer*, *string*, or *function*) and internal data. In practice this makes the language very flexible, as even functions can be treated like any other object.

Comments

Any text preceded by the hash mark (pound sign) # is ignored by the Python interpreter. This is often used to add comments to code. At times you may also want to exclude certain blocks of code without deleting them. One solution is to *comment out* the code:

```
results = []
for line in file_handle:
    # keep the empty lines for now
    # if len(line) == 0:
    #   continue
    results.append(line.replace("foo", "bar"))
```

Comments can also occur after a line of executed code. While some programmers prefer comments to be placed in the line preceding a particular line of code, this can be useful at times:

```
print("Reached this line")  # Simple status report
```

Function and object method calls

You call functions using parentheses and passing zero or more arguments, optionally assigning the returned value to a variable:

```
result = f(x, y, z)
g()
```

Almost every object in Python has attached functions, known as *methods*, that have access to the object's internal contents. You can call them using the following syntax:

```
obj.some_method(x, y, z)
```

Functions can take both *positional* and *keyword* arguments:

```
result = f(a, b, c, d=5, e="foo")
```

We will look at this in more detail later.

Variables and argument passing

When assigning a variable (or *name*) in Python, you are creating a *reference* to the object shown on the righthand side of the equals sign. In practical terms, consider a list of integers:

```
In [8]: a = [1, 2, 3]
```

Suppose we assign a to a new variable b:

```
In [9]: b = a

In [10]: b
Out[10]: [1, 2, 3]
```

In some languages, the assignment if b will cause the data [1, 2, 3] to be copied. In Python, a and b actually now refer to the same object, the original list [1, 2, 3] (see Figure 2-5 for a mock-up). You can prove this to yourself by appending an element to a and then examining b:

```
In [11]: a.append(4)

In [12]: b
Out[12]: [1, 2, 3, 4]
```

Figure 2-5. Two references for the same object

Understanding the semantics of references in Python, and when, how, and why data is copied, is especially critical when you are working with larger datasets in Python.

Assignment is also referred to as *binding*, as we are binding a name to an object. Variable names that have been assigned may occasionally be referred to as bound variables.

When you pass objects as arguments to a function, new local variables are created referencing the original objects without any copying. If you bind a new object to a variable inside a function, that will not overwrite a variable of the same name in the "scope" outside of the function (the "parent scope"). It is therefore possible to alter the internals of a mutable argument. Suppose we had the following function:

```
In [13]: def append_element(some_list, element):
   ....:     some_list.append(element)
```

Then we have:

```
In [14]: data = [1, 2, 3]

In [15]: append_element(data, 4)

In [16]: data
Out[16]: [1, 2, 3, 4]
```

Dynamic references, strong types

Variables in Python have no inherent type associated with them; a variable can refer to a different type of object simply by doing an assignment. There is no problem with the following:

```
In [17]: a = 5

In [18]: type(a)
Out[18]: int

In [19]: a = "foo"

In [20]: type(a)
Out[20]: str
```

Variables are names for objects within a particular namespace; the type information is stored in the object itself. Some observers might hastily conclude that Python is not a "typed language." This is not true; consider this example:

```
In [21]: "5" + 5
---------------------------------------------------------------------------
TypeError                                 Traceback (most recent call last)
<ipython-input-21-7fe5aa79f268> in <module>
----> 1 "5" + 5
TypeError: can only concatenate str (not "int") to str
```

In some languages, the string '5' might get implicitly converted (or *cast*) to an integer, thus yielding 10. In other languages the integer 5 might be cast to a string, yielding the concatenated string '55'. In Python, such implicit casts are not allowed. In this regard we say that Python is a *strongly typed* language, which means that every object has a specific type (or *class*), and implicit conversions will occur only in certain permitted circumstances, such as:

```
In [22]: a = 4.5

In [23]: b = 2

# String formatting, to be visited later
In [24]: print(f"a is {type(a)}, b is {type(b)}")
a is <class 'float'>, b is <class 'int'>

In [25]: a / b
Out[25]: 2.25
```

Here, even though b is an integer, it is implicitly converted to a float for the division operation.

Knowing the type of an object is important, and it's useful to be able to write functions that can handle many different kinds of input. You can check that an object is an instance of a particular type using the isinstance function:

```
In [26]: a = 5

In [27]: isinstance(a, int)
Out[27]: True
```

isinstance can accept a tuple of types if you want to check that an object's type is among those present in the tuple:

```
In [28]: a = 5; b = 4.5

In [29]: isinstance(a, (int, float))
Out[29]: True

In [30]: isinstance(b, (int, float))
Out[30]: True
```

Attributes and methods

Objects in Python typically have both attributes (other Python objects stored "inside" the object) and methods (functions associated with an object that can have access to the object's internal data). Both of them are accessed via the syntax *obj.attribute_name*:

```
In [1]: a = "foo"

In [2]: a.<Press Tab>
```

```
capitalize()   index()          isspace()        removesuffix()   startswith()
casefold()     isprintable()    istitle()        replace()        strip()
center()       isalnum()        isupper()        rfind()          swapcase()
count()        isalpha()        join()           rindex()         title()
encode()       isascii()        ljust()          rjust()          translate()
endswith()     isdecimal()      lower()          rpartition()
expandtabs()   isdigit()        lstrip()         rsplit()
find()         isidentifier()   maketrans()      rstrip()
format()       islower()        partition()      split()
format_map()   isnumeric()      removeprefix()   splitlines()
```

Attributes and methods can also be accessed by name via the getattr function:

```
In [32]: getattr(a, "split")
Out[32]: <function str.split(sep=None, maxsplit=-1)>
```

While we will not extensively use the functions getattr and related functions hasattr and setattr in this book, they can be used very effectively to write generic, reusable code.

Duck typing

Often you may not care about the type of an object but rather only whether it has certain methods or behavior. This is sometimes called *duck typing*, after the saying "If it walks like a duck and quacks like a duck, then it's a duck." For example, you can verify that an object is iterable if it implements the *iterator protocol*. For many objects, this means it has an __iter__ "magic method," though an alternative and better way to check is to try using the iter function:

```
In [33]: def isiterable(obj):
   ....:     try:
   ....:         iter(obj)
   ....:         return True
   ....:     except TypeError: # not iterable
   ....:         return False
```

This function would return True for strings as well as most Python collection types:

```
In [34]: isiterable("a string")
Out[34]: True

In [35]: isiterable([1, 2, 3])
Out[35]: True

In [36]: isiterable(5)
Out[36]: False
```

Imports

In Python, a *module* is simply a file with the *.py* extension containing Python code. Suppose we had the following module:

```
# some_module.py
PI = 3.14159

def f(x):
    return x + 2

def g(a, b):
    return a + b
```

If we wanted to access the variables and functions defined in *some_module.py*, from another file in the same directory we could do:

```
import some_module
result = some_module.f(5)
pi = some_module.PI
```

Or alternately:

```
from some_module import g, PI
result = g(5, PI)
```

By using the **as** keyword, you can give imports different variable names:

```
import some_module as sm
from some_module import PI as pi, g as gf

r1 = sm.f(pi)
r2 = gf(6, pi)
```

Binary operators and comparisons

Most of the binary math operations and comparisons use familiar mathematical syntax used in other programming languages:

```
In [37]: 5 - 7
Out[37]: -2

In [38]: 12 + 21.5
Out[38]: 33.5

In [39]: 5 <= 2
Out[39]: False
```

See Table 2-1 for all of the available binary operators.

Table 2-1. Binary operators

Operation	Description
a + b	Add a and b
a - b	Subtract b from a
a * b	Multiply a by b
a / b	Divide a by b
a // b	Floor-divide a by b, dropping any fractional remainder
a ** b	Raise a to the b power
a & b	True if both a and b are True; for integers, take the bitwise AND
a | b	True if either a or b is True; for integers, take the bitwise OR
a ^ b	For Booleans, True if a or b is True, but not both; for integers, take the bitwise EXCLUSIVE-OR
a == b	True if a equals b
a != b	True if a is not equal to b
a < b, a <= b	True if a is less than (less than or equal to) b
a > b, a >= b	True if a is greater than (greater than or equal to) b
a is b	True if a and b reference the same Python object
a is not b	True if a and b reference different Python objects

To check if two variables refer to the same object, use the is keyword. Use is not to check that two objects are not the same:

```
In [40]: a = [1, 2, 3]

In [41]: b = a

In [42]: c = list(a)

In [43]: a is b
Out[43]: True

In [44]: a is not c
Out[44]: True
```

Since the list function always creates a new Python list (i.e., a copy), we can be sure that c is distinct from a. Comparing with is is not the same as the == operator, because in this case we have:

```
In [45]: a == c
Out[45]: True
```

A common use of `is` and `is not` is to check if a variable is None, since there is only one instance of None:

```
In [46]: a = None

In [47]: a is None
Out[47]: True
```

Mutable and immutable objects

Many objects in Python, such as lists, dictionaries, NumPy arrays, and most user-defined types (classes), are *mutable*. This means that the object or values that they contain can be modified:

```
In [48]: a_list = ["foo", 2, [4, 5]]

In [49]: a_list[2] = (3, 4)

In [50]: a_list
Out[50]: ['foo', 2, (3, 4)]
```

Others, like strings and tuples, are immutable, which means their internal data cannot be changed:

```
In [51]: a_tuple = (3, 5, (4, 5))

In [52]: a_tuple[1] = "four"
---------------------------------------------------------------------------
TypeError                                 Traceback (most recent call last)
<ipython-input-52-cd2a018a7529> in <module>
----> 1 a_tuple[1] = "four"
TypeError: 'tuple' object does not support item assignment
```

Remember that just because you *can* mutate an object does not mean that you always *should*. Such actions are known as *side effects*. For example, when writing a function, any side effects should be explicitly communicated to the user in the function's documentation or comments. If possible, I recommend trying to avoid side effects and *favor immutability*, even though there may be mutable objects involved.

Scalar Types

Python has a small set of built-in types for handling numerical data, strings, Boolean (`True` or `False`) values, and dates and time. These "single value" types are sometimes called *scalar types*, and we refer to them in this book as *scalars* . See Table 2-2 for a list of the main scalar types. Date and time handling will be discussed separately, as these are provided by the `datetime` module in the standard library.

Table 2-2. Standard Python scalar types

Type	Description
None	The Python "null" value (only one instance of the None object exists)
str	String type; holds Unicode strings
bytes	Raw binary data
float	Double-precision floating-point number (note there is no separate double type)
bool	A Boolean True or False value
int	Arbitrary precision integer

Numeric types

The primary Python types for numbers are `int` and `float`. An `int` can store arbitrarily large numbers:

```
In [53]: ival = 17239871

In [54]: ival ** 6
Out[54]: 26254519291092456596965462913230729701102721
```

Floating-point numbers are represented with the Python `float` type. Under the hood, each one is a double-precision value. They can also be expressed with scientific notation:

```
In [55]: fval = 7.243

In [56]: fval2 = 6.78e-5
```

Integer division not resulting in a whole number will always yield a floating-point number:

```
In [57]: 3 / 2
Out[57]: 1.5
```

To get C-style integer division (which drops the fractional part if the result is not a whole number), use the floor division operator `//`:

```
In [58]: 3 // 2
Out[58]: 1
```

Strings

Many people use Python for its built-in string handling capabilities. You can write *string literals* using either single quotes `'` or double quotes `"` (double quotes are generally favored):

```
a = 'one way of writing a string'
b = "another way"
```

The Python string type is `str`.

For multiline strings with line breaks, you can use triple quotes, either ''' or """:

```
c = """
This is a longer string that
spans multiple lines
"""
```

It may surprise you that this string c actually contains four lines of text; the line breaks after """ and after lines are included in the string. We can count the new line characters with the count method on c:

```
In [60]: c.count("\n")
Out[60]: 3
```

Python strings are immutable; you cannot modify a string:

```
In [61]: a = "this is a string"

In [62]: a[10] = "f"
---------------------------------------------------------------------------
TypeError                                 Traceback (most recent call last)
<ipython-input-62-3b2d95f10db4> in <module>
----> 1 a[10] = "f"
TypeError: 'str' object does not support item assignment
```

To interpret this error message, read from the bottom up. We tried to replace the character (the "item") at position 10 with the letter "f", but this is not allowed for string objects. If we need to modify a string, we have to use a function or method that creates a new string, such as the string **replace** method:

```
In [63]: b = a.replace("string", "longer string")

In [64]: b
Out[64]: 'this is a longer string'
```

Afer this operation, the variable a is unmodified:

```
In [65]: a
Out[65]: 'this is a string'
```

Many Python objects can be converted to a string using the str function:

```
In [66]: a = 5.6

In [67]: s = str(a)

In [68]: print(s)
5.6
```

Strings are a sequence of Unicode characters and therefore can be treated like other sequences, such as lists and tuples:

```
In [69]: s = "python"
```

```
In [70]: list(s)
Out[70]: ['p', 'y', 't', 'h', 'o', 'n']

In [71]: s[:3]
Out[71]: 'pyt'
```

The syntax s[:3] is called *slicing* and is implemented for many kinds of Python sequences. This will be explained in more detail later on, as it is used extensively in this book.

The backslash character \ is an *escape character*, meaning that it is used to specify special characters like newline \n or Unicode characters. To write a string literal with backslashes, you need to escape them:

```
In [72]: s = "12\\34"

In [73]: print(s)
12\34
```

If you have a string with a lot of backslashes and no special characters, you might find this a bit annoying. Fortunately you can preface the leading quote of the string with r, which means that the characters should be interpreted as is:

```
In [74]: s = r"this\has\no\special\characters"

In [75]: s
Out[75]: 'this\\has\\no\\special\\characters'
```

The r stands for *raw*.

Adding two strings together concatenates them and produces a new string:

```
In [76]: a = "this is the first half "

In [77]: b = "and this is the second half"

In [78]: a + b
Out[78]: 'this is the first half and this is the second half'
```

String templating or formatting is another important topic. The number of ways to do so has expanded with the advent of Python 3, and here I will briefly describe the mechanics of one of the main interfaces. String objects have a format method that can be used to substitute formatted arguments into the string, producing a new string:

```
In [79]: template = "{0:.2f} {1:s} are worth US${2:d}"
```

In this string:

- {0:.2f} means to format the first argument as a floating-point number with two decimal places.

- {1:s} means to format the second argument as a string.

- {2:d} means to format the third argument as an exact integer.

To substitute arguments for these format parameters, we pass a sequence of arguments to the `format` method:

```
In [80]: template.format(88.46, "Argentine Pesos", 1)
Out[80]: '88.46 Argentine Pesos are worth US$1'
```

Python 3.6 introduced a new feature called *f-strings* (short for *formatted string literals*) which can make creating formatted strings even more convenient. To create an f-string, write the character `f` immediately preceding a string literal. Within the string, enclose Python expressions in curly braces to substitute the value of the expression into the formatted string:

```
In [81]: amount = 10

In [82]: rate = 88.46

In [83]: currency = "Pesos"

In [84]: result = f"{amount} {currency} is worth US${amount / rate}"
```

Format specifiers can be added after each expression using the same syntax as with the string templates above:

```
In [85]: f"{amount} {currency} is worth US${amount / rate:.2f}"
Out[85]: '10 Pesos is worth US$0.11'
```

String formatting is a deep topic; there are multiple methods and numerous options and tweaks available to control how values are formatted in the resulting string. To learn more, consult the official Python documentation (*https://docs.python.org/3/library/string.html*).

Bytes and Unicode

In modern Python (i.e., Python 3.0 and up), Unicode has become the first-class string type to enable more consistent handling of ASCII and non-ASCII text. In older versions of Python, strings were all bytes without any explicit Unicode encoding. You could convert to Unicode assuming you knew the character encoding. Here is an example Unicode string with non-ASCII characters:

```
In [86]: val = "español"

In [87]: val
Out[87]: 'español'
```

We can convert this Unicode string to its UTF-8 bytes representation using the encode method:

```
In [88]: val_utf8 = val.encode("utf-8")

In [89]: val_utf8
Out[89]: b'espa\xc3\xb1ol'

In [90]: type(val_utf8)
Out[90]: bytes
```

Assuming you know the Unicode encoding of a bytes object, you can go back using the decode method:

```
In [91]: val_utf8.decode("utf-8")
Out[91]: 'español'
```

While it is now preferable to use UTF-8 for any encoding, for historical reasons you may encounter data in any number of different encodings:

```
In [92]: val.encode("latin1")
Out[92]: b'espa\xf1ol'

In [93]: val.encode("utf-16")
Out[93]: b'\xff\xfee\x00s\x00p\x00a\x00\xf1\x00o\x00l\x00'

In [94]: val.encode("utf-16le")
Out[94]: b'e\x00s\x00p\x00a\x00\xf1\x00o\x00l\x00'
```

It is most common to encounter bytes objects in the context of working with files, where implicitly decoding all data to Unicode strings may not be desired.

Booleans

The two Boolean values in Python are written as True and False. Comparisons and other conditional expressions evaluate to either True or False. Boolean values are combined with the and and or keywords:

```
In [95]: True and True
Out[95]: True

In [96]: False or True
Out[96]: True
```

When converted to numbers, False becomes 0 and True becomes 1:

```
In [97]: int(False)
Out[97]: 0

In [98]: int(True)
Out[98]: 1
```

The keyword not flips a Boolean value from True to False or vice versa:

```
In [99]: a = True
```

```
In [100]: b = False

In [101]: not a
Out[101]: False

In [102]: not b
Out[102]: True
```

Type casting

The `str`, `bool`, `int`, and `float` types are also functions that can be used to cast values to those types:

```
In [103]: s = "3.14159"

In [104]: fval = float(s)

In [105]: type(fval)
Out[105]: float

In [106]: int(fval)
Out[106]: 3

In [107]: bool(fval)
Out[107]: True

In [108]: bool(0)
Out[108]: False
```

Note that most nonzero values when cast to `bool` become `True`.

None

None is the Python null value type:

```
In [109]: a = None

In [110]: a is None
Out[110]: True

In [111]: b = 5

In [112]: b is not None
Out[112]: True
```

None is also a common default value for function arguments:

```
def add_and_maybe_multiply(a, b, c=None):
    result = a + b

    if c is not None:
        result = result * c
```

```
    return result
```

Dates and times

The built-in Python datetime module provides datetime, date, and time types. The datetime type combines the information stored in date and time and is the most commonly used:

```
In [113]: from datetime import datetime, date, time

In [114]: dt = datetime(2011, 10, 29, 20, 30, 21)

In [115]: dt.day
Out[115]: 29

In [116]: dt.minute
Out[116]: 30
```

Given a datetime instance, you can extract the equivalent date and time objects by calling methods on the datetime of the same name:

```
In [117]: dt.date()
Out[117]: datetime.date(2011, 10, 29)

In [118]: dt.time()
Out[118]: datetime.time(20, 30, 21)
```

The strftime method formats a datetime as a string:

```
In [119]: dt.strftime("%Y-%m-%d %H:%M")
Out[119]: '2011-10-29 20:30'
```

Strings can be converted (parsed) into datetime objects with the strptime function:

```
In [120]: datetime.strptime("20091031", "%Y%m%d")
Out[120]: datetime.datetime(2009, 10, 31, 0, 0)
```

See Table 11-2 for a full list of format specifications.

When you are aggregating or otherwise grouping time series data, it will occasionally be useful to replace time fields of a series of datetimes—for example, replacing the minute and second fields with zero:

```
In [121]: dt_hour = dt.replace(minute=0, second=0)

In [122]: dt_hour
Out[122]: datetime.datetime(2011, 10, 29, 20, 0)
```

Since datetime.datetime is an immutable type, methods like these always produce new objects. So in the previous example, dt is not modified by replace:

```
In [123]: dt
Out[123]: datetime.datetime(2011, 10, 29, 20, 30, 21)
```

The difference of two datetime objects produces a datetime.timedelta type:

```
In [124]: dt2 = datetime(2011, 11, 15, 22, 30)

In [125]: delta = dt2 - dt

In [126]: delta
Out[126]: datetime.timedelta(days=17, seconds=7179)

In [127]: type(delta)
Out[127]: datetime.timedelta
```

The output timedelta(17, 7179) indicates that the timedelta encodes an offset of 17 days and 7,179 seconds.

Adding a timedelta to a datetime produces a new shifted datetime:

```
In [128]: dt
Out[128]: datetime.datetime(2011, 10, 29, 20, 30, 21)

In [129]: dt + delta
Out[129]: datetime.datetime(2011, 11, 15, 22, 30)
```

Control Flow

Python has several built-in keywords for conditional logic, loops, and other standard *control flow* concepts found in other programming languages.

if, elif, and else

The if statement is one of the most well-known control flow statement types. It checks a condition that, if True, evaluates the code in the block that follows:

```
x = -5
if x < 0:
    print("It's negative")
```

An if statement can be optionally followed by one or more elif blocks and a catchall else block if all of the conditions are False:

```
if x < 0:
    print("It's negative")
elif x == 0:
    print("Equal to zero")
elif 0 < x < 5:
    print("Positive but smaller than 5")
else:
    print("Positive and larger than or equal to 5")
```

If any of the conditions are True, no further elif or else blocks will be reached. With a compound condition using and or or, conditions are evaluated left to right and will short-circuit:

```
In [130]: a = 5; b = 7

In [131]: c = 8; d = 4

In [132]: if a < b or c > d:
   .....:     print("Made it")
Made it
```

In this example, the comparison `c > d` never gets evaluated because the first comparison was `True`.

It is also possible to chain comparisons:

```
In [133]: 4 > 3 > 2 > 1
Out[133]: True
```

for loops

`for` loops are for iterating over a collection (like a list or tuple) or an iterater. The standard syntax for a `for` loop is:

```
for value in collection:
    # do something with value
```

You can advance a `for` loop to the next iteration, skipping the remainder of the block, using the `continue` keyword. Consider this code, which sums up integers in a list and skips `None` values:

```
sequence = [1, 2, None, 4, None, 5]
total = 0
for value in sequence:
    if value is None:
        continue
    total += value
```

A `for` loop can be exited altogether with the `break` keyword. This code sums elements of the list until a 5 is reached:

```
sequence = [1, 2, 0, 4, 6, 5, 2, 1]
total_until_5 = 0
for value in sequence:
    if value == 5:
        break
    total_until_5 += value
```

The `break` keyword only terminates the innermost `for` loop; any outer `for` loops will continue to run:

```
In [134]: for i in range(4):
   .....:     for j in range(4):
   .....:         if j > i:
   .....:             break
   .....:         print((i, j))
```

```
   .....:
(0, 0)
(1, 0)
(1, 1)
(2, 0)
(2, 1)
(2, 2)
(3, 0)
(3, 1)
(3, 2)
(3, 3)
```

As we will see in more detail, if the elements in the collection or iterator are sequences (tuples or lists, say), they can be conveniently *unpacked* into variables in the for loop statement:

```
for a, b, c in iterator:
    # do something
```

while loops

A while loop specifies a condition and a block of code that is to be executed until the condition evaluates to False or the loop is explicitly ended with break:

```
x = 256
total = 0
while x > 0:
    if total > 500:
        break
    total += x
    x = x // 2
```

pass

pass is the "no-op" (or "do nothing") statement in Python. It can be used in blocks where no action is to be taken (or as a placeholder for code not yet implemented); it is required only because Python uses whitespace to delimit blocks:

```
if x < 0:
    print("negative!")
elif x == 0:
    # TODO: put something smart here
    pass
else:
    print("positive!")
```

range

The range function generates a sequence of evenly spaced integers:

```
In [135]: range(10)
Out[135]: range(0, 10)
```

```
In [136]: list(range(10))
Out[136]: [0, 1, 2, 3, 4, 5, 6, 7, 8, 9]
```

A start, end, and step (which may be negative) can be given:

```
In [137]: list(range(0, 20, 2))
Out[137]: [0, 2, 4, 6, 8, 10, 12, 14, 16, 18]

In [138]: list(range(5, 0, -1))
Out[138]: [5, 4, 3, 2, 1]
```

As you can see, range produces integers up to but not including the endpoint. A common use of range is for iterating through sequences by index:

```
In [139]: seq = [1, 2, 3, 4]

In [140]: for i in range(len(seq)):
   .....:     print(f"element {i}: {seq[i]}")
element 0: 1
element 1: 2
element 2: 3
element 3: 4
```

While you can use functions like list to store all the integers generated by range in some other data structure, often the default iterator form will be what you want. This snippet sums all numbers from 0 to 99,999 that are multiples of 3 or 5:

```
In [141]: total = 0

In [142]: for i in range(100_000):
   .....:     # % is the modulo operator
   .....:     if i % 3 == 0 or i % 5 == 0:
   .....:         total += i

In [143]: print(total)
2333316668
```

While the range generated can be arbitrarily large, the memory use at any given time may be very small.

2.4 Conclusion

This chapter provided a brief introduction to some basic Python language concepts and the IPython and Jupyter programming environments. In the next chapter, I will discuss many built-in data types, functions, and input-output utilities that will be used continuously throughout the rest of the book.

## CHAPTER 3

Built-In Data Structures, Functions, and Files

This chapter discusses capabilities built into the Python language that will be used ubiquitously throughout the book. While add-on libraries like pandas and NumPy add advanced computational functionality for larger datasets, they are designed to be used together with Python's built-in data manipulation tools.

We'll start with Python's workhorse data structures: tuples, lists, dictionaries, and sets. Then, we'll discuss creating your own reusable Python functions. Finally, we'll look at the mechanics of Python file objects and interacting with your local hard drive.

3.1 Data Structures and Sequences

Python's data structures are simple but powerful. Mastering their use is a critical part of becoming a proficient Python programmer. We start with tuple, list, and dictionary, which are some of the most frequently used *sequence* types.

Tuple

A *tuple* is a fixed-length, immutable sequence of Python objects which, once assigned, cannot be changed. The easiest way to create one is with a comma-separated sequence of values wrapped in parentheses:

```
In [2]: tup = (4, 5, 6)

In [3]: tup
Out[3]: (4, 5, 6)
```

In many contexts, the parentheses can be omitted, so here we could also have written:

```
In [4]: tup = 4, 5, 6
```

```
In [5]: tup
Out[5]: (4, 5, 6)
```

You can convert any sequence or iterator to a tuple by invoking `tuple`:

```
In [6]: tuple([4, 0, 2])
Out[6]: (4, 0, 2)
```

```
In [7]: tup = tuple('string')
```

```
In [8]: tup
Out[8]: ('s', 't', 'r', 'i', 'n', 'g')
```

Elements can be accessed with square brackets [ ] as with most other sequence types. As in C, C++, Java, and many other languages, sequences are 0-indexed in Python:

```
In [9]: tup[0]
Out[9]: 's'
```

When you're defining tuples within more complicated expressions, it's often necessary to enclose the values in parentheses, as in this example of creating a tuple of tuples:

```
In [10]: nested_tup = (4, 5, 6), (7, 8)
```

```
In [11]: nested_tup
Out[11]: ((4, 5, 6), (7, 8))
```

```
In [12]: nested_tup[0]
Out[12]: (4, 5, 6)
```

```
In [13]: nested_tup[1]
Out[13]: (7, 8)
```

While the objects stored in a tuple may be mutable themselves, once the tuple is created it's not possible to modify which object is stored in each slot:

```
In [14]: tup = tuple(['foo', [1, 2], True])
```

```
In [15]: tup[2] = False
---------------------------------------------------------------
TypeError                                 Traceback (most recent call last)
<ipython-input-15-b89d0c4ae599> in <module>
----> 1 tup[2] = False
TypeError: 'tuple' object does not support item assignment
```

If an object inside a tuple is mutable, such as a list, you can modify it in place:

```
In [16]: tup[1].append(3)
```

```
In [17]: tup
Out[17]: ('foo', [1, 2, 3], True)
```

You can concatenate tuples using the + operator to produce longer tuples:

```
In [18]: (4, None, 'foo') + (6, 0) + ('bar',)
Out[18]: (4, None, 'foo', 6, 0, 'bar')
```

Multiplying a tuple by an integer, as with lists, has the effect of concatenating that many copies of the tuple:

```
In [19]: ('foo', 'bar') * 4
Out[19]: ('foo', 'bar', 'foo', 'bar', 'foo', 'bar', 'foo', 'bar')
```

Note that the objects themselves are not copied, only the references to them.

Unpacking tuples

If you try to *assign* to a tuple-like expression of variables, Python will attempt to *unpack* the value on the righthand side of the equals sign:

```
In [20]: tup = (4, 5, 6)

In [21]: a, b, c = tup

In [22]: b
Out[22]: 5
```

Even sequences with nested tuples can be unpacked:

```
In [23]: tup = 4, 5, (6, 7)

In [24]: a, b, (c, d) = tup

In [25]: d
Out[25]: 7
```

Using this functionality you can easily swap variable names, a task that in many languages might look like:

```
tmp = a
a = b
b = tmp
```

But, in Python, the swap can be done like this:

```
In [26]: a, b = 1, 2

In [27]: a
Out[27]: 1

In [28]: b
Out[28]: 2

In [29]: b, a = a, b
```

```
In [30]: a
Out[30]: 2

In [31]: b
Out[31]: 1
```

A common use of variable unpacking is iterating over sequences of tuples or lists:

```
In [32]: seq = [(1, 2, 3), (4, 5, 6), (7, 8, 9)]

In [33]: for a, b, c in seq:
   ....:     print(f'a={a}, b={b}, c={c}')
a=1, b=2, c=3
a=4, b=5, c=6
a=7, b=8, c=9
```

Another common use is returning multiple values from a function. I'll cover this in more detail later.

There are some situations where you may want to "pluck" a few elements from the beginning of a tuple. There is a special syntax that can do this, *rest, which is also used in function signatures to capture an arbitrarily long list of positional arguments:

```
In [34]: values = 1, 2, 3, 4, 5

In [35]: a, b, *rest = values

In [36]: a
Out[36]: 1

In [37]: b
Out[37]: 2

In [38]: rest
Out[38]: [3, 4, 5]
```

This rest bit is sometimes something you want to discard; there is nothing special about the rest name. As a matter of convention, many Python programmers will use the underscore (_) for unwanted variables:

```
In [39]: a, b, *_ = values
```

Tuple methods

Since the size and contents of a tuple cannot be modified, it is very light on instance methods. A particularly useful one (also available on lists) is count, which counts the number of occurrences of a value:

```
In [40]: a = (1, 2, 2, 2, 3, 4, 2)

In [41]: a.count(2)
Out[41]: 4
```

List

In contrast with tuples, lists are variable length and their contents can be modified in place. Lists are mutable. You can define them using square brackets [] or using the `list` type function:

```
In [42]: a_list = [2, 3, 7, None]

In [43]: tup = ("foo", "bar", "baz")

In [44]: b_list = list(tup)

In [45]: b_list
Out[45]: ['foo', 'bar', 'baz']

In [46]: b_list[1] = "peekaboo"

In [47]: b_list
Out[47]: ['foo', 'peekaboo', 'baz']
```

Lists and tuples are semantically similar (though tuples cannot be modified) and can be used interchangeably in many functions.

The `list` built-in function is frequently used in data processing as a way to material-ize an iterator or generator expression:

```
In [48]: gen = range(10)

In [49]: gen
Out[49]: range(0, 10)

In [50]: list(gen)
Out[50]: [0, 1, 2, 3, 4, 5, 6, 7, 8, 9]
```

Adding and removing elements

Elements can be appended to the end of the list with the append method:

```
In [51]: b_list.append("dwarf")

In [52]: b_list
Out[52]: ['foo', 'peekaboo', 'baz', 'dwarf']
```

Using `insert` you can insert an element at a specific location in the list:

```
In [53]: b_list.insert(1, "red")

In [54]: b_list
Out[54]: ['foo', 'red', 'peekaboo', 'baz', 'dwarf']
```

The insertion index must be between 0 and the length of the list, inclusive.

insert is computationally expensive compared with append, because references to subsequent elements have to be shifted internally to make room for the new element. If you need to insert elements at both the beginning and end of a sequence, you may wish to explore collections.deque, a double-ended queue, which is optimized for this purpose and found in the Python Standard Library.

The inverse operation to insert is pop, which removes and returns an element at a particular index:

```
In [55]: b_list.pop(2)
Out[55]: 'peekaboo'

In [56]: b_list
Out[56]: ['foo', 'red', 'baz', 'dwarf']
```

Elements can be removed by value with remove, which locates the first such value and removes it from the list:

```
In [57]: b_list.append("foo")

In [58]: b_list
Out[58]: ['foo', 'red', 'baz', 'dwarf', 'foo']

In [59]: b_list.remove("foo")

In [60]: b_list
Out[60]: ['red', 'baz', 'dwarf', 'foo']
```

If performance is not a concern, by using append and remove, you can use a Python list as a set-like data structure (although Python has actual set objects, discussed later).

Check if a list contains a value using the in keyword:

```
In [61]: "dwarf" in b_list
Out[61]: True
```

The keyword not can be used to negate in:

```
In [62]: "dwarf" not in b_list
Out[62]: False
```

Checking whether a list contains a value is a lot slower than doing so with dictionaries and sets (to be introduced shortly), as Python makes a linear scan across the values of the list, whereas it can check the others (based on hash tables) in constant time.

Concatenating and combining lists

Similar to tuples, adding two lists together with + concatenates them:

```
In [63]: [4, None, "foo"] + [7, 8, (2, 3)]
Out[63]: [4, None, 'foo', 7, 8, (2, 3)]
```

If you have a list already defined, you can append multiple elements to it using the extend method:

```
In [64]: x = [4, None, "foo"]

In [65]: x.extend([7, 8, (2, 3)])

In [66]: x
Out[66]: [4, None, 'foo', 7, 8, (2, 3)]
```

Note that list concatenation by addition is a comparatively expensive operation since a new list must be created and the objects copied over. Using extend to append elements to an existing list, especially if you are building up a large list, is usually preferable. Thus:

```
everything = []
for chunk in list_of_lists:
    everything.extend(chunk)
```

is faster than the concatenative alternative:

```
everything = []
for chunk in list_of_lists:
    everything = everything + chunk
```

Sorting

You can sort a list in place (without creating a new object) by calling its sort function:

```
In [67]: a = [7, 2, 5, 1, 3]

In [68]: a.sort()

In [69]: a
Out[69]: [1, 2, 3, 5, 7]
```

sort has a few options that will occasionally come in handy. One is the ability to pass a secondary *sort key*—that is, a function that produces a value to use to sort the objects. For example, we could sort a collection of strings by their lengths:

```
In [70]: b = ["saw", "small", "He", "foxes", "six"]

In [71]: b.sort(key=len)

In [72]: b
Out[72]: ['He', 'saw', 'six', 'small', 'foxes']
```

Soon, we'll look at the sorted function, which can produce a sorted copy of a general sequence.

Slicing

You can select sections of most sequence types by using slice notation, which in its basic form consists of start:stop passed to the indexing operator []:

```
In [73]: seq = [7, 2, 3, 7, 5, 6, 0, 1]

In [74]: seq[1:5]
Out[74]: [2, 3, 7, 5]
```

Slices can also be assigned with a sequence:

```
In [75]: seq[3:5] = [6, 3]

In [76]: seq
Out[76]: [7, 2, 3, 6, 3, 6, 0, 1]
```

While the element at the start index is included, the stop index is *not included*, so that the number of elements in the result is stop - start.

Either the start or stop can be omitted, in which case they default to the start of the sequence and the end of the sequence, respectively:

```
In [77]: seq[:5]
Out[77]: [7, 2, 3, 6, 3]

In [78]: seq[3:]
Out[78]: [6, 3, 6, 0, 1]
```

Negative indices slice the sequence relative to the end:

```
In [79]: seq[-4:]
Out[79]: [3, 6, 0, 1]

In [80]: seq[-6:-2]
Out[80]: [3, 6, 3, 6]
```

Slicing semantics takes a bit of getting used to, especially if you're coming from R or MATLAB. See Figure 3-1 for a helpful illustration of slicing with positive and negative integers. In the figure, the indices are shown at the "bin edges" to help show where the slice selections start and stop using positive or negative indices.

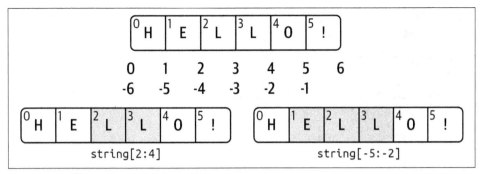

Figure 3-1. Illustration of Python slicing conventions

A `step` can also be used after a second colon to, say, take every other element:

```
In [81]: seq[::2]
Out[81]: [7, 3, 3, 0]
```

A clever use of this is to pass -1, which has the useful effect of reversing a list or tuple:

```
In [82]: seq[::-1]
Out[82]: [1, 0, 6, 3, 6, 3, 2, 7]
```

Dictionary

The dictionary or dict may be the most important built-in Python data structure. In other programming languages, dictionaries are sometimes called *hash maps* or *associative arrays*. A dictionary stores a collection of *key-value* pairs, where *key* and *value* are Python objects. Each key is associated with a value so that a value can be conveniently retrieved, inserted, modified, or deleted given a particular key. One approach for creating a dictionary is to use curly braces {} and colons to separate keys and values:

```
In [83]: empty_dict = {}

In [84]: d1 = {"a": "some value", "b": [1, 2, 3, 4]}

In [85]: d1
Out[85]: {'a': 'some value', 'b': [1, 2, 3, 4]}
```

You can access, insert, or set elements using the same syntax as for accessing elements of a list or tuple:

```
In [86]: d1[7] = "an integer"

In [87]: d1
Out[87]: {'a': 'some value', 'b': [1, 2, 3, 4], 7: 'an integer'}

In [88]: d1["b"]
Out[88]: [1, 2, 3, 4]
```

You can check if a dictionary contains a key using the same syntax used for checking whether a list or tuple contains a value:

```
In [89]: "b" in d1
Out[89]: True
```

You can delete values using either the del keyword or the pop method (which simultaneously returns the value and deletes the key):

```
In [90]: d1[5] = "some value"

In [91]: d1
Out[91]:
{'a': 'some value',
 'b': [1, 2, 3, 4],
 7: 'an integer',
 5: 'some value'}

In [92]: d1["dummy"] = "another value"

In [93]: d1
Out[93]:
{'a': 'some value',
 'b': [1, 2, 3, 4],
 7: 'an integer',
 5: 'some value',
 'dummy': 'another value'}

In [94]: del d1[5]

In [95]: d1
Out[95]:
{'a': 'some value',
 'b': [1, 2, 3, 4],
 7: 'an integer',
 'dummy': 'another value'}

In [96]: ret = d1.pop("dummy")

In [97]: ret
Out[97]: 'another value'

In [98]: d1
Out[98]: {'a': 'some value', 'b': [1, 2, 3, 4], 7: 'an integer'}
```

The keys and values method gives you iterators of the dictionary's keys and values, respectively. The order of the keys depends on the order of their insertion, and these functions output the keys and values in the same respective order:

```
In [99]: list(d1.keys())
Out[99]: ['a', 'b', 7]
```

```
In [100]: list(d1.values())
Out[100]: ['some value', [1, 2, 3, 4], 'an integer']
```

If you need to iterate over both the keys and values, you can use the items method to iterate over the keys and values as 2-tuples:

```
In [101]: list(d1.items())
Out[101]: [('a', 'some value'), ('b', [1, 2, 3, 4]), (7, 'an integer')]
```

You can merge one dictionary into another using the update method:

```
In [102]: d1.update({"b": "foo", "c": 12})

In [103]: d1
Out[103]: {'a': 'some value', 'b': 'foo', 7: 'an integer', 'c': 12}
```

The update method changes dictionaries in place, so any existing keys in the data passed to update will have their old values discarded.

Creating dictionaries from sequences

It's common to occasionally end up with two sequences that you want to pair up element-wise in a dictionary. As a first cut, you might write code like this:

```
mapping = {}
for key, value in zip(key_list, value_list):
    mapping[key] = value
```

Since a dictionary is essentially a collection of 2-tuples, the dict function accepts a list of 2-tuples:

```
In [104]: tuples = zip(range(5), reversed(range(5)))

In [105]: tuples
Out[105]: <zip at 0x7fefe4553a00>

In [106]: mapping = dict(tuples)

In [107]: mapping
Out[107]: {0: 4, 1: 3, 2: 2, 3: 1, 4: 0}
```

Later we'll talk about *dictionary comprehensions*, which are another way to construct dictionaries.

Default values

It's common to have logic like:

```
if key in some_dict:
    value = some_dict[key]
else:
    value = default_value
```

Thus, the dictionary methods `get` and `pop` can take a default value to be returned, so that the above `if-else` block can be written simply as:

```
value = some_dict.get(key, default_value)
```

`get` by default will return `None` if the key is not present, while `pop` will raise an exception. With *setting* values, it may be that the values in a dictionary are another kind of collection, like a list. For example, you could imagine categorizing a list of words by their first letters as a dictionary of lists:

```
In [108]: words = ["apple", "bat", "bar", "atom", "book"]

In [109]: by_letter = {}

In [110]: for word in words:
   .....:     letter = word[0]
   .....:     if letter not in by_letter:
   .....:         by_letter[letter] = [word]
   .....:     else:
   .....:         by_letter[letter].append(word)
   .....:

In [111]: by_letter
Out[111]: {'a': ['apple', 'atom'], 'b': ['bat', 'bar', 'book']}
```

The `setdefault` dictionary method can be used to simplify this workflow. The preceding for loop can be rewritten as:

```
In [112]: by_letter = {}

In [113]: for word in words:
   .....:     letter = word[0]
   .....:     by_letter.setdefault(letter, []).append(word)
   .....:

In [114]: by_letter
Out[114]: {'a': ['apple', 'atom'], 'b': ['bat', 'bar', 'book']}
```

The built-in `collections` module has a useful class, `defaultdict`, which makes this even easier. To create one, you pass a type or function for generating the default value for each slot in the dictionary:

```
In [115]: from collections import defaultdict

In [116]: by_letter = defaultdict(list)

In [117]: for word in words:
   .....:     by_letter[word[0]].append(word)
```

Valid dictionary key types

While the values of a dictionary can be any Python object, the keys generally have to be immutable objects like scalar types (int, float, string) or tuples (all the objects in the tuple need to be immutable, too). The technical term here is *hashability*. You can check whether an object is hashable (can be used as a key in a dictionary) with the hash function:

```
In [118]: hash("string")
Out[118]: 3634226001988967898

In [119]: hash((1, 2, (2, 3)))
Out[119]: -9209053662355515447

In [120]: hash((1, 2, [2, 3])) # fails because lists are mutable
---------------------------------------------------------------------------
TypeError                                 Traceback (most recent call last)
<ipython-input-120-473c35a62c0b> in <module>
----> 1 hash((1, 2, [2, 3])) # fails because lists are mutable
TypeError: unhashable type: 'list'
```

The hash values you see when using the hash function in general will depend on the Python version you are using.

To use a list as a key, one option is to convert it to a tuple, which can be hashed as long as its elements also can be:

```
In [121]: d = {}

In [122]: d[tuple([1, 2, 3])] = 5

In [123]: d
Out[123]: {(1, 2, 3): 5}
```

Set

A *set* is an unordered collection of unique elements. A set can be created in two ways: via the set function or via a *set literal* with curly braces:

```
In [124]: set([2, 2, 2, 1, 3, 3])
Out[124]: {1, 2, 3}

In [125]: {2, 2, 2, 1, 3, 3}
Out[125]: {1, 2, 3}
```

Sets support mathematical *set operations* like union, intersection, difference, and symmetric difference. Consider these two example sets:

```
In [126]: a = {1, 2, 3, 4, 5}

In [127]: b = {3, 4, 5, 6, 7, 8}
```

The union of these two sets is the set of distinct elements occurring in either set. This can be computed with either the union method or the | binary operator:

```
In [128]: a.union(b)
Out[128]: {1, 2, 3, 4, 5, 6, 7, 8}

In [129]: a | b
Out[129]: {1, 2, 3, 4, 5, 6, 7, 8}
```

The intersection contains the elements occurring in both sets. The & operator or the intersection method can be used:

```
In [130]: a.intersection(b)
Out[130]: {3, 4, 5}

In [131]: a & b
Out[131]: {3, 4, 5}
```

See Table 3-1 for a list of commonly used set methods.

Table 3-1. Python set operations

Function	Alternative syntax	Description
a.add(x)	N/A	Add element x to set a
a.clear()	N/A	Reset set a to an empty state, discarding all of its elements
a.remove(x)	N/A	Remove element x from set a
a.pop()	N/A	Remove an arbitrary element from set a, raising KeyError if the set is empty
a.union(b)	a	b	All of the unique elements in a and b
a.update(b)	a |= b	Set the contents of a to be the union of the elements in a and b
a.intersection(b)	a & b	All of the elements in *both* a and b
a.intersection_update(b)	a &= b	Set the contents of a to be the intersection of the elements in a and b
a.difference(b)	a - b	The elements in a that are not in b
a.difference_update(b)	a -= b	Set a to the elements in a that are not in b
a.symmetric_difference(b)	a ^ b	All of the elements in either a or b but *not both*
a.symmetric_difference_update(b)	a ^= b	Set a to contain the elements in either a or b but *not both*
a.issubset(b)	<=	True if the elements of a are all contained in b
a.issuperset(b)	>=	True if the elements of b are all contained in a
a.isdisjoint(b)	N/A	True if a and b have no elements in common

If you pass an input that is not a set to methods like `union` and `intersection`, Python will convert the input to a set before executing the operation. When using the binary operators, both objects must already be sets.

All of the logical set operations have in-place counterparts, which enable you to replace the contents of the set on the left side of the operation with the result. For very large sets, this may be more efficient:

```
In [132]: c = a.copy()

In [133]: c |= b

In [134]: c
Out[134]: {1, 2, 3, 4, 5, 6, 7, 8}

In [135]: d = a.copy()

In [136]: d &= b

In [137]: d
Out[137]: {3, 4, 5}
```

Like dictionary keys, set elements generally must be immutable, and they must be *hashable* (which means that calling `hash` on a value does not raise an exception). In order to store list-like elements (or other mutable sequences) in a set, you can convert them to tuples:

```
In [138]: my_data = [1, 2, 3, 4]

In [139]: my_set = {tuple(my_data)}

In [140]: my_set
Out[140]: {(1, 2, 3, 4)}
```

You can also check if a set is a subset of (is contained in) or a superset of (contains all elements of) another set:

```
In [141]: a_set = {1, 2, 3, 4, 5}

In [142]: {1, 2, 3}.issubset(a_set)
Out[142]: True

In [143]: a_set.issuperset({1, 2, 3})
Out[143]: True
```

Sets are equal if and only if their contents are equal:

```
In [144]: {1, 2, 3} == {3, 2, 1}
Out[144]: True
```

Built-In Sequence Functions

Python has a handful of useful sequence functions that you should familiarize your-self with and use at any opportunity.

enumerate

It's common when iterating over a sequence to want to keep track of the index of the current item. A do-it-yourself approach would look like:

```
index = 0
for value in collection:
    # do something with value
    index += 1
```

Since this is so common, Python has a built-in function, enumerate, which returns a sequence of (i, value) tuples:

```
for index, value in enumerate(collection):
    # do something with value
```

sorted

The sorted function returns a new sorted list from the elements of any sequence:

```
In [145]: sorted([7, 1, 2, 6, 0, 3, 2])
Out[145]: [0, 1, 2, 2, 3, 6, 7]

In [146]: sorted("horse race")
Out[146]: [' ', 'a', 'c', 'e', 'e', 'h', 'o', 'r', 'r', 's']
```

The sorted function accepts the same arguments as the sort method on lists.

zip

zip "pairs" up the elements of a number of lists, tuples, or other sequences to create a list of tuples:

```
In [147]: seq1 = ["foo", "bar", "baz"]

In [148]: seq2 = ["one", "two", "three"]

In [149]: zipped = zip(seq1, seq2)

In [150]: list(zipped)
Out[150]: [('foo', 'one'), ('bar', 'two'), ('baz', 'three')]
```

zip can take an arbitrary number of sequences, and the number of elements it produces is determined by the *shortest* sequence:

```
In [151]: seq3 = [False, True]
```

```
In [152]: list(zip(seq1, seq2, seq3))
Out[152]: [('foo', 'one', False), ('bar', 'two', True)]
```

A common use of `zip` is simultaneously iterating over multiple sequences, possibly also combined with `enumerate`:

```
In [153]: for index, (a, b) in enumerate(zip(seq1, seq2)):
   .....:     print(f"{index}: {a}, {b}")
   .....:
0: foo, one
1: bar, two
2: baz, three
```

reversed

`reversed` iterates over the elements of a sequence in reverse order:

```
In [154]: list(reversed(range(10)))
Out[154]: [9, 8, 7, 6, 5, 4, 3, 2, 1, 0]
```

Keep in mind that `reversed` is a generator (to be discussed in some more detail later), so it does not create the reversed sequence until materialized (e.g., with `list` or a `for` loop).

List, Set, and Dictionary Comprehensions

List comprehensions are a convenient and widely used Python language feature. They allow you to concisely form a new list by filtering the elements of a collection, transforming the elements passing the filter into one concise expression. They take the basic form:

```
[expr for value in collection if condition]
```

This is equivalent to the following `for` loop:

```
result = []
for value in collection:
    if condition:
        result.append(expr)
```

The filter condition can be omitted, leaving only the expression. For example, given a list of strings, we could filter out strings with length 2 or less and convert them to uppercase like this:

```
In [155]: strings = ["a", "as", "bat", "car", "dove", "python"]
```

```
In [156]: [x.upper() for x in strings if len(x) > 2]
Out[156]: ['BAT', 'CAR', 'DOVE', 'PYTHON']
```

Set and dictionary comprehensions are a natural extension, producing sets and dictionaries in an idiomatically similar way instead of lists.

A dictionary comprehension looks like this:

```
dict_comp = {key-expr: value-expr for value in collection
             if condition}
```

A set comprehension looks like the equivalent list comprehension except with curly braces instead of square brackets:

```
set_comp = {expr for value in collection if condition}
```

Like list comprehensions, set and dictionary comprehensions are mostly conveniences, but they similarly can make code both easier to write and read. Consider the list of strings from before. Suppose we wanted a set containing just the lengths of the strings contained in the collection; we could easily compute this using a set comprehension:

```
In [157]: unique_lengths = {len(x) for x in strings}
```

```
In [158]: unique_lengths
Out[158]: {1, 2, 3, 4, 6}
```

We could also express this more functionally using the map function, introduced shortly:

```
In [159]: set(map(len, strings))
Out[159]: {1, 2, 3, 4, 6}
```

As a simple dictionary comprehension example, we could create a lookup map of these strings for their locations in the list:

```
In [160]: loc_mapping = {value: index for index, value in enumerate(strings)}
```

```
In [161]: loc_mapping
Out[161]: {'a': 0, 'as': 1, 'bat': 2, 'car': 3, 'dove': 4, 'python': 5}
```

Nested list comprehensions

Suppose we have a list of lists containing some English and Spanish names:

```
In [162]: all_data = [["John", "Emily", "Michael", "Mary", "Steven"],
     ....:            ["Maria", "Juan", "Javier", "Natalia", "Pilar"]]
```

Suppose we wanted to get a single list containing all names with two or more a's in them. We could certainly do this with a simple for loop:

```
In [163]: names_of_interest = []
```

```
In [164]: for names in all_data:
     ....:     enough_as = [name for name in names if name.count("a") >= 2]
     ....:     names_of_interest.extend(enough_as)
     ....:
```

```
In [165]: names_of_interest
Out[165]: ['Maria', 'Natalia']
```

You can actually wrap this whole operation up in a single *nested list comprehension*, which will look like:

```
In [166]: result = [name for names in all_data for name in names
    .....:          if name.count("a") >= 2]

In [167]: result
Out[167]: ['Maria', 'Natalia']
```

At first, nested list comprehensions are a bit hard to wrap your head around. The for parts of the list comprehension are arranged according to the order of nesting, and any filter condition is put at the end as before. Here is another example where we "flatten" a list of tuples of integers into a simple list of integers:

```
In [168]: some_tuples = [(1, 2, 3), (4, 5, 6), (7, 8, 9)]

In [169]: flattened = [x for tup in some_tuples for x in tup]

In [170]: flattened
Out[170]: [1, 2, 3, 4, 5, 6, 7, 8, 9]
```

Keep in mind that the order of the for expressions would be the same if you wrote a nested for loop instead of a list comprehension:

```
flattened = []

for tup in some_tuples:
    for x in tup:
        flattened.append(x)
```

You can have arbitrarily many levels of nesting, though if you have more than two or three levels of nesting, you should probably start to question whether this makes sense from a code readability standpoint. It's important to distinguish the syntax just shown from a list comprehension inside a list comprehension, which is also perfectly valid:

```
In [172]: [[x for x in tup] for tup in some_tuples]
Out[172]: [[1, 2, 3], [4, 5, 6], [7, 8, 9]]
```

This produces a list of lists, rather than a flattened list of all of the inner elements.

3.2 Functions

Functions are the primary and most important method of code organization and reuse in Python. As a rule of thumb, if you anticipate needing to repeat the same or very similar code more than once, it may be worth writing a reusable function. Functions can also help make your code more readable by giving a name to a group of Python statements.

Functions are declared with the def keyword. A function contains a block of code with an optional use of the return keyword:

```
In [173]: def my_function(x, y):
     .....:     return x + y
```

When a line with return is reached, the value or expression after return is sent to the context where the function was called, for example:

```
In [174]: my_function(1, 2)
Out[174]: 3

In [175]: result = my_function(1, 2)

In [176]: result
Out[176]: 3
```

There is no issue with having multiple return statements. If Python reaches the end of a function without encountering a return statement, None is returned automatically. For example:

```
In [177]: def function_without_return(x):
     .....:     print(x)

In [178]: result = function_without_return("hello!")
hello!

In [179]: print(result)
None
```

Each function can have *positional* arguments and *keyword* arguments. Keyword arguments are most commonly used to specify default values or optional arguments. Here we will define a function with an optional z argument with the default value 1.5:

```
def my_function2(x, y, z=1.5):
    if z > 1:
        return z * (x + y)
    else:
        return z / (x + y)
```

While keyword arguments are optional, all positional arguments must be specified when calling a function.

You can pass values to the z argument with or without the keyword provided, though using the keyword is encouraged:

```
In [181]: my_function2(5, 6, z=0.7)
Out[181]: 0.06363636363636363

In [182]: my_function2(3.14, 7, 3.5)
Out[182]: 35.49
```

```
In [183]: my_function2(10, 20)
Out[183]: 45.0
```

The main restriction on function arguments is that the keyword arguments *must* follow the positional arguments (if any). You can specify keyword arguments in any order. This frees you from having to remember the order in which the function arguments were specified. You need to remember only what their names are.

Namespaces, Scope, and Local Functions

Functions can access variables created inside the function as well as those outside the function in higher (or even *global*) scopes. An alternative and more descriptive name describing a variable scope in Python is a *namespace*. Any variables that are assigned within a function by default are assigned to the local namespace. The local namespace is created when the function is called and is immediately populated by the function's arguments. After the function is finished, the local namespace is destroyed (with some exceptions that are outside the purview of this chapter). Consider the following function:

```
def func():
    a = []
    for i in range(5):
        a.append(i)
```

When func() is called, the empty list a is created, five elements are appended, and then a is destroyed when the function exits. Suppose instead we had declared a as follows:

```
In [184]: a = []

In [185]: def func():
   .....:         for i in range(5):
   .....:             a.append(i)
```

Each call to func will modify list a:

```
In [186]: func()

In [187]: a
Out[187]: [0, 1, 2, 3, 4]

In [188]: func()

In [189]: a
Out[189]: [0, 1, 2, 3, 4, 0, 1, 2, 3, 4]
```

Assigning variables outside of the function's scope is possible, but those variables must be declared explicitly using either the global or nonlocal keywords:

```
In [190]: a = None
```

```
In [191]: def bind_a_variable():
     .....:     global a
     .....:     a = []
     .....: bind_a_variable()
     .....:

In [192]: print(a)
[]
```

`nonlocal` allows a function to modify variables defined in a higher-level scope that is not global. Since its use is somewhat esoteric (I never use it in this book), I refer you to the Python documentation to learn more about it.

 I generally discourage use of the `global` keyword. Typically, global variables are used to store some kind of state in a system. If you find yourself using a lot of them, it may indicate a need for object-oriented programming (using classes).

Returning Multiple Values

When I first programmed in Python after having programmed in Java and C++, one of my favorite features was the ability to return multiple values from a function with simple syntax. Here's an example:

```
def f():
    a = 5
    b = 6
    c = 7
    return a, b, c

a, b, c = f()
```

In data analysis and other scientific applications, you may find yourself doing this often. What's happening here is that the function is actually just returning *one* object, a tuple, which is then being unpacked into the result variables. In the preceding example, we could have done this instead:

```
return_value = f()
```

In this case, `return_value` would be a 3-tuple with the three returned variables. A potentially attractive alternative to returning multiple values like before might be to return a dictionary instead:

```
def f():
    a = 5
    b = 6
    c = 7
    return {"a" : a, "b" : b, "c" : c}
```

This alternative technique can be useful depending on what you are trying to do.

Functions Are Objects

Since Python functions are objects, many constructs can be easily expressed that are difficult to do in other languages. Suppose we were doing some data cleaning and needed to apply a bunch of transformations to the following list of strings:

```
In [193]: states = ["   Alabama ", "Georgia!", "Georgia", "georgia", "FlOrIda",
   .....:            "south   carolina##", "West virginia?"]
```

Anyone who has ever worked with user-submitted survey data has seen messy results like these. Lots of things need to happen to make this list of strings uniform and ready for analysis: stripping whitespace, removing punctuation symbols, and standardizing proper capitalization. One way to do this is to use built-in string methods along with the re standard library module for regular expressions:

```python
import re

def clean_strings(strings):
    result = []
    for value in strings:
        value = value.strip()
        value = re.sub("[!#?]", "", value)
        value = value.title()
        result.append(value)
    return result
```

The result looks like this:

```
In [195]: clean_strings(states)
Out[195]:
['Alabama',
 'Georgia',
 'Georgia',
 'Georgia',
 'Florida',
 'South   Carolina',
 'West Virginia']
```

An alternative approach that you may find useful is to make a list of the operations you want to apply to a particular set of strings:

```python
def remove_punctuation(value):
    return re.sub("[!#?]", "", value)

clean_ops = [str.strip, remove_punctuation, str.title]

def clean_strings(strings, ops):
    result = []
    for value in strings:
        for func in ops:
            value = func(value)
        result.append(value)
    return result
```

Then we have the following:

```
In [197]: clean_strings(states, clean_ops)
Out[197]:
['Alabama',
 'Georgia',
 'Georgia',
 'Georgia',
 'Florida',
 'South   Carolina',
 'West Virginia']
```

A more *functional* pattern like this enables you to easily modify how the strings are transformed at a very high level. The `clean_strings` function is also now more reusable and generic.

You can use functions as arguments to other functions like the built-in `map` function, which applies a function to a sequence of some kind:

```
In [198]: for x in map(remove_punctuation, states):
   .....:        print(x)
Alabama
Georgia
Georgia
georgia
FlOrIda
south   carolina
West virginia
```

`map` can be used as an alternative to list comprehensions without any filter.

Anonymous (Lambda) Functions

Python has support for so-called *anonymous* or *lambda* functions, which are a way of writing functions consisting of a single statement, the result of which is the return value. They are defined with the `lambda` keyword, which has no meaning other than "we are declaring an anonymous function":

```
In [199]: def short_function(x):
   .....:        return x * 2

In [200]: equiv_anon = lambda x: x * 2
```

I usually refer to these as lambda functions in the rest of the book. They are especially convenient in data analysis because, as you'll see, there are many cases where data transformation functions will take functions as arguments. It's often less typing (and clearer) to pass a lambda function as opposed to writing a full-out function declaration or even assigning the lambda function to a local variable. Consider this example:

```
In [201]: def apply_to_list(some_list, f):
   .....:        return [f(x) for x in some_list]
```

```
In [202]: ints = [4, 0, 1, 5, 6]

In [203]: apply_to_list(ints, lambda x: x * 2)
Out[203]: [8, 0, 2, 10, 12]
```

You could also have written [x * 2 for x in ints], but here we were able to succinctly pass a custom operator to the apply_to_list function.

As another example, suppose you wanted to sort a collection of strings by the number of distinct letters in each string:

```
In [204]: strings = ["foo", "card", "bar", "aaaa", "abab"]
```

Here we could pass a lambda function to the list's sort method:

```
In [205]: strings.sort(key=lambda x: len(set(x)))

In [206]: strings
Out[206]: ['aaaa', 'foo', 'abab', 'bar', 'card']
```

Generators

Many objects in Python support iteration, such as over objects in a list or lines in a file. This is accomplished by means of the *iterator protocol*, a generic way to make objects iterable. For example, iterating over a dictionary yields the dictionary keys:

```
In [207]: some_dict = {"a": 1, "b": 2, "c": 3}

In [208]: for key in some_dict:
   .....:     print(key)
a
b
c
```

When you write for key in some_dict, the Python interpreter first attempts to create an iterator out of some_dict:

```
In [209]: dict_iterator = iter(some_dict)

In [210]: dict_iterator
Out[210]: <dict_keyiterator at 0x7fefe45465c0>
```

An iterator is any object that will yield objects to the Python interpreter when used in a context like a for loop. Most methods expecting a list or list-like object will also accept any iterable object. This includes built-in methods such as min, max, and sum, and type constructors like list and tuple:

```
In [211]: list(dict_iterator)
Out[211]: ['a', 'b', 'c']
```

A *generator* is a convenient way, similar to writing a normal function, to construct a new iterable object. Whereas normal functions execute and return a single result at a time, generators can return a sequence of multiple values by pausing and resuming execution each time the generator is used. To create a generator, use the `yield` keyword instead of `return` in a function:

```
def squares(n=10):
    print(f"Generating squares from 1 to {n ** 2}")
    for i in range(1, n + 1):
        yield i ** 2
```

When you actually call the generator, no code is immediately executed:

```
In [213]: gen = squares()
```

```
In [214]: gen
Out[214]: <generator object squares at 0x7fefe437d620>
```

It is not until you request elements from the generator that it begins executing its code:

```
In [215]: for x in gen:
   .....:         print(x, end=" ")
Generating squares from 1 to 100
1 4 9 16 25 36 49 64 81 100
```

 Since generators produce output one element at a time versus an entire list all at once, it can help your program use less memory.

Generator expressions

Another way to make a generator is by using a *generator expression*. This is a generator analogue to list, dictionary, and set comprehensions. To create one, enclose what would otherwise be a list comprehension within parentheses instead of brackets:

```
In [216]: gen = (x ** 2 for x in range(100))
```

```
In [217]: gen
Out[217]: <generator object <genexpr> at 0x7fefe437d000>
```

This is equivalent to the following more verbose generator:

```
def _make_gen():
    for x in range(100):
        yield x ** 2
gen = _make_gen()
```

Generator expressions can be used instead of list comprehensions as function arguments in some cases:

```
In [218]: sum(x ** 2 for x in range(100))
Out[218]: 328350

In [219]: dict((i, i ** 2) for i in range(5))
Out[219]: {0: 0, 1: 1, 2: 4, 3: 9, 4: 16}
```

Depending on the number of elements produced by the comprehension expression, the generator version can sometimes be meaningfully faster.

itertools module

The standard library itertools module has a collection of generators for many common data algorithms. For example, groupby takes any sequence and a function, grouping consecutive elements in the sequence by return value of the function. Here's an example:

```
In [220]: import itertools

In [221]: def first_letter(x):
   .....:         return x[0]

In [222]: names = ["Alan", "Adam", "Wes", "Will", "Albert", "Steven"]

In [223]: for letter, names in itertools.groupby(names, first_letter):
   .....:         print(letter, list(names)) # names is a generator
A ['Alan', 'Adam']
W ['Wes', 'Will']
A ['Albert']
S ['Steven']
```

See Table 3-2 for a list of a few other itertools functions I've frequently found helpful. You may like to check out the official Python documentation (*https://docs.python.org/3/library/itertools.html*) for more on this useful built-in utility module.

Table 3-2. Some useful itertools functions

Function	Description
chain(*iterables)	Generates a sequence by chaining iterators together. Once elements from the first iterator are exhausted, elements from the next iterator are returned, and so on.
combinations(iterable, k)	Generates a sequence of all possible k-tuples of elements in the iterable, ignoring order and without replacement (see also the companion function combinations_with_replacement).
permutations(iterable, k)	Generates a sequence of all possible k-tuples of elements in the iterable, respecting order.
groupby(iterable[, keyfunc])	Generates (key, sub-iterator) for each unique key.
product(*iterables, repeat=1)	Generates the Cartesian product of the input iterables as tuples, similar to a nested for loop.

Errors and Exception Handling

Handling Python errors or *exceptions* gracefully is an important part of building robust programs. In data analysis applications, many functions work only on certain kinds of input. As an example, Python's float function is capable of casting a string to a floating-point number, but it fails with ValueError on improper inputs:

```
In [224]: float("1.2345")
Out[224]: 1.2345

In [225]: float("something")
---------------------------------------------------------------------------
ValueError                                Traceback (most recent call last)
<ipython-input-225-5ccfe07933f4> in <module>
----> 1 float("something")
ValueError: could not convert string to float: 'something'
```

Suppose we wanted a version of float that fails gracefully, returning the input argument. We can do this by writing a function that encloses the call to float in a try/except block (execute this code in IPython):

```
def attempt_float(x):
    try:
        return float(x)
    except:
        return x
```

The code in the except part of the block will only be executed if float(x) raises an exception:

```
In [227]: attempt_float("1.2345")
Out[227]: 1.2345

In [228]: attempt_float("something")
Out[228]: 'something'
```

You might notice that float can raise exceptions other than ValueError:

```
In [229]: float((1, 2))
---------------------------------------------------------------------------
TypeError                                 Traceback (most recent call last)
<ipython-input-229-82f777b0e564> in <module>
----> 1 float((1, 2))
TypeError: float() argument must be a string or a real number, not 'tuple'
```

You might want to suppress only ValueError, since a TypeError (the input was not a string or numeric value) might indicate a legitimate bug in your program. To do that, write the exception type after except:

```
def attempt_float(x):
    try:
        return float(x)
```

```
        except ValueError:
            return x
```

We have then:

```
In [231]: attempt_float((1, 2))
- - - - - - - - - - - - - - - - - - - - - - - - - - - - - - - - - - - - - - - - - - - - - - - - - - - - - - - - -
TypeError                              Traceback (most recent call last)
<ipython-input-231-8b0026e9e6b7> in <module>
----> 1 attempt_float((1, 2))
<ipython-input-230-6209ddecd2b5> in attempt_float(x)
      1 def attempt_float(x):
      2     try:
----> 3         return float(x)
      4     except ValueError:
      5         return x
TypeError: float() argument must be a string or a real number, not 'tuple'
```

You can catch multiple exception types by writing a tuple of exception types instead (the parentheses are required):

```
def attempt_float(x):
    try:
        return float(x)
    except (TypeError, ValueError):
        return x
```

In some cases, you may not want to suppress an exception, but you want some code to be executed regardless of whether or not the code in the try block succeeds. To do this, use finally:

```
f = open(path, mode="w")

try:
    write_to_file(f)
finally:
    f.close()
```

Here, the file object f will *always* get closed. Similarly, you can have code that executes only if the try: block succeeds using else:

```
f = open(path, mode="w")

try:
    write_to_file(f)
except:
    print("Failed")
else:
    print("Succeeded")
finally:
    f.close()
```

Exceptions in IPython

If an exception is raised while you are %run-ing a script or executing any statement, IPython will by default print a full call stack trace (traceback) with a few lines of context around the position at each point in the stack:

```
In [10]: %run examples/ipython_bug.py
---------------------------------------------------------------------------
AssertionError                            Traceback (most recent call last)
/home/wesm/code/pydata-book/examples/ipython_bug.py in <module>()
     13      throws_an_exception()
     14
---> 15 calling_things()

/home/wesm/code/pydata-book/examples/ipython_bug.py in calling_things()
     11 def calling_things():
     12      works_fine()
---> 13      throws_an_exception()
     14
     15 calling_things()

/home/wesm/code/pydata-book/examples/ipython_bug.py in throws_an_exception()
      7      a = 5
      8      b = 6
----> 9      assert(a + b == 10)
     10
     11 def calling_things():

AssertionError:
```

Having additional context by itself is a big advantage over the standard Python interpreter (which does not provide any additional context). You can control the amount of context shown using the %xmode magic command, from Plain (same as the standard Python interpreter) to Verbose (which inlines function argument values and more). As you will see later in Appendix B, you can step *into the stack* (using the %debug or %pdb magics) after an error has occurred for interactive postmortem debugging.

3.3 Files and the Operating System

Most of this book uses high-level tools like pandas.read_csv to read data files from disk into Python data structures. However, it's important to understand the basics of how to work with files in Python. Fortunately, it's relatively straightforward, which is one reason Python is so popular for text and file munging.

To open a file for reading or writing, use the built-in open function with either a relative or absolute file path and an optional file encoding:

```
In [233]: path = "examples/segismundo.txt"

In [234]: f = open(path, encoding="utf-8")
```

Here, I pass `encoding="utf-8"` as a best practice because the default Unicode encoding for reading files varies from platform to platform.

By default, the file is opened in read-only mode `"r"`. We can then treat the file object `f` like a list and iterate over the lines like so:

```
for line in f:
    print(line)
```

The lines come out of the file with the end-of-line (EOL) markers intact, so you'll often see code to get an EOL-free list of lines in a file like:

```
In [235]: lines = [x.rstrip() for x in open(path, encoding="utf-8")]

In [236]: lines
Out[236]:
['Sueña el rico en su riqueza,',
 'que más cuidados le ofrece;',
 '',
 'sueña el pobre que padece',
 'su miseria y su pobreza;',
 '',
 'sueña el que a medrar empieza,',
 'sueña el que afana y pretende,',
 'sueña el que agravia y ofende,',
 '',
 'y en el mundo, en conclusión,',
 'todos sueñan lo que son,',
 'aunque ninguno lo entiende.',
 '']
```

When you use `open` to create file objects, it is recommended to close the file when you are finished with it. Closing the file releases its resources back to the operating system:

```
In [237]: f.close()
```

One of the ways to make it easier to clean up open files is to use the `with` statement:

```
In [238]: with open(path, encoding="utf-8") as f:
   .....:     lines = [x.rstrip() for x in f]
```

This will automatically close the file `f` when exiting the `with` block. Failing to ensure that files are closed will not cause problems in many small programs or scripts, but it can be an issue in programs that need to interact with a large number of files.

If we had typed `f = open(path, "w")`, a *new file* at *examples/segismundo.txt* would have been created (be careful!), overwriting any file in its place. There is also the "x" file mode, which creates a writable file but fails if the file path already exists. See Table 3-3 for a list of all valid file read/write modes.

Table 3-3. Python file modes

Mode	Description
r	Read-only mode
w	Write-only mode; creates a new file (erasing the data for any file with the same name)
x	Write-only mode; creates a new file but fails if the file path already exists
a	Append to existing file (creates the file if it does not already exist)
r+	Read and write
b	Add to mode for binary files (i.e., "rb" or "wb")
t	Text mode for files (automatically decoding bytes to Unicode); this is the default if not specified

For readable files, some of the most commonly used methods are read, seek, and tell. read returns a certain number of characters from the file. What constitutes a "character" is determined by the file encoding or simply raw bytes if the file is opened in binary mode:

```
In [239]: f1 = open(path)

In [240]: f1.read(10)
Out[240]: 'Sueña el r'

In [241]: f2 = open(path, mode="rb")  # Binary mode

In [242]: f2.read(10)
Out[242]: b'Sue\xc3\xb1a el '
```

The read method advances the file object position by the number of bytes read. tell gives you the current position:

```
In [243]: f1.tell()
Out[243]: 11

In [244]: f2.tell()
Out[244]: 10
```

Even though we read 10 characters from the file f1 opened in text mode, the position is 11 because it took that many bytes to decode 10 characters using the default encoding. You can check the default encoding in the sys module:

```
In [245]: import sys

In [246]: sys.getdefaultencoding()
Out[246]: 'utf-8'
```

To get consistent behavior across platforms, it is best to pass an encoding (such as encoding="utf-8", which is widely used) when opening files.

seek changes the file position to the indicated byte in the file:

```
In [247]: f1.seek(3)
Out[247]: 3

In [248]: f1.read(1)
Out[248]: 'ñ'

In [249]: f1.tell()
Out[249]: 5
```

Lastly, we remember to close the files:

```
In [250]: f1.close()

In [251]: f2.close()
```

To write text to a file, you can use the file's write or writelines methods. For example, we could create a version of *examples/segismundo.txt* with no blank lines like so:

```
In [252]: path
Out[252]: 'examples/segismundo.txt'

In [253]: with open("tmp.txt", mode="w") as handle:
   .....:     handle.writelines(x for x in open(path) if len(x) > 1)

In [254]: with open("tmp.txt") as f:
   .....:     lines = f.readlines()

In [255]: lines
Out[255]:
['Sueña el rico en su riqueza,\n',
 'que más cuidados le ofrece;\n',
 'sueña el pobre que padece\n',
 'su miseria y su pobreza;\n',
 'sueña el que a medrar empieza,\n',
 'sueña el que afana y pretende,\n',
 'sueña el que agravia y ofende,\n',
 'y en el mundo, en conclusión,\n',
 'todos sueñan lo que son,\n',
 'aunque ninguno lo entiende.\n']
```

See Table 3-4 for many of the most commonly used file methods.

Table 3-4. Important Python file methods or attributes

Method/attribute	Description
read([size])	Return data from file as bytes or string depending on the file mode, with optional size argument indicating the number of bytes or string characters to read
readable()	Return True if the file supports read operations
readlines([size])	Return list of lines in the file, with optional size argument

Method/attribute	Description
write(string)	Write passed string to file
writable()	Return True if the file supports write operations
writelines(strings)	Write passed sequence of strings to the file
close()	Close the file object
flush()	Flush the internal I/O buffer to disk
seek(pos)	Move to indicated file position (integer)
seekable()	Return True if the file object supports seeking and thus random access (some file-like objects do not)
tell()	Return current file position as integer
closed	True if the file is closed
encoding	The encoding used to interpret bytes in the file as Unicode (typically UTF-8)

Bytes and Unicode with Files

The default behavior for Python files (whether readable or writable) is *text mode*, which means that you intend to work with Python strings (i.e., Unicode). This contrasts with *binary mode*, which you can obtain by appending b to the file mode. Revisiting the file (which contains non-ASCII characters with UTF-8 encoding) from the previous section, we have:

```
In [258]: with open(path) as f:
   .....:     chars = f.read(10)

In [259]: chars
Out[259]: 'Sueña el r'

In [260]: len(chars)
Out[260]: 10
```

UTF-8 is a variable-length Unicode encoding, so when I request some number of characters from the file, Python reads enough bytes (which could be as few as 10 or as many as 40 bytes) from the file to decode that many characters. If I open the file in "rb" mode instead, read requests that exact number of bytes:

```
In [261]: with open(path, mode="rb") as f:
   .....:     data = f.read(10)

In [262]: data
Out[262]: b'Sue\xc3\xb1a el '
```

Depending on the text encoding, you may be able to decode the bytes to a str object yourself, but only if each of the encoded Unicode characters is fully formed:

```
In [263]: data.decode("utf-8")
Out[263]: 'Sueña el '

In [264]: data[:4].decode("utf-8")
```

```
-------------------------------------------------------------------
UnicodeDecodeError                          Traceback (most recent call last)
<ipython-input-264-846a5c2fed34> in <module>
----> 1 data[:4].decode("utf-8")
UnicodeDecodeError: 'utf-8' codec can't decode byte 0xc3 in position 3: unexpecte
d end of data
```

Text mode, combined with the encoding option of open, provides a convenient way
to convert from one Unicode encoding to another:

```
In [265]: sink_path = "sink.txt"

In [266]: with open(path) as source:
     ....:     with open(sink_path, "x", encoding="iso-8859-1") as sink:
     ....:         sink.write(source.read())

In [267]: with open(sink_path, encoding="iso-8859-1") as f:
     ....:     print(f.read(10))
Sueña el r
```

Beware using seek when opening files in any mode other than binary. If the file
position falls in the middle of the bytes defining a Unicode character, then subsequent
reads will result in an error:

```
In [269]: f = open(path, encoding='utf-8')

In [270]: f.read(5)
Out[270]: 'Sueña'

In [271]: f.seek(4)
Out[271]: 4

In [272]: f.read(1)
-------------------------------------------------------------------
UnicodeDecodeError                          Traceback (most recent call last)
<ipython-input-272-5a354f952aa4> in <module>
----> 1 f.read(1)
/miniconda/envs/book-env/lib/python3.10/codecs.py in decode(self, input, final)
    320         # decode input (taking the buffer into account)
    321         data = self.buffer + input
--> 322         (result, consumed) = self._buffer_decode(data, self.errors, final
)
    323         # keep undecoded input until the next call
    324         self.buffer = data[consumed:]
UnicodeDecodeError: 'utf-8' codec can't decode byte 0xb1 in position 0: invalid s
tart byte

In [273]: f.close()
```

If you find yourself regularly doing data analysis on non-ASCII text data, mastering
Python's Unicode functionality will prove valuable. See Python's online documentation (*https://docs.python.org*) for much more.

3.4 Conclusion

With some of the basics of the Python environment and language now under your belt, it is time to move on and learn about NumPy and array-oriented computing in Python.

## CHAPTER 4

NumPy Basics: Arrays and Vectorized Computation

NumPy, short for Numerical Python, is one of the most important foundational packages for numerical computing in Python. Many computational packages providing scientific functionality use NumPy's array objects as one of the standard interface *lingua francas* for data exchange. Much of the knowledge about NumPy that I cover is transferable to pandas as well.

Here are some of the things you'll find in NumPy:

- ndarray, an efficient multidimensional array providing fast array-oriented arithmetic operations and flexible *broadcasting* capabilities
- Mathematical functions for fast operations on entire arrays of data without having to write loops
- Tools for reading/writing array data to disk and working with memory-mapped files
- Linear algebra, random number generation, and Fourier transform capabilities
- A C API for connecting NumPy with libraries written in C, C++, or FORTRAN

Because NumPy provides a comprehensive and well-documented C API, it is straightforward to pass data to external libraries written in a low-level language, and for external libraries to return data to Python as NumPy arrays. This feature has made Python a language of choice for wrapping legacy C, C++, or FORTRAN codebases and giving them a dynamic and accessible interface.

While NumPy by itself does not provide modeling or scientific functionality, having an understanding of NumPy arrays and array-oriented computing will help you use tools with array computing semantics, like pandas, much more effectively. Since

NumPy is a large topic, I will cover many advanced NumPy features like broadcasting in more depth later (see Appendix A). Many of these advanced features are not needed to follow the rest of this book, but they may help you as you go deeper into scientific computing in Python.

For most data analysis applications, the main areas of functionality I'll focus on are:

- Fast array-based operations for data munging and cleaning, subsetting and filtering, transformation, and any other kind of computation
- Common array algorithms like sorting, unique, and set operations
- Efficient descriptive statistics and aggregating/summarizing data
- Data alignment and relational data manipulations for merging and joining heterogeneous datasets
- Expressing conditional logic as array expressions instead of loops with `if-elif-else` branches
- Group-wise data manipulations (aggregation, transformation, and function application)

While NumPy provides a computational foundation for general numerical data processing, many readers will want to use pandas as the basis for most kinds of statistics or analytics, especially on tabular data. Also, pandas provides some more domain-specific functionality like time series manipulation, which is not present in NumPy.

 Array-oriented computing in Python traces its roots back to 1995, when Jim Hugunin created the Numeric library. Over the next 10 years, many scientific programming communities began doing array programming in Python, but the library ecosystem had become fragmented in the early 2000s. In 2005, Travis Oliphant was able to forge the NumPy project from the then Numeric and Numarray projects to bring the community together around a single array computing framework.

One of the reasons NumPy is so important for numerical computations in Python is because it is designed for efficiency on large arrays of data. There are a number of reasons for this:

- NumPy internally stores data in a contiguous block of memory, independent of other built-in Python objects. NumPy's library of algorithms written in the C language can operate on this memory without any type checking or other overhead. NumPy arrays also use much less memory than built-in Python sequences.

- NumPy operations perform complex computations on entire arrays without the need for Python for loops, which can be slow for large sequences. NumPy is faster than regular Python code because its C-based algorithms avoid overhead present with regular interpreted Python code.

To give you an idea of the performance difference, consider a NumPy array of one million integers, and the equivalent Python list:

```
In [7]: import numpy as np

In [8]: my_arr = np.arange(1_000_000)

In [9]: my_list = list(range(1_000_000))
```

Now let's multiply each sequence by 2:

```
In [10]: %timeit my_arr2 = my_arr * 2
715 us +- 13.2 us per loop (mean +- std. dev. of 7 runs, 1000 loops each)

In [11]: %timeit my_list2 = [x * 2 for x in my_list]
48.8 ms +- 298 us per loop (mean +- std. dev. of 7 runs, 10 loops each)
```

NumPy-based algorithms are generally 10 to 100 times faster (or more) than their pure Python counterparts and use significantly less memory.

4.1 The NumPy ndarray: A Multidimensional Array Object

One of the key features of NumPy is its N-dimensional array object, or ndarray, which is a fast, flexible container for large datasets in Python. Arrays enable you to perform mathematical operations on whole blocks of data using similar syntax to the equivalent operations between scalar elements.

To give you a flavor of how NumPy enables batch computations with similar syntax to scalar values on built-in Python objects, I first import NumPy and create a small array:

```
In [12]: import numpy as np

In [13]: data = np.array([[1.5, -0.1, 3], [0, -3, 6.5]])

In [14]: data
Out[14]:
array([[ 1.5, -0.1,  3. ],
       [ 0. , -3. ,  6.5]])
```

I then write mathematical operations with data:

```
In [15]: data * 10
Out[15]:
array([[ 15.,  -1.,  30.],
       [  0., -30.,  65.]])
```

```
In [16]: data + data
Out[16]:
array([[ 3. , -0.2,  6. ],
       [ 0. , -6. , 13. ]])
```

In the first example, all of the elements have been multiplied by 10. In the second, the corresponding values in each "cell" in the array have been added to each other.

> In this chapter and throughout the book, I use the standard NumPy convention of always using `import numpy as np`. It would be possible to put `from numpy import *` in your code to avoid having to write `np.`, but I advise against making a habit of this. The `numpy` namespace is large and contains a number of functions whose names conflict with built-in Python functions (like `min` and `max`). Following standard conventions like these is almost always a good idea.

An ndarray is a generic multidimensional container for homogeneous data; that is, all of the elements must be the same type. Every array has a `shape`, a tuple indicating the size of each dimension, and a `dtype`, an object describing the *data type* of the array:

```
In [17]: data.shape
Out[17]: (2, 3)

In [18]: data.dtype
Out[18]: dtype('float64')
```

This chapter will introduce you to the basics of using NumPy arrays, and it should be sufficient for following along with the rest of the book. While it's not necessary to have a deep understanding of NumPy for many data analytical applications, becoming proficient in array-oriented programming and thinking is a key step along the way to becoming a scientific Python guru.

> Whenever you see "array," "NumPy array," or "ndarray" in the book text, in most cases they all refer to the ndarray object.

Creating ndarrays

The easiest way to create an array is to use the `array` function. This accepts any sequence-like object (including other arrays) and produces a new NumPy array containing the passed data. For example, a list is a good candidate for conversion:

```
In [19]: data1 = [6, 7.5, 8, 0, 1]
```

```
In [20]: arr1 = np.array(data1)

In [21]: arr1
Out[21]: array([6. , 7.5, 8. , 0. , 1. ])
```

Nested sequences, like a list of equal-length lists, will be converted into a multidimensional array:

```
In [22]: data2 = [[1, 2, 3, 4], [5, 6, 7, 8]]

In [23]: arr2 = np.array(data2)

In [24]: arr2
Out[24]:
array([[1, 2, 3, 4],
       [5, 6, 7, 8]])
```

Since `data2` was a list of lists, the NumPy array `arr2` has two dimensions, with shape inferred from the data. We can confirm this by inspecting the `ndim` and `shape` attributes:

```
In [25]: arr2.ndim
Out[25]: 2

In [26]: arr2.shape
Out[26]: (2, 4)
```

Unless explicitly specified (discussed in "Data Types for ndarrays" on page 88), `numpy.array` tries to infer a good data type for the array that it creates. The data type is stored in a special `dtype` metadata object; for example, in the previous two examples we have:

```
In [27]: arr1.dtype
Out[27]: dtype('float64')

In [28]: arr2.dtype
Out[28]: dtype('int64')
```

In addition to `numpy.array`, there are a number of other functions for creating new arrays. As examples, `numpy.zeros` and `numpy.ones` create arrays of 0s or 1s, respectively, with a given length or shape. `numpy.empty` creates an array without initializing its values to any particular value. To create a higher dimensional array with these methods, pass a tuple for the shape:

```
In [29]: np.zeros(10)
Out[29]: array([0., 0., 0., 0., 0., 0., 0., 0., 0., 0.])

In [30]: np.zeros((3, 6))
Out[30]:
array([[0., 0., 0., 0., 0., 0.],
       [0., 0., 0., 0., 0., 0.],
       [0., 0., 0., 0., 0., 0.]])
```

```
In [31]: np.empty((2, 3, 2))
Out[31]:
array([[[0., 0.],
        [0., 0.],
        [0., 0.]],
       [[0., 0.],
        [0., 0.],
        [0., 0.]]])
```

 It's not safe to assume that numpy.empty will return an array of all zeros. This function returns uninitialized memory and thus may contain nonzero "garbage" values. You should use this function only if you intend to populate the new array with data.

numpy.arange is an array-valued version of the built-in Python range function:

```
In [32]: np.arange(15)
Out[32]: array([ 0,  1,  2,  3,  4,  5,  6,  7,  8,  9, 10, 11, 12, 13, 14])
```

See Table 4-1 for a short list of standard array creation functions. Since NumPy is focused on numerical computing, the data type, if not specified, will in many cases be float64 (floating point).

Table 4-1. Some important NumPy array creation functions

Function	Description
array	Convert input data (list, tuple, array, or other sequence type) to an ndarray either by inferring a data type or explicitly specifying a data type; copies the input data by default
asarray	Convert input to ndarray, but do not copy if the input is already an ndarray
arange	Like the built-in range but returns an ndarray instead of a list
ones, ones_like	Produce an array of all 1s with the given shape and data type; ones_like takes another array and produces a ones array of the same shape and data type
zeros, zeros_like	Like ones and ones_like but producing arrays of 0s instead
empty, empty_like	Create new arrays by allocating new memory, but do not populate with any values like ones and zeros
full, full_like	Produce an array of the given shape and data type with all values set to the indicated "fill value"; full_like takes another array and produces a filled array of the same shape and data type
eye, identity	Create a square N × N identity matrix (1s on the diagonal and 0s elsewhere)

Data Types for ndarrays

The *data type* or dtype is a special object containing the information (or *metadata*, data about data) the ndarray needs to interpret a chunk of memory as a particular type of data:

```
In [33]: arr1 = np.array([1, 2, 3], dtype=np.float64)

In [34]: arr2 = np.array([1, 2, 3], dtype=np.int32)

In [35]: arr1.dtype
Out[35]: dtype('float64')

In [36]: arr2.dtype
Out[36]: dtype('int32')
```

Data types are a source of NumPy's flexibility for interacting with data coming from other systems. In most cases they provide a mapping directly onto an underlying disk or memory representation, which makes it possible to read and write binary streams of data to disk and to connect to code written in a low-level language like C or FORTRAN. The numerical data types are named the same way: a type name, like float or int, followed by a number indicating the number of bits per element. A standard double-precision floating-point value (what's used under the hood in Python's float object) takes up 8 bytes or 64 bits. Thus, this type is known in NumPy as float64. See Table 4-2 for a full listing of NumPy's supported data types.

 Don't worry about memorizing the NumPy data types, especially if you're a new user. It's often only necessary to care about the general *kind* of data you're dealing with, whether floating point, complex, integer, Boolean, string, or general Python object. When you need more control over how data is stored in memory and on disk, especially large datasets, it is good to know that you have control over the storage type.

Table 4-2. NumPy data types

Type	Type code	Description
int8, uint8	i1, u1	Signed and unsigned 8-bit (1 byte) integer types
int16, uint16	i2, u2	Signed and unsigned 16-bit integer types
int32, uint32	i4, u4	Signed and unsigned 32-bit integer types
int64, uint64	i8, u8	Signed and unsigned 64-bit integer types
float16	f2	Half-precision floating point
float32	f4 or f	Standard single-precision floating point; compatible with C float
float64	f8 or d	Standard double-precision floating point; compatible with C double and Python float object
float128	f16 or g	Extended-precision floating point
complex64, complex128, complex256	c8, c16, c32	Complex numbers represented by two 32, 64, or 128 floats, respectively
bool	?	Boolean type storing True and False values
object	O	Python object type; a value can be any Python object

Type	Type code	Description
string_	S	Fixed-length ASCII string type (1 byte per character); for example, to create a string data type with length 10, use 'S10'
unicode_	U	Fixed-length Unicode type (number of bytes platform specific); same specification semantics as string_ (e.g., 'U10')

 There are both *signed* and *unsigned* integer types, and many readers will not be familiar with this terminology. A *signed* integer can represent both positive and negative integers, while an *unsigned* integer can only represent nonzero integers. For example, int8 (signed 8-bit integer) can represent integers from -128 to 127 (inclusive), while uint8 (unsigned 8-bit integer) can represent 0 through 255.

You can explicitly convert or *cast* an array from one data type to another using ndarray's astype method:

```
In [37]: arr = np.array([1, 2, 3, 4, 5])

In [38]: arr.dtype
Out[38]: dtype('int64')

In [39]: float_arr = arr.astype(np.float64)

In [40]: float_arr
Out[40]: array([1., 2., 3., 4., 5.])

In [41]: float_arr.dtype
Out[41]: dtype('float64')
```

In this example, integers were cast to floating point. If I cast some floating-point numbers to be of integer data type, the decimal part will be truncated:

```
In [42]: arr = np.array([3.7, -1.2, -2.6, 0.5, 12.9, 10.1])

In [43]: arr
Out[43]: array([ 3.7, -1.2, -2.6,  0.5, 12.9, 10.1])

In [44]: arr.astype(np.int32)
Out[44]: array([ 3, -1, -2,  0, 12, 10], dtype=int32)
```

If you have an array of strings representing numbers, you can use astype to convert them to numeric form:

```
In [45]: numeric_strings = np.array(["1.25", "-9.6", "42"], dtype=np.string_)

In [46]: numeric_strings.astype(float)
Out[46]: array([ 1.25, -9.6 , 42.  ])
```

Be cautious when using the `numpy.string_` type, as string data in NumPy is fixed size and may truncate input without warning. pandas has more intuitive out-of-the-box behavior on non-numeric data.

If casting were to fail for some reason (like a string that cannot be converted to `float64`), a `ValueError` will be raised. Before, I was a bit lazy and wrote `float` instead of `np.float64`; NumPy aliases the Python types to its own equivalent data types.

You can also use another array's `dtype` attribute:

```
In [47]: int_array = np.arange(10)

In [48]: calibers = np.array([.22, .270, .357, .380, .44, .50], dtype=np.float64)

In [49]: int_array.astype(calibers.dtype)
Out[49]: array([0., 1., 2., 3., 4., 5., 6., 7., 8., 9.])
```

There are shorthand type code strings you can also use to refer to a `dtype`:

```
In [50]: zeros_uint32 = np.zeros(8, dtype="u4")

In [51]: zeros_uint32
Out[51]: array([0, 0, 0, 0, 0, 0, 0, 0], dtype=uint32)
```

Calling `astype` *always* creates a new array (a copy of the data), even if the new data type is the same as the old data type.

Arithmetic with NumPy Arrays

Arrays are important because they enable you to express batch operations on data without writing any `for` loops. NumPy users call this *vectorization*. Any arithmetic operations between equal-size arrays apply the operation element-wise:

```
In [52]: arr = np.array([[1., 2., 3.], [4., 5., 6.]])

In [53]: arr
Out[53]:
array([[1., 2., 3.],
       [4., 5., 6.]])

In [54]: arr * arr
Out[54]:
array([[ 1.,  4.,  9.],
       [16., 25., 36.]])
```

```
In [55]: arr - arr
Out[55]:
array([[0., 0., 0.],
       [0., 0., 0.]])
```

Arithmetic operations with scalars propagate the scalar argument to each element in the array:

```
In [56]: 1 / arr
Out[56]:
array([[1.    , 0.5   , 0.3333],
       [0.25  , 0.2   , 0.1667]])

In [57]: arr ** 2
Out[57]:
array([[ 1.,  4.,  9.],
       [16., 25., 36.]])
```

Comparisons between arrays of the same size yield Boolean arrays:

```
In [58]: arr2 = np.array([[0., 4., 1.], [7., 2., 12.]])

In [59]: arr2
Out[59]:
array([[ 0.,  4.,  1.],
       [ 7.,  2., 12.]])

In [60]: arr2 > arr
Out[60]:
array([[False,  True, False],
       [ True, False,  True]])
```

Evaluating operations between differently sized arrays is called *broadcasting* and will be discussed in more detail in Appendix A. Having a deep understanding of broadcasting is not necessary for most of this book.

Basic Indexing and Slicing

NumPy array indexing is a deep topic, as there are many ways you may want to select a subset of your data or individual elements. One-dimensional arrays are simple; on the surface they act similarly to Python lists:

```
In [61]: arr = np.arange(10)

In [62]: arr
Out[62]: array([0, 1, 2, 3, 4, 5, 6, 7, 8, 9])

In [63]: arr[5]
Out[63]: 5

In [64]: arr[5:8]
Out[64]: array([5, 6, 7])
```

```
In [65]: arr[5:8] = 12
```

```
In [66]: arr
Out[66]: array([ 0,  1,  2,  3,  4, 12, 12, 12,  8,  9])
```

As you can see, if you assign a scalar value to a slice, as in arr[5:8] = 12, the value is propagated (or *broadcast* henceforth) to the entire selection.

 An important first distinction from Python's built-in lists is that array slices are views on the original array. This means that the data is not copied, and any modifications to the view will be reflected in the source array.

To give an example of this, I first create a slice of arr:

```
In [67]: arr_slice = arr[5:8]
```

```
In [68]: arr_slice
Out[68]: array([12, 12, 12])
```

Now, when I change values in arr_slice, the mutations are reflected in the original array arr:

```
In [69]: arr_slice[1] = 12345
```

```
In [70]: arr
Out[70]:
array([    0,     1,     2,     3,     4,    12, 12345,    12,     8,
           9])
```

The "bare" slice [:] will assign to all values in an array:

```
In [71]: arr_slice[:] = 64
```

```
In [72]: arr
Out[72]: array([ 0,  1,  2,  3,  4, 64, 64, 64,  8,  9])
```

If you are new to NumPy, you might be surprised by this, especially if you have used other array programming languages that copy data more eagerly. As NumPy has been designed to be able to work with very large arrays, you could imagine performance and memory problems if NumPy insisted on always copying data.

 If you want a copy of a slice of an ndarray instead of a view, you will need to explicitly copy the array—for example, arr[5:8].copy(). As you will see, pandas works this way, too.

With higher dimensional arrays, you have many more options. In a two-dimensional array, the elements at each index are no longer scalars but rather one-dimensional arrays:

```
In [73]: arr2d = np.array([[1, 2, 3], [4, 5, 6], [7, 8, 9]])

In [74]: arr2d[2]
Out[74]: array([7, 8, 9])
```

Thus, individual elements can be accessed recursively. But that is a bit too much work, so you can pass a comma-separated list of indices to select individual elements. So these are equivalent:

```
In [75]: arr2d[0][2]
Out[75]: 3

In [76]: arr2d[0, 2]
Out[76]: 3
```

See Figure 4-1 for an illustration of indexing on a two-dimensional array. I find it helpful to think of axis 0 as the "rows" of the array and axis 1 as the "columns."

Figure 4-1. Indexing elements in a NumPy array

In multidimensional arrays, if you omit later indices, the returned object will be a lower dimensional ndarray consisting of all the data along the higher dimensions. So in the $2 \times 2 \times 3$ array arr3d:

```
In [77]: arr3d = np.array([[[1, 2, 3], [4, 5, 6]], [[7, 8, 9], [10, 11, 12]]])

In [78]: arr3d
Out[78]:
array([[[ 1,  2,  3],
        [ 4,  5,  6]],
       [[ 7,  8,  9],
        [10, 11, 12]]])
```

arr3d[0] is a 2×3 array:

```
In [79]: arr3d[0]
Out[79]:
array([[1, 2, 3],
       [4, 5, 6]])
```

Both scalar values and arrays can be assigned to `arr3d[0]`:

```
In [80]: old_values = arr3d[0].copy()

In [81]: arr3d[0] = 42

In [82]: arr3d
Out[82]:
array([[[42, 42, 42],
        [42, 42, 42]],
       [[ 7,  8,  9],
        [10, 11, 12]]])

In [83]: arr3d[0] = old_values

In [84]: arr3d
Out[84]:
array([[[ 1,  2,  3],
        [ 4,  5,  6]],
       [[ 7,  8,  9],
        [10, 11, 12]]])
```

Similarly, `arr3d[1, 0]` gives you all of the values whose indices start with `(1, 0)`, forming a one-dimensional array:

```
In [85]: arr3d[1, 0]
Out[85]: array([7, 8, 9])
```

This expression is the same as though we had indexed in two steps:

```
In [86]: x = arr3d[1]

In [87]: x
Out[87]:
array([[ 7,  8,  9],
       [10, 11, 12]])

In [88]: x[0]
Out[88]: array([7, 8, 9])
```

Note that in all of these cases where subsections of the array have been selected, the returned arrays are views.

> This multidimensional indexing syntax for NumPy arrays will not work with regular Python objects, such as lists of lists.

Indexing with slices

Like one-dimensional objects such as Python lists, ndarrays can be sliced with the familiar syntax:

```
In [89]: arr
Out[89]: array([ 0,  1,  2,  3,  4, 64, 64, 64,  8,  9])

In [90]: arr[1:6]
Out[90]: array([ 1,  2,  3,  4, 64])
```

Consider the two-dimensional array from before, arr2d. Slicing this array is a bit different:

```
In [91]: arr2d
Out[91]:
array([[1, 2, 3],
       [4, 5, 6],
       [7, 8, 9]])

In [92]: arr2d[:2]
Out[92]:
array([[1, 2, 3],
       [4, 5, 6]])
```

As you can see, it has sliced along axis 0, the first axis. A slice, therefore, selects a range of elements along an axis. It can be helpful to read the expression arr2d[:2] as "select the first two rows of arr2d."

You can pass multiple slices just like you can pass multiple indexes:

```
In [93]: arr2d[:2, 1:]
Out[93]:
array([[2, 3],
       [5, 6]])
```

When slicing like this, you always obtain array views of the same number of dimensions. By mixing integer indexes and slices, you get lower dimensional slices.

For example, I can select the second row but only the first two columns, like so:

```
In [94]: lower_dim_slice = arr2d[1, :2]
```

Here, while arr2d is two-dimensional, lower_dim_slice is one-dimensional, and its shape is a tuple with one axis size:

```
In [95]: lower_dim_slice.shape
Out[95]: (2,)
```

Similarly, I can select the third column but only the first two rows, like so:

```
In [96]: arr2d[:2, 2]
Out[96]: array([3, 6])
```

See Figure 4-2 for an illustration. Note that a colon by itself means to take the entire axis, so you can slice only higher dimensional axes by doing:

```
In [97]: arr2d[:, :1]
Out[97]:
array([[1],
       [4],
       [7]])
```

Of course, assigning to a slice expression assigns to the whole selection:

```
In [98]: arr2d[:2, 1:] = 0

In [99]: arr2d
Out[99]:
array([[1, 0, 0],
       [4, 0, 0],
       [7, 8, 9]])
```

Figure 4-2. Two-dimensional array slicing

	Expression	Shape
	arr[:2,1:]	(2,2)
	arr[2]	(3,)
	arr[2, :]	(3,)
	arr[2:, :]	(1,3)
	arr[:, :2]	(3,2)
	arr[1, :2]	(2,)
	arr[1:2, :2]	(1,2)

Boolean Indexing

Let's consider an example where we have some data in an array and an array of names with duplicates:

```
In [100]: names = np.array(["Bob", "Joe", "Will", "Bob", "Will", "Joe", "Joe"])

In [101]: data = np.array([[4, 7], [0, 2], [-5, 6], [0, 0], [1, 2],
   .....:                  [-12, -4], [3, 4]])

In [102]: names
Out[102]: array(['Bob', 'Joe', 'Will', 'Bob', 'Will', 'Joe', 'Joe'], dtype='<U4')

In [103]: data
Out[103]:
array([[  4,   7],
       [  0,   2],
       [ -5,   6],
       [  0,   0],
       [  1,   2],
       [-12,  -4],
       [  3,   4]])
```

Suppose each name corresponds to a row in the data array and we wanted to select all the rows with the corresponding name "Bob". Like arithmetic operations, comparisons (such as ==) with arrays are also vectorized. Thus, comparing names with the string "Bob" yields a Boolean array:

```
In [104]: names == "Bob"
Out[104]: array([ True, False, False,  True, False, False, False])
```

This Boolean array can be passed when indexing the array:

```
In [105]: data[names == "Bob"]
Out[105]:
array([[4, 7],
       [0, 0]])
```

The Boolean array must be of the same length as the array axis it's indexing. You can even mix and match Boolean arrays with slices or integers (or sequences of integers; more on this later).

In these examples, I select from the rows where names == "Bob" and index the columns, too:

```
In [106]: data[names == "Bob", 1:]
Out[106]:
array([[7],
       [0]])

In [107]: data[names == "Bob", 1]
Out[107]: array([7, 0])
```

To select everything but "Bob" you can either use != or negate the condition using ~:

```
In [108]: names != "Bob"
Out[108]: array([False,  True,  True, False,  True,  True,  True])
```

```
In [109]: ~(names == "Bob")
Out[109]: array([False,  True,  True, False,  True,  True,  True])

In [110]: data[~(names == "Bob")]
Out[110]:
array([[  0,    2],
       [ -5,    6],
       [  1,    2],
       [-12,   -4],
       [  3,    4]])
```

The ~ operator can be useful when you want to invert a Boolean array referenced by a variable:

```
In [111]: cond = names == "Bob"

In [112]: data[~cond]
Out[112]:
array([[  0,    2],
       [ -5,    6],
       [  1,    2],
       [-12,   -4],
       [  3,    4]])
```

To select two of the three names to combine multiple Boolean conditions, use Boolean arithmetic operators like & (and) and | (or):

```
In [113]: mask = (names == "Bob") | (names == "Will")

In [114]: mask
Out[114]: array([ True, False,  True,  True,  True, False, False])

In [115]: data[mask]
Out[115]:
array([[ 4,  7],
       [-5,  6],
       [ 0,  0],
       [ 1,  2]])
```

Selecting data from an array by Boolean indexing and assigning the result to a new variable *always* creates a copy of the data, even if the returned array is unchanged.

> The Python keywords and and or do not work with Boolean arrays. Use & (and) and | (or) instead.

Setting values with Boolean arrays works by substituting the value or values on the righthand side into the locations where the Boolean array's values are True. To set all of the negative values in data to 0, we need only do:

```
In [116]: data[data < 0] = 0
```

```
In [117]: data
Out[117]:
array([[4, 7],
       [0, 2],
       [0, 6],
       [0, 0],
       [1, 2],
       [0, 0],
       [3, 4]])
```

You can also set whole rows or columns using a one-dimensional Boolean array:

```
In [118]: data[names != "Joe"] = 7
```

```
In [119]: data
Out[119]:
array([[7, 7],
       [0, 2],
       [7, 7],
       [7, 7],
       [7, 7],
       [0, 0],
       [3, 4]])
```

As we will see later, these types of operations on two-dimensional data are convenient to do with pandas.

Fancy Indexing

Fancy indexing is a term adopted by NumPy to describe indexing using integer arrays. Suppose we had an 8 × 4 array:

```
In [120]: arr = np.zeros((8, 4))
```

```
In [121]: for i in range(8):
   .....:     arr[i] = i
```

```
In [122]: arr
Out[122]:
array([[0., 0., 0., 0.],
       [1., 1., 1., 1.],
       [2., 2., 2., 2.],
       [3., 3., 3., 3.],
       [4., 4., 4., 4.],
       [5., 5., 5., 5.],
       [6., 6., 6., 6.],
       [7., 7., 7., 7.]])
```

To select a subset of the rows in a particular order, you can simply pass a list or ndarray of integers specifying the desired order:

```
In [123]: arr[[4, 3, 0, 6]]
Out[123]:
array([[4., 4., 4., 4.],
       [3., 3., 3., 3.],
       [0., 0., 0., 0.],
       [6., 6., 6., 6.]])
```

Hopefully this code did what you expected! Using negative indices selects rows from the end:

```
In [124]: arr[[-3, -5, -7]]
Out[124]:
array([[5., 5., 5., 5.],
       [3., 3., 3., 3.],
       [1., 1., 1., 1.]])
```

Passing multiple index arrays does something slightly different; it selects a one-dimensional array of elements corresponding to each tuple of indices:

```
In [125]: arr = np.arange(32).reshape((8, 4))

In [126]: arr
Out[126]:
array([[ 0,  1,  2,  3],
       [ 4,  5,  6,  7],
       [ 8,  9, 10, 11],
       [12, 13, 14, 15],
       [16, 17, 18, 19],
       [20, 21, 22, 23],
       [24, 25, 26, 27],
       [28, 29, 30, 31]])

In [127]: arr[[1, 5, 7, 2], [0, 3, 1, 2]]
Out[127]: array([ 4, 23, 29, 10])
```

To learn more about the reshape method, have a look at Appendix A.

Here the elements (1, 0), (5, 3), (7, 1), and (2, 2) were selected. The result of fancy indexing with as many integer arrays as there are axes is always one-dimensional.

The behavior of fancy indexing in this case is a bit different from what some users might have expected (myself included), which is the rectangular region formed by selecting a subset of the matrix's rows and columns. Here is one way to get that:

```
In [128]: arr[[1, 5, 7, 2]][:, [0, 3, 1, 2]]
Out[128]:
array([[ 4,  7,  5,  6],
       [20, 23, 21, 22],
       [28, 31, 29, 30],
       [ 8, 11,  9, 10]])
```

Keep in mind that fancy indexing, unlike slicing, always copies the data into a new array when assigning the result to a new variable. If you assign values with fancy indexing, the indexed values will be modified:

```
In [129]: arr[[1, 5, 7, 2], [0, 3, 1, 2]]
Out[129]: array([ 4, 23, 29, 10])

In [130]: arr[[1, 5, 7, 2], [0, 3, 1, 2]] = 0

In [131]: arr
Out[131]:
array([[ 0,  1,  2,  3],
       [ 0,  5,  6,  7],
       [ 8,  9,  0, 11],
       [12, 13, 14, 15],
       [16, 17, 18, 19],
       [20, 21, 22,  0],
       [24, 25, 26, 27],
       [28,  0, 30, 31]])
```

Transposing Arrays and Swapping Axes

Transposing is a special form of reshaping that similarly returns a view on the underlying data without copying anything. Arrays have the transpose method and the special T attribute:

```
In [132]: arr = np.arange(15).reshape((3, 5))

In [133]: arr
Out[133]:
array([[ 0,  1,  2,  3,  4],
       [ 5,  6,  7,  8,  9],
       [10, 11, 12, 13, 14]])

In [134]: arr.T
Out[134]:
array([[ 0,  5, 10],
       [ 1,  6, 11],
       [ 2,  7, 12],
       [ 3,  8, 13],
       [ 4,  9, 14]])
```

When doing matrix computations, you may do this very often—for example, when computing the inner matrix product using numpy.dot:

```
In [135]: arr = np.array([[0, 1, 0], [1, 2, -2], [6, 3, 2], [-1, 0, -1], [1, 0, 1
]])

In [136]: arr
Out[136]:
array([[ 0,  1,  0],
       [ 1,  2, -2],
```

```
       [ 6,   3,   2],
       [-1,   0,  -1],
       [ 1,   0,   1]])

In [137]: np.dot(arr.T, arr)
Out[137]:
array([[39, 20, 12],
       [20, 14,  2],
       [12,  2, 10]])
```

The @ infix operator is another way to do matrix multiplication:

```
In [138]: arr.T @ arr
Out[138]:
array([[39, 20, 12],
       [20, 14,  2],
       [12,  2, 10]])
```

Simple transposing with .T is a special case of swapping axes. ndarray has the method swapaxes, which takes a pair of axis numbers and switches the indicated axes to rearrange the data:

```
In [139]: arr
Out[139]:
array([[ 0,  1,  0],
       [ 1,  2, -2],
       [ 6,  3,  2],
       [-1,  0, -1],
       [ 1,  0,  1]])

In [140]: arr.swapaxes(0, 1)
Out[140]:
array([[ 0,  1,  6, -1,  1],
       [ 1,  2,  3,  0,  0],
       [ 0, -2,  2, -1,  1]])
```

swapaxes similarly returns a view on the data without making a copy.

4.2 Pseudorandom Number Generation

The numpy.random module supplements the built-in Python random module with functions for efficiently generating whole arrays of sample values from many kinds of probability distributions. For example, you can get a 4 × 4 array of samples from the standard normal distribution using numpy.random.standard_normal:

```
In [141]: samples = np.random.standard_normal(size=(4, 4))

In [142]: samples
Out[142]:
array([[-0.2047,  0.4789, -0.5194, -0.5557],
       [ 1.9658,  1.3934,  0.0929,  0.2817],
```

```
      [ 0.769 ,  1.2464,  1.0072, -1.2962],
      [ 0.275 ,  0.2289,  1.3529,  0.8864]]])
```

Python's built-in `random` module, by contrast, samples only one value at a time. As you can see from this benchmark, `numpy.random` is well over an order of magnitude faster for generating very large samples:

```
In [143]: from random import normalvariate

In [144]: N = 1_000_000

In [145]: %timeit samples = [normalvariate(0, 1) for _ in range(N)]
1.04 s +- 11.4 ms per loop (mean +- std. dev. of 7 runs, 1 loop each)

In [146]: %timeit np.random.standard_normal(N)
21.9 ms +- 155 us per loop (mean +- std. dev. of 7 runs, 10 loops each)
```

These random numbers are not truly random (rather, *pseudorandom*) but instead are generated by a configurable random number generator that determines deterministically what values are created. Functions like `numpy.random.standard_normal` use the `numpy.random` module's default random number generator, but your code can be configured to use an explicit generator:

```
In [147]: rng = np.random.default_rng(seed=12345)

In [148]: data = rng.standard_normal((2, 3))
```

The `seed` argument is what determines the initial state of the generator, and the state changes each time the `rng` object is used to generate data. The generator object `rng` is also isolated from other code which might use the `numpy.random` module:

```
In [149]: type(rng)
Out[149]: numpy.random._generator.Generator
```

See Table 4-3 for a partial list of methods available on random generator objects like `rng`. I will use the `rng` object I created above to generate random data throughout the rest of the chapter.

Table 4-3. NumPy random number generator methods

Method	Description
permutation	Return a random permutation of a sequence, or return a permuted range
shuffle	Randomly permute a sequence in place
uniform	Draw samples from a uniform distribution
integers	Draw random integers from a given low-to-high range
standard_normal	Draw samples from a normal distribution with mean 0 and standard deviation 1
binomial	Draw samples from a binomial distribution
normal	Draw samples from a normal (Gaussian) distribution
beta	Draw samples from a beta distribution

Method	Description
chisquare	Draw samples from a chi-square distribution
gamma	Draw samples from a gamma distribution
uniform	Draw samples from a uniform [0, 1) distribution

4.3 Universal Functions: Fast Element-Wise Array Functions

A universal function, or *ufunc*, is a function that performs element-wise operations on data in ndarrays. You can think of them as fast vectorized wrappers for simple functions that take one or more scalar values and produce one or more scalar results.

Many ufuncs are simple element-wise transformations, like `numpy.sqrt` or `numpy.exp`:

```
In [150]: arr = np.arange(10)

In [151]: arr
Out[151]: array([0, 1, 2, 3, 4, 5, 6, 7, 8, 9])

In [152]: np.sqrt(arr)
Out[152]:
array([0.    , 1.    , 1.4142, 1.7321, 2.    , 2.2361, 2.4495, 2.6458,
       2.8284, 3.    ])

In [153]: np.exp(arr)
Out[153]:
array([   1.    ,    2.7183,    7.3891,   20.0855,   54.5982,  148.4132,
        403.4288, 1096.6332, 2980.958 , 8103.0839])
```

These are referred to as *unary* ufuncs. Others, such as `numpy.add` or `numpy.maximum`, take two arrays (thus, *binary* ufuncs) and return a single array as the result:

```
In [154]: x = rng.standard_normal(8)

In [155]: y = rng.standard_normal(8)

In [156]: x
Out[156]:
array([-1.3678,  0.6489,  0.3611, -1.9529,  2.3474,  0.9685, -0.7594,
        0.9022])

In [157]: y
Out[157]:
array([-0.467 , -0.0607,  0.7888, -1.2567,  0.5759,  1.399 ,  1.3223,
       -0.2997])

In [158]: np.maximum(x, y)
Out[158]:
```

```
array([-0.467 ,  0.6489,  0.7888, -1.2567,  2.3474,  1.399 ,  1.3223,
        0.9022])
```

In this example, `numpy.maximum` computed the element-wise maximum of the elements in x and y.

While not common, a ufunc can return multiple arrays. `numpy.modf` is one example: a vectorized version of the built-in Python `math.modf`, it returns the fractional and integral parts of a floating-point array:

```
In [159]: arr = rng.standard_normal(7) * 5

In [160]: arr
Out[160]: array([ 4.5146, -8.1079, -0.7909,  2.2474, -6.718 , -0.4084,  8.6237])

In [161]: remainder, whole_part = np.modf(arr)

In [162]: remainder
Out[162]: array([ 0.5146, -0.1079, -0.7909,  0.2474, -0.718 , -0.4084,  0.6237])

In [163]: whole_part
Out[163]: array([ 4., -8., -0.,  2., -6., -0.,  8.])
```

Ufuncs accept an optional out argument that allows them to assign their results into an existing array rather than create a new one:

```
In [164]: arr
Out[164]: array([ 4.5146, -8.1079, -0.7909,  2.2474, -6.718 , -0.4084,  8.6237])

In [165]: out = np.zeros_like(arr)

In [166]: np.add(arr, 1)
Out[166]: array([ 5.5146, -7.1079,  0.2091,  3.2474, -5.718 ,  0.5916,  9.6237])

In [167]: np.add(arr, 1, out=out)
Out[167]: array([ 5.5146, -7.1079,  0.2091,  3.2474, -5.718 ,  0.5916,  9.6237])

In [168]: out
Out[168]: array([ 5.5146, -7.1079,  0.2091,  3.2474, -5.718 ,  0.5916,  9.6237])
```

See Tables 4-4 and 4-5 for a listing of some of NumPy's ufuncs. New ufuncs continue to be added to NumPy, so consulting the online NumPy documentation is the best way to get a comprehensive listing and stay up to date.

Table 4-4. Some unary universal functions

Function	Description
abs, fabs	Compute the absolute value element-wise for integer, floating-point, or complex values
sqrt	Compute the square root of each element (equivalent to arr ** 0.5)
square	Compute the square of each element (equivalent to arr ** 2)
exp	Compute the exponent e^x of each element
log, log10, log2, log1p	Natural logarithm (base *e*), log base 10, log base 2, and log(1 + x), respectively
sign	Compute the sign of each element: 1 (positive), 0 (zero), or −1 (negative)
ceil	Compute the ceiling of each element (i.e., the smallest integer greater than or equal to that number)
floor	Compute the floor of each element (i.e., the largest integer less than or equal to each element)
rint	Round elements to the nearest integer, preserving the dtype
modf	Return fractional and integral parts of array as separate arrays
isnan	Return Boolean array indicating whether each value is NaN (Not a Number)
isfinite, isinf	Return Boolean array indicating whether each element is finite (non-inf, non-NaN) or infinite, respectively
cos, cosh, sin, sinh, tan, tanh	Regular and hyperbolic trigonometric functions
arccos, arccosh, arcsin, arcsinh, arctan, arctanh	Inverse trigonometric functions
logical_not	Compute truth value of not x element-wise (equivalent to ~arr)

Table 4-5. Some binary universal functions

Function	Description
add	Add corresponding elements in arrays
subtract	Subtract elements in second array from first array
multiply	Multiply array elements
divide, floor_divide	Divide or floor divide (truncating the remainder)
power	Raise elements in first array to powers indicated in second array
maximum, fmax	Element-wise maximum; fmax ignores NaN
minimum, fmin	Element-wise minimum; fmin ignores NaN
mod	Element-wise modulus (remainder of division)
copysign	Copy sign of values in second argument to values in first argument
greater, greater_equal, less, less_equal, equal, not_equal	Perform element-wise comparison, yielding Boolean array (equivalent to infix operators >, >=, <, <=, ==, !=)
logical_and	Compute element-wise truth value of AND (&) logical operation
logical_or	Compute element-wise truth value of OR (|) logical operation
logical_xor	Compute element-wise truth value of XOR (^) logical operation

4.4 Array-Oriented Programming with Arrays

Using NumPy arrays enables you to express many kinds of data processing tasks as concise array expressions that might otherwise require writing loops. This practice of replacing explicit loops with array expressions is referred to by some people as *vectorization*. In general, vectorized array operations will usually be significantly faster than their pure Python equivalents, with the biggest impact in any kind of numerical computations. Later, in Appendix A, I explain *broadcasting*, a powerful method for vectorizing computations.

As a simple example, suppose we wished to evaluate the function sqrt(x^2 + y^2) across a regular grid of values. The numpy.meshgrid function takes two one-dimensional arrays and produces two two-dimensional matrices corresponding to all pairs of (x, y) in the two arrays:

```
In [169]: points = np.arange(-5, 5, 0.01) # 100 equally spaced points

In [170]: xs, ys = np.meshgrid(points, points)

In [171]: ys
Out[171]:
array([[-5.  , -5.  , -5.  , ..., -5.  , -5.  , -5.  ],
       [-4.99, -4.99, -4.99, ..., -4.99, -4.99, -4.99],
       [-4.98, -4.98, -4.98, ..., -4.98, -4.98, -4.98],
       ...,
       [ 4.97,  4.97,  4.97, ...,  4.97,  4.97,  4.97],
       [ 4.98,  4.98,  4.98, ...,  4.98,  4.98,  4.98],
       [ 4.99,  4.99,  4.99, ...,  4.99,  4.99,  4.99]])
```

Now, evaluating the function is a matter of writing the same expression you would write with two points:

```
In [172]: z = np.sqrt(xs ** 2 + ys ** 2)

In [173]: z
Out[173]:
array([[7.0711, 7.064 , 7.0569, ..., 7.0499, 7.0569, 7.064 ],
       [7.064 , 7.0569, 7.0499, ..., 7.0428, 7.0499, 7.0569],
       [7.0569, 7.0499, 7.0428, ..., 7.0357, 7.0428, 7.0499],
       ...,
       [7.0499, 7.0428, 7.0357, ..., 7.0286, 7.0357, 7.0428],
       [7.0569, 7.0499, 7.0428, ..., 7.0357, 7.0428, 7.0499],
       [7.064 , 7.0569, 7.0499, ..., 7.0428, 7.0499, 7.0569]])
```

As a preview of Chapter 9, I use matplotlib to create visualizations of this two-dimensional array:

```
In [174]: import matplotlib.pyplot as plt

In [175]: plt.imshow(z, cmap=plt.cm.gray, extent=[-5, 5, -5, 5])
Out[175]: <matplotlib.image.AxesImage at 0x7f624ae73b20>
```

```
In [176]: plt.colorbar()
Out[176]: <matplotlib.colorbar.Colorbar at 0x7f6253e43ee0>

In [177]: plt.title("Image plot of $\sqrt{x^2 + y^2}$ for a grid of values")
Out[177]: Text(0.5, 1.0, 'Image plot of $\\sqrt{x^2 + y^2}$ for a grid of values'
)
```

In Figure 4-3, I used the matplotlib function imshow to create an image plot from a two-dimensional array of function values.

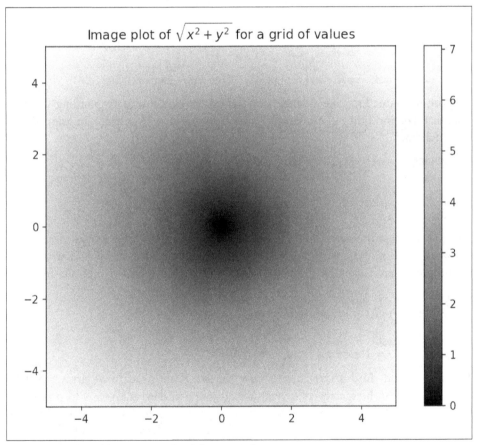

Figure 4-3. Plot of function evaluated on a grid

If you're working in IPython, you can close all open plot windows by executing plt.close("all"):

```
In [179]: plt.close("all")
```

The term *vectorization* is used to describe some other computer science concepts, but in this book I use it to describe operations on whole arrays of data at once rather than going value by value using a Python for loop.

Expressing Conditional Logic as Array Operations

The numpy.where function is a vectorized version of the ternary expression x if condition else y. Suppose we had a Boolean array and two arrays of values:

```
In [180]: xarr = np.array([1.1, 1.2, 1.3, 1.4, 1.5])

In [181]: yarr = np.array([2.1, 2.2, 2.3, 2.4, 2.5])

In [182]: cond = np.array([True, False, True, True, False])
```

Suppose we wanted to take a value from xarr whenever the corresponding value in cond is True, and otherwise take the value from yarr. A list comprehension doing this might look like:

```
In [183]: result = [(x if c else y)
    .....:           for x, y, c in zip(xarr, yarr, cond)]

In [184]: result
Out[184]: [1.1, 2.2, 1.3, 1.4, 2.5]
```

This has multiple problems. First, it will not be very fast for large arrays (because all the work is being done in interpreted Python code). Second, it will not work with multidimensional arrays. With numpy.where you can do this with a single function call:

```
In [185]: result = np.where(cond, xarr, yarr)

In [186]: result
Out[186]: array([1.1, 2.2, 1.3, 1.4, 2.5])
```

The second and third arguments to numpy.where don't need to be arrays; one or both of them can be scalars. A typical use of where in data analysis is to produce a new array of values based on another array. Suppose you had a matrix of randomly generated data and you wanted to replace all positive values with 2 and all negative values with –2. This is possible to do with numpy.where:

```
In [187]: arr = rng.standard_normal((4, 4))

In [188]: arr
Out[188]:
array([[ 2.6182,  0.7774,  0.8286, -0.959 ],
       [-1.2094, -1.4123,  0.5415,  0.7519],
       [-0.6588, -1.2287,  0.2576,  0.3129],
       [-0.1308,  1.27  , -0.093 , -0.0662]])
```

```
In [189]: arr > 0
Out[189]:
array([[ True,  True,  True, False],
       [False, False,  True,  True],
       [False, False,  True,  True],
       [False,  True, False, False]])

In [190]: np.where(arr > 0, 2, -2)
Out[190]:
array([[ 2,  2,  2, -2],
       [-2, -2,  2,  2],
       [-2, -2,  2,  2],
       [-2,  2, -2, -2]])
```

You can combine scalars and arrays when using numpy.where. For example, I can replace all positive values in arr with the constant 2, like so:

```
In [191]: np.where(arr > 0, 2, arr) # set only positive values to 2
Out[191]:
array([[ 2.    ,  2.    ,  2.    , -0.959 ],
       [-1.2094, -1.4123,  2.    ,  2.    ],
       [-0.6588, -1.2287,  2.    ,  2.    ],
       [-0.1308,  2.    , -0.093 , -0.0662]])
```

Mathematical and Statistical Methods

A set of mathematical functions that compute statistics about an entire array or about the data along an axis are accessible as methods of the array class. You can use aggregations (sometimes called *reductions*) like sum, mean, and std (standard deviation) either by calling the array instance method or using the top-level NumPy function. When you use the NumPy function, like numpy.sum, you have to pass the array you want to aggregate as the first argument.

Here I generate some normally distributed random data and compute some aggregate statistics:

```
In [192]: arr = rng.standard_normal((5, 4))

In [193]: arr
Out[193]:
array([[-1.1082,  0.136 ,  1.3471,  0.0611],
       [ 0.0709,  0.4337,  0.2775,  0.5303],
       [ 0.5367,  0.6184, -0.795 ,  0.3   ],
       [-1.6027,  0.2668, -1.2616, -0.0713],
       [ 0.474 , -0.4149,  0.0977, -1.6404]])

In [194]: arr.mean()
Out[194]: -0.08719744457434529

In [195]: np.mean(arr)
```

```
Out[195]: -0.08719744457434529

In [196]: arr.sum()
Out[196]: -1.743948891486906
```

Functions like `mean` and `sum` take an optional `axis` argument that computes the statistic over the given axis, resulting in an array with one less dimension:

```
In [197]: arr.mean(axis=1)
Out[197]: array([ 0.109 ,  0.3281,  0.165 , -0.6672, -0.3709])

In [198]: arr.sum(axis=0)
Out[198]: array([-1.6292,  1.0399, -0.3344, -0.8203])
```

Here, `arr.mean(axis=1)` means "compute mean across the columns," where `arr.sum(axis=0)` means "compute sum down the rows."

Other methods like `cumsum` and `cumprod` do not aggregate, instead producing an array of the intermediate results:

```
In [199]: arr = np.array([0, 1, 2, 3, 4, 5, 6, 7])

In [200]: arr.cumsum()
Out[200]: array([ 0,  1,  3,  6, 10, 15, 21, 28])
```

In multidimensional arrays, accumulation functions like `cumsum` return an array of the same size but with the partial aggregates computed along the indicated axis according to each lower dimensional slice:

```
In [201]: arr = np.array([[0, 1, 2], [3, 4, 5], [6, 7, 8]])

In [202]: arr
Out[202]:
array([[0, 1, 2],
       [3, 4, 5],
       [6, 7, 8]])
```

The expression `arr.cumsum(axis=0)` computes the cumulative sum along the rows, while `arr.cumsum(axis=1)` computes the sums along the columns:

```
In [203]: arr.cumsum(axis=0)
Out[203]:
array([[ 0,  1,  2],
       [ 3,  5,  7],
       [ 9, 12, 15]])

In [204]: arr.cumsum(axis=1)
Out[204]:
array([[ 0,  1,  3],
       [ 3,  7, 12],
       [ 6, 13, 21]])
```

See Table 4-6 for a full listing. We'll see many examples of these methods in action in later chapters.

Table 4-6. Basic array statistical methods

Method	Description
sum	Sum of all the elements in the array or along an axis; zero-length arrays have sum 0
mean	Arithmetic mean; invalid (returns NaN) on zero-length arrays
std, var	Standard deviation and variance, respectively
min, max	Minimum and maximum
argmin, argmax	Indices of minimum and maximum elements, respectively
cumsum	Cumulative sum of elements starting from 0
cumprod	Cumulative product of elements starting from 1

Methods for Boolean Arrays

Boolean values are coerced to 1 (True) and 0 (False) in the preceding methods. Thus, sum is often used as a means of counting True values in a Boolean array:

```
In [205]: arr = rng.standard_normal(100)

In [206]: (arr > 0).sum() # Number of positive values
Out[206]: 48

In [207]: (arr <= 0).sum() # Number of non-positive values
Out[207]: 52
```

The parentheses here in the expression (arr > 0).sum() are necessary to be able to call sum() on the temporary result of arr > 0.

Two additional methods, any and all, are useful especially for Boolean arrays. any tests whether one or more values in an array is True, while all checks if every value is True:

```
In [208]: bools = np.array([False, False, True, False])

In [209]: bools.any()
Out[209]: True

In [210]: bools.all()
Out[210]: False
```

These methods also work with non-Boolean arrays, where nonzero elements are treated as True.

Sorting

Like Python's built-in list type, NumPy arrays can be sorted in place with the `sort` method:

```
In [211]: arr = rng.standard_normal(6)

In [212]: arr
Out[212]: array([ 0.0773, -0.6839, -0.7208,  1.1206, -0.0548, -0.0824])

In [213]: arr.sort()

In [214]: arr
Out[214]: array([-0.7208, -0.6839, -0.0824, -0.0548,  0.0773,  1.1206])
```

You can sort each one-dimensional section of values in a multidimensional array in place along an axis by passing the axis number to `sort`. In this example data:

```
In [215]: arr = rng.standard_normal((5, 3))

In [216]: arr
Out[216]:
array([[ 0.936 ,  1.2385,  1.2728],
       [ 0.4059, -0.0503,  0.2893],
       [ 0.1793,  1.3975,  0.292 ],
       [ 0.6384, -0.0279,  1.3711],
       [-2.0528,  0.3805,  0.7554]])
```

`arr.sort(axis=0)` sorts the values within each column, while `arr.sort(axis=1)` sorts across each row:

```
In [217]: arr.sort(axis=0)

In [218]: arr
Out[218]:
array([[-2.0528, -0.0503,  0.2893],
       [ 0.1793, -0.0279,  0.292 ],
       [ 0.4059,  0.3805,  0.7554],
       [ 0.6384,  1.2385,  1.2728],
       [ 0.936 ,  1.3975,  1.3711]])

In [219]: arr.sort(axis=1)

In [220]: arr
Out[220]:
array([[-2.0528, -0.0503,  0.2893],
       [-0.0279,  0.1793,  0.292 ],
       [ 0.3805,  0.4059,  0.7554],
       [ 0.6384,  1.2385,  1.2728],
       [ 0.936 ,  1.3711,  1.3975]])
```

The top-level method `numpy.sort` returns a sorted copy of an array (like the Python built-in function `sorted`) instead of modifying the array in place. For example:

```
In [221]: arr2 = np.array([5, -10, 7, 1, 0, -3])

In [222]: sorted_arr2 = np.sort(arr2)

In [223]: sorted_arr2
Out[223]: array([-10,  -3,   0,   1,   5,   7])
```

For more details on using NumPy's sorting methods, and more advanced techniques like indirect sorts, see Appendix A. Several other kinds of data manipulations related to sorting (e.g., sorting a table of data by one or more columns) can also be found in pandas.

Unique and Other Set Logic

NumPy has some basic set operations for one-dimensional ndarrays. A commonly used one is numpy.unique, which returns the sorted unique values in an array:

```
In [224]: names = np.array(["Bob", "Will", "Joe", "Bob", "Will", "Joe", "Joe"])

In [225]: np.unique(names)
Out[225]: array(['Bob', 'Joe', 'Will'], dtype='<U4')

In [226]: ints = np.array([3, 3, 3, 2, 2, 1, 1, 4, 4])

In [227]: np.unique(ints)
Out[227]: array([1, 2, 3, 4])
```

Contrast numpy.unique with the pure Python alternative:

```
In [228]: sorted(set(names))
Out[228]: ['Bob', 'Joe', 'Will']
```

In many cases, the NumPy version is faster and returns a NumPy array rather than a Python list.

Another function, numpy.in1d, tests membership of the values in one array in another, returning a Boolean array:

```
In [229]: values = np.array([6, 0, 0, 3, 2, 5, 6])

In [230]: np.in1d(values, [2, 3, 6])
Out[230]: array([ True, False, False,  True,  True, False,  True])
```

See Table 4-7 for a listing of array set operations in NumPy.

Table 4-7. Array set operations

Method	Description
unique(x)	Compute the sorted, unique elements in x
intersect1d(x, y)	Compute the sorted, common elements in x and y
union1d(x, y)	Compute the sorted union of elements

Method	Description
`in1d(x, y)`	Compute a Boolean array indicating whether each element of x is contained in y
`setdiff1d(x, y)`	Set difference, elements in x that are not in y
`setxor1d(x, y)`	Set symmetric differences; elements that are in either of the arrays, but not both

4.5 File Input and Output with Arrays

NumPy is able to save and load data to and from disk in some text or binary formats. In this section I discuss only NumPy's built-in binary format, since most users will prefer pandas and other tools for loading text or tabular data (see Chapter 6 for much more).

`numpy.save` and `numpy.load` are the two workhorse functions for efficiently saving and loading array data on disk. Arrays are saved by default in an uncompressed raw binary format with file extension *.npy*:

```
In [231]: arr = np.arange(10)

In [232]: np.save("some_array", arr)
```

If the file path does not already end in *.npy*, the extension will be appended. The array on disk can then be loaded with `numpy.load`:

```
In [233]: np.load("some_array.npy")
Out[233]: array([0, 1, 2, 3, 4, 5, 6, 7, 8, 9])
```

You can save multiple arrays in an uncompressed archive using `numpy.savez` and passing the arrays as keyword arguments:

```
In [234]: np.savez("array_archive.npz", a=arr, b=arr)
```

When loading an *.npz* file, you get back a dictionary-like object that loads the individual arrays lazily:

```
In [235]: arch = np.load("array_archive.npz")

In [236]: arch["b"]
Out[236]: array([0, 1, 2, 3, 4, 5, 6, 7, 8, 9])
```

If your data compresses well, you may wish to use `numpy.savez_compressed` instead:

```
In [237]: np.savez_compressed("arrays_compressed.npz", a=arr, b=arr)
```

4.6 Linear Algebra

Linear algebra operations, like matrix multiplication, decompositions, determinants, and other square matrix math, are an important part of many array libraries. Multiplying two two-dimensional arrays with * is an element-wise product, while matrix multiplications require using a function. Thus, there is a function dot, both an array method and a function in the numpy namespace, for matrix multiplication:

```
In [241]: x = np.array([[1., 2., 3.], [4., 5., 6.]])
```

```
In [242]: y = np.array([[6., 23.], [-1, 7], [8, 9]])
```

```
In [243]: x
Out[243]:
array([[1., 2., 3.],
       [4., 5., 6.]])
```

```
In [244]: y
Out[244]:
array([[ 6., 23.],
       [-1.,  7.],
       [ 8.,  9.]])
```

```
In [245]: x.dot(y)
Out[245]:
array([[ 28.,  64.],
       [ 67., 181.]])
```

x.dot(y) is equivalent to np.dot(x, y):

```
In [246]: np.dot(x, y)
Out[246]:
array([[ 28.,  64.],
       [ 67., 181.]])
```

A matrix product between a two-dimensional array and a suitably sized one-dimensional array results in a one-dimensional array:

```
In [247]: x @ np.ones(3)
Out[247]: array([ 6., 15.])
```

numpy.linalg has a standard set of matrix decompositions and things like inverse and determinant:

```
In [248]: from numpy.linalg import inv, qr
```

```
In [249]: X = rng.standard_normal((5, 5))
```

```
In [250]: mat = X.T @ X
```

```
In [251]: inv(mat)
Out[251]:
array([[  3.4993,   2.8444,   3.5956, -16.5538,   4.4733],
       [  2.8444,   2.5667,   2.9002, -13.5774,   3.7678],
       [  3.5956,   2.9002,   4.4823, -18.3453,   4.7066],
       [-16.5538, -13.5774, -18.3453,  84.0102, -22.0484],
       [  4.4733,   3.7678,   4.7066, -22.0484,   6.0525]])
```

```
In [252]: mat @ inv(mat)
Out[252]:
array([[ 1.,   0.,  -0.,   0.,  -0.],
       [ 0.,   1.,   0.,   0.,  -0.],
       [ 0.,  -0.,   1.,  -0.,  -0.],
       [ 0.,  -0.,   0.,   1.,  -0.],
       [ 0.,  -0.,   0.,  -0.,   1.]])
```

The expression X.T.dot(X) computes the dot product of X with its transpose X.T.

See Table 4-8 for a list of some of the most commonly used linear algebra functions.

Table 4-8. Commonly used numpy.linalg functions

Function	Description
diag	Return the diagonal (or off-diagonal) elements of a square matrix as a 1D array, or convert a 1D array into a square matrix with zeros on the off-diagonal
dot	Matrix multiplication
trace	Compute the sum of the diagonal elements
det	Compute the matrix determinant
eig	Compute the eigenvalues and eigenvectors of a square matrix
inv	Compute the inverse of a square matrix
pinv	Compute the Moore-Penrose pseudoinverse of a matrix
qr	Compute the QR decomposition
svd	Compute the singular value decomposition (SVD)
solve	Solve the linear system Ax = b for x, where A is a square matrix
lstsq	Compute the least-squares solution to Ax = b

4.7 Example: Random Walks

The simulation of *random walks* (*https://en.wikipedia.org/wiki/Random_walk*) provides an illustrative application of utilizing array operations. Let's first consider a simple random walk starting at 0 with steps of 1 and –1 occurring with equal probability.

Here is a pure Python way to implement a single random walk with 1,000 steps using the built-in random module:

```
#! blockstart
import random
position = 0
walk = [position]
nsteps = 1000
for _ in range(nsteps):
    step = 1 if random.randint(0, 1) else -1
    position += step
    walk.append(position)
#! blockend
```

See Figure 4-4 for an example plot of the first 100 values on one of these random walks:

```
In [255]: plt.plot(walk[:100])
```

Figure 4-4. A simple random walk

You might make the observation that `walk` is the cumulative sum of the random steps and could be evaluated as an array expression. Thus, I use the `numpy.random` module to draw 1,000 coin flips at once, set these to 1 and –1, and compute the cumulative sum:

```
In [256]: nsteps = 1000

In [257]: rng = np.random.default_rng(seed=12345)  # fresh random generator

In [258]: draws = rng.integers(0, 2, size=nsteps)

In [259]: steps = np.where(draws == 0, 1, -1)

In [260]: walk = steps.cumsum()
```

From this we can begin to extract statistics like the minimum and maximum value along the walk's trajectory:

```
In [261]: walk.min()
Out[261]: -8

In [262]: walk.max()
Out[262]: 50
```

A more complicated statistic is the *first crossing time*, the step at which the random walk reaches a particular value. Here we might want to know how long it took the random walk to get at least 10 steps away from the origin 0 in either direction. np.abs(walk) >= 10 gives us a Boolean array indicating where the walk has reached or exceeded 10, but we want the index of the *first* 10 or –10. Turns out, we can compute this using argmax, which returns the first index of the maximum value in the Boolean array (True is the maximum value):

```
In [263]: (np.abs(walk) >= 10).argmax()
Out[263]: 155
```

Note that using argmax here is not always efficient because it always makes a full scan of the array. In this special case, once a True is observed we know it to be the maximum value.

Simulating Many Random Walks at Once

If your goal was to simulate many random walks, say five thousand of them, you can generate all of the random walks with minor modifications to the preceding code. If passed a 2-tuple, the numpy.random functions will generate a two-dimensional array of draws, and we can compute the cumulative sum for each row to compute all five thousand random walks in one shot:

```
In [264]: nwalks = 5000

In [265]: nsteps = 1000

In [266]: draws = rng.integers(0, 2, size=(nwalks, nsteps)) # 0 or 1

In [267]: steps = np.where(draws > 0, 1, -1)

In [268]: walks = steps.cumsum(axis=1)

In [269]: walks
Out[269]:
array([[  1,   2,   3, ...,  22,  23,  22],
       [  1,   0,  -1, ..., -50, -49, -48],
       [  1,   2,   3, ...,  50,  49,  48],
       ...,
       [ -1,  -2,  -1, ..., -10,  -9, -10],
       [ -1,  -2,  -3, ...,   8,   9,   8],
       [ -1,   0,   1, ...,  -4,  -3,  -2]])
```

Now, we can compute the maximum and minimum values obtained over all of the walks:

```
In [270]: walks.max()
Out[270]: 114
```

```
In [271]: walks.min()
Out[271]: -120
```

Out of these walks, let's compute the minimum crossing time to 30 or –30. This is slightly tricky because not all 5,000 of them reach 30. We can check this using the any method:

```
In [272]: hits30 = (np.abs(walks) >= 30).any(axis=1)
```

```
In [273]: hits30
Out[273]: array([False,  True,  True, ...,  True, False,  True])
```

```
In [274]: hits30.sum() # Number that hit 30 or -30
Out[274]: 3395
```

We can use this Boolean array to select the rows of walks that actually cross the absolute 30 level, and call argmax across axis 1 to get the crossing times:

```
In [275]: crossing_times = (np.abs(walks[hits30]) >= 30).argmax(axis=1)
```

```
In [276]: crossing_times
Out[276]: array([201, 491, 283, ..., 219, 259, 541])
```

Lastly, we compute the average minimum crossing time:

```
In [277]: crossing_times.mean()
Out[277]: 500.5699558173785
```

Feel free to experiment with other distributions for the steps other than equal-sized coin flips. You need only use a different random generator method, like stan dard_normal to generate normally distributed steps with some mean and standard deviation:

```
In [278]: draws = 0.25 * rng.standard_normal((nwalks, nsteps))
```

 Keep in mind that this vectorized approach requires creating an array with nwalks * nsteps elements, which may use a large amount of memory for large simulations. If memory is more constrained, then a different approach will be required.

4.8 Conclusion

While much of the rest of the book will focus on building data wrangling skills with pandas, we will continue to work in a similar array-based style. In Appendix A, we will dig deeper into NumPy features to help you further develop your array computing skills.

## CHAPTER 5

Getting Started with pandas

pandas will be a major tool of interest throughout much of the rest of the book. It contains data structures and data manipulation tools designed to make data cleaning and analysis fast and convenient in Python. pandas is often used in tandem with numerical computing tools like NumPy and SciPy, analytical libraries like statsmodels and scikit-learn, and data visualization libraries like matplotlib. pandas adopts significant parts of NumPy's idiomatic style of array-based computing, especially array-based functions and a preference for data processing without `for` loops.

While pandas adopts many coding idioms from NumPy, the biggest difference is that pandas is designed for working with tabular or heterogeneous data. NumPy, by contrast, is best suited for working with homogeneously typed numerical array data.

Since becoming an open source project in 2010, pandas has matured into a quite large library that's applicable in a broad set of real-world use cases. The developer community has grown to over 2,500 distinct contributors, who've been helping build the project as they used it to solve their day-to-day data problems. The vibrant pandas developer and user communities have been a key part of its success.

Many people don't know that I haven't been actively involved in day-to-day pandas development since 2013; it has been an entirely community-managed project since then. Be sure to pass on your thanks to the core development and all the contributors for their hard work!

Throughout the rest of the book, I use the following import conventions for NumPy and pandas:

```
In [1]: import numpy as np
```

```
In [2]: import pandas as pd
```

Thus, whenever you see `pd.` in code, it's referring to pandas. You may also find it easier to import Series and DataFrame into the local namespace since they are so frequently used:

```
In [3]: from pandas import Series, DataFrame
```

5.1 Introduction to pandas Data Structures

To get started with pandas, you will need to get comfortable with its two workhorse data structures: *Series* and *DataFrame*. While they are not a universal solution for every problem, they provide a solid foundation for a wide variety of data tasks.

Series

A Series is a one-dimensional array-like object containing a sequence of values (of similar types to NumPy types) of the same type and an associated array of data labels, called its *index*. The simplest Series is formed from only an array of data:

```
In [14]: obj = pd.Series([4, 7, -5, 3])
```

```
In [15]: obj
Out[15]:
0    4
1    7
2   -5
3    3
dtype: int64
```

The string representation of a Series displayed interactively shows the index on the left and the values on the right. Since we did not specify an index for the data, a default one consisting of the integers 0 through N - 1 (where N is the length of the data) is created. You can get the array representation and index object of the Series via its `array` and `index` attributes, respectively:

```
In [16]: obj.array
Out[16]:
<PandasArray>
[4, 7, -5, 3]
Length: 4, dtype: int64
```

```
In [17]: obj.index
Out[17]: RangeIndex(start=0, stop=4, step=1)
```

The result of the .array attribute is a PandasArray which usually wraps a NumPy array but can also contain special extension array types which will be discussed more in Section 7.3, "Extension Data Types," on page 224.

Often, you'll want to create a Series with an index identifying each data point with a label:

```
In [18]: obj2 = pd.Series([4, 7, -5, 3], index=["d", "b", "a", "c"])

In [19]: obj2
Out[19]:
d    4
b    7
a   -5
c    3
dtype: int64

In [20]: obj2.index
Out[20]: Index(['d', 'b', 'a', 'c'], dtype='object')
```

Compared with NumPy arrays, you can use labels in the index when selecting single values or a set of values:

```
In [21]: obj2["a"]
Out[21]: -5

In [22]: obj2["d"] = 6

In [23]: obj2[["c", "a", "d"]]
Out[23]:
c    3
a   -5
d    6
dtype: int64
```

Here ["c", "a", "d"] is interpreted as a list of indices, even though it contains strings instead of integers.

Using NumPy functions or NumPy-like operations, such as filtering with a Boolean array, scalar multiplication, or applying math functions, will preserve the index-value link:

```
In [24]: obj2[obj2 > 0]
Out[24]:
d    6
b    7
c    3
dtype: int64

In [25]: obj2 * 2
Out[25]:
d   12
```

```
b     14
a    -10
c      6
dtype: int64

In [26]: import numpy as np

In [27]: np.exp(obj2)
Out[27]:
d       403.428793
b      1096.633158
a         0.006738
c        20.085537
dtype: float64
```

Another way to think about a Series is as a fixed-length, ordered dictionary, as it is a mapping of index values to data values. It can be used in many contexts where you might use a dictionary:

```
In [28]: "b" in obj2
Out[28]: True

In [29]: "e" in obj2
Out[29]: False
```

Should you have data contained in a Python dictionary, you can create a Series from it by passing the dictionary:

```
In [30]: sdata = {"Ohio": 35000, "Texas": 71000, "Oregon": 16000, "Utah": 5000}

In [31]: obj3 = pd.Series(sdata)

In [32]: obj3
Out[32]:
Ohio      35000
Texas     71000
Oregon    16000
Utah       5000
dtype: int64
```

A Series can be converted back to a dictionary with its to_dict method:

```
In [33]: obj3.to_dict()
Out[33]: {'Ohio': 35000, 'Texas': 71000, 'Oregon': 16000, 'Utah': 5000}
```

When you are only passing a dictionary, the index in the resulting Series will respect the order of the keys according to the dictionary's keys method, which depends on the key insertion order. You can override this by passing an index with the dictionary keys in the order you want them to appear in the resulting Series:

```
In [34]: states = ["California", "Ohio", "Oregon", "Texas"]

In [35]: obj4 = pd.Series(sdata, index=states)
```

```
In [36]: obj4
Out[36]:
California        NaN
Ohio         35000.0
Oregon       16000.0
Texas        71000.0
dtype: float64
```

Here, three values found in sdata were placed in the appropriate locations, but since no value for "California" was found, it appears as NaN (Not a Number), which is considered in pandas to mark missing or *NA* values. Since "Utah" was not included in states, it is excluded from the resulting object.

I will use the terms "missing," "NA," or "null" interchangeably to refer to missing data. The isna and notna functions in pandas should be used to detect missing data:

```
In [37]: pd.isna(obj4)
Out[37]:
California     True
Ohio          False
Oregon        False
Texas         False
dtype: bool

In [38]: pd.notna(obj4)
Out[38]:
California     False
Ohio           True
Oregon         True
Texas          True
dtype: bool
```

Series also has these as instance methods:

```
In [39]: obj4.isna()
Out[39]:
California     True
Ohio          False
Oregon        False
Texas         False
dtype: bool
```

I discuss working with missing data in more detail in Chapter 7.

A useful Series feature for many applications is that it automatically aligns by index label in arithmetic operations:

```
In [40]: obj3
Out[40]:
Ohio      35000
Texas     71000
Oregon    16000
```

```
Utah        5000
dtype: int64

In [41]: obj4
Out[41]:
California        NaN
Ohio         35000.0
Oregon       16000.0
Texas        71000.0
dtype: float64

In [42]: obj3 + obj4
Out[42]:
California        NaN
Ohio         70000.0
Oregon       32000.0
Texas       142000.0
Utah             NaN
dtype: float64
```

Data alignment features will be addressed in more detail later. If you have experience with databases, you can think about this as being similar to a join operation.

Both the Series object itself and its index have a `name` attribute, which integrates with other areas of pandas functionality:

```
In [43]: obj4.name = "population"

In [44]: obj4.index.name = "state"

In [45]: obj4
Out[45]:
state
California        NaN
Ohio         35000.0
Oregon       16000.0
Texas        71000.0
Name: population, dtype: float64
```

A Series's index can be altered in place by assignment:

```
In [46]: obj
Out[46]:
0    4
1    7
2   -5
3    3
dtype: int64

In [47]: obj.index = ["Bob", "Steve", "Jeff", "Ryan"]

In [48]: obj
Out[48]:
```

```
Bob       4
Steve     7
Jeff     -5
Ryan      3
dtype: int64
```

DataFrame

A DataFrame represents a rectangular table of data and contains an ordered, named collection of columns, each of which can be a different value type (numeric, string, Boolean, etc.). The DataFrame has both a row and column index; it can be thought of as a dictionary of Series all sharing the same index.

 While a DataFrame is physically two-dimensional, you can use it to represent higher dimensional data in a tabular format using hierarchical indexing, a subject we will discuss in Chapter 8 and an ingredient in some of the more advanced data-handling features in pandas.

There are many ways to construct a DataFrame, though one of the most common is from a dictionary of equal-length lists or NumPy arrays:

```
data = {"state": ["Ohio", "Ohio", "Ohio", "Nevada", "Nevada", "Nevada"],
        "year": [2000, 2001, 2002, 2001, 2002, 2003],
        "pop": [1.5, 1.7, 3.6, 2.4, 2.9, 3.2]}
frame = pd.DataFrame(data)
```

The resulting DataFrame will have its index assigned automatically, as with Series, and the columns are placed according to the order of the keys in `data` (which depends on their insertion order in the dictionary):

```
In [50]: frame
Out[50]:
    state  year  pop
0    Ohio  2000  1.5
1    Ohio  2001  1.7
2    Ohio  2002  3.6
3  Nevada  2001  2.4
4  Nevada  2002  2.9
5  Nevada  2003  3.2
```

 If you are using the Jupyter notebook, pandas DataFrame objects will be displayed as a more browser-friendly HTML table. See Figure 5-1 for an example.

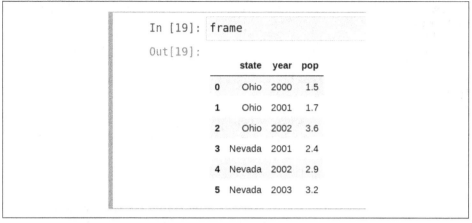

```
In [19]: frame
Out[19]:
         state  year  pop
    0     Ohio  2000  1.5
    1     Ohio  2001  1.7
    2     Ohio  2002  3.6
    3   Nevada  2001  2.4
    4   Nevada  2002  2.9
    5   Nevada  2003  3.2
```

Figure 5-1. How pandas DataFrame objects look in Jupyter

For large DataFrames, the head method selects only the first five rows:

```
In [51]: frame.head()
Out[51]:
     state  year  pop
0     Ohio  2000  1.5
1     Ohio  2001  1.7
2     Ohio  2002  3.6
3   Nevada  2001  2.4
4   Nevada  2002  2.9
```

Similarly, tail returns the last five rows:

```
In [52]: frame.tail()
Out[52]:
     state  year  pop
1     Ohio  2001  1.7
2     Ohio  2002  3.6
3   Nevada  2001  2.4
4   Nevada  2002  2.9
5   Nevada  2003  3.2
```

If you specify a sequence of columns, the DataFrame's columns will be arranged in that order:

```
In [53]: pd.DataFrame(data, columns=["year", "state", "pop"])
Out[53]:
   year   state  pop
0  2000    Ohio  1.5
1  2001    Ohio  1.7
2  2002    Ohio  3.6
3  2001  Nevada  2.4
4  2002  Nevada  2.9
5  2003  Nevada  3.2
```

If you pass a column that isn't contained in the dictionary, it will appear with missing values in the result:

```
In [54]: frame2 = pd.DataFrame(data, columns=["year", "state", "pop", "debt"])

In [55]: frame2
Out[55]:
   year   state  pop debt
0  2000    Ohio  1.5  NaN
1  2001    Ohio  1.7  NaN
2  2002    Ohio  3.6  NaN
3  2001  Nevada  2.4  NaN
4  2002  Nevada  2.9  NaN
5  2003  Nevada  3.2  NaN

In [56]: frame2.columns
Out[56]: Index(['year', 'state', 'pop', 'debt'], dtype='object')
```

A column in a DataFrame can be retrieved as a Series either by dictionary-like notation or by using the dot attribute notation:

```
In [57]: frame2["state"]
Out[57]:
0      Ohio
1      Ohio
2      Ohio
3    Nevada
4    Nevada
5    Nevada
Name: state, dtype: object

In [58]: frame2.year
Out[58]:
0    2000
1    2001
2    2002
3    2001
4    2002
5    2003
Name: year, dtype: int64
```

Attribute-like access (e.g., frame2.year) and tab completion of column names in IPython are provided as a convenience.

frame2[column] works for any column name, but frame2.column works only when the column name is a valid Python variable name and does not conflict with any of the method names in DataFrame. For example, if a column's name contains whitespace or symbols other than underscores, it cannot be accessed with the dot attribute method.

Note that the returned Series have the same index as the DataFrame, and their `name` attribute has been appropriately set.

Rows can also be retrieved by position or name with the special `iloc` and `loc` attributes (more on this later in "Selection on DataFrame with loc and iloc" on page 147):

```
In [59]: frame2.loc[1]
Out[59]:
year     2001
state    Ohio
pop       1.7
debt      NaN
Name: 1, dtype: object

In [60]: frame2.iloc[2]
Out[60]:
year     2002
state    Ohio
pop       3.6
debt      NaN
Name: 2, dtype: object
```

Columns can be modified by assignment. For example, the empty `debt` column could be assigned a scalar value or an array of values:

```
In [61]: frame2["debt"] = 16.5

In [62]: frame2
Out[62]:
   year   state  pop  debt
0  2000    Ohio  1.5  16.5
1  2001    Ohio  1.7  16.5
2  2002    Ohio  3.6  16.5
3  2001  Nevada  2.4  16.5
4  2002  Nevada  2.9  16.5
5  2003  Nevada  3.2  16.5

In [63]: frame2["debt"] = np.arange(6.)

In [64]: frame2
Out[64]:
   year   state  pop  debt
0  2000    Ohio  1.5   0.0
1  2001    Ohio  1.7   1.0
2  2002    Ohio  3.6   2.0
3  2001  Nevada  2.4   3.0
4  2002  Nevada  2.9   4.0
5  2003  Nevada  3.2   5.0
```

When you are assigning lists or arrays to a column, the value's length must match the length of the DataFrame. If you assign a Series, its labels will be realigned exactly to the DataFrame's index, inserting missing values in any index values not present:

```
In [65]: val = pd.Series([-1.2, -1.5, -1.7], index=["two", "four", "five"])

In [66]: frame2["debt"] = val

In [67]: frame2
Out[67]:
   year   state  pop  debt
0  2000    Ohio  1.5   NaN
1  2001    Ohio  1.7   NaN
2  2002    Ohio  3.6   NaN
3  2001  Nevada  2.4   NaN
4  2002  Nevada  2.9   NaN
5  2003  Nevada  3.2   NaN
```

Assigning a column that doesn't exist will create a new column.

The del keyword will delete columns like with a dictionary. As an example, I first add a new column of Boolean values where the state column equals "Ohio":

```
In [68]: frame2["eastern"] = frame2["state"] == "Ohio"

In [69]: frame2
Out[69]:
   year   state  pop  debt  eastern
0  2000    Ohio  1.5   NaN     True
1  2001    Ohio  1.7   NaN     True
2  2002    Ohio  3.6   NaN     True
3  2001  Nevada  2.4   NaN    False
4  2002  Nevada  2.9   NaN    False
5  2003  Nevada  3.2   NaN    False
```

New columns cannot be created with the frame2.eastern dot attribute notation.

The del method can then be used to remove this column:

```
In [70]: del frame2["eastern"]

In [71]: frame2.columns
Out[71]: Index(['year', 'state', 'pop', 'debt'], dtype='object')
```

The column returned from indexing a DataFrame is a *view* on the underlying data, not a copy. Thus, any in-place modifications to the Series will be reflected in the DataFrame. The column can be explicitly copied with the Series's copy method.

Another common form of data is a nested dictionary of dictionaries:

```
In [72]: populations = {"Ohio": {2000: 1.5, 2001: 1.7, 2002: 3.6},
   ....:                "Nevada": {2001: 2.4, 2002: 2.9}}
```

If the nested dictionary is passed to the DataFrame, pandas will interpret the outer dictionary keys as the columns, and the inner keys as the row indices:

```
In [73]: frame3 = pd.DataFrame(populations)

In [74]: frame3
Out[74]:
      Ohio  Nevada
2000   1.5     NaN
2001   1.7     2.4
2002   3.6     2.9
```

You can transpose the DataFrame (swap rows and columns) with similar syntax to a NumPy array:

```
In [75]: frame3.T
Out[75]:
         2000  2001  2002
Ohio      1.5   1.7   3.6
Nevada    NaN   2.4   2.9
```

Note that transposing discards the column data types if the columns do not all have the same data type, so transposing and then transposing back may lose the previous type information. The columns become arrays of pure Python objects in this case.

The keys in the inner dictionaries are combined to form the index in the result. This isn't true if an explicit index is specified:

```
In [76]: pd.DataFrame(populations, index=[2001, 2002, 2003])
Out[76]:
      Ohio  Nevada
2001   1.7     2.4
2002   3.6     2.9
2003   NaN     NaN
```

Dictionaries of Series are treated in much the same way:

```
In [77]: pdata = {"Ohio": frame3["Ohio"][:-1],
   ....:          "Nevada": frame3["Nevada"][:2]}
```

```
In [78]: pd.DataFrame(pdata)
Out[78]:
      Ohio  Nevada
2000  1.5     NaN
2001  1.7     2.4
```

For a list of many of the things you can pass to the DataFrame constructor, see Table 5-1.

Table 5-1. Possible data inputs to the DataFrame constructor

Type	Notes
2D ndarray	A matrix of data, passing optional row and column labels
Dictionary of arrays, lists, or tuples	Each sequence becomes a column in the DataFrame; all sequences must be the same length
NumPy structured/record array	Treated as the "dictionary of arrays" case
Dictionary of Series	Each value becomes a column; indexes from each Series are unioned together to form the result's row index if no explicit index is passed
Dictionary of dictionaries	Each inner dictionary becomes a column; keys are unioned to form the row index as in the "dictionary of Series" case
List of dictionaries or Series	Each item becomes a row in the DataFrame; unions of dictionary keys or Series indexes become the DataFrame's column labels
List of lists or tuples	Treated as the "2D ndarray" case
Another DataFrame	The DataFrame's indexes are used unless different ones are passed
NumPy MaskedArray	Like the "2D ndarray" case except masked values are missing in the DataFrame result

If a DataFrame's `index` and `columns` have their `name` attributes set, these will also be displayed:

```
In [79]: frame3.index.name = "year"

In [80]: frame3.columns.name = "state"

In [81]: frame3
Out[81]:
state  Ohio  Nevada
year
2000    1.5     NaN
2001    1.7     2.4
2002    3.6     2.9
```

Unlike Series, DataFrame does not have a `name` attribute. DataFrame's `to_numpy` method returns the data contained in the DataFrame as a two-dimensional ndarray:

```
In [82]: frame3.to_numpy()
Out[82]:
array([[1.5, nan],
```

```
       [1.7, 2.4],
       [3.6, 2.9]])
```

If the DataFrame's columns are different data types, the data type of the returned array will be chosen to accommodate all of the columns:

```
In [83]: frame2.to_numpy()
Out[83]:
array([[2000, 'Ohio', 1.5, nan],
       [2001, 'Ohio', 1.7, nan],
       [2002, 'Ohio', 3.6, nan],
       [2001, 'Nevada', 2.4, nan],
       [2002, 'Nevada', 2.9, nan],
       [2003, 'Nevada', 3.2, nan]], dtype=object)
```

Index Objects

pandas's Index objects are responsible for holding the axis labels (including a Data-Frame's column names) and other metadata (like the axis name or names). Any array or other sequence of labels you use when constructing a Series or DataFrame is internally converted to an Index:

```
In [84]: obj = pd.Series(np.arange(3), index=["a", "b", "c"])

In [85]: index = obj.index

In [86]: index
Out[86]: Index(['a', 'b', 'c'], dtype='object')

In [87]: index[1:]
Out[87]: Index(['b', 'c'], dtype='object')
```

Index objects are immutable and thus can't be modified by the user:

```
index[1] = "d"  # TypeError
```

Immutability makes it safer to share Index objects among data structures:

```
In [88]: labels = pd.Index(np.arange(3))

In [89]: labels
Out[89]: Int64Index([0, 1, 2], dtype='int64')

In [90]: obj2 = pd.Series([1.5, -2.5, 0], index=labels)

In [91]: obj2
Out[91]:
0    1.5
1   -2.5
2    0.0
dtype: float64
```

```
In [92]: obj2.index is labels
Out[92]: True
```

 Some users will not often take advantage of the capabilities provided by an Index, but because some operations will yield results
containing indexed data, it's important to understand how they
work.

In addition to being array-like, an Index also behaves like a fixed-size set:

```
In [93]: frame3
Out[93]:
state  Ohio  Nevada
year
2000    1.5     NaN
2001    1.7     2.4
2002    3.6     2.9

In [94]: frame3.columns
Out[94]: Index(['Ohio', 'Nevada'], dtype='object', name='state')

In [95]: "Ohio" in frame3.columns
Out[95]: True

In [96]: 2003 in frame3.index
Out[96]: False
```

Unlike Python sets, a pandas Index can contain duplicate labels:

```
In [97]: pd.Index(["foo", "foo", "bar", "bar"])
Out[97]: Index(['foo', 'foo', 'bar', 'bar'], dtype='object')
```

Selections with duplicate labels will select all occurrences of that label.

Each Index has a number of methods and properties for set logic, which answer other
common questions about the data it contains. Some useful ones are summarized in
Table 5-2.

Table 5-2. Some Index methods and properties

Method/Property	Description
append()	Concatenate with additional Index objects, producing a new Index
difference()	Compute set difference as an Index
intersection()	Compute set intersection
union()	Compute set union
isin()	Compute Boolean array indicating whether each value is contained in the passed collection
delete()	Compute new Index with element at Index i deleted
drop()	Compute new Index by deleting passed values
insert()	Compute new Index by inserting element at Index i

Method/Property	Description
is_monotonic	Returns True if each element is greater than or equal to the previous element
is_unique	Returns True if the Index has no duplicate values
unique()	Compute the array of unique values in the Index

5.2 Essential Functionality

This section will walk you through the fundamental mechanics of interacting with the data contained in a Series or DataFrame. In the chapters to come, we will delve more deeply into data analysis and manipulation topics using pandas. This book is not intended to serve as exhaustive documentation for the pandas library; instead, we'll focus on familiarizing you with heavily used features, leaving the less common (i.e., more esoteric) things for you to learn more about by reading the online pandas documentation.

Reindexing

An important method on pandas objects is reindex, which means to create a new object with the values rearranged to align with the new index. Consider an example:

```
In [98]: obj = pd.Series([4.5, 7.2, -5.3, 3.6], index=["d", "b", "a", "c"])

In [99]: obj
Out[99]:
d    4.5
b    7.2
a   -5.3
c    3.6
dtype: float64
```

Calling reindex on this Series rearranges the data according to the new index, introducing missing values if any index values were not already present:

```
In [100]: obj2 = obj.reindex(["a", "b", "c", "d", "e"])

In [101]: obj2
Out[101]:
a   -5.3
b    7.2
c    3.6
d    4.5
e    NaN
dtype: float64
```

For ordered data like time series, you may want to do some interpolation or filling of values when reindexing. The method option allows us to do this, using a method such as ffill, which forward-fills the values:

```
In [102]: obj3 = pd.Series(["blue", "purple", "yellow"], index=[0, 2, 4])

In [103]: obj3
Out[103]:
0       blue
2     purple
4     yellow
dtype: object

In [104]: obj3.reindex(np.arange(6), method="ffill")
Out[104]:
0       blue
1       blue
2     purple
3     purple
4     yellow
5     yellow
dtype: object
```

With DataFrame, reindex can alter the (row) index, columns, or both. When passed only a sequence, it reindexes the rows in the result:

```
In [105]: frame = pd.DataFrame(np.arange(9).reshape((3, 3)),
   .....:                      index=["a", "c", "d"],
   .....:                      columns=["Ohio", "Texas", "California"])

In [106]: frame
Out[106]:
   Ohio  Texas  California
a     0      1           2
c     3      4           5
d     6      7           8

In [107]: frame2 = frame.reindex(index=["a", "b", "c", "d"])

In [108]: frame2
Out[108]:
   Ohio  Texas  California
a   0.0    1.0         2.0
b   NaN    NaN         NaN
c   3.0    4.0         5.0
d   6.0    7.0         8.0
```

The columns can be reindexed with the columns keyword:

```
In [109]: states = ["Texas", "Utah", "California"]

In [110]: frame.reindex(columns=states)
Out[110]:
   Texas  Utah  California
a      1   NaN           2
c      4   NaN           5
d      7   NaN           8
```

Because "Ohio" was not in states, the data for that column is dropped from the result.

Another way to reindex a particular axis is to pass the new axis labels as a positional argument and then specify the axis to reindex with the axis keyword:

```
In [111]: frame.reindex(states, axis="columns")
Out[111]:
   Texas  Utah  California
a      1   NaN           2
c      4   NaN           5
d      7   NaN           8
```

See Table 5-3 for more about the arguments to reindex.

Table 5-3. reindex function arguments

Argument	Description
labels	New sequence to use as an index. Can be Index instance or any other sequence-like Python data structure. An Index will be used exactly as is without any copying.
index	Use the passed sequence as the new index labels.
columns	Use the passed sequence as the new column labels.
axis	The axis to reindex, whether "index" (rows) or "columns". The default is "index". You can alternately do reindex(index=new_labels) or reindex(columns=new_labels).
method	Interpolation (fill) method; "ffill" fills forward, while "bfill" fills backward.
fill_value	Substitute value to use when introducing missing data by reindexing. Use fill_value="missing" (the default behavior) when you want absent labels to have null values in the result.
limit	When forward filling or backfilling, the maximum size gap (in number of elements) to fill.
tolerance	When forward filling or backfilling, the maximum size gap (in absolute numeric distance) to fill for inexact matches.
level	Match simple Index on level of MultiIndex; otherwise select subset of.
copy	If True, always copy underlying data even if the new index is equivalent to the old index; if False, do not copy the data when the indexes are equivalent.

As we'll explore later in "Selection on DataFrame with loc and iloc" on page 147, you can also reindex by using the loc operator, and many users prefer to always do it this way. This works only if all of the new index labels already exist in the DataFrame (whereas reindex will insert missing data for new labels):

```
In [112]: frame.loc[["a", "d", "c"], ["California", "Texas"]]
Out[112]:
   California  Texas
a          2      1
d          8      7
c          5      4
```

Dropping Entries from an Axis

Dropping one or more entries from an axis is simple if you already have an index array or list without those entries, since you can use the `reindex` method or `.loc`-based indexing. As that can require a bit of munging and set logic, the `drop` method will return a new object with the indicated value or values deleted from an axis:

```
In [113]: obj = pd.Series(np.arange(5.), index=["a", "b", "c", "d", "e"])

In [114]: obj
Out[114]:
a    0.0
b    1.0
c    2.0
d    3.0
e    4.0
dtype: float64

In [115]: new_obj = obj.drop("c")

In [116]: new_obj
Out[116]:
a    0.0
b    1.0
d    3.0
e    4.0
dtype: float64

In [117]: obj.drop(["d", "c"])
Out[117]:
a    0.0
b    1.0
e    4.0
dtype: float64
```

With DataFrame, index values can be deleted from either axis. To illustrate this, we first create an example DataFrame:

```
In [118]: data = pd.DataFrame(np.arange(16).reshape((4, 4)),
   .....:                     index=["Ohio", "Colorado", "Utah", "New York"],
   .....:                     columns=["one", "two", "three", "four"])

In [119]: data
Out[119]:
          one  two  three  four
Ohio        0    1      2     3
Colorado    4    5      6     7
Utah        8    9     10    11
New York   12   13     14    15
```

Calling `drop` with a sequence of labels will drop values from the row labels (axis 0):

```
In [120]: data.drop(index=["Colorado", "Ohio"])
Out[120]:
          one  two  three  four
Utah        8    9     10    11
New York   12   13     14    15
```

To drop labels from the columns, instead use the `columns` keyword:

```
In [121]: data.drop(columns=["two"])
Out[121]:
          one  three  four
Ohio        0      2     3
Colorado    4      6     7
Utah        8     10    11
New York   12     14    15
```

You can also drop values from the columns by passing `axis=1` (which is like NumPy) or `axis="columns"`:

```
In [122]: data.drop("two", axis=1)
Out[122]:
          one  three  four
Ohio        0      2     3
Colorado    4      6     7
Utah        8     10    11
New York   12     14    15

In [123]: data.drop(["two", "four"], axis="columns")
Out[123]:
          one  three
Ohio        0      2
Colorado    4      6
Utah        8     10
New York   12     14
```

Indexing, Selection, and Filtering

Series indexing (`obj[...]`) works analogously to NumPy array indexing, except you can use the Series's index values instead of only integers. Here are some examples of this:

```
In [124]: obj = pd.Series(np.arange(4.), index=["a", "b", "c", "d"])

In [125]: obj
Out[125]:
a    0.0
b    1.0
c    2.0
d    3.0
dtype: float64
```

```
In [126]: obj["b"]
Out[126]: 1.0

In [127]: obj[1]
Out[127]: 1.0

In [128]: obj[2:4]
Out[128]:
c    2.0
d    3.0
dtype: float64

In [129]: obj[["b", "a", "d"]]
Out[129]:
b    1.0
a    0.0
d    3.0
dtype: float64

In [130]: obj[[1, 3]]
Out[130]:
b    1.0
d    3.0
dtype: float64

In [131]: obj[obj < 2]
Out[131]:
a    0.0
b    1.0
dtype: float64
```

While you can select data by label this way, the preferred way to select index values is with the special loc operator:

```
In [132]: obj.loc[["b", "a", "d"]]
Out[132]:
b    1.0
a    0.0
d    3.0
dtype: float64
```

The reason to prefer loc is because of the different treatment of integers when indexing with []. Regular []-based indexing will treat integers as labels if the index contains integers, so the behavior differs depending on the data type of the index. For example:

```
In [133]: obj1 = pd.Series([1, 2, 3], index=[2, 0, 1])

In [134]: obj2 = pd.Series([1, 2, 3], index=["a", "b", "c"])

In [135]: obj1
Out[135]:
```

```
2    1
0    2
1    3
dtype: int64

In [136]: obj2
Out[136]:
a    1
b    2
c    3
dtype: int64

In [137]: obj1[[0, 1, 2]]
Out[137]:
0    2
1    3
2    1
dtype: int64

In [138]: obj2[[0, 1, 2]]
Out[138]:
a    1
b    2
c    3
dtype: int64
```

When using loc, the expression obj.loc[[0, 1, 2]] will fail when the index does not contain integers:

```
In [134]: obj2.loc[[0, 1]]
---------------------------------------------------------------------------
KeyError                                  Traceback (most recent call last)
/tmp/ipykernel_804589/4185657903.py in <module>
----> 1 obj2.loc[[0, 1]]

^ LONG EXCEPTION ABBREVIATED ^

KeyError: "None of [Int64Index([0, 1], dtype="int64")] are in the [index]"
```

Since loc operator indexes exclusively with labels, there is also an iloc operator that indexes exclusively with integers to work consistently whether or not the index contains integers:

```
In [139]: obj1.iloc[[0, 1, 2]]
Out[139]:
2    1
0    2
1    3
dtype: int64

In [140]: obj2.iloc[[0, 1, 2]]
Out[140]:
a    1
```

```
b    2
c    3
dtype: int64
```

You can also slice with labels, but it works differently from normal Python slicing in that the endpoint is inclusive:

```
In [141]: obj2.loc["b":"c"]
Out[141]:
b    2
c    3
dtype: int64
```

Assigning values using these methods modifies the corresponding section of the Series:

```
In [142]: obj2.loc["b":"c"] = 5

In [143]: obj2
Out[143]:
a    1
b    5
c    5
dtype: int64
```

It can be a common newbie error to try to call loc or iloc like functions rather than "indexing into" them with square brackets. The square bracket notation is used to enable slice operations and to allow for indexing on multiple axes with DataFrame objects.

Indexing into a DataFrame retrieves one or more columns either with a single value or sequence:

```
In [144]: data = pd.DataFrame(np.arange(16).reshape((4, 4)),
   .....:                     index=["Ohio", "Colorado", "Utah", "New York"],
   .....:                     columns=["one", "two", "three", "four"])

In [145]: data
Out[145]:
          one  two  three  four
Ohio        0    1      2     3
Colorado    4    5      6     7
Utah        8    9     10    11
New York   12   13     14    15

In [146]: data["two"]
Out[146]:
Ohio        1
Colorado    5
Utah        9
```

```
New York    13
Name: two, dtype: int64

In [147]: data[["three", "one"]]
Out[147]:
          three  one
Ohio          2    0
Colorado      6    4
Utah         10    8
New York     14   12
```

Indexing like this has a few special cases. The first is slicing or selecting data with a Boolean array:

```
In [148]: data[:2]
Out[148]:
          one  two  three  four
Ohio        0    1      2     3
Colorado    4    5      6     7

In [149]: data[data["three"] > 5]
Out[149]:
          one  two  three  four
Colorado    4    5      6     7
Utah        8    9     10    11
New York   12   13     14    15
```

The row selection syntax `data[:2]` is provided as a convenience. Passing a single element or a list to the [ ] operator selects columns.

Another use case is indexing with a Boolean DataFrame, such as one produced by a scalar comparison. Consider a DataFrame with all Boolean values produced by comparing with a scalar value:

```
In [150]: data < 5
Out[150]:
            one    two  three   four
Ohio       True   True   True   True
Colorado   True  False  False  False
Utah      False  False  False  False
New York  False  False  False  False
```

We can use this DataFrame to assign the value 0 to each location with the value `True`, like so:

```
In [151]: data[data < 5] = 0

In [152]: data
Out[152]:
          one  two  three  four
Ohio        0    0      0     0
Colorado    0    5      6     7
```

```
Utah        8    9    10   11
New York   12   13    14   15
```

Selection on DataFrame with loc and iloc

Like Series, DataFrame has special attributes loc and iloc for label-based and integer-based indexing, respectively. Since DataFrame is two-dimensional, you can select a subset of the rows and columns with NumPy-like notation using either axis labels (loc) or integers (iloc).

As a first example, let's select a single row by label:

```
In [153]: data
Out[153]:
          one  two  three  four
Ohio        0    0      0     0
Colorado    0    5      6     7
Utah        8    9     10    11
New York   12   13     14    15

In [154]: data.loc["Colorado"]
Out[154]:
one      0
two      5
three    6
four     7
Name: Colorado, dtype: int64
```

The result of selecting a single row is a Series with an index that contains the DataFrame's column labels. To select multiple roles, creating a new DataFrame, pass a sequence of labels:

```
In [155]: data.loc[["Colorado", "New York"]]
Out[155]:
          one  two  three  four
Colorado    0    5      6     7
New York   12   13     14    15
```

You can combine both row and column selection in loc by separating the selections with a comma:

```
In [156]: data.loc["Colorado", ["two", "three"]]
Out[156]:
two      5
three    6
Name: Colorado, dtype: int64
```

We'll then perform some similar selections with integers using iloc:

```
In [157]: data.iloc[2]
Out[157]:
one      8
two      9
```

```
three    10
four     11
Name: Utah, dtype: int64

In [158]: data.iloc[[2, 1]]
Out[158]:
          one  two  three  four
Utah        8    9     10    11
Colorado    0    5      6     7

In [159]: data.iloc[2, [3, 0, 1]]
Out[159]:
four     11
one       8
two       9
Name: Utah, dtype: int64

In [160]: data.iloc[[1, 2], [3, 0, 1]]
Out[160]:
          four  one  two
Colorado     7    0    5
Utah        11    8    9
```

Both indexing functions work with slices in addition to single labels or lists of labels:

```
In [161]: data.loc[:"Utah", "two"]
Out[161]:
Ohio        0
Colorado    5
Utah        9
Name: two, dtype: int64

In [162]: data.iloc[:, :3][data.three > 5]
Out[162]:
          one  two  three
Colorado    0    5      6
Utah        8    9     10
New York   12   13     14
```

Boolean arrays can be used with loc but not iloc:

```
In [163]: data.loc[data.three >= 2]
Out[163]:
          one  two  three  four
Colorado    0    5      6     7
Utah        8    9     10    11
New York   12   13     14    15
```

There are many ways to select and rearrange the data contained in a pandas object. For DataFrame, Table 5-4 provides a short summary of many of them. As you will see later, there are a number of additional options for working with hierarchical indexes.

Table 5-4. Indexing options with DataFrame

Type	Notes
df[column]	Select single column or sequence of columns from the DataFrame; special case conveniences: Boolean array (filter rows), slice (slice rows), or Boolean DataFrame (set values based on some criterion)
df.loc[rows]	Select single row or subset of rows from the DataFrame by label
df.loc[:, cols]	Select single column or subset of columns by label
df.loc[rows, cols]	Select both row(s) and column(s) by label
df.iloc[rows]	Select single row or subset of rows from the DataFrame by integer position
df.iloc[:, cols]	Select single column or subset of columns by integer position
df.iloc[rows, cols]	Select both row(s) and column(s) by integer position
df.at[row, col]	Select a single scalar value by row and column label
df.iat[row, col]	Select a single scalar value by row and column position (integers)
reindex method	Select either rows or columns by labels

Integer indexing pitfalls

Working with pandas objects indexed by integers can be a stumbling block for new users since they work differently from built-in Python data structures like lists and tuples. For example, you might not expect the following code to generate an error:

```
In [164]: ser = pd.Series(np.arange(3.))

In [165]: ser
Out[165]:
0    0.0
1    1.0
2    2.0
dtype: float64

In [166]: ser[-1]
---------------------------------------------------------------------------
ValueError                                Traceback (most recent call last)
/miniconda/envs/book-env/lib/python3.10/site-packages/pandas/core/indexes/range.p
y in get_loc(self, key, method, tolerance)
    384                 try:
--> 385                     return self._range.index(new_key)
    386                 except ValueError as err:
ValueError: -1 is not in range
The above exception was the direct cause of the following exception:
KeyError                                  Traceback (most recent call last)
<ipython-input-166-44969a759c20> in <module>
----> 1 ser[-1]
/miniconda/envs/book-env/lib/python3.10/site-packages/pandas/core/series.py in __
getitem__(self, key)
    956
    957         elif key_is_scalar:
--> 958             return self._get_value(key)
```

```
   959
   960            if is_hashable(key):
/miniconda/envs/book-env/lib/python3.10/site-packages/pandas/core/series.py in _g
et_value(self, label, takeable)
   1067
   1068            # Similar to Index.get_value, but we do not fall back to position
al
-> 1069            loc = self.index.get_loc(label)
   1070            return self.index._get_values_for_loc(self, loc, label)
   1071
/miniconda/envs/book-env/lib/python3.10/site-packages/pandas/core/indexes/range.p
y in get_loc(self, key, method, tolerance)
   385                    return self._range.index(new_key)
   386                except ValueError as err:
--> 387                    raise KeyError(key) from err
   388            self._check_indexing_error(key)
   389            raise KeyError(key)
KeyError: -1
```

In this case, pandas could "fall back" on integer indexing, but it is difficult to do this in general without introducing subtle bugs into the user code. Here we have an index containing 0, 1, and 2, but pandas does not want to guess what the user wants (label-based indexing or position-based):

```
In [167]: ser
Out[167]:
0    0.0
1    1.0
2    2.0
dtype: float64
```

On the other hand, with a noninteger index, there is no such ambiguity:

```
In [168]: ser2 = pd.Series(np.arange(3.), index=["a", "b", "c"])

In [169]: ser2[-1]
Out[169]: 2.0
```

If you have an axis index containing integers, data selection will always be label oriented. As I said above, if you use loc (for labels) or iloc (for integers) you will get exactly what you want:

```
In [170]: ser.iloc[-1]
Out[170]: 2.0
```

On the other hand, slicing with integers is always integer oriented:

```
In [171]: ser[:2]
Out[171]:
0    0.0
1    1.0
dtype: float64
```

As a result of these pitfalls, it is best to always prefer indexing with loc and iloc to avoid ambiguity.

Pitfalls with chained indexing

In the previous section we looked at how you can do flexible selections on a Data-Frame using loc and iloc. These indexing attributes can also be used to modify DataFrame objects in place, but doing so requires some care.

For example, in the example DataFrame above, we can assign to a column or row by label or integer position:

```
In [172]: data.loc[:, "one"] = 1

In [173]: data
Out[173]:
          one  two  three  four
Ohio        1    0      0     0
Colorado    1    5      6     7
Utah        1    9     10    11
New York    1   13     14    15

In [174]: data.iloc[2] = 5

In [175]: data
Out[175]:
          one  two  three  four
Ohio        1    0      0     0
Colorado    1    5      6     7
Utah        5    5      5     5
New York    1   13     14    15

In [176]: data.loc[data["four"] > 5] = 3

In [177]: data
Out[177]:
          one  two  three  four
Ohio        1    0      0     0
Colorado    3    3      3     3
Utah        5    5      5     5
New York    3    3      3     3
```

A common gotcha for new pandas users is to chain selections when assigning, like this:

```
In [177]: data.loc[data.three == 5]["three"] = 6
<ipython-input-11-0ed1cf2155d5>:1: SettingWithCopyWarning:
A value is trying to be set on a copy of a slice from a DataFrame.
Try using .loc[row_indexer,col_indexer] = value instead
```

Depending on the data contents, this may print a special SettingWithCopyWarning, which warns you that you are trying to modify a temporary value (the nonempty result of `data.loc[data.three == 5])` instead of the original DataFrame `data`, which might be what you were intending. Here, `data` was unmodified:

```
In [179]: data
Out[179]:
          one  two  three  four
Ohio        1    0      0     0
Colorado    3    3      3     3
Utah        5    5      5     5
New York    3    3      3     3
```

In these scenarios, the fix is to rewrite the chained assignment to use a single `loc` operation:

```
In [180]: data.loc[data.three == 5, "three"] = 6
```

```
In [181]: data
Out[181]:
          one  two  three  four
Ohio        1    0      0     0
Colorado    3    3      3     3
Utah        5    5      6     5
New York    3    3      3     3
```

A good rule of thumb is to avoid chained indexing when doing assignments. There are other cases where pandas will generate `SettingWithCopyWarning` that have to do with chained indexing. I refer you to this topic in the online pandas documentation.

Arithmetic and Data Alignment

pandas can make it much simpler to work with objects that have different indexes. For example, when you add objects, if any index pairs are not the same, the respective index in the result will be the union of the index pairs. Let's look at an example:

```
In [182]: s1 = pd.Series([7.3, -2.5, 3.4, 1.5], index=["a", "c", "d", "e"])
```

```
In [183]: s2 = pd.Series([-2.1, 3.6, -1.5, 4, 3.1],
   .....:                 index=["a", "c", "e", "f", "g"])
```

```
In [184]: s1
Out[184]:
a    7.3
c   -2.5
d    3.4
e    1.5
dtype: float64
```

```
In [185]: s2
Out[185]:
a   -2.1
c    3.6
e   -1.5
```

```
f    4.0
g    3.1
dtype: float64
```

Adding these yields:

```
In [186]: s1 + s2
Out[186]:
a    5.2
c    1.1
d    NaN
e    0.0
f    NaN
g    NaN
dtype: float64
```

The internal data alignment introduces missing values in the label locations that don't overlap. Missing values will then propagate in further arithmetic computations.

In the case of DataFrame, alignment is performed on both rows and columns:

```
In [187]: df1 = pd.DataFrame(np.arange(9.).reshape((3, 3)), columns=list("bcd"),
   .....:                    index=["Ohio", "Texas", "Colorado"])

In [188]: df2 = pd.DataFrame(np.arange(12.).reshape((4, 3)), columns=list("bde"),
   .....:                    index=["Utah", "Ohio", "Texas", "Oregon"])

In [189]: df1
Out[189]:
            b    c    d
Ohio      0.0  1.0  2.0
Texas     3.0  4.0  5.0
Colorado  6.0  7.0  8.0

In [190]: df2
Out[190]:
          b    d     e
Utah    0.0  1.0   2.0
Ohio    3.0  4.0   5.0
Texas   6.0  7.0   8.0
Oregon  9.0  10.0  11.0
```

Adding these returns a DataFrame with index and columns that are the unions of the ones in each DataFrame:

```
In [191]: df1 + df2
Out[191]:
            b    c     d    e
Colorado  NaN  NaN   NaN  NaN
Ohio      3.0  NaN   6.0  NaN
Oregon    NaN  NaN   NaN  NaN
Texas     9.0  NaN  12.0  NaN
Utah      NaN  NaN   NaN  NaN
```

Since the "c" and "e" columns are not found in both DataFrame objects, they appear as missing in the result. The same holds for the rows with labels that are not common to both objects.

If you add DataFrame objects with no column or row labels in common, the result will contain all nulls:

```
In [192]: df1 = pd.DataFrame({"A": [1, 2]})

In [193]: df2 = pd.DataFrame({"B": [3, 4]})

In [194]: df1
Out[194]:
   A
0  1
1  2

In [195]: df2
Out[195]:
   B
0  3
1  4

In [196]: df1 + df2
Out[196]:
    A    B
0 NaN  NaN
1 NaN  NaN
```

Arithmetic methods with fill values

In arithmetic operations between differently indexed objects, you might want to fill with a special value, like 0, when an axis label is found in one object but not the other. Here is an example where we set a particular value to NA (null) by assigning np.nan to it:

```
In [197]: df1 = pd.DataFrame(np.arange(12.).reshape((3, 4)),
   .....:                    columns=list("abcd"))

In [198]: df2 = pd.DataFrame(np.arange(20.).reshape((4, 5)),
   .....:                    columns=list("abcde"))

In [199]: df2.loc[1, "b"] = np.nan

In [200]: df1
Out[200]:
     a    b     c     d
0  0.0  1.0   2.0   3.0
1  4.0  5.0   6.0   7.0
2  8.0  9.0  10.0  11.0
```

```
In [201]: df2
Out[201]:
      a     b     c     d     e
0   0.0   1.0   2.0   3.0   4.0
1   5.0   NaN   7.0   8.0   9.0
2  10.0  11.0  12.0  13.0  14.0
3  15.0  16.0  17.0  18.0  19.0
```

Adding these results in missing values in the locations that don't overlap:

```
In [202]: df1 + df2
Out[202]:
      a     b     c     d    e
0   0.0   2.0   4.0   6.0  NaN
1   9.0   NaN  13.0  15.0  NaN
2  18.0  20.0  22.0  24.0  NaN
3   NaN   NaN   NaN   NaN  NaN
```

Using the add method on df1, I pass df2 and an argument to fill_value, which substitutes the passed value for any missing values in the operation:

```
In [203]: df1.add(df2, fill_value=0)
Out[203]:
      a     b     c     d     e
0   0.0   2.0   4.0   6.0   4.0
1   9.0   5.0  13.0  15.0   9.0
2  18.0  20.0  22.0  24.0  14.0
3  15.0  16.0  17.0  18.0  19.0
```

See Table 5-5 for a listing of Series and DataFrame methods for arithmetic. Each has a counterpart, starting with the letter r, that has arguments reversed. So these two statements are equivalent:

```
In [204]: 1 / df1
Out[204]:
       a         b         c         d
0    inf  1.000000  0.500000  0.333333
1  0.250  0.200000  0.166667  0.142857
2  0.125  0.111111  0.100000  0.090909

In [205]: df1.rdiv(1)
Out[205]:
       a         b         c         d
0    inf  1.000000  0.500000  0.333333
1  0.250  0.200000  0.166667  0.142857
2  0.125  0.111111  0.100000  0.090909
```

Relatedly, when reindexing a Series or DataFrame, you can also specify a different fill value:

```
In [206]: df1.reindex(columns=df2.columns, fill_value=0)
Out[206]:
     a    b    c    d  e
0  0.0  1.0  2.0  3.0  0
```

```
1   4.0  5.0   6.0   7.0  0
2   8.0  9.0  10.0  11.0  0
```

Table 5-5. Flexible arithmetic methods

Method	Description
add, radd	Methods for addition (+)
sub, rsub	Methods for subtraction (-)
div, rdiv	Methods for division (/)
floordiv, rfloordiv	Methods for floor division (//)
mul, rmul	Methods for multiplication (*)
pow, rpow	Methods for exponentiation (**)

Operations between DataFrame and Series

As with NumPy arrays of different dimensions, arithmetic between DataFrame and Series is also defined. First, as a motivating example, consider the difference between a two-dimensional array and one of its rows:

```
In [207]: arr = np.arange(12.).reshape((3, 4))

In [208]: arr
Out[208]:
array([[ 0.,   1.,   2.,   3.],
       [ 4.,   5.,   6.,   7.],
       [ 8.,   9.,  10.,  11.]])

In [209]: arr[0]
Out[209]: array([0., 1., 2., 3.])

In [210]: arr - arr[0]
Out[210]:
array([[0., 0., 0., 0.],
       [4., 4., 4., 4.],
       [8., 8., 8., 8.]])
```

When we subtract `arr[0]` from `arr`, the subtraction is performed once for each row. This is referred to as *broadcasting* and is explained in more detail as it relates to general NumPy arrays in Appendix A. Operations between a DataFrame and a Series are similar:

```
In [211]: frame = pd.DataFrame(np.arange(12.).reshape((4, 3)),
   .....:                      columns=list("bde"),
   .....:                      index=["Utah", "Ohio", "Texas", "Oregon"])

In [212]: series = frame.iloc[0]

In [213]: frame
Out[213]:
        b   d   e
```

```
Utah    0.0   1.0   2.0
Ohio    3.0   4.0   5.0
Texas   6.0   7.0   8.0
Oregon  9.0  10.0  11.0

In [214]: series
Out[214]:
b    0.0
d    1.0
e    2.0
Name: Utah, dtype: float64
```

By default, arithmetic between DataFrame and Series matches the index of the Series on the columns of the DataFrame, broadcasting down the rows:

```
In [215]: frame - series
Out[215]:
          b    d    e
Utah    0.0  0.0  0.0
Ohio    3.0  3.0  3.0
Texas   6.0  6.0  6.0
Oregon  9.0  9.0  9.0
```

If an index value is not found in either the DataFrame's columns or the Series's index, the objects will be reindexed to form the union:

```
In [216]: series2 = pd.Series(np.arange(3), index=["b", "e", "f"])

In [217]: series2
Out[217]:
b    0
e    1
f    2
dtype: int64

In [218]: frame + series2
Out[218]:
          b   d     e   f
Utah    0.0 NaN   3.0 NaN
Ohio    3.0 NaN   6.0 NaN
Texas   6.0 NaN   9.0 NaN
Oregon  9.0 NaN  12.0 NaN
```

If you want to instead broadcast over the columns, matching on the rows, you have to use one of the arithmetic methods and specify to match over the index. For example:

```
In [219]: series3 = frame["d"]

In [220]: frame
Out[220]:
          b    d    e
Utah    0.0  1.0  2.0
Ohio    3.0  4.0  5.0
```

```
Texas    6.0   7.0   8.0
Oregon   9.0  10.0  11.0

In [221]: series3
Out[221]:
Utah        1.0
Ohio        4.0
Texas       7.0
Oregon     10.0
Name: d, dtype: float64

In [222]: frame.sub(series3, axis="index")
Out[222]:
          b    d    e
Utah   -1.0  0.0  1.0
Ohio   -1.0  0.0  1.0
Texas  -1.0  0.0  1.0
Oregon -1.0  0.0  1.0
```

The axis that you pass is the *axis to match on*. In this case we mean to match on the DataFrame's row index (axis="index") and broadcast across the columns.

Function Application and Mapping

NumPy ufuncs (element-wise array methods) also work with pandas objects:

```
In [223]: frame = pd.DataFrame(np.random.standard_normal((4, 3)),
   .....:                      columns=list("bde"),
   .....:                      index=["Utah", "Ohio", "Texas", "Oregon"])

In [224]: frame
Out[224]:
              b         d         e
Utah   -0.204708  0.478943 -0.519439
Ohio   -0.555730  1.965781  1.393406
Texas   0.092908  0.281746  0.769023
Oregon  1.246435  1.007189 -1.296221

In [225]: np.abs(frame)
Out[225]:
              b         d         e
Utah    0.204708  0.478943  0.519439
Ohio    0.555730  1.965781  1.393406
Texas   0.092908  0.281746  0.769023
Oregon  1.246435  1.007189  1.296221
```

Another frequent operation is applying a function on one-dimensional arrays to each column or row. DataFrame's apply method does exactly this:

```
In [226]: def f1(x):
   .....:     return x.max() - x.min()
```

```
In [227]: frame.apply(f1)
Out[227]:
b    1.802165
d    1.684034
e    2.689627
dtype: float64
```

Here the function f, which computes the difference between the maximum and minimum of a Series, is invoked once on each column in frame. The result is a Series having the columns of frame as its index.

If you pass axis="columns" to apply, the function will be invoked once per row instead. A helpful way to think about this is as "apply across the columns":

```
In [228]: frame.apply(f1, axis="columns")
Out[228]:
Utah      0.998382
Ohio      2.521511
Texas     0.676115
Oregon    2.542656
dtype: float64
```

Many of the most common array statistics (like sum and mean) are DataFrame methods, so using apply is not necessary.

The function passed to apply need not return a scalar value; it can also return a Series with multiple values:

```
In [229]: def f2(x):
   .....:     return pd.Series([x.min(), x.max()], index=["min", "max"])

In [230]: frame.apply(f2)
Out[230]:
            b         d         e
min -0.555730  0.281746 -1.296221
max  1.246435  1.965781  1.393406
```

Element-wise Python functions can be used, too. Suppose you wanted to compute a formatted string from each floating-point value in frame. You can do this with applymap:

```
In [231]: def my_format(x):
   .....:     return f"{x:.2f}"

In [232]: frame.applymap(my_format)
Out[232]:
            b     d     e
Utah    -0.20  0.48 -0.52
Ohio    -0.56  1.97  1.39
Texas    0.09  0.28  0.77
Oregon   1.25  1.01 -1.30
```

The reason for the name `applymap` is that Series has a `map` method for applying an element-wise function:

```
In [233]: frame["e"].map(my_format)
Out[233]:
Utah      -0.52
Ohio       1.39
Texas      0.77
Oregon    -1.30
Name: e, dtype: object
```

Sorting and Ranking

Sorting a dataset by some criterion is another important built-in operation. To sort lexicographically by row or column label, use the `sort_index` method, which returns a new, sorted object:

```
In [234]: obj = pd.Series(np.arange(4), index=["d", "a", "b", "c"])

In [235]: obj
Out[235]:
d    0
a    1
b    2
c    3
dtype: int64

In [236]: obj.sort_index()
Out[236]:
a    1
b    2
c    3
d    0
dtype: int64
```

With a DataFrame, you can sort by index on either axis:

```
In [237]: frame = pd.DataFrame(np.arange(8).reshape((2, 4)),
   .....:                      index=["three", "one"],
   .....:                      columns=["d", "a", "b", "c"])

In [238]: frame
Out[238]:
       d  a  b  c
three  0  1  2  3
one    4  5  6  7

In [239]: frame.sort_index()
Out[239]:
       d  a  b  c
one    4  5  6  7
three  0  1  2  3
```

```
In [240]: frame.sort_index(axis="columns")
Out[240]:
        a  b  c  d
three   1  2  3  0
one     5  6  7  4
```

The data is sorted in ascending order by default but can be sorted in descending order, too:

```
In [241]: frame.sort_index(axis="columns", ascending=False)
Out[241]:
        d  c  b  a
three   0  3  2  1
one     4  7  6  5
```

To sort a Series by its values, use its sort_values method:

```
In [242]: obj = pd.Series([4, 7, -3, 2])

In [243]: obj.sort_values()
Out[243]:
2   -3
3    2
0    4
1    7
dtype: int64
```

Any missing values are sorted to the end of the Series by default:

```
In [244]: obj = pd.Series([4, np.nan, 7, np.nan, -3, 2])

In [245]: obj.sort_values()
Out[245]:
4   -3.0
5    2.0
0    4.0
2    7.0
1    NaN
3    NaN
dtype: float64
```

Missing values can be sorted to the start instead by using the na_position option:

```
In [246]: obj.sort_values(na_position="first")
Out[246]:
1    NaN
3    NaN
4   -3.0
5    2.0
0    4.0
2    7.0
dtype: float64
```

When sorting a DataFrame, you can use the data in one or more columns as the sort keys. To do so, pass one or more column names to sort_values:

```
In [247]: frame = pd.DataFrame({"b": [4, 7, -3, 2], "a": [0, 1, 0, 1]})

In [248]: frame
Out[248]:
   b  a
0  4  0
1  7  1
2 -3  0
3  2  1

In [249]: frame.sort_values("b")
Out[249]:
   b  a
2 -3  0
3  2  1
0  4  0
1  7  1
```

To sort by multiple columns, pass a list of names:

```
In [250]: frame.sort_values(["a", "b"])
Out[250]:
   b  a
2 -3  0
0  4  0
3  2  1
1  7  1
```

Ranking assigns ranks from one through the number of valid data points in an array, starting from the lowest value. The rank methods for Series and DataFrame are the place to look; by default, rank breaks ties by assigning each group the mean rank:

```
In [251]: obj = pd.Series([7, -5, 7, 4, 2, 0, 4])

In [252]: obj.rank()
Out[252]:
0    6.5
1    1.0
2    6.5
3    4.5
4    3.0
5    2.0
6    4.5
dtype: float64
```

Ranks can also be assigned according to the order in which they're observed in the data:

```
In [253]: obj.rank(method="first")
Out[253]:
0    6.0
1    1.0
2    7.0
3    4.0
4    3.0
5    2.0
6    5.0
dtype: float64
```

Here, instead of using the average rank 6.5 for the entries 0 and 2, they instead have been set to 6 and 7 because label 0 precedes label 2 in the data.

You can rank in descending order, too:

```
In [254]: obj.rank(ascending=False)
Out[254]:
0    1.5
1    7.0
2    1.5
3    3.5
4    5.0
5    6.0
6    3.5
dtype: float64
```

See Table 5-6 for a list of tie-breaking methods available.

DataFrame can compute ranks over the rows or the columns:

```
In [255]: frame = pd.DataFrame({"b": [4.3, 7, -3, 2], "a": [0, 1, 0, 1],
   .....:                       "c": [-2, 5, 8, -2.5]})

In [256]: frame
Out[256]:
     b  a    c
0  4.3  0 -2.0
1  7.0  1  5.0
2 -3.0  0  8.0
3  2.0  1 -2.5

In [257]: frame.rank(axis="columns")
Out[257]:
     b    a    c
0  3.0  2.0  1.0
1  3.0  1.0  2.0
2  1.0  2.0  3.0
3  3.0  2.0  1.0
```

Table 5-6. Tie-breaking methods with rank

Method	Description
"average"	Default: assign the average rank to each entry in the equal group
"min"	Use the minimum rank for the whole group
"max"	Use the maximum rank for the whole group
"first"	Assign ranks in the order the values appear in the data
"dense"	Like method="min", but ranks always increase by 1 between groups rather than the number of equal elements in a group

Axis Indexes with Duplicate Labels

Up until now almost all of the examples we have looked at have unique axis labels (index values). While many pandas functions (like reindex) require that the labels be unique, it's not mandatory. Let's consider a small Series with duplicate indices:

```
In [258]: obj = pd.Series(np.arange(5), index=["a", "a", "b", "b", "c"])
```

```
In [259]: obj
Out[259]:
a    0
a    1
b    2
b    3
c    4
dtype: int64
```

The is_unique property of the index can tell you whether or not its labels are unique:

```
In [260]: obj.index.is_unique
Out[260]: False
```

Data selection is one of the main things that behaves differently with duplicates. Indexing a label with multiple entries returns a Series, while single entries return a scalar value:

```
In [261]: obj["a"]
Out[261]:
a    0
a    1
dtype: int64
```

```
In [262]: obj["c"]
Out[262]: 4
```

This can make your code more complicated, as the output type from indexing can vary based on whether or not a label is repeated.

The same logic extends to indexing rows (or columns) in a DataFrame:

```
In [263]: df = pd.DataFrame(np.random.standard_normal((5, 3)),
   .....:                    index=["a", "a", "b", "b", "c"])

In [264]: df
Out[264]:
          0         1         2
a  0.274992  0.228913  1.352917
a  0.886429 -2.001637 -0.371843
b  1.669025 -0.438570 -0.539741
b  0.476985  3.248944 -1.021228
c -0.577087  0.124121  0.302614

In [265]: df.loc["b"]
Out[265]:
          0         1         2
b  1.669025 -0.438570 -0.539741
b  0.476985  3.248944 -1.021228

In [266]: df.loc["c"]
Out[266]:
0   -0.577087
1    0.124121
2    0.302614
Name: c, dtype: float64
```

5.3 Summarizing and Computing Descriptive Statistics

pandas objects are equipped with a set of common mathematical and statistical methods. Most of these fall into the category of *reductions* or *summary statistics*, methods that extract a single value (like the sum or mean) from a Series, or a Series of values from the rows or columns of a DataFrame. Compared with the similar methods found on NumPy arrays, they have built-in handling for missing data. Consider a small DataFrame:

```
In [267]: df = pd.DataFrame([[1.4, np.nan], [7.1, -4.5],
   .....:                    [np.nan, np.nan], [0.75, -1.3]],
   .....:                    index=["a", "b", "c", "d"],
   .....:                    columns=["one", "two"])

In [268]: df
Out[268]:
    one  two
a  1.40  NaN
b  7.10 -4.5
c   NaN  NaN
d  0.75 -1.3
```

Calling DataFrame's sum method returns a Series containing column sums:

```
In [269]: df.sum()
Out[269]:
one    9.25
two   -5.80
dtype: float64
```

Passing axis="columns" or axis=1 sums across the columns instead:

```
In [270]: df.sum(axis="columns")
Out[270]:
a    1.40
b    2.60
c    0.00
d   -0.55
dtype: float64
```

When an entire row or column contains all NA values, the sum is 0, whereas if any value is not NA, then the result is NA. This can be disabled with the skipna option, in which case any NA value in a row or column names the corresponding result NA:

```
In [271]: df.sum(axis="index", skipna=False)
Out[271]:
one   NaN
two   NaN
dtype: float64

In [272]: df.sum(axis="columns", skipna=False)
Out[272]:
a     NaN
b    2.60
c     NaN
d   -0.55
dtype: float64
```

Some aggregations, like mean, require at least one non-NA value to yield a value result, so here we have:

```
In [273]: df.mean(axis="columns")
Out[273]:
a    1.400
b    1.300
c     NaN
d   -0.275
dtype: float64
```

See Table 5-7 for a list of common options for each reduction method.

Table 5-7. Options for reduction methods

Method	Description
axis	Axis to reduce over; "index" for DataFrame's rows and "columns" for columns
skipna	Exclude missing values; True by default
level	Reduce grouped by level if the axis is hierarchically indexed (MultiIndex)

Some methods, like idxmin and idxmax, return indirect statistics, like the index value where the minimum or maximum values are attained:

```
In [274]: df.idxmax()
Out[274]:
one    b
two    d
dtype: object
```

Other methods are *accumulations*:

```
In [275]: df.cumsum()
Out[275]:
    one   two
a  1.40   NaN
b  8.50  -4.5
c   NaN   NaN
d  9.25  -5.8
```

Some methods are neither reductions nor accumulations. describe is one such example, producing multiple summary statistics in one shot:

```
In [276]: df.describe()
Out[276]:
            one       two
count  3.000000  2.000000
mean   3.083333 -2.900000
std    3.493685  2.262742
min    0.750000 -4.500000
25%    1.075000 -3.700000
50%    1.400000 -2.900000
75%    4.250000 -2.100000
max    7.100000 -1.300000
```

On nonnumeric data, describe produces alternative summary statistics:

```
In [277]: obj = pd.Series(["a", "a", "b", "c"] * 4)

In [278]: obj.describe()
Out[278]:
count     16
unique     3
top        a
freq       8
dtype: object
```

See Table 5-8 for a full list of summary statistics and related methods.

Table 5-8. Descriptive and summary statistics

Method	Description
count	Number of non-NA values
describe	Compute set of summary statistics
min, max	Compute minimum and maximum values
argmin, argmax	Compute index locations (integers) at which minimum or maximum value is obtained, respectively; not available on DataFrame objects
idxmin, idxmax	Compute index labels at which minimum or maximum value is obtained, respectively
quantile	Compute sample quantile ranging from 0 to 1 (default: 0.5)
sum	Sum of values
mean	Mean of values
median	Arithmetic median (50% quantile) of values
mad	Mean absolute deviation from mean value
prod	Product of all values
var	Sample variance of values
std	Sample standard deviation of values
skew	Sample skewness (third moment) of values
kurt	Sample kurtosis (fourth moment) of values
cumsum	Cumulative sum of values
cummin, cummax	Cumulative minimum or maximum of values, respectively
cumprod	Cumulative product of values
diff	Compute first arithmetic difference (useful for time series)
pct_change	Compute percent changes

Correlation and Covariance

Some summary statistics, like correlation and covariance, are computed from pairs of arguments. Let's consider some DataFrames of stock prices and volumes originally obtained from Yahoo! Finance and available in binary Python pickle files you can find in the accompanying datasets for the book:

```
In [279]: price = pd.read_pickle("examples/yahoo_price.pkl")

In [280]: volume = pd.read_pickle("examples/yahoo_volume.pkl")
```

I now compute percent changes of the prices, a time series operation that will be explored further in Chapter 11:

```
In [281]: returns = price.pct_change()

In [282]: returns.tail()
Out[282]:
                AAPL      GOOG      IBM       MSFT
```

```
Date
2016-10-17 -0.000680  0.001837  0.002072 -0.003483
2016-10-18 -0.000681  0.019616 -0.026168  0.007690
2016-10-19 -0.002979  0.007846  0.003583 -0.002255
2016-10-20 -0.000512 -0.005652  0.001719 -0.004867
2016-10-21 -0.003930  0.003011 -0.012474  0.042096
```

The corr method of Series computes the correlation of the overlapping, non-NA, aligned-by-index values in two Series. Relatedly, cov computes the covariance:

```
In [283]: returns["MSFT"].corr(returns["IBM"])
Out[283]: 0.49976361144151144

In [284]: returns["MSFT"].cov(returns["IBM"])
Out[284]: 8.870655479703546e-05
```

Since MSFT is a valid Python variable name, we can also select these columns using more concise syntax:

```
In [285]: returns["MSFT"].corr(returns["IBM"])
Out[285]: 0.49976361144151144
```

DataFrame's corr and cov methods, on the other hand, return a full correlation or covariance matrix as a DataFrame, respectively:

```
In [286]: returns.corr()
Out[286]:
          AAPL      GOOG       IBM      MSFT
AAPL  1.000000  0.407919  0.386817  0.389695
GOOG  0.407919  1.000000  0.405099  0.465919
IBM   0.386817  0.405099  1.000000  0.499764
MSFT  0.389695  0.465919  0.499764  1.000000

In [287]: returns.cov()
Out[287]:
          AAPL      GOOG       IBM      MSFT
AAPL  0.000277  0.000107  0.000078  0.000095
GOOG  0.000107  0.000251  0.000078  0.000108
IBM   0.000078  0.000078  0.000146  0.000089
MSFT  0.000095  0.000108  0.000089  0.000215
```

Using DataFrame's corrwith method, you can compute pair-wise correlations between a DataFrame's columns or rows with another Series or DataFrame. Passing a Series returns a Series with the correlation value computed for each column:

```
In [288]: returns.corrwith(returns["IBM"])
Out[288]:
AAPL    0.386817
GOOG    0.405099
IBM     1.000000
MSFT    0.499764
dtype: float64
```

Passing a DataFrame computes the correlations of matching column names. Here, I compute correlations of percent changes with volume:

```
In [289]: returns.corrwith(volume)
Out[289]:
AAPL   -0.075565
GOOG   -0.007067
IBM    -0.204849
MSFT   -0.092950
dtype: float64
```

Passing axis="columns" does things row-by-row instead. In all cases, the data points are aligned by label before the correlation is computed.

Unique Values, Value Counts, and Membership

Another class of related methods extracts information about the values contained in a one-dimensional Series. To illustrate these, consider this example:

```
In [290]: obj = pd.Series(["c", "a", "d", "a", "a", "b", "b", "c", "c"])
```

The first function is unique, which gives you an array of the unique values in a Series:

```
In [291]: uniques = obj.unique()

In [292]: uniques
Out[292]: array(['c', 'a', 'd', 'b'], dtype=object)
```

The unique values are not necessarily returned in the order in which they first appear, and not in sorted order, but they could be sorted after the fact if needed (uniques.sort()). Relatedly, value_counts computes a Series containing value frequencies:

```
In [293]: obj.value_counts()
Out[293]:
c    3
a    3
b    2
d    1
dtype: int64
```

The Series is sorted by value in descending order as a convenience. value_counts is also available as a top-level pandas method that can be used with NumPy arrays or other Python sequences:

```
In [294]: pd.value_counts(obj.to_numpy(), sort=False)
Out[294]:
c    3
a    3
d    1
b    2
dtype: int64
```

`isin` performs a vectorized set membership check and can be useful in filtering a dataset down to a subset of values in a Series or column in a DataFrame:

```
In [295]: obj
Out[295]:
0    c
1    a
2    d
3    a
4    a
5    b
6    b
7    c
8    c
dtype: object

In [296]: mask = obj.isin(["b", "c"])

In [297]: mask
Out[297]:
0     True
1    False
2    False
3    False
4    False
5     True
6     True
7     True
8     True
dtype: bool

In [298]: obj[mask]
Out[298]:
0    c
5    b
6    b
7    c
8    c
dtype: object
```

Related to `isin` is the `Index.get_indexer` method, which gives you an index array from an array of possibly nondistinct values into another array of distinct values:

```
In [299]: to_match = pd.Series(["c", "a", "b", "b", "c", "a"])

In [300]: unique_vals = pd.Series(["c", "b", "a"])

In [301]: indices = pd.Index(unique_vals).get_indexer(to_match)

In [302]: indices
Out[302]: array([0, 2, 1, 1, 0, 2])
```

See Table 5-9 for a reference on these methods.

Table 5-9. Unique, value counts, and set membership methods

Method	Description
isin	Compute a Boolean array indicating whether each Series or DataFrame value is contained in the passed sequence of values
get_indexer	Compute integer indices for each value in an array into another array of distinct values; helpful for data alignment and join-type operations
unique	Compute an array of unique values in a Series, returned in the order observed
value_counts	Return a Series containing unique values as its index and frequencies as its values, ordered count in descending order

In some cases, you may want to compute a histogram on multiple related columns in a DataFrame. Here's an example:

```
In [303]: data = pd.DataFrame({"Qu1": [1, 3, 4, 3, 4],
   .....:                      "Qu2": [2, 3, 1, 2, 3],
   .....:                      "Qu3": [1, 5, 2, 4, 4]})

In [304]: data
Out[304]:
   Qu1  Qu2  Qu3
0    1    2    1
1    3    3    5
2    4    1    2
3    3    2    4
4    4    3    4
```

We can compute the value counts for a single column, like so:

```
In [305]: data["Qu1"].value_counts().sort_index()
Out[305]:
1    1
3    2
4    2
Name: Qu1, dtype: int64
```

To compute this for all columns, pass `pandas.value_counts` to the DataFrame's `apply` method:

```
In [306]: result = data.apply(pd.value_counts).fillna(0)

In [307]: result
Out[307]:
   Qu1  Qu2  Qu3
1  1.0  1.0  1.0
2  0.0  2.0  1.0
3  2.0  2.0  0.0
4  2.0  0.0  2.0
5  0.0  0.0  1.0
```

Here, the row labels in the result are the distinct values occurring in all of the columns. The values are the respective counts of these values in each column.

There is also a `DataFrame.value_counts` method, but it computes counts considering each row of the DataFrame as a tuple to determine the number of occurrences of each distinct row:

```
In [308]: data = pd.DataFrame({"a": [1, 1, 1, 2, 2], "b": [0, 0, 1, 0, 0]})

In [309]: data
Out[309]:
   a  b
0  1  0
1  1  0
2  1  1
3  2  0
4  2  0

In [310]: data.value_counts()
Out[310]:
a  b
1  0    2
2  0    2
1  1    1
dtype: int64
```

In this case, the result has an index representing the distinct rows as a hierarchical index, a topic we will explore in greater detail in Chapter 8.

5.4 Conclusion

In the next chapter, we will discuss tools for reading (or *loading*) and writing datasets with pandas. After that, we will dig deeper into data cleaning, wrangling, analysis, and visualization tools using pandas.

## CHAPTER 6

Data Loading, Storage, and File Formats

Reading data and making it accessible (often called *data loading*) is a necessary first step for using most of the tools in this book. The term *parsing* is also sometimes used to describe loading text data and interpreting it as tables and different data types. I'm going to focus on data input and output using pandas, though there are numerous tools in other libraries to help with reading and writing data in various formats.

Input and output typically fall into a few main categories: reading text files and other more efficient on-disk formats, loading data from databases, and interacting with network sources like web APIs.

6.1 Reading and Writing Data in Text Format

pandas features a number of functions for reading tabular data as a DataFrame object. Table 6-1 summarizes some of them; `pandas.read_csv` is one of the most frequently used in this book. We will look at binary data formats later in Section 6.2, "Binary Data Formats," on page 193.

Table 6-1. Text and binary data loading functions in pandas

Function	Description
read_csv	Load delimited data from a file, URL, or file-like object; use comma as default delimiter
read_fwf	Read data in fixed-width column format (i.e., no delimiters)
read_clipboard	Variation of read_csv that reads data from the clipboard; useful for converting tables from web pages
read_excel	Read tabular data from an Excel XLS or XLSX file
read_hdf	Read HDF5 files written by pandas
read_html	Read all tables found in the given HTML document
read_json	Read data from a JSON (JavaScript Object Notation) string representation, file, URL, or file-like object

Function	Description
read_feather	Read the Feather binary file format
read_orc	Read the Apache ORC binary file format
read_parquet	Read the Apache Parquet binary file format
read_pickle	Read an object stored by pandas using the Python pickle format
read_sas	Read a SAS dataset stored in one of the SAS system's custom storage formats
read_spss	Read a data file created by SPSS
read_sql	Read the results of a SQL query (using SQLAlchemy)
read_sql_table	Read a whole SQL table (using SQLAlchemy); equivalent to using a query that selects everything in that table using read_sql
read_stata	Read a dataset from Stata file format
read_xml	Read a table of data from an XML file

I'll give an overview of the mechanics of these functions, which are meant to convert text data into a DataFrame. The optional arguments for these functions may fall into a few categories:

Indexing

Can treat one or more columns as the returned DataFrame, and whether to get column names from the file, arguments you provide, or not at all.

Type inference and data conversion

Includes the user-defined value conversions and custom list of missing value markers.

Date and time parsing

Includes a combining capability, including combining date and time information spread over multiple columns into a single column in the result.

Iterating

Support for iterating over chunks of very large files.

Unclean data issues

Includes skipping rows or a footer, comments, or other minor things like numeric data with thousands separated by commas.

Because of how messy data in the real world can be, some of the data loading functions (especially pandas.read_csv) have accumulated a long list of optional arguments over time. It's normal to feel overwhelmed by the number of different parameters (pandas.read_csv has around 50). The online pandas documentation has many examples about how each of these works, so if you're struggling to read a particular file, there might be a similar enough example to help you find the right parameters.

Some of these functions perform *type inference*, because the column data types are not part of the data format. That means you don't necessarily have to specify which columns are numeric, integer, Boolean, or string. Other data formats, like HDF5, ORC, and Parquet, have the data type information embedded in the format.

Handling dates and other custom types can require extra effort.

Let's start with a small comma-separated values (CSV) text file:

```
In [10]: !cat examples/ex1.csv
a,b,c,d,message
1,2,3,4,hello
5,6,7,8,world
9,10,11,12,foo
```

 Here I used the Unix `cat` shell command to print the raw contents of the file to the screen. If you're on Windows, you can use `type` instead of `cat` to achieve the same effect within a Windows terminal (or command line).

Since this is comma-delimited, we can then use `pandas.read_csv` to read it into a DataFrame:

```
In [11]: df = pd.read_csv("examples/ex1.csv")

In [12]: df
Out[12]:
   a   b   c   d message
0  1   2   3   4   hello
1  5   6   7   8   world
2  9  10  11  12     foo
```

A file will not always have a header row. Consider this file:

```
In [13]: !cat examples/ex2.csv
1,2,3,4,hello
5,6,7,8,world
9,10,11,12,foo
```

To read this file, you have a couple of options. You can allow pandas to assign default column names, or you can specify names yourself:

```
In [14]: pd.read_csv("examples/ex2.csv", header=None)
Out[14]:
   0   1   2   3      4
0  1   2   3   4  hello
1  5   6   7   8  world
2  9  10  11  12    foo

In [15]: pd.read_csv("examples/ex2.csv", names=["a", "b", "c", "d", "message"])
Out[15]:
```

```
   a   b   c    d message
0  1   2   3    4   hello
1  5   6   7    8   world
2  9  10  11   12     foo
```

Suppose you wanted the message column to be the index of the returned DataFrame. You can either indicate you want the column at index 4 or named "message" using the index_col argument:

```
In [16]: names = ["a", "b", "c", "d", "message"]

In [17]: pd.read_csv("examples/ex2.csv", names=names, index_col="message")
Out[17]:
         a   b   c   d
message
hello    1   2   3   4
world    5   6   7   8
foo      9  10  11  12
```

If you want to form a hierarchical index (discussed in Section 8.1, "Hierarchical Indexing," on page 247) from multiple columns, pass a list of column numbers or names:

```
In [18]: !cat examples/csv_mindex.csv
key1,key2,value1,value2
one,a,1,2
one,b,3,4
one,c,5,6
one,d,7,8
two,a,9,10
two,b,11,12
two,c,13,14
two,d,15,16

In [19]: parsed = pd.read_csv("examples/csv_mindex.csv",
   ....:                       index_col=["key1", "key2"])

In [20]: parsed
Out[20]:
           value1  value2
key1 key2
one  a          1       2
     b          3       4
     c          5       6
     d          7       8
two  a          9      10
     b         11      12
     c         13      14
     d         15      16
```

In some cases, a table might not have a fixed delimiter, using whitespace or some other pattern to separate fields. Consider a text file that looks like this:

```
In [21]: !cat examples/ex3.txt
A          B          C
aaa -0.264438 -1.026059 -0.619500
bbb  0.927272  0.302904 -0.032399
ccc -0.264273 -0.386314 -0.217601
ddd -0.871858 -0.348382  1.100491
```

While you could do some munging by hand, the fields here are separated by a variable amount of whitespace. In these cases, you can pass a regular expression as a delimiter for pandas.read_csv. This can be expressed by the regular expression \s+, so we have then:

```
In [22]: result = pd.read_csv("examples/ex3.txt", sep="\s+")
```

```
In [23]: result
Out[23]:
               A          B          C
aaa -0.264438 -1.026059 -0.619500
bbb  0.927272  0.302904 -0.032399
ccc -0.264273 -0.386314 -0.217601
ddd -0.871858 -0.348382  1.100491
```

Because there was one fewer column name than the number of data rows, pandas.read_csv infers that the first column should be the DataFrame's index in this special case.

The file parsing functions have many additional arguments to help you handle the wide variety of exception file formats that occur (see a partial listing in Table 6-2). For example, you can skip the first, third, and fourth rows of a file with skiprows:

```
In [24]: !cat examples/ex4.csv
# hey!
a,b,c,d,message
# just wanted to make things more difficult for you
# who reads CSV files with computers, anyway?
1,2,3,4,hello
5,6,7,8,world
9,10,11,12,foo
```

```
In [25]: pd.read_csv("examples/ex4.csv", skiprows=[0, 2, 3])
Out[25]:
   a   b   c   d message
0  1   2   3   4   hello
1  5   6   7   8   world
2  9  10  11  12     foo
```

Handling missing values is an important and frequently nuanced part of the file reading process. Missing data is usually either not present (empty string) or marked by some *sentinel* (placeholder) value. By default, pandas uses a set of commonly occurring sentinels, such as NA and NULL:

```
In [26]: !cat examples/ex5.csv
something,a,b,c,d,message
one,1,2,3,4,NA
two,5,6,,8,world
three,9,10,11,12,foo
In [27]: result = pd.read_csv("examples/ex5.csv")

In [28]: result
Out[28]:
  something  a   b     c   d message
0       one  1   2   3.0   4     NaN
1       two  5   6   NaN   8   world
2     three  9  10  11.0  12     foo
```

Recall that pandas outputs missing values as NaN, so we have two null or missing values in result:

```
In [29]: pd.isna(result)
Out[29]:
  something      a      b      c      d message
0     False  False  False  False  False    True
1     False  False  False   True  False   False
2     False  False  False  False  False   False
```

The na_values option accepts a sequence of strings to add to the default list of strings recognized as missing:

```
In [30]: result = pd.read_csv("examples/ex5.csv", na_values=["NULL"])

In [31]: result
Out[31]:
  something  a   b     c   d message
0       one  1   2   3.0   4     NaN
1       two  5   6   NaN   8   world
2     three  9  10  11.0  12     foo
```

pandas.read_csv has a list of many default NA value representations, but these defaults can be disabled with the keep_default_na option:

```
In [32]: result2 = pd.read_csv("examples/ex5.csv", keep_default_na=False)

In [33]: result2
Out[33]:
  something  a   b   c   d message
0       one  1   2   3   4      NA
1       two  5   6       8   world
2     three  9  10  11  12     foo

In [34]: result2.isna()
Out[34]:
```

```
        something        a       b       c       d  message
0          False   False   False   False   False    False
1          False   False   False   False   False    False
2          False   False   False   False   False    False

In [35]: result3 = pd.read_csv("examples/ex5.csv", keep_default_na=False,
   ....:                        na_values=["NA"])

In [36]: result3
Out[36]:
  something    a   b   c   d message
0       one    1   2   3   4     NaN
1       two    5   6       8   world
2     three    9  10  11  12     foo

In [37]: result3.isna()
Out[37]:
  something        a       b       c       d  message
0      False   False   False   False   False     True
1      False   False   False   False   False    False
2      False   False   False   False   False    False
```

Different NA sentinels can be specified for each column in a dictionary:

```
In [38]: sentinels = {"message": ["foo", "NA"], "something": ["two"]}

In [39]: pd.read_csv("examples/ex5.csv", na_values=sentinels,
   ....:             keep_default_na=False)
Out[39]:
  something    a   b   c   d message
0       one    1   2   3   4     NaN
1       NaN    5   6       8   world
2     three    9  10  11  12     NaN
```

Table 6-2 lists some frequently used options in pandas.read_csv.

Table 6-2. Some pandas.read_csv function arguments

Argument	Description
path	String indicating filesystem location, URL, or file-like object.
sep or delimiter	Character sequence or regular expression to use to split fields in each row.
header	Row number to use as column names; defaults to 0 (first row), but should be None if there is no header row.
index_col	Column numbers or names to use as the row index in the result; can be a single name/number or a list of them for a hierarchical index.
names	List of column names for result.
skiprows	Number of rows at beginning of file to ignore or list of row numbers (starting from 0) to skip.
na_values	Sequence of values to replace with NA. They are added to the default list unless keep_default_na=False is passed.
keep_default_na	Whether to use the default NA value list or not (True by default).

Argument	Description
`comment`	Character(s) to split comments off the end of lines.
`parse_dates`	Attempt to parse data to `datetime`; `False` by default. If `True`, will attempt to parse all columns. Otherwise, can specify a list of column numbers or names to parse. If element of list is tuple or list, will combine multiple columns together and parse to date (e.g., if date/time split across two columns).
`keep_date_col`	If joining columns to parse date, keep the joined columns; `False` by default.
`converters`	Dictionary containing column number or name mapping to functions (e.g., `{"foo": f}` would apply the function `f` to all values in the `"foo"` column).
`dayfirst`	When parsing potentially ambiguous dates, treat as international format (e.g., 7/6/2012 -> June 7, 2012); `False` by default.
`date_parser`	Function to use to parse dates.
`nrows`	Number of rows to read from beginning of file (not counting the header).
`iterator`	Return a `TextFileReader` object for reading the file piecemeal. This object can also be used with the `with` statement.
`chunksize`	For iteration, size of file chunks.
`skip_footer`	Number of lines to ignore at end of file.
`verbose`	Print various parsing information, like the time spent in each stage of the file conversion and memory use information.
`encoding`	Text encoding (e.g., `"utf-8` for UTF-8 encoded text). Defaults to `"utf-8"` if None.
`squeeze`	If the parsed data contains only one column, return a Series.
`thousands`	Separator for thousands (e.g., `","` or `"."`); default is None.
`decimal`	Decimal separator in numbers (e.g., `"."` or `","`); default is `"."`.
`engine`	CSV parsing and conversion engine to use; can be one of `"c"`, `"python"`, or `"pyarrow"`. The default is `"c"`, though the newer `"pyarrow"` engine can parse some files much faster. The `"python"` engine is slower but supports some features that the other engines do not.

Reading Text Files in Pieces

When processing very large files or figuring out the right set of arguments to correctly process a large file, you may want to read only a small piece of a file or iterate through smaller chunks of the file.

Before we look at a large file, we make the pandas display settings more compact:

```
In [40]: pd.options.display.max_rows = 10
```

Now we have:

```
In [41]: result = pd.read_csv("examples/ex6.csv")

In [42]: result
Out[42]:
            one       two     three      four key
0      0.467976 -0.038649 -0.295344 -1.824726   L
1     -0.358893  1.404453  0.704965 -0.200638   B
2     -0.501840  0.659254 -0.421691 -0.057688   G
```

```
3     0.204886   1.074134   1.388361 -0.982404   R
4     0.354628  -0.133116   0.283763 -0.837063   Q
...        ...        ...        ...       ...   ..
9995  2.311896  -0.417070  -1.409599 -0.515821   L
9996 -0.479893  -0.650419   0.745152 -0.646038   E
9997  0.523331   0.787112   0.486066  1.093156   K
9998 -0.362559   0.598894  -1.843201  0.887292   G
9999 -0.096376  -1.012999  -0.657431 -0.573315   0
[10000 rows x 5 columns]
```

The elipsis marks ... indicate that rows in the middle of the DataFrame have been omitted.

If you want to read only a small number of rows (avoiding reading the entire file), specify that with nrows:

```
In [43]: pd.read_csv("examples/ex6.csv", nrows=5)
Out[43]:
        one       two     three      four key
0  0.467976 -0.038649 -0.295344 -1.824726   L
1 -0.358893  1.404453  0.704965 -0.200638   B
2 -0.501840  0.659254 -0.421691 -0.057688   G
3  0.204886  1.074134  1.388361 -0.982404   R
4  0.354628 -0.133116  0.283763 -0.837063   Q
```

To read a file in pieces, specify a chunksize as a number of rows:

```
In [44]: chunker = pd.read_csv("examples/ex6.csv", chunksize=1000)

In [45]: type(chunker)
Out[45]: pandas.io.parsers.readers.TextFileReader
```

The TextFileReader object returned by pandas.read_csv allows you to iterate over the parts of the file according to the chunksize. For example, we can iterate over ex6.csv, aggregating the value counts in the "key" column, like so:

```
chunker = pd.read_csv("examples/ex6.csv", chunksize=1000)

tot = pd.Series([], dtype='int64')
for piece in chunker:
    tot = tot.add(piece["key"].value_counts(), fill_value=0)

tot = tot.sort_values(ascending=False)
```

We have then:

```
In [47]: tot[:10]
Out[47]:
E    368.0
X    364.0
L    346.0
0    343.0
Q    340.0
M    338.0
```

```
J    337.0
F    335.0
K    334.0
H    330.0
dtype: float64
```

TextFileReader is also equipped with a get_chunk method that enables you to read pieces of an arbitrary size.

Writing Data to Text Format

Data can also be exported to a delimited format. Let's consider one of the CSV files read before:

```
In [48]: data = pd.read_csv("examples/ex5.csv")

In [49]: data
Out[49]:
  something  a   b     c   d message
0       one  1   2   3.0   4     NaN
1       two  5   6   NaN   8   world
2     three  9  10  11.0  12     foo
```

Using DataFrame's to_csv method, we can write the data out to a comma-separated file:

```
In [50]: data.to_csv("examples/out.csv")

In [51]: !cat examples/out.csv
,something,a,b,c,d,message
0,one,1,2,3.0,4,
1,two,5,6,,8,world
2,three,9,10,11.0,12,foo
```

Other delimiters can be used, of course (writing to sys.stdout so it prints the text result to the console rather than a file):

```
In [52]: import sys

In [53]: data.to_csv(sys.stdout, sep="|")
|something|a|b|c|d|message
0|one|1|2|3.0|4|
1|two|5|6||8|world
2|three|9|10|11.0|12|foo
```

Missing values appear as empty strings in the output. You might want to denote them by some other sentinel value:

```
In [54]: data.to_csv(sys.stdout, na_rep="NULL")
,something,a,b,c,d,message
0,one,1,2,3.0,4,NULL
1,two,5,6,NULL,8,world
2,three,9,10,11.0,12,foo
```

With no other options specified, both the row and column labels are written. Both of these can be disabled:

```
In [55]: data.to_csv(sys.stdout, index=False, header=False)
one,1,2,3.0,4,
two,5,6,,8,world
three,9,10,11.0,12,foo
```

You can also write only a subset of the columns, and in an order of your choosing:

```
In [56]: data.to_csv(sys.stdout, index=False, columns=["a", "b", "c"])
a,b,c
1,2,3.0
5,6,
9,10,11.0
```

Working with Other Delimited Formats

It's possible to load most forms of tabular data from disk using functions like pandas.read_csv. In some cases, however, some manual processing may be necessary. It's not uncommon to receive a file with one or more malformed lines that trip up pandas.read_csv. To illustrate the basic tools, consider a small CSV file:

```
In [57]: !cat examples/ex7.csv
"a","b","c"
"1","2","3"
"1","2","3"
```

For any file with a single-character delimiter, you can use Python's built-in csv module. To use it, pass any open file or file-like object to csv.reader:

```
In [58]: import csv
```

```
In [59]: f = open("examples/ex7.csv")
```

```
In [60]: reader = csv.reader(f)
```

Iterating through the reader like a file yields lists of values with any quote characters removed:

```
In [61]: for line in reader:
   ....:     print(line)
['a', 'b', 'c']
['1', '2', '3']
['1', '2', '3']
```

```
In [62]: f.close()
```

From there, it's up to you to do the wrangling necessary to put the data in the form that you need. Let's take this step by step. First, we read the file into a list of lines:

```
In [63]: with open("examples/ex7.csv") as f:
   ....:     lines = list(csv.reader(f))
```

Then we split the lines into the header line and the data lines:

```
In [64]: header, values = lines[0], lines[1:]
```

Then we can create a dictionary of data columns using a dictionary comprehension and the expression `zip(*values)` (beware that this will use a lot of memory on large files), which transposes rows to columns:

```
In [65]: data_dict = {h: v for h, v in zip(header, zip(*values))}
```

```
In [66]: data_dict
Out[66]: {'a': ('1', '1'), 'b': ('2', '2'), 'c': ('3', '3')}
```

CSV files come in many different flavors. To define a new format with a different delimiter, string quoting convention, or line terminator, we could define a simple subclass of `csv.Dialect`:

```
class my_dialect(csv.Dialect):
    lineterminator = "\n"
    delimiter = ";"
    quotechar = '"'
    quoting = csv.QUOTE_MINIMAL

reader = csv.reader(f, dialect=my_dialect)
```

We could also give individual CSV dialect parameters as keywords to `csv.reader` without having to define a subclass:

```
reader = csv.reader(f, delimiter="|")
```

The possible options (attributes of `csv.Dialect`) and what they do can be found in Table 6-3.

Table 6-3. CSV dialect options

Argument	Description
`delimiter`	One-character string to separate fields; defaults to `","`.
`lineterminator`	Line terminator for writing; defaults to `"\r\n"`. Reader ignores this and recognizes cross-platform line terminators.
`quotechar`	Quote character for fields with special characters (like a delimiter); default is `'"'`.
`quoting`	Quoting convention. Options include `csv.QUOTE_ALL` (quote all fields), `csv.QUOTE_MINIMAL` (only fields with special characters like the delimiter), `csv.QUOTE_NONNUMERIC`, and `csv.QUOTE_NONE` (no quoting). See Python's documentation for full details. Defaults to `QUOTE_MINIMAL`.
`skipinitialspace`	Ignore whitespace after each delimiter; default is `False`.
`doublequote`	How to handle quoting character inside a field; if `True`, it is doubled (see online documentation for full detail and behavior).
`escapechar`	String to escape the delimiter if `quoting` is set to `csv.QUOTE_NONE`; disabled by default.

For files with more complicated or fixed multicharacter delimiters, you will not be able to use the `csv` module. In those cases, you'll have to do the line splitting and other cleanup using the string's `split` method or the regular expression method `re.split`. Thankfully, `pandas.read_csv` is capable of doing almost anything you need if you pass the necessary options, so you only rarely will have to parse files by hand.

To *write* delimited files manually, you can use `csv.writer`. It accepts an open, writable file object and the same dialect and format options as `csv.reader`:

```
with open("mydata.csv", "w") as f:
    writer = csv.writer(f, dialect=my_dialect)
    writer.writerow(("one", "two", "three"))
    writer.writerow(("1", "2", "3"))
    writer.writerow(("4", "5", "6"))
    writer.writerow(("7", "8", "9"))
```

JSON Data

JSON (short for JavaScript Object Notation) has become one of the standard formats for sending data by HTTP request between web browsers and other applications. It is a much more free-form data format than a tabular text form like CSV. Here is an example:

```
obj = """
{"name": "Wes",
 "cities_lived": ["Akron", "Nashville", "New York", "San Francisco"],
 "pet": null,
 "siblings": [{"name": "Scott", "age": 34, "hobbies": ["guitars", "soccer"]},
              {"name": "Katie", "age": 42, "hobbies": ["diving", "art"]}]
}
"""
```

JSON is very nearly valid Python code with the exception of its null value `null` and some other nuances (such as disallowing trailing commas at the end of lists). The basic types are objects (dictionaries), arrays (lists), strings, numbers, Booleans, and nulls. All of the keys in an object must be strings. There are several Python libraries for reading and writing JSON data. I'll use `json` here, as it is built into the Python standard library. To convert a JSON string to Python form, use `json.loads`:

```
In [68]: import json

In [69]: result = json.loads(obj)

In [70]: result
Out[70]:
{'name': 'Wes',
 'cities_lived': ['Akron', 'Nashville', 'New York', 'San Francisco'],
```

```
 'pet': None,
 'siblings': [{'name': 'Scott',
   'age': 34,
   'hobbies': ['guitars', 'soccer']},
  {'name': 'Katie', 'age': 42, 'hobbies': ['diving', 'art']}]}
```

json.dumps, on the other hand, converts a Python object back to JSON:

```
In [71]: asjson = json.dumps(result)
```

```
In [72]: asjson
Out[72]: '{"name": "Wes", "cities_lived": ["Akron", "Nashville", "New York", "San
 Francisco"], "pet": null, "siblings": [{"name": "Scott", "age": 34, "hobbies": [
 "guitars", "soccer"]}, {"name": "Katie", "age": 42, "hobbies": ["diving", "art"]}
 ]}'
```

How you convert a JSON object or list of objects to a DataFrame or some other data structure for analysis will be up to you. Conveniently, you can pass a list of dictionaries (which were previously JSON objects) to the DataFrame constructor and select a subset of the data fields:

```
In [73]: siblings = pd.DataFrame(result["siblings"], columns=["name", "age"])
```

```
In [74]: siblings
Out[74]:
    name  age
0  Scott   34
1  Katie   42
```

The pandas.read_json can automatically convert JSON datasets in specific arrangements into a Series or DataFrame. For example:

```
In [75]: !cat examples/example.json
[{"a": 1, "b": 2, "c": 3},
 {"a": 4, "b": 5, "c": 6},
 {"a": 7, "b": 8, "c": 9}]
```

The default options for pandas.read_json assume that each object in the JSON array is a row in the table:

```
In [76]: data = pd.read_json("examples/example.json")
```

```
In [77]: data
Out[77]:
   a  b  c
0  1  2  3
1  4  5  6
2  7  8  9
```

For an extended example of reading and manipulating JSON data (including nested records), see the USDA food database example in Chapter 13.

If you need to export data from pandas to JSON, one way is to use the to_json methods on Series and DataFrame:

```
In [78]: data.to_json(sys.stdout)
{"a":{"0":1,"1":4,"2":7},"b":{"0":2,"1":5,"2":8},"c":{"0":3,"1":6,"2":9}}
In [79]: data.to_json(sys.stdout, orient="records")
[{"a":1,"b":2,"c":3},{"a":4,"b":5,"c":6},{"a":7,"b":8,"c":9}]
```

XML and HTML: Web Scraping

Python has many libraries for reading and writing data in the ubiquitous HTML and XML formats. Examples include lxml, Beautiful Soup, and html5lib. While lxml is comparatively much faster in general, the other libraries can better handle malformed HTML or XML files.

pandas has a built-in function, pandas.read_html, which uses all of these libraries to automatically parse tables out of HTML files as DataFrame objects. To show how this works, I downloaded an HTML file (used in the pandas documentation) from the US FDIC showing bank failures.[1] First, you must install some additional libraries used by read_html:

```
conda install lxml beautifulsoup4 html5lib
```

If you are not using conda, pip install lxml should also work.

The pandas.read_html function has a number of options, but by default it searches for and attempts to parse all tabular data contained within <table> tags. The result is a list of DataFrame objects:

```
In [80]: tables = pd.read_html("examples/fdic_failed_bank_list.html")

In [81]: len(tables)
Out[81]: 1

In [82]: failures = tables[0]

In [83]: failures.head()
Out[83]:
                       Bank Name            City  ST   CERT  \
0                     Allied Bank        Mulberry  AR     91
1     The Woodbury Banking Company        Woodbury  GA  11297
2         First CornerStone Bank  King of Prussia  PA  35312
3             Trust Company Bank         Memphis  TN   9956
4     North Milwaukee State Bank       Milwaukee  WI  20364
              Acquiring Institution        Closing Date       Updated Date
0                       Today's Bank  September 23, 2016  November 17, 2016
1                        United Bank     August 19, 2016  November 17, 2016
```

---

1 For the full list, see *https://www.fdic.gov/bank/individual/failed/banklist.html*.

```
2  First-Citizens Bank & Trust Company      May 6, 2016  September 6, 2016
3              The Bank of Fayette County   April 29, 2016  September 6, 2016
4  First-Citizens Bank & Trust Company    March 11, 2016      June 16, 2016
```

Because `failures` has many columns, pandas inserts a line break character \.

As you will learn in later chapters, from here we could proceed to do some data cleaning and analysis, like computing the number of bank failures by year:

```
In [84]: close_timestamps = pd.to_datetime(failures["Closing Date"])

In [85]: close_timestamps.dt.year.value_counts()
Out[85]:
2010    157
2009    140
2011     92
2012     51
2008     25
        ...
2004      4
2001      4
2007      3
2003      3
2000      2
Name: Closing Date, Length: 15, dtype: int64
```

Parsing XML with lxml.objectify

XML is another common structured data format supporting hierarchical, nested data with metadata. The book you are currently reading was actually created from a series of large XML documents.

Earlier, I showed the `pandas.read_html` function, which uses either lxml or Beautiful Soup under the hood to parse data from HTML. XML and HTML are structurally similar, but XML is more general. Here, I will show an example of how to use lxml to parse data from a more general XML format.

For many years, the New York Metropolitan Transportation Authority (MTA) published a number of data series about its bus and train services in XML format. Here we'll look at the performance data, which is contained in a set of XML files. Each train or bus service has a different file (like *Performance_MNR.xml* for the Metro-North Railroad) containing monthly data as a series of XML records that look like this:

```
<INDICATOR>
  <INDICATOR_SEQ>373889</INDICATOR_SEQ>
  <PARENT_SEQ></PARENT_SEQ>
  <AGENCY_NAME>Metro-North Railroad</AGENCY_NAME>
  <INDICATOR_NAME>Escalator Availability</INDICATOR_NAME>
  <DESCRIPTION>Percent of the time that escalators are operational
  systemwide. The availability rate is based on physical observations performed
  the morning of regular business days only. This is a new indicator the agency
```

```
        began reporting in 2009.</DESCRIPTION>
        <PERIOD_YEAR>2011</PERIOD_YEAR>
        <PERIOD_MONTH>12</PERIOD_MONTH>
        <CATEGORY>Service Indicators</CATEGORY>
        <FREQUENCY>M</FREQUENCY>
        <DESIRED_CHANGE>U</DESIRED_CHANGE>
        <INDICATOR_UNIT>%</INDICATOR_UNIT>
        <DECIMAL_PLACES>1</DECIMAL_PLACES>
        <YTD_TARGET>97.00</YTD_TARGET>
        <YTD_ACTUAL></YTD_ACTUAL>
        <MONTHLY_TARGET>97.00</MONTHLY_TARGET>
        <MONTHLY_ACTUAL></MONTHLY_ACTUAL>
    </INDICATOR>
```

Using `lxml.objectify`, we parse the file and get a reference to the root node of the XML file with `getroot`:

```
In [86]: from lxml import objectify

In [87]: path = "datasets/mta_perf/Performance_MNR.xml"

In [88]: with open(path) as f:
   ....:     parsed = objectify.parse(f)

In [89]: root = parsed.getroot()
```

`root.INDICATOR` returns a generator yielding each `<INDICATOR>` XML element. For each record, we can populate a dictionary of tag names (like `YTD_ACTUAL`) to data values (excluding a few tags) by running the following code:

```
data = []

skip_fields = ["PARENT_SEQ", "INDICATOR_SEQ",
               "DESIRED_CHANGE", "DECIMAL_PLACES"]

for elt in root.INDICATOR:
    el_data = {}
    for child in elt.getchildren():
        if child.tag in skip_fields:
            continue
        el_data[child.tag] = child.pyval
    data.append(el_data)
```

Lastly, convert this list of dictionaries into a DataFrame:

```
In [91]: perf = pd.DataFrame(data)

In [92]: perf.head()
Out[92]:
            AGENCY_NAME                        INDICATOR_NAME  \
0  Metro-North Railroad  On-Time Performance (West of Hudson)
1  Metro-North Railroad  On-Time Performance (West of Hudson)
2  Metro-North Railroad  On-Time Performance (West of Hudson)
```

```
3  Metro-North Railroad  On-Time Performance (West of Hudson)
4  Metro-North Railroad  On-Time Performance (West of Hudson)
                                                             DESCRIPTION  \
0  Percent of commuter trains that arrive at their destinations within 5 m...
1  Percent of commuter trains that arrive at their destinations within 5 m...
2  Percent of commuter trains that arrive at their destinations within 5 m...
3  Percent of commuter trains that arrive at their destinations within 5 m...
4  Percent of commuter trains that arrive at their destinations within 5 m...
   PERIOD_YEAR  PERIOD_MONTH            CATEGORY FREQUENCY INDICATOR_UNIT  \
0         2008             1  Service Indicators         M              %
1         2008             2  Service Indicators         M              %
2         2008             3  Service Indicators         M              %
3         2008             4  Service Indicators         M              %
4         2008             5  Service Indicators         M              %
   YTD_TARGET YTD_ACTUAL MONTHLY_TARGET MONTHLY_ACTUAL
0        95.0       96.9           95.0           96.9
1        95.0       96.0           95.0           95.0
2        95.0       96.3           95.0           96.9
3        95.0       96.8           95.0           98.3
4        95.0       96.6           95.0           95.8
```

pandas's `pandas.read_xml` function turns this process into a one-line expression:

```
In [93]: perf2 = pd.read_xml(path)

In [94]: perf2.head()
Out[94]:
   INDICATOR_SEQ  PARENT_SEQ          AGENCY_NAME  \
0          28445         NaN  Metro-North Railroad
1          28445         NaN  Metro-North Railroad
2          28445         NaN  Metro-North Railroad
3          28445         NaN  Metro-North Railroad
4          28445         NaN  Metro-North Railroad
                      INDICATOR_NAME  \
0  On-Time Performance (West of Hudson)
1  On-Time Performance (West of Hudson)
2  On-Time Performance (West of Hudson)
3  On-Time Performance (West of Hudson)
4  On-Time Performance (West of Hudson)
                                                             DESCRIPTION  \
0  Percent of commuter trains that arrive at their destinations within 5 m...
1  Percent of commuter trains that arrive at their destinations within 5 m...
2  Percent of commuter trains that arrive at their destinations within 5 m...
3  Percent of commuter trains that arrive at their destinations within 5 m...
4  Percent of commuter trains that arrive at their destinations within 5 m...
   PERIOD_YEAR  PERIOD_MONTH            CATEGORY FREQUENCY DESIRED_CHANGE  \
0         2008             1  Service Indicators         M              U
1         2008             2  Service Indicators         M              U
2         2008             3  Service Indicators         M              U
3         2008             4  Service Indicators         M              U
4         2008             5  Service Indicators         M              U
   INDICATOR_UNIT  DECIMAL_PLACES YTD_TARGET YTD_ACTUAL MONTHLY_TARGET  \
0              %               1      95.00      96.90          95.00
```

```
1             %          1     95.00    96.00      95.00
2             %          1     95.00    96.30      95.00
3             %          1     95.00    96.80      95.00
4             %          1     95.00    96.60      95.00
   MONTHLY_ACTUAL
0         96.90
1         95.00
2         96.90
3         98.30
4         95.80
```

For more complex XML documents, refer to the docstring for pandas.read_xml which describes how to do selections and filters to extract a particular table of interest.

6.2 Binary Data Formats

One simple way to store (or *serialize*) data in binary format is using Python's built-in pickle module. pandas objects all have a to_pickle method that writes the data to disk in pickle format:

```
In [95]: frame = pd.read_csv("examples/ex1.csv")

In [96]: frame
Out[96]:
   a   b   c   d message
0  1   2   3   4   hello
1  5   6   7   8   world
2  9  10  11  12     foo

In [97]: frame.to_pickle("examples/frame_pickle")
```

Pickle files are in general readable only in Python. You can read any "pickled" object stored in a file by using the built-in pickle directly, or even more conveniently using pandas.read_pickle:

```
In [98]: pd.read_pickle("examples/frame_pickle")
Out[98]:
   a   b   c   d message
0  1   2   3   4   hello
1  5   6   7   8   world
2  9  10  11  12     foo
```

pickle is recommended only as a short-term storage format. The problem is that it is hard to guarantee that the format will be stable over time; an object pickled today may not unpickle with a later version of a library. pandas has tried to maintain backward compatibility when possible, but at some point in the future it may be necessary to "break" the pickle format.

pandas has built-in support for several other open source binary data formats, such as HDF5, ORC, and Apache Parquet. For example, if you install the `pyarrow` package (`conda install pyarrow`), then you can read Parquet files with `pandas.read_par quet`:

```
In [100]: fec = pd.read_parquet('datasets/fec/fec.parquet')
```

I will give some HDF5 examples in "Using HDF5 Format" on page 195. I encourage you to explore different file formats to see how fast they are and how well they work for your analysis.

Reading Microsoft Excel Files

pandas also supports reading tabular data stored in Excel 2003 (and higher) files using either the `pandas.ExcelFile` class or `pandas.read_excel` function. Internally, these tools use the add-on packages `xlrd` and `openpyxl` to read old-style XLS and newer XLSX files, respectively. These must be installed separately from pandas using pip or conda:

```
conda install openpyxl xlrd
```

To use `pandas.ExcelFile`, create an instance by passing a path to an `xls` or `xlsx` file:

```
In [101]: xlsx = pd.ExcelFile("examples/ex1.xlsx")
```

This object can show you the list of available sheet names in the file:

```
In [102]: xlsx.sheet_names
Out[102]: ['Sheet1']
```

Data stored in a sheet can then be read into DataFrame with `parse`:

```
In [103]: xlsx.parse(sheet_name="Sheet1")
Out[103]:
   Unnamed: 0  a   b   c   d message
0           0  1   2   3   4   hello
1           1  5   6   7   8   world
2           2  9  10  11  12     foo
```

This Excel table has an index column, so we can indicate that with the `index_col` argument:

```
In [104]: xlsx.parse(sheet_name="Sheet1", index_col=0)
Out[104]:
   a   b   c   d message
0  1   2   3   4   hello
1  5   6   7   8   world
2  9  10  11  12     foo
```

If you are reading multiple sheets in a file, then it is faster to create the `pandas.Excel File`, but you can also simply pass the filename to `pandas.read_excel`:

```
In [105]: frame = pd.read_excel("examples/ex1.xlsx", sheet_name="Sheet1")

In [106]: frame
Out[106]:
   Unnamed: 0  a   b   c   d message
0           0  1   2   3   4   hello
1           1  5   6   7   8   world
2           2  9  10  11  12     foo
```

To write pandas data to Excel format, you must first create an ExcelWriter, then write data to it using the pandas object's to_excel method:

```
In [107]: writer = pd.ExcelWriter("examples/ex2.xlsx")

In [108]: frame.to_excel(writer, "Sheet1")

In [109]: writer.save()
```

You can also pass a file path to to_excel and avoid the ExcelWriter:

```
In [110]: frame.to_excel("examples/ex2.xlsx")
```

Using HDF5 Format

HDF5 is a respected file format intended for storing large quantities of scientific array data. It is available as a C library, and it has interfaces available in many other languages, including Java, Julia, MATLAB, and Python. The "HDF" in HDF5 stands for *hierarchical data format*. Each HDF5 file can store multiple datasets and supporting metadata. Compared with simpler formats, HDF5 supports on-the-fly compression with a variety of compression modes, enabling data with repeated patterns to be stored more efficiently. HDF5 can be a good choice for working with datasets that don't fit into memory, as you can efficiently read and write small sections of much larger arrays.

To get started with HDF5 and pandas, you must first install PyTables by installing the tables package with conda:

```
conda install pytables
```

 Note that the PyTables package is called "tables" in PyPI, so if you install with pip you will have to run pip install tables.

While it's possible to directly access HDF5 files using either the PyTables or h5py libraries, pandas provides a high-level interface that simplifies storing Series and DataFrame objects. The HDFStore class works like a dictionary and handles the low-level details:

```
In [113]: frame = pd.DataFrame({"a": np.random.standard_normal(100)})

In [114]: store = pd.HDFStore("examples/mydata.h5")

In [115]: store["obj1"] = frame

In [116]: store["obj1_col"] = frame["a"]

In [117]: store
Out[117]:
<class 'pandas.io.pytables.HDFStore'>
File path: examples/mydata.h5
```

Objects contained in the HDF5 file can then be retrieved with the same dictionary-like API:

```
In [118]: store["obj1"]
Out[118]:
           a
0   -0.204708
1    0.478943
2   -0.519439
3   -0.555730
4    1.965781
..       ...
95   0.795253
96   0.118110
97  -0.748532
98   0.584970
99   0.152677
[100 rows x 1 columns]
```

HDFStore supports two storage schemas, "fixed" and "table" (the default is "fixed"). The latter is generally slower, but it supports query operations using a special syntax:

```
In [119]: store.put("obj2", frame, format="table")

In [120]: store.select("obj2", where=["index >= 10 and index <= 15"])
Out[120]:
           a
10   1.007189
11  -1.296221
12   0.274992
13   0.228913
14   1.352917
15   0.886429

In [121]: store.close()
```

The put is an explicit version of the store["obj2"] = frame method but allows us to set other options like the storage format.

The `pandas.read_hdf` function gives you a shortcut to these tools:

```
In [122]: frame.to_hdf("examples/mydata.h5", "obj3", format="table")

In [123]: pd.read_hdf("examples/mydata.h5", "obj3", where=["index < 5"])
Out[123]:
          a
0 -0.204708
1  0.478943
2 -0.519439
3 -0.555730
4  1.965781
```

If you'd like, you can delete the HDF5 file you created, like so:

```
In [124]: import os

In [125]: os.remove("examples/mydata.h5")
```

> If you are processing data that is stored on remote servers, like Amazon S3 or HDFS, using a different binary format designed for distributed storage like Apache Parquet (*http://parquet.apache.org*) may be more suitable.

If you work with large quantities of data locally, I would encourage you to explore PyTables and h5py to see how they can suit your needs. Since many data analysis problems are I/O-bound (rather than CPU-bound), using a tool like HDF5 can massively accelerate your applications.

> HDF5 is *not* a database. It is best suited for write-once, read-many datasets. While data can be added to a file at any time, if multiple writers do so simultaneously, the file can become corrupted.

6.3 Interacting with Web APIs

Many websites have public APIs providing data feeds via JSON or some other format. There are a number of ways to access these APIs from Python; one method that I recommend is the `requests` package (*http://docs.python-requests.org*), which can be installed with pip or conda:

```
conda install requests
```

To find the last 30 GitHub issues for pandas on GitHub, we can make a GET HTTP request using the add-on `requests` library:

```
In [126]: import requests
```

```
In [127]: url = "https://api.github.com/repos/pandas-dev/pandas/issues"

In [128]: resp = requests.get(url)

In [129]: resp.raise_for_status()

In [130]: resp
Out[130]: <Response [200]>
```

It's a good practice to always call `raise_for_status` after using `requests.get` to check for HTTP errors.

The response object's `json` method will return a Python object containing the parsed JSON data as a dictionary or list (depending on what JSON is returned):

```
In [131]: data = resp.json()

In [132]: data[0]["title"]
Out[132]: 'REF: make copy keyword non-stateful'
```

Since the results retrieved are based on real-time data, what you see when you run this code will almost definitely be different.

Each element in `data` is a dictionary containing all of the data found on a GitHub issue page (except for the comments). We can pass `data` directly to `pandas.Data Frame` and extract fields of interest:

```
In [133]: issues = pd.DataFrame(data, columns=["number", "title",
   .....:                                      "labels", "state"])

In [134]: issues
Out[134]:
    number  \
0    48062
1    48061
2    48060
3    48059
4    48058
..     ...
25   48032
26   48030
27   48028
28   48027
29   48026

                                                          title  \
0                           REF: make copy keyword non-stateful
1                                        STYLE: upgrade flake8
2   DOC: "Creating a Python environment" in "Creating a development environ...
3                              REGR: Avoid overflow with groupby sum
4   REGR: fix reset_index (Index.insert) regression with custom Index subcl...
..                                                          ...
25                    BUG: Union of multi index with EA types can lose EA dtype
```

```
26                                    ENH: Add rolling.prod()
27                              CLN: Refactor groupby's _make_wrapper
28                              ENH: Support masks in groupby prod
29                              DEP: Add pip to environment.yml
                                                            labels  \
0                                                               []
1   [{'id': 106935113, 'node_id': 'MDU6TGFiZWwxMDY5MzUxMTM=', 'url': 'https...
2   [{'id': 134699, 'node_id': 'MDU6TGFiZWwxMzQ2OTk=', 'url': 'https://api....
3   [{'id': 233160, 'node_id': 'MDU6TGFiZWwyMzMxNjA=', 'url': 'https://api....
4   [{'id': 32815646, 'node_id': 'MDU6TGFiZWwzMjgxNTY0Ng==', 'url': 'https:...
..                                                             ...
25  [{'id': 76811, 'node_id': 'MDU6TGFiZWw3NjgxMQ==', 'url': 'https://api.g...
26  [{'id': 76812, 'node_id': 'MDU6TGFiZWw3NjgxMg==', 'url': 'https://api.g...
27  [{'id': 233160, 'node_id': 'MDU6TGFiZWwyMzMxNjA=', 'url': 'https://api....
28  [{'id': 233160, 'node_id': 'MDU6TGFiZWwyMzMxNjA=', 'url': 'https://api....
29  [{'id': 76811, 'node_id': 'MDU6TGFiZWw3NjgxMQ==', 'url': 'https://api.g...
    state
0   open
1   open
2   open
3   open
4   open
..   ...
25  open
26  open
27  open
28  open
29  open
[30 rows x 4 columns]
```

With a bit of elbow grease, you can create some higher-level interfaces to common web APIs that return DataFrame objects for more convenient analysis.

6.4 Interacting with Databases

In a business setting, a lot of data may not be stored in text or Excel files. SQL-based relational databases (such as SQL Server, PostgreSQL, and MySQL) are in wide use, and many alternative databases have become quite popular. The choice of database is usually dependent on the performance, data integrity, and scalability needs of an application.

pandas has some functions to simplify loading the results of a SQL query into a DataFrame. As an example, I'll create a SQLite3 database using Python's built-in sqlite3 driver:

```
In [135]: import sqlite3

In [136]: query = """
   .....: CREATE TABLE test
   .....: (a VARCHAR(20), b VARCHAR(20),
```

```
.....:    c REAL,        d INTEGER
.....: );"""

In [137]: con = sqlite3.connect("mydata.sqlite")

In [138]: con.execute(query)
Out[138]: <sqlite3.Cursor at 0x7fdfd73b69c0>

In [139]: con.commit()
```

Then, insert a few rows of data:

```
In [140]: data = [("Atlanta", "Georgia", 1.25, 6),
.....:            ("Tallahassee", "Florida", 2.6, 3),
.....:            ("Sacramento", "California", 1.7, 5)]

In [141]: stmt = "INSERT INTO test VALUES(?, ?, ?, ?)"

In [142]: con.executemany(stmt, data)
Out[142]: <sqlite3.Cursor at 0x7fdfd73a00c0>

In [143]: con.commit()
```

Most Python SQL drivers return a list of tuples when selecting data from a table:

```
In [144]: cursor = con.execute("SELECT * FROM test")

In [145]: rows = cursor.fetchall()

In [146]: rows
Out[146]:
[('Atlanta', 'Georgia', 1.25, 6),
 ('Tallahassee', 'Florida', 2.6, 3),
 ('Sacramento', 'California', 1.7, 5)]
```

You can pass the list of tuples to the DataFrame constructor, but you also need
the column names, contained in the cursor's `description` attribute. Note that for
SQLite3, the cursor `description` only provides column names (the other fields,
which are part of Python's Database API specification, are None), but for some other
database drivers, more column information is provided:

```
In [147]: cursor.description
Out[147]:
(('a', None, None, None, None, None, None),
 ('b', None, None, None, None, None, None),
 ('c', None, None, None, None, None, None),
 ('d', None, None, None, None, None, None))

In [148]: pd.DataFrame(rows, columns=[x[0] for x in cursor.description])
Out[148]:
         a         b     c  d
0    Atlanta   Georgia  1.25  6
```

```
1   Tallahassee    Florida  2.60  3
2   Sacramento  California  1.70  5
```

This is quite a bit of munging that you'd rather not repeat each time you query the database. The SQLAlchemy project (*http://www.sqlalchemy.org/*) is a popular Python SQL toolkit that abstracts away many of the common differences between SQL databases. pandas has a `read_sql` function that enables you to read data easily from a general SQLAlchemy connection. You can install SQLAlchemy with conda like so:

```
conda install sqlalchemy
```

Now, we'll connect to the same SQLite database with SQLAlchemy and read data from the table created before:

```
In [149]: import sqlalchemy as sqla

In [150]: db = sqla.create_engine("sqlite:///mydata.sqlite")

In [151]: pd.read_sql("SELECT * FROM test", db)
Out[151]:
            a           b     c  d
0       Atlanta     Georgia  1.25  6
1   Tallahassee     Florida  2.60  3
2   Sacramento  California  1.70  5
```

6.5 Conclusion

Getting access to data is frequently the first step in the data analysis process. We have looked at a number of useful tools in this chapter that should help you get started. In the upcoming chapters we will dig deeper into data wrangling, data visualization, time series analysis, and other topics.

Data Cleaning and Preparation

During the course of doing data analysis and modeling, a significant amount of time is spent on data preparation: loading, cleaning, transforming, and rearranging. Such tasks are often reported to take up 80% or more of an analyst's time. Sometimes the way that data is stored in files or databases is not in the right format for a particular task. Many researchers choose to do ad hoc processing of data from one form to another using a general-purpose programming language, like Python, Perl, R, or Java, or Unix text-processing tools like sed or awk. Fortunately, pandas, along with the built-in Python language features, provides you with a high-level, flexible, and fast set of tools to enable you to manipulate data into the right form.

If you identify a type of data manipulation that isn't anywhere in this book or elsewhere in the pandas library, feel free to share your use case on one of the Python mailing lists or on the pandas GitHub site. Indeed, much of the design and implementation of pandas have been driven by the needs of real-world applications.

In this chapter I discuss tools for missing data, duplicate data, string manipulation, and some other analytical data transformations. In the next chapter, I focus on combining and rearranging datasets in various ways.

7.1 Handling Missing Data

Missing data occurs commonly in many data analysis applications. One of the goals of pandas is to make working with missing data as painless as possible. For example, all of the descriptive statistics on pandas objects exclude missing data by default.

The way that missing data is represented in pandas objects is somewhat imperfect, but it is sufficient for most real-world use. For data with float64 dtype, pandas uses the floating-point value NaN (Not a Number) to represent missing data.

We call this a *sentinel value*: when present, it indicates a missing (or *null*) value:

```
In [14]: float_data = pd.Series([1.2, -3.5, np.nan, 0])
```

```
In [15]: float_data
Out[15]:
0    1.2
1   -3.5
2    NaN
3    0.0
dtype: float64
```

The isna method gives us a Boolean Series with True where values are null:

```
In [16]: float_data.isna()
Out[16]:
0    False
1    False
2     True
3    False
dtype: bool
```

In pandas, we've adopted a convention used in the R programming language by referring to missing data as NA, which stands for *not available*. In statistics applications, NA data may either be data that does not exist or that exists but was not observed (through problems with data collection, for example). When cleaning up data for analysis, it is often important to do analysis on the missing data itself to identify data collection problems or potential biases in the data caused by missing data.

The built-in Python None value is also treated as NA:

```
In [17]: string_data = pd.Series(["aardvark", np.nan, None, "avocado"])
```

```
In [18]: string_data
Out[18]:
0    aardvark
1         NaN
2        None
3     avocado
dtype: object
```

```
In [19]: string_data.isna()
Out[19]:
0    False
1     True
2     True
3    False
dtype: bool
```

```
In [20]: float_data = pd.Series([1, 2, None], dtype='float64')
```

```
In [21]: float_data
Out[21]:
```

```
0    1.0
1    2.0
2    NaN
dtype: float64

In [22]: float_data.isna()
Out[22]:
0    False
1    False
2     True
dtype: bool
```

The pandas project has attempted to make working with missing data consistent across data types. Functions like `pandas.isna` abstract away many of the annoying details. See Table 7-1 for a list of some functions related to missing data handling.

Table 7-1. NA handling object methods

Method	Description
dropna	Filter axis labels based on whether values for each label have missing data, with varying thresholds for how much missing data to tolerate.
fillna	Fill in missing data with some value or using an interpolation method such as "ffill" or "bfill".
isna	Return Boolean values indicating which values are missing/NA.
notna	Negation of isna, returns True for non-NA values and False for NA values.

Filtering Out Missing Data

There are a few ways to filter out missing data. While you always have the option to do it by hand using `pandas.isna` and Boolean indexing, `dropna` can be helpful. On a Series, it returns the Series with only the nonnull data and index values:

```
In [23]: data = pd.Series([1, np.nan, 3.5, np.nan, 7])

In [24]: data.dropna()
Out[24]:
0    1.0
2    3.5
4    7.0
dtype: float64
```

This is the same thing as doing:

```
In [25]: data[data.notna()]
Out[25]:
0    1.0
2    3.5
4    7.0
dtype: float64
```

With DataFrame objects, there are different ways to remove missing data. You may want to drop rows or columns that are all NA, or only those rows or columns containing any NAs at all. dropna by default drops any row containing a missing value:

```
In [26]: data = pd.DataFrame([[1., 6.5, 3.], [1., np.nan, np.nan],
   ....:                       [np.nan, np.nan, np.nan], [np.nan, 6.5, 3.]])

In [27]: data
Out[27]:
     0    1    2
0  1.0  6.5  3.0
1  1.0  NaN  NaN
2  NaN  NaN  NaN
3  NaN  6.5  3.0

In [28]: data.dropna()
Out[28]:
     0    1    2
0  1.0  6.5  3.0
```

Passing how="all" will drop only rows that are all NA:

```
In [29]: data.dropna(how="all")
Out[29]:
     0    1    2
0  1.0  6.5  3.0
1  1.0  NaN  NaN
3  NaN  6.5  3.0
```

Keep in mind that these functions return new objects by default and do not modify the contents of the original object.

To drop columns in the same way, pass axis="columns":

```
In [30]: data[4] = np.nan

In [31]: data
Out[31]:
     0    1    2    4
0  1.0  6.5  3.0  NaN
1  1.0  NaN  NaN  NaN
2  NaN  NaN  NaN  NaN
3  NaN  6.5  3.0  NaN

In [32]: data.dropna(axis="columns", how="all")
Out[32]:
     0    1    2
0  1.0  6.5  3.0
1  1.0  NaN  NaN
2  NaN  NaN  NaN
3  NaN  6.5  3.0
```

Suppose you want to keep only rows containing at most a certain number of missing observations. You can indicate this with the `thresh` argument:

```
In [33]: df = pd.DataFrame(np.random.standard_normal((7, 3)))

In [34]: df.iloc[:4, 1] = np.nan

In [35]: df.iloc[:2, 2] = np.nan

In [36]: df
Out[36]:
          0         1         2
0 -0.204708       NaN       NaN
1 -0.555730       NaN       NaN
2  0.092908       NaN  0.769023
3  1.246435       NaN -1.296221
4  0.274992  0.228913  1.352917
5  0.886429 -2.001637 -0.371843
6  1.669025 -0.438570 -0.539741

In [37]: df.dropna()
Out[37]:
          0         1         2
4  0.274992  0.228913  1.352917
5  0.886429 -2.001637 -0.371843
6  1.669025 -0.438570 -0.539741

In [38]: df.dropna(thresh=2)
Out[38]:
          0         1         2
2  0.092908       NaN  0.769023
3  1.246435       NaN -1.296221
4  0.274992  0.228913  1.352917
5  0.886429 -2.001637 -0.371843
6  1.669025 -0.438570 -0.539741
```

Filling In Missing Data

Rather than filtering out missing data (and potentially discarding other data along with it), you may want to fill in the "holes" in any number of ways. For most purposes, the `fillna` method is the workhorse function to use. Calling `fillna` with a constant replaces missing values with that value:

```
In [39]: df.fillna(0)
Out[39]:
          0         1         2
0 -0.204708  0.000000  0.000000
1 -0.555730  0.000000  0.000000
2  0.092908  0.000000  0.769023
3  1.246435  0.000000 -1.296221
4  0.274992  0.228913  1.352917
```

```
5  0.886429 -2.001637 -0.371843
6  1.669025 -0.438570 -0.539741
```

Calling `fillna` with a dictionary, you can use a different fill value for each column:

```
In [40]: df.fillna({1: 0.5, 2: 0})
Out[40]:
          0         1         2
0 -0.204708  0.500000  0.000000
1 -0.555730  0.500000  0.000000
2  0.092908  0.500000  0.769023
3  1.246435  0.500000 -1.296221
4  0.274992  0.228913  1.352917
5  0.886429 -2.001637 -0.371843
6  1.669025 -0.438570 -0.539741
```

The same interpolation methods available for reindexing (see Table 5-3) can be used with `fillna`:

```
In [41]: df = pd.DataFrame(np.random.standard_normal((6, 3)))

In [42]: df.iloc[2:, 1] = np.nan

In [43]: df.iloc[4:, 2] = np.nan

In [44]: df
Out[44]:
          0         1         2
0  0.476985  3.248944 -1.021228
1 -0.577087  0.124121  0.302614
2  0.523772       NaN  1.343810
3 -0.713544       NaN -2.370232
4 -1.860761       NaN       NaN
5 -1.265934       NaN       NaN

In [45]: df.fillna(method="ffill")
Out[45]:
          0         1         2
0  0.476985  3.248944 -1.021228
1 -0.577087  0.124121  0.302614
2  0.523772  0.124121  1.343810
3 -0.713544  0.124121 -2.370232
4 -1.860761  0.124121 -2.370232
5 -1.265934  0.124121 -2.370232

In [46]: df.fillna(method="ffill", limit=2)
Out[46]:
          0         1         2
0  0.476985  3.248944 -1.021228
1 -0.577087  0.124121  0.302614
2  0.523772  0.124121  1.343810
3 -0.713544  0.124121 -2.370232
```

```
4 -1.860761      NaN -2.370232
5 -1.265934      NaN -2.370232
```

With `fillna` you can do lots of other things such as simple data imputation using the median or mean statistics:

```
In [47]: data = pd.Series([1., np.nan, 3.5, np.nan, 7])

In [48]: data.fillna(data.mean())
Out[48]:
0    1.000000
1    3.833333
2    3.500000
3    3.833333
4    7.000000
dtype: float64
```

See Table 7-2 for a reference on `fillna` function arguments.

Table 7-2. fillna function arguments

Argument	Description
value	Scalar value or dictionary-like object to use to fill missing values
method	Interpolation method: one of "bfill" (backward fill) or "ffill" (forward fill); default is None
axis	Axis to fill on ("index" or "columns"); default is axis="index"
limit	For forward and backward filling, maximum number of consecutive periods to fill

7.2 Data Transformation

So far in this chapter we've been concerned with handling missing data. Filtering, cleaning, and other transformations are another class of important operations.

Removing Duplicates

Duplicate rows may be found in a DataFrame for any number of reasons. Here is an example:

```
In [49]: data = pd.DataFrame({"k1": ["one", "two"] * 3 + ["two"],
   ....:                       "k2": [1, 1, 2, 3, 3, 4, 4]})

In [50]: data
Out[50]:
    k1  k2
0  one   1
1  two   1
2  one   2
3  two   3
4  one   3
5  two   4
6  two   4
```

The DataFrame method `duplicated` returns a Boolean Series indicating whether each row is a duplicate (its column values are exactly equal to those in an earlier row) or not:

```
In [51]: data.duplicated()
Out[51]:
0    False
1    False
2    False
3    False
4    False
5    False
6     True
dtype: bool
```

Relatedly, `drop_duplicates` returns a DataFrame with rows where the `duplicated` array is `False` filtered out:

```
In [52]: data.drop_duplicates()
Out[52]:
    k1  k2
0  one   1
1  two   1
2  one   2
3  two   3
4  one   3
5  two   4
```

Both methods by default consider all of the columns; alternatively, you can specify any subset of them to detect duplicates. Suppose we had an additional column of values and wanted to filter duplicates based only on the "k1" column:

```
In [53]: data["v1"] = range(7)

In [54]: data
Out[54]:
    k1  k2  v1
0  one   1   0
1  two   1   1
2  one   2   2
3  two   3   3
4  one   3   4
5  two   4   5
6  two   4   6

In [55]: data.drop_duplicates(subset=["k1"])
Out[55]:
    k1  k2  v1
0  one   1   0
1  two   1   1
```

duplicated and drop_duplicates by default keep the first observed value combination. Passing keep="last" will return the last one:

```
In [56]: data.drop_duplicates(["k1", "k2"], keep="last")
Out[56]:
    k1  k2  v1
0  one   1   0
1  two   1   1
2  one   2   2
3  two   3   3
4  one   3   4
6  two   4   6
```

Transforming Data Using a Function or Mapping

For many datasets, you may wish to perform some transformation based on the values in an array, Series, or column in a DataFrame. Consider the following hypothetical data collected about various kinds of meat:

```
In [57]: data = pd.DataFrame({"food": ["bacon", "pulled pork", "bacon",
    ....:                               "pastrami", "corned beef", "bacon",
    ....:                               "pastrami", "honey ham", "nova lox"],
    ....:                     "ounces": [4, 3, 12, 6, 7.5, 8, 3, 5, 6]})

In [58]: data
Out[58]:
          food  ounces
0        bacon     4.0
1  pulled pork     3.0
2        bacon    12.0
3     pastrami     6.0
4  corned beef     7.5
5        bacon     8.0
6     pastrami     3.0
7    honey ham     5.0
8     nova lox     6.0
```

Suppose you wanted to add a column indicating the type of animal that each food came from. Let's write down a mapping of each distinct meat type to the kind of animal:

```
meat_to_animal = {
  "bacon": "pig",
  "pulled pork": "pig",
  "pastrami": "cow",
  "corned beef": "cow",
  "honey ham": "pig",
  "nova lox": "salmon"
}
```

The map method on a Series (also discussed in "Function Application and Mapping" on page 158) accepts a function or dictionary-like object containing a mapping to do the transformation of values:

```
In [60]: data["animal"] = data["food"].map(meat_to_animal)

In [61]: data
Out[61]:
          food  ounces  animal
0         bacon    4.0     pig
1   pulled pork    3.0     pig
2         bacon   12.0     pig
3      pastrami    6.0     cow
4   corned beef    7.5     cow
5         bacon    8.0     pig
6      pastrami    3.0     cow
7     honey ham    5.0     pig
8      nova lox    6.0  salmon
```

We could also have passed a function that does all the work:

```
In [62]: def get_animal(x):
   ....:     return meat_to_animal[x]

In [63]: data["food"].map(get_animal)
Out[63]:
0       pig
1       pig
2       pig
3       cow
4       cow
5       pig
6       cow
7       pig
8    salmon
Name: food, dtype: object
```

Using map is a convenient way to perform element-wise transformations and other data cleaning-related operations.

Replacing Values

Filling in missing data with the fillna method is a special case of more general value replacement. As you've already seen, map can be used to modify a subset of values in an object, but replace provides a simpler and more flexible way to do so. Let's consider this Series:

```
In [64]: data = pd.Series([1., -999., 2., -999., -1000., 3.])

In [65]: data
Out[65]:
0       1.0
```

```
1     -999.0
2        2.0
3     -999.0
4    -1000.0
5        3.0
dtype: float64
```

The -999 values might be sentinel values for missing data. To replace these with NA values that pandas understands, we can use replace, producing a new Series:

```
In [66]: data.replace(-999, np.nan)
Out[66]:
0        1.0
1        NaN
2        2.0
3        NaN
4    -1000.0
5        3.0
dtype: float64
```

If you want to replace multiple values at once, you instead pass a list and then the substitute value:

```
In [67]: data.replace([-999, -1000], np.nan)
Out[67]:
0    1.0
1    NaN
2    2.0
3    NaN
4    NaN
5    3.0
dtype: float64
```

To use a different replacement for each value, pass a list of substitutes:

```
In [68]: data.replace([-999, -1000], [np.nan, 0])
Out[68]:
0    1.0
1    NaN
2    2.0
3    NaN
4    0.0
5    3.0
dtype: float64
```

The argument passed can also be a dictionary:

```
In [69]: data.replace({-999: np.nan, -1000: 0})
Out[69]:
0    1.0
1    NaN
2    2.0
3    NaN
4    0.0
```

```
5    3.0
dtype: float64
```

 The `data.replace` method is distinct from `data.str.replace`, which performs element-wise string substitution. We look at these string methods on Series later in the chapter.

Renaming Axis Indexes

Like values in a Series, axis labels can be similarly transformed by a function or mapping of some form to produce new, differently labeled objects. You can also modify the axes in place without creating a new data structure. Here's a simple example:

```
In [70]: data = pd.DataFrame(np.arange(12).reshape((3, 4)),
   ....:                      index=["Ohio", "Colorado", "New York"],
   ....:                      columns=["one", "two", "three", "four"])
```

Like a Series, the axis indexes have a `map` method:

```
In [71]: def transform(x):
   ....:     return x[:4].upper()

In [72]: data.index.map(transform)
Out[72]: Index(['OHIO', 'COLO', 'NEW '], dtype='object')
```

You can assign to the `index` attribute, modifying the DataFrame in place:

```
In [73]: data.index = data.index.map(transform)

In [74]: data
Out[74]:
      one  two  three  four
OHIO    0    1      2     3
COLO    4    5      6     7
NEW     8    9     10    11
```

If you want to create a transformed version of a dataset without modifying the original, a useful method is `rename`:

```
In [75]: data.rename(index=str.title, columns=str.upper)
Out[75]:
      ONE  TWO  THREE  FOUR
Ohio    0    1      2     3
Colo    4    5      6     7
New     8    9     10    11
```

Notably, `rename` can be used in conjunction with a dictionary-like object, providing new values for a subset of the axis labels:

```
In [76]: data.rename(index={"OHIO": "INDIANA"},
   ....:             columns={"three": "peekaboo"})
Out[76]:
         one  two  peekaboo  four
INDIANA    0    1         2     3
COLO       4    5         6     7
NEW        8    9        10    11
```

rename saves you from the chore of copying the DataFrame manually and assigning new values to its index and columns attributes.

Discretization and Binning

Continuous data is often discretized or otherwise separated into "bins" for analysis. Suppose you have data about a group of people in a study, and you want to group them into discrete age buckets:

```
In [77]: ages = [20, 22, 25, 27, 21, 23, 37, 31, 61, 45, 41, 32]
```

Let's divide these into bins of 18 to 25, 26 to 35, 36 to 60, and finally 61 and older. To do so, you have to use pandas.cut:

```
In [78]: bins = [18, 25, 35, 60, 100]

In [79]: age_categories = pd.cut(ages, bins)

In [80]: age_categories
Out[80]:
[(18, 25], (18, 25], (18, 25], (25, 35], (18, 25], ..., (25, 35], (60, 100], (35,
 60], (35, 60], (25, 35]]
Length: 12
Categories (4, interval[int64, right]): [(18, 25] < (25, 35] < (35, 60] < (60, 10
0]]
```

The object pandas returns is a special Categorical object. The output you see describes the bins computed by pandas.cut. Each bin is identified by a special (unique to pandas) interval value type containing the lower and upper limit of each bin:

```
In [81]: age_categories.codes
Out[81]: array([0, 0, 0, 1, 0, 0, 2, 1, 3, 2, 2, 1], dtype=int8)

In [82]: age_categories.categories
Out[82]: IntervalIndex([(18, 25], (25, 35], (35, 60], (60, 100]], dtype='interval
[int64, right]')

In [83]: age_categories.categories[0]
Out[83]: Interval(18, 25, closed='right')

In [84]: pd.value_counts(age_categories)
Out[84]:
(18, 25]     5
```

```
(25, 35]    3
(35, 60]    3
(60, 100]   1
dtype: int64
```

Note that `pd.value_counts(categories)` are the bin counts for the result of `pandas.cut`.

In the string representation of an interval, a parenthesis means that the side is *open* (exclusive), while the square bracket means it is *closed* (inclusive). You can change which side is closed by passing `right=False`:

```
In [85]: pd.cut(ages, bins, right=False)
Out[85]:
[[18, 25), [18, 25), [25, 35), [25, 35), [18, 25), ..., [25, 35), [60, 100), [35,
 60), [35, 60), [25, 35)]
Length: 12
Categories (4, interval[int64, left]): [[18, 25) < [25, 35) < [35, 60) < [60, 100
)]
```

You can override the default interval-based bin labeling by passing a list or array to the `labels` option:

```
In [86]: group_names = ["Youth", "YoungAdult", "MiddleAged", "Senior"]
```

```
In [87]: pd.cut(ages, bins, labels=group_names)
Out[87]:
['Youth', 'Youth', 'Youth', 'YoungAdult', 'Youth', ..., 'YoungAdult', 'Senior', '
MiddleAged', 'MiddleAged', 'YoungAdult']
Length: 12
Categories (4, object): ['Youth' < 'YoungAdult' < 'MiddleAged' < 'Senior']
```

If you pass an integer number of bins to `pandas.cut` instead of explicit bin edges, it will compute equal-length bins based on the minimum and maximum values in the data. Consider the case of some uniformly distributed data chopped into fourths:

```
In [88]: data = np.random.uniform(size=20)
```

```
In [89]: pd.cut(data, 4, precision=2)
Out[89]:
[(0.34, 0.55], (0.34, 0.55], (0.76, 0.97], (0.76, 0.97], (0.34, 0.55], ..., (0.34
, 0.55], (0.34, 0.55], (0.55, 0.76], (0.34, 0.55], (0.12, 0.34]]
Length: 20
Categories (4, interval[float64, right]): [(0.12, 0.34] < (0.34, 0.55] < (0.55, 0
.76] <
                                    (0.76, 0.97]]
```

The `precision=2` option limits the decimal precision to two digits.

A closely related function, `pandas.qcut`, bins the data based on sample quantiles. Depending on the distribution of the data, using `pandas.cut` will not usually result in each bin having the same number of data points. Since `pandas.qcut` uses sample quantiles instead, you will obtain roughly equally sized bins:

```
In [90]: data = np.random.standard_normal(1000)

In [91]: quartiles = pd.qcut(data, 4, precision=2)

In [92]: quartiles
Out[92]:
[(-0.026, 0.62], (0.62, 3.93], (-0.68, -0.026], (0.62, 3.93], (-0.026, 0.62], ...
, (-0.68, -0.026], (-0.68, -0.026], (-2.96, -0.68], (0.62, 3.93], (-0.68, -0.026]
]
Length: 1000
Categories (4, interval[float64, right]): [(-2.96, -0.68] < (-0.68, -0.026] < (-0
.026, 0.62] <
                                           (0.62, 3.93]]

In [93]: pd.value_counts(quartiles)
Out[93]:
(-2.96, -0.68]     250
(-0.68, -0.026]    250
(-0.026, 0.62]     250
(0.62, 3.93]       250
dtype: int64
```

Similar to `pandas.cut`, you can pass your own quantiles (numbers between 0 and 1, inclusive):

```
In [94]: pd.qcut(data, [0, 0.1, 0.5, 0.9, 1.]).value_counts()
Out[94]:
(-2.9499999999999997, -1.187]    100
(-1.187, -0.0265]                400
(-0.0265, 1.286]                 400
(1.286, 3.928]                   100
dtype: int64
```

We'll return to `pandas.cut` and `pandas.qcut` later in the chapter during our discussion of aggregation and group operations, as these discretization functions are especially useful for quantile and group analysis.

Detecting and Filtering Outliers

Filtering or transforming outliers is largely a matter of applying array operations. Consider a DataFrame with some normally distributed data:

```
In [95]: data = pd.DataFrame(np.random.standard_normal((1000, 4)))

In [96]: data.describe()
Out[96]:
                 0            1            2            3
count  1000.000000  1000.000000  1000.000000  1000.000000
mean      0.049091     0.026112    -0.002544    -0.051827
```

```
std       0.996947    1.007458    0.995232    0.998311
min      -3.645860   -3.184377   -3.745356   -3.428254
25%      -0.599807   -0.612162   -0.687373   -0.747478
50%       0.047101   -0.013609   -0.022158   -0.088274
75%       0.756646    0.695298    0.699046    0.623331
max       2.653656    3.525865    2.735527    3.366626
```

Suppose you wanted to find values in one of the columns exceeding 3 in absolute value:

```
In [97]: col = data[2]

In [98]: col[col.abs() > 3]
Out[98]:
41     -3.399312
136    -3.745356
Name: 2, dtype: float64
```

To select all rows having a value exceeding 3 or –3, you can use the any method on a Boolean DataFrame:

```
In [99]: data[(data.abs() > 3).any(axis="columns")]
Out[99]:
            0          1          2          3
41    0.457246  -0.025907  -3.399312  -0.974657
60    1.951312   3.260383   0.963301   1.201206
136   0.508391  -0.196713  -3.745356  -1.520113
235  -0.242459  -3.056990   1.918403  -0.578828
258   0.682841   0.326045   0.425384  -3.428254
322   1.179227  -3.184377   1.369891  -1.074833
544  -3.548824   1.553205  -2.186301   1.277104
635  -0.578093   0.193299   1.397822   3.366626
782  -0.207434   3.525865   0.283070   0.544635
803  -3.645860   0.255475  -0.549574  -1.907459
```

The parentheses around data.abs() > 3 are necessary in order to call the any method on the result of the comparison operation.

Values can be set based on these criteria. Here is code to cap values outside the interval –3 to 3:

```
In [100]: data[data.abs() > 3] = np.sign(data) * 3

In [101]: data.describe()
Out[101]:
                  0             1             2             3
count   1000.000000   1000.000000   1000.000000   1000.000000
mean       0.050286      0.025567     -0.001399     -0.051765
std        0.992920      1.004214      0.991414      0.995761
min       -3.000000     -3.000000     -3.000000     -3.000000
25%       -0.599807     -0.612162     -0.687373     -0.747478
50%        0.047101     -0.013609     -0.022158     -0.088274
```

```
75%     0.756646    0.695298    0.699046    0.623331
max     2.653656    3.000000    2.735527    3.000000
```

The statement np.sign(data) produces 1 and –1 values based on whether the values in data are positive or negative:

```
In [102]: np.sign(data).head()
Out[102]:
      0    1    2    3
0  -1.0  1.0 -1.0  1.0
1   1.0 -1.0  1.0 -1.0
2   1.0  1.0  1.0 -1.0
3  -1.0 -1.0  1.0 -1.0
4  -1.0  1.0 -1.0 -1.0
```

Permutation and Random Sampling

Permuting (randomly reordering) a Series or the rows in a DataFrame is possible using the numpy.random.permutation function. Calling permutation with the length of the axis you want to permute produces an array of integers indicating the new ordering:

```
In [103]: df = pd.DataFrame(np.arange(5 * 7).reshape((5, 7)))

In [104]: df
Out[104]:
    0   1   2   3   4   5   6
0   0   1   2   3   4   5   6
1   7   8   9  10  11  12  13
2  14  15  16  17  18  19  20
3  21  22  23  24  25  26  27
4  28  29  30  31  32  33  34

In [105]: sampler = np.random.permutation(5)

In [106]: sampler
Out[106]: array([3, 1, 4, 2, 0])
```

That array can then be used in iloc-based indexing or the equivalent take function:

```
In [107]: df.take(sampler)
Out[107]:
    0   1   2   3   4   5   6
3  21  22  23  24  25  26  27
1   7   8   9  10  11  12  13
4  28  29  30  31  32  33  34
2  14  15  16  17  18  19  20
0   0   1   2   3   4   5   6

In [108]: df.iloc[sampler]
Out[108]:
    0   1   2   3   4   5   6
```

```
3  21  22  23  24  25  26  27
1   7   8   9  10  11  12  13
4  28  29  30  31  32  33  34
2  14  15  16  17  18  19  20
0   0   1   2   3   4   5   6
```

By invoking take with axis="columns", we could also select a permutation of the columns:

```
In [109]: column_sampler = np.random.permutation(7)

In [110]: column_sampler
Out[110]: array([4, 6, 3, 2, 1, 0, 5])

In [111]: df.take(column_sampler, axis="columns")
Out[111]:
    4   6   3   2   1   0   5
0   4   6   3   2   1   0   5
1  11  13  10   9   8   7  12
2  18  20  17  16  15  14  19
3  25  27  24  23  22  21  26
4  32  34  31  30  29  28  33
```

To select a random subset without replacement (the same row cannot appear twice), you can use the sample method on Series and DataFrame:

```
In [112]: df.sample(n=3)
Out[112]:
    0   1   2   3   4   5   6
2  14  15  16  17  18  19  20
4  28  29  30  31  32  33  34
0   0   1   2   3   4   5   6
```

To generate a sample *with* replacement (to allow repeat choices), pass replace=True to sample:

```
In [113]: choices = pd.Series([5, 7, -1, 6, 4])

In [114]: choices.sample(n=10, replace=True)
Out[114]:
2   -1
0    5
3    6
1    7
4    4
0    5
4    4
0    5
4    4
4    4
dtype: int64
```

Computing Indicator/Dummy Variables

Another type of transformation for statistical modeling or machine learning applications is converting a categorical variable into a *dummy* or *indicator* matrix. If a column in a DataFrame has k distinct values, you would derive a matrix or DataFrame with k columns containing all 1s and 0s. pandas has a pandas.get_dummies function for doing this, though you could also devise one yourself. Let's consider an example DataFrame:

```
In [115]: df = pd.DataFrame({"key": ["b", "b", "a", "c", "a", "b"],
   .....:                     "data1": range(6)})

In [116]: df
Out[116]:
  key  data1
0   b      0
1   b      1
2   a      2
3   c      3
4   a      4
5   b      5

In [117]: pd.get_dummies(df["key"])
Out[117]:
   a  b  c
0  0  1  0
1  0  1  0
2  1  0  0
3  0  0  1
4  1  0  0
5  0  1  0
```

In some cases, you may want to add a prefix to the columns in the indicator DataFrame, which can then be merged with the other data. pandas.get_dummies has a prefix argument for doing this:

```
In [118]: dummies = pd.get_dummies(df["key"], prefix="key")

In [119]: df_with_dummy = df[["data1"]].join(dummies)

In [120]: df_with_dummy
Out[120]:
   data1  key_a  key_b  key_c
0      0      0      1      0
1      1      0      1      0
2      2      1      0      0
3      3      0      0      1
4      4      1      0      0
5      5      0      1      0
```

The DataFrame.join method will be explained in more detail in the next chapter.

If a row in a DataFrame belongs to multiple categories, we have to use a different approach to create the dummy variables. Let's look at the MovieLens 1M dataset, which is investigated in more detail in Chapter 13:

```
In [121]: mnames = ["movie_id", "title", "genres"]

In [122]: movies = pd.read_table("datasets/movielens/movies.dat", sep="::",
   .....:                        header=None, names=mnames, engine="python")

In [123]: movies[:10]
Out[123]:
   movie_id                               title                        genres
0         1                    Toy Story (1995)   Animation|Children's|Comedy
1         2                      Jumanji (1995)  Adventure|Children's|Fantasy
2         3             Grumpier Old Men (1995)                Comedy|Romance
3         4            Waiting to Exhale (1995)                  Comedy|Drama
4         5  Father of the Bride Part II (1995)                        Comedy
5         6                         Heat (1995)         Action|Crime|Thriller
6         7                      Sabrina (1995)                Comedy|Romance
7         8                 Tom and Huck (1995)            Adventure|Children's
8         9                 Sudden Death (1995)                        Action
9        10                    GoldenEye (1995)     Action|Adventure|Thriller
```

pandas has implemented a special Series method `str.get_dummies` (methods that start with `str.` are discussed in more detail later in Section 7.4, "String Manipulation," on page 227) that handles this scenario of multiple group membership encoded as a delimited string:

```
In [124]: dummies = movies["genres"].str.get_dummies("|")

In [125]: dummies.iloc[:10, :6]
Out[125]:
   Action  Adventure  Animation  Children's  Comedy  Crime
0       0          0          1           1       1      0
1       0          1          0           0       1      0
2       0          0          0           0       1      0
3       0          0          0           0       1      0
4       0          0          0           0       1      0
5       1          0          0           0       0      1
6       0          0          0           0       1      0
7       0          1          0           1       0      0
8       1          0          0           0       0      0
9       1          1          0           0       0      0
```

Then, as before, you can combine this with `movies` while adding a `"Genre_"` to the column names in the `dummies` DataFrame with the `add_prefix` method:

```
In [126]: movies_windic = movies.join(dummies.add_prefix("Genre_"))

In [127]: movies_windic.iloc[0]
Out[127]:
movie_id                                           1
```

```
title                          Toy Story (1995)
genres               Animation|Children's|Comedy
Genre_Action                                   0
Genre_Adventure                                0
Genre_Animation                                1
Genre_Children's                               1
Genre_Comedy                                   1
Genre_Crime                                    0
Genre_Documentary                              0
Genre_Drama                                    0
Genre_Fantasy                                  0
Genre_Film-Noir                                0
Genre_Horror                                   0
Genre_Musical                                  0
Genre_Mystery                                  0
Genre_Romance                                  0
Genre_Sci-Fi                                   0
Genre_Thriller                                 0
Genre_War                                      0
Genre_Western                                  0
Name: 0, dtype: object
```

 For much larger data, this method of constructing indicator variables with multiple membership is not especially speedy. It would be better to write a lower-level function that writes directly to a NumPy array, and then wrap the result in a DataFrame.

A useful recipe for statistical applications is to combine pandas.get_dummies with a discretization function like pandas.cut:

```
In [128]: np.random.seed(12345) # to make the example repeatable

In [129]: values = np.random.uniform(size=10)

In [130]: values
Out[130]:
array([0.9296, 0.3164, 0.1839, 0.2046, 0.5677, 0.5955, 0.9645, 0.6532,
       0.7489, 0.6536])

In [131]: bins = [0, 0.2, 0.4, 0.6, 0.8, 1]

In [132]: pd.get_dummies(pd.cut(values, bins))
Out[132]:
   (0.0, 0.2]  (0.2, 0.4]  (0.4, 0.6]  (0.6, 0.8]  (0.8, 1.0]
0           0           0           0           0           1
1           0           1           0           0           0
2           1           0           0           0           0
3           0           1           0           0           0
4           0           0           1           0           0
5           0           0           1           0           0
```

6	0	0	0	0	1
7	0	0	0	1	0
8	0	0	0	1	0
9	0	0	0	1	0

We will look again at `pandas.get_dummies` later in "Creating dummy variables for modeling" on page 245.

7.3 Extension Data Types

 This is a newer and more advanced topic that many pandas users do not need to know a lot about, but I present it here for completeness since I will reference and use extension data types in various places in the upcoming chapters.

pandas was originally built upon the capabilities present in NumPy, an array computing library used primarily for working with numerical data. Many pandas concepts, such as missing data, were implemented using what was available in NumPy while trying to maximize compatibility between libraries that used NumPy and pandas together.

Building on NumPy led to a number of shortcomings, such as:

- Missing data handling for some numerical data types, such as integers and Booleans, was incomplete. As a result, when missing data was introduced into such data, pandas converted the data type to `float64` and used `np.nan` to represent null values. This had compounding effects by introducing subtle issues into many pandas algorithms.

- Datasets with a lot of string data were computationally expensive and used a lot of memory.

- Some data types, like time intervals, timedeltas, and timestamps with time zones, could not be supported efficiently without using computationally expensive arrays of Python objects.

More recently, pandas has developed an *extension type* system allowing for new data types to be added even if they are not supported natively by NumPy. These new data types can be treated as first class alongside data coming from NumPy arrays.

Let's look at an example where we create a Series of integers with a missing value:

```
In [133]: s = pd.Series([1, 2, 3, None])

In [134]: s
Out[134]:
0    1.0
```

```
1    2.0
2    3.0
3    NaN
dtype: float64

In [135]: s.dtype
Out[135]: dtype('float64')
```

Mainly for backward compatibility reasons, Series uses the legacy behavior of using a float64 data type and np.nan for the missing value. We could create this Series instead using pandas.Int64Dtype:

```
In [136]: s = pd.Series([1, 2, 3, None], dtype=pd.Int64Dtype())

In [137]: s
Out[137]:
0       1
1       2
2       3
3    <NA>
dtype: Int64

In [138]: s.isna()
Out[138]:
0    False
1    False
2    False
3     True
dtype: bool

In [139]: s.dtype
Out[139]: Int64Dtype()
```

The output <NA> indicates that a value is missing for an extension type array. This uses the special pandas.NA sentinel value:

```
In [140]: s[3]
Out[140]: <NA>

In [141]: s[3] is pd.NA
Out[141]: True
```

We also could have used the shorthand "Int64" instead of pd.Int64Dtype() to specify the type. The capitalization is necessary, otherwise it will be a NumPy-based nonextension type:

```
In [142]: s = pd.Series([1, 2, 3, None], dtype="Int64")
```

pandas also has an extension type specialized for string data that does not use NumPy object arrays (it requires the pyarrow library, which you may need to install separately):

```
In [143]: s = pd.Series(['one', 'two', None, 'three'], dtype=pd.StringDtype())

In [144]: s
Out[144]:
0      one
1      two
2      <NA>
3    three
dtype: string
```

These string arrays generally use much less memory and are frequently computationally more efficient for doing operations on large datasets.

Another important extension type is `Categorical`, which we discuss in more detail in Section 7.5, "Categorical Data," on page 235. A reasonably complete list of extension types available as of this writing is in Table 7-3.

Extension types can be passed to the Series `astype` method, allowing you to convert easily as part of your data cleaning process:

```
In [145]: df = pd.DataFrame({"A": [1, 2, None, 4],
   .....:                     "B": ["one", "two", "three", None],
   .....:                     "C": [False, None, False, True]})

In [146]: df
Out[146]:
     A      B      C
0  1.0    one  False
1  2.0    two   None
2  NaN  three  False
3  4.0   None   True

In [147]: df["A"] = df["A"].astype("Int64")

In [148]: df["B"] = df["B"].astype("string")

In [149]: df["C"] = df["C"].astype("boolean")

In [150]: df
Out[150]:
      A      B      C
0     1    one  False
1     2    two   <NA>
2  <NA>  three  False
3     4   <NA>   True
```

Table 7-3. pandas extension data types

Extension type	Description
BooleanDtype	Nullable Boolean data, use "boolean" when passing as string
CategoricalDtype	Categorical data type, use "category" when passing as string
DatetimeTZDtype	Datetime with time zone
Float32Dtype	32-bit nullable floating point, use "Float32" when passing as string
Float64Dtype	64-bit nullable floating point, use "Float64" when passing as string
Int8Dtype	8-bit nullable signed integer, use "Int8" when passing as string
Int16Dtype	16-bit nullable signed integer, use "Int16" when passing as string
Int32Dtype	32-bit nullable signed integer, use "Int32" when passing as string
Int64Dtype	64-bit nullable signed integer, use "Int64" when passing as string
UInt8Dtype	8-bit nullable unsigned integer, use "UInt8" when passing as string
UInt16Dtype	16-bit nullable unsigned integer, use "UInt16" when passing as string
UInt32Dtype	32-bit nullable unsigned integer, use "UInt32" when passing as string
UInt64Dtype	64-bit nullable unsigned integer, use "UInt64" when passing as string

7.4 String Manipulation

Python has long been a popular raw data manipulation language in part due to its ease of use for string and text processing. Most text operations are made simple with the string object's built-in methods. For more complex pattern matching and text manipulations, regular expressions may be needed. pandas adds to the mix by enabling you to apply string and regular expressions concisely on whole arrays of data, additionally handling the annoyance of missing data.

Python Built-In String Object Methods

In many string munging and scripting applications, built-in string methods are sufficient. As an example, a comma-separated string can be broken into pieces with split:

```
In [151]: val = "a,b,  guido"

In [152]: val.split(",")
Out[152]: ['a', 'b', '  guido']
```

split is often combined with strip to trim whitespace (including line breaks):

```
In [153]: pieces = [x.strip() for x in val.split(",")]

In [154]: pieces
Out[154]: ['a', 'b', 'guido']
```

These substrings could be concatenated together with a two-colon delimiter using addition:

```
In [155]: first, second, third = pieces

In [156]: first + "::" + second + "::" + third
Out[156]: 'a::b::guido'
```

But this isn't a practical generic method. A faster and more Pythonic way is to pass a list or tuple to the `join` method on the string "::":

```
In [157]: "::".join(pieces)
Out[157]: 'a::b::guido'
```

Other methods are concerned with locating substrings. Using Python's `in` keyword is the best way to detect a substring, though `index` and `find` can also be used:

```
In [158]: "guido" in val
Out[158]: True

In [159]: val.index(",")
Out[159]: 1

In [160]: val.find(":")
Out[160]: -1
```

Note that the difference between `find` and `index` is that `index` raises an exception if the string isn't found (versus returning –1):

```
In [161]: val.index(":")
---------------------------------------------------------------------------
ValueError                                Traceback (most recent call last)
<ipython-input-161-bea4c4c30248> in <module>
----> 1 val.index(":")
ValueError: substring not found
```

Relatedly, `count` returns the number of occurrences of a particular substring:

```
In [162]: val.count(",")
Out[162]: 2
```

`replace` will substitute occurrences of one pattern for another. It is commonly used to delete patterns, too, by passing an empty string:

```
In [163]: val.replace(",", "::")
Out[163]: 'a::b::  guido'

In [164]: val.replace(",", "")
Out[164]: 'ab  guido'
```

See Table 7-4 for a listing of some of Python's string methods.

Regular expressions can also be used with many of these operations, as you'll see.

Table 7-4. Python built-in string methods

Method	Description
count	Return the number of nonoverlapping occurrences of substring in the string
endswith	Return True if string ends with suffix
startswith	Return True if string starts with prefix
join	Use string as delimiter for concatenating a sequence of other strings
index	Return starting index of the first occurrence of passed substring if found in the string; otherwise, raises ValueError if not found
find	Return position of first character of *first* occurrence of substring in the string; like index, but returns −1 if not found
rfind	Return position of first character of *last* occurrence of substring in the string; returns −1 if not found
replace	Replace occurrences of string with another string
strip, rstrip, lstrip	Trim whitespace, including newlines on both sides, on the right side, or on the left side, respectively
split	Break string into list of substrings using passed delimiter
lower	Convert alphabet characters to lowercase
upper	Convert alphabet characters to uppercase
casefold	Convert characters to lowercase, and convert any region-specific variable character combinations to a common comparable form
ljust, rjust	Left justify or right justify, respectively; pad opposite side of string with spaces (or some other fill character) to return a string with a minimum width

Regular Expressions

Regular expressions provide a flexible way to search or match (often more complex) string patterns in text. A single expression, commonly called a *regex*, is a string formed according to the regular expression language. Python's built-in re module is responsible for applying regular expressions to strings; I'll give a number of examples of its use here.

The art of writing regular expressions could be a chapter of its own and thus is outside the book's scope. There are many excellent tutorials and references available on the internet and in other books.

The re module functions fall into three categories: pattern matching, substitution, and splitting. Naturally these are all related; a regex describes a pattern to locate in the text, which can then be used for many purposes. Let's look at a simple example: suppose we wanted to split a string with a variable number of whitespace characters (tabs, spaces, and newlines).

The regex describing one or more whitespace characters is `\s+`:

```
In [165]: import re

In [166]: text = "foo    bar\t baz  \tqux"

In [167]: re.split(r"\s+", text)
Out[167]: ['foo', 'bar', 'baz', 'qux']
```

When you call `re.split(r"\s+", text)`, the regular expression is first *compiled*, and then its `split` method is called on the passed text. You can compile the regex yourself with `re.compile`, forming a reusable regex object:

```
In [168]: regex = re.compile(r"\s+")

In [169]: regex.split(text)
Out[169]: ['foo', 'bar', 'baz', 'qux']
```

If, instead, you wanted to get a list of all patterns matching the regex, you can use the `findall` method:

```
In [170]: regex.findall(text)
Out[170]: ['    ', '\t ', '  \t']
```

> To avoid unwanted escaping with \ in a regular expression, use *raw* string literals like `r"C:\x"` instead of the equivalent `"C:\\x"`.

Creating a regex object with `re.compile` is highly recommended if you intend to apply the same expression to many strings; doing so will save CPU cycles.

`match` and `search` are closely related to `findall`. While `findall` returns all matches in a string, `search` returns only the first match. More rigidly, `match` *only* matches at the beginning of the string. As a less trivial example, let's consider a block of text and a regular expression capable of identifying most email addresses:

```
text = """Dave dave@google.com
Steve steve@gmail.com
Rob rob@gmail.com
Ryan ryan@yahoo.com"""
pattern = r"[A-Z0-9._%+-]+@[A-Z0-9.-]+\.[A-Z]{2,4}"

# re.IGNORECASE makes the regex case insensitive
regex = re.compile(pattern, flags=re.IGNORECASE)
```

Using `findall` on the text produces a list of the email addresses:

```
In [172]: regex.findall(text)
Out[172]:
['dave@google.com',
```

```
'steve@gmail.com',
'rob@gmail.com',
'ryan@yahoo.com']
```

search returns a special match object for the first email address in the text. For the preceding regex, the match object can only tell us the start and end position of the pattern in the string:

```
In [173]: m = regex.search(text)

In [174]: m
Out[174]: <re.Match object; span=(5, 20), match='dave@google.com'>

In [175]: text[m.start():m.end()]
Out[175]: 'dave@google.com'
```

regex.match returns None, as it will match only if the pattern occurs at the start of the string:

```
In [176]: print(regex.match(text))
None
```

Relatedly, sub will return a new string with occurrences of the pattern replaced by a new string:

```
In [177]: print(regex.sub("REDACTED", text))
Dave REDACTED
Steve REDACTED
Rob REDACTED
Ryan REDACTED
```

Suppose you wanted to find email addresses and simultaneously segment each address into its three components: username, domain name, and domain suffix. To do this, put parentheses around the parts of the pattern to segment:

```
In [178]: pattern = r"([A-Z0-9._%+-]+)@([A-Z0-9.-]+)\.([A-Z]{2,4})"

In [179]: regex = re.compile(pattern, flags=re.IGNORECASE)
```

A match object produced by this modified regex returns a tuple of the pattern components with its groups method:

```
In [180]: m = regex.match("wesm@bright.net")

In [181]: m.groups()
Out[181]: ('wesm', 'bright', 'net')
```

findall returns a list of tuples when the pattern has groups:

```
In [182]: regex.findall(text)
Out[182]:
[('dave', 'google', 'com'),
 ('steve', 'gmail', 'com'),
```

```
                ('rob', 'gmail', 'com'),
                ('ryan', 'yahoo', 'com')]
```

sub also has access to groups in each match using special symbols like \1 and \2. The symbol \1 corresponds to the first matched group, \2 corresponds to the second, and so forth:

```
In [183]: print(regex.sub(r"Username: \1, Domain: \2, Suffix: \3", text))
Dave Username: dave, Domain: google, Suffix: com
Steve Username: steve, Domain: gmail, Suffix: com
Rob Username: rob, Domain: gmail, Suffix: com
Ryan Username: ryan, Domain: yahoo, Suffix: com
```

There is much more to regular expressions in Python, most of which is outside the book's scope. Table 7-5 provides a brief summary.

Table 7-5. Regular expression methods

Method	Description
findall	Return all nonoverlapping matching patterns in a string as a list
finditer	Like findall, but returns an iterator
match	Match pattern at start of string and optionally segment pattern components into groups; if the pattern matches, return a match object, and otherwise None
search	Scan string for match to pattern, returning a match object if so; unlike match, the match can be anywhere in the string as opposed to only at the beginning
split	Break string into pieces at each occurrence of pattern
sub, subn	Replace all (sub) or first n occurrences (subn) of pattern in string with replacement expression; use symbols \1, \2, ... to refer to match group elements in the replacement string

String Functions in pandas

Cleaning up a messy dataset for analysis often requires a lot of string manipulation. To complicate matters, a column containing strings will sometimes have missing data:

```
In [184]: data = {"Dave": "dave@google.com", "Steve": "steve@gmail.com",
   .....:         "Rob": "rob@gmail.com", "Wes": np.nan}

In [185]: data = pd.Series(data)

In [186]: data
Out[186]:
Dave      dave@google.com
Steve     steve@gmail.com
Rob         rob@gmail.com
Wes                   NaN
dtype: object

In [187]: data.isna()
Out[187]:
Dave      False
```

```
Steve    False
Rob      False
Wes       True
dtype: bool
```

String and regular expression methods can be applied (passing a lambda or other function) to each value using data.map, but it will fail on the NA (null) values. To cope with this, Series has array-oriented methods for string operations that skip over and propagate NA values. These are accessed through Series's str attribute; for example, we could check whether each email address has "gmail" in it with str.contains:

```
In [188]: data.str.contains("gmail")
Out[188]:
Dave     False
Steve     True
Rob       True
Wes        NaN
dtype: object
```

Note that the result of this operation has an object dtype. pandas has *extension types* that provide for specialized treatment of strings, integers, and Boolean data which until recently have had some rough edges when working with missing data:

```
In [189]: data_as_string_ext = data.astype('string')

In [190]: data_as_string_ext
Out[190]:
Dave      dave@google.com
Steve     steve@gmail.com
Rob        rob@gmail.com
Wes                  <NA>
dtype: string

In [191]: data_as_string_ext.str.contains("gmail")
Out[191]:
Dave     False
Steve     True
Rob       True
Wes       <NA>
dtype: boolean
```

Extension types are discussed in more detail in Section 7.3, "Extension Data Types," on page 224.

Regular expressions can be used, too, along with any re options like IGNORECASE:

```
In [192]: pattern = r"([A-Z0-9._%+-]+)@([A-Z0-9.-]+)\.([A-Z]{2,4})"

In [193]: data.str.findall(pattern, flags=re.IGNORECASE)
Out[193]:
Dave     [(dave, google, com)]
```

```
Steve     [(steve, gmail, com)]
Rob         [(rob, gmail, com)]
Wes                         NaN
dtype: object
```

There are a couple of ways to do vectorized element retrieval. Either use `str.get` or index into the `str` attribute:

```
In [194]: matches = data.str.findall(pattern, flags=re.IGNORECASE).str[0]
```

```
In [195]: matches
Out[195]:
Dave     (dave, google, com)
Steve     (steve, gmail, com)
Rob         (rob, gmail, com)
Wes                         NaN
dtype: object
```

```
In [196]: matches.str.get(1)
Out[196]:
Dave       google
Steve       gmail
Rob         gmail
Wes           NaN
dtype: object
```

You can similarly slice strings using this syntax:

```
In [197]: data.str[:5]
Out[197]:
Dave       dave@
Steve       steve
Rob         rob@g
Wes           NaN
dtype: object
```

The `str.extract` method will return the captured groups of a regular expression as a DataFrame:

```
In [198]: data.str.extract(pattern, flags=re.IGNORECASE)
Out[198]:
            0       1     2
Dave     dave  google   com
Steve   steve   gmail   com
Rob       rob   gmail   com
Wes       NaN     NaN   NaN
```

See Table 7-6 for more pandas string methods.

Table 7-6. Partial listing of Series string methods

Method	Description
cat	Concatenate strings element-wise with optional delimiter
contains	Return Boolean array if each string contains pattern/regex
count	Count occurrences of pattern
extract	Use a regular expression with groups to extract one or more strings from a Series of strings; the result will be a DataFrame with one column per group
endswith	Equivalent to x.endswith(pattern) for each element
startswith	Equivalent to x.startswith(pattern) for each element
findall	Compute list of all occurrences of pattern/regex for each string
get	Index into each element (retrieve i-th element)
isalnum	Equivalent to built-in str.alnum
isalpha	Equivalent to built-in str.isalpha
isdecimal	Equivalent to built-in str.isdecimal
isdigit	Equivalent to built-in str.isdigit
islower	Equivalent to built-in str.islower
isnumeric	Equivalent to built-in str.isnumeric
isupper	Equivalent to built-in str.isupper
join	Join strings in each element of the Series with passed separator
len	Compute length of each string
lower, upper	Convert cases; equivalent to x.lower() or x.upper() for each element
match	Use re.match with the passed regular expression on each element, returning True or False whether it matches
pad	Add whitespace to left, right, or both sides of strings
center	Equivalent to pad(side="both")
repeat	Duplicate values (e.g., s.str.repeat(3) is equivalent to x * 3 for each string)
replace	Replace occurrences of pattern/regex with some other string
slice	Slice each string in the Series
split	Split strings on delimiter or regular expression
strip	Trim whitespace from both sides, including newlines
rstrip	Trim whitespace on right side
lstrip	Trim whitespace on left side

7.5 Categorical Data

This section introduces the pandas Categorical type. I will show how you can achieve better performance and memory use in some pandas operations by using it. I also introduce some tools that may help with using categorical data in statistics and machine learning applications.

Background and Motivation

Frequently, a column in a table may contain repeated instances of a smaller set of distinct values. We have already seen functions like `unique` and `value_counts`, which enable us to extract the distinct values from an array and compute their frequencies, respectively:

```
In [199]: values = pd.Series(['apple', 'orange', 'apple',
    .....:                     'apple'] * 2)

In [200]: values
Out[200]:
0     apple
1    orange
2     apple
3     apple
4     apple
5    orange
6     apple
7     apple
dtype: object

In [201]: pd.unique(values)
Out[201]: array(['apple', 'orange'], dtype=object)

In [202]: pd.value_counts(values)
Out[202]:
apple     6
orange    2
dtype: int64
```

Many data systems (for data warehousing, statistical computing, or other uses) have developed specialized approaches for representing data with repeated values for more efficient storage and computation. In data warehousing, a best practice is to use so-called *dimension tables* containing the distinct values and storing the primary observations as integer keys referencing the dimension table:

```
In [203]: values = pd.Series([0, 1, 0, 0] * 2)

In [204]: dim = pd.Series(['apple', 'orange'])

In [205]: values
Out[205]:
0    0
1    1
2    0
3    0
4    0
5    1
6    0
7    0
```

```
dtype: int64

In [206]: dim
Out[206]:
0     apple
1    orange
dtype: object
```

We can use the `take` method to restore the original Series of strings:

```
In [207]: dim.take(values)
Out[207]:
0     apple
1    orange
0     apple
0     apple
0     apple
1    orange
0     apple
0     apple
dtype: object
```

This representation as integers is called the *categorical* or *dictionary-encoded* representation. The array of distinct values can be called the *categories*, *dictionary*, or *levels* of the data. In this book we will use the terms *categorical* and *categories*. The integer values that reference the categories are called the *category codes* or simply *codes*.

The categorical representation can yield significant performance improvements when you are doing analytics. You can also perform transformations on the categories while leaving the codes unmodified. Some example transformations that can be made at relatively low cost are:

- Renaming categories
- Appending a new category without changing the order or position of the existing categories

Categorical Extension Type in pandas

pandas has a special `Categorical` extension type for holding data that uses the integer-based categorical representation or *encoding*. This is a popular data compression technique for data with many occurrences of similar values and can provide significantly faster performance with lower memory use, especially for string data.

Let's consider the example Series from before:

```
In [208]: fruits = ['apple', 'orange', 'apple', 'apple'] * 2

In [209]: N = len(fruits)

In [210]: rng = np.random.default_rng(seed=12345)
```

```
In [211]: df = pd.DataFrame({'fruit': fruits,
   .....:                     'basket_id': np.arange(N),
   .....:                     'count': rng.integers(3, 15, size=N),
   .....:                     'weight': rng.uniform(0, 4, size=N)},
   .....:                    columns=['basket_id', 'fruit', 'count', 'weight'])

In [212]: df
Out[212]:
   basket_id   fruit  count    weight
0          0   apple     11  1.564438
1          1  orange      5  1.331256
2          2   apple     12  2.393235
3          3   apple      6  0.746937
4          4   apple      5  2.691024
5          5  orange     12  3.767211
6          6   apple     10  0.992983
7          7   apple     11  3.795525
```

Here, df['fruit'] is an array of Python string objects. We can convert it to categorical by calling:

```
In [213]: fruit_cat = df['fruit'].astype('category')

In [214]: fruit_cat
Out[214]:
0     apple
1    orange
2     apple
3     apple
4     apple
5    orange
6     apple
7     apple
Name: fruit, dtype: category
Categories (2, object): ['apple', 'orange']
```

The values for fruit_cat are now an instance of pandas.Categorical, which you can access via the .array attribute:

```
In [215]: c = fruit_cat.array

In [216]: type(c)
Out[216]: pandas.core.arrays.categorical.Categorical
```

The Categorical object has categories and codes attributes:

```
In [217]: c.categories
Out[217]: Index(['apple', 'orange'], dtype='object')

In [218]: c.codes
Out[218]: array([0, 1, 0, 0, 0, 1, 0, 0], dtype=int8)
```

These can be accessed more easily using the `cat` accessor, which will be explained soon in "Categorical Methods" on page 242.

A useful trick to get a mapping between codes and categories is:

```
In [219]: dict(enumerate(c.categories))
Out[219]: {0: 'apple', 1: 'orange'}
```

You can convert a DataFrame column to categorical by assigning the converted result:

```
In [220]: df['fruit'] = df['fruit'].astype('category')
```

```
In [221]: df["fruit"]
Out[221]:
0     apple
1    orange
2     apple
3     apple
4     apple
5    orange
6     apple
7     apple
Name: fruit, dtype: category
Categories (2, object): ['apple', 'orange']
```

You can also create `pandas.Categorical` directly from other types of Python sequences:

```
In [222]: my_categories = pd.Categorical(['foo', 'bar', 'baz', 'foo', 'bar'])
```

```
In [223]: my_categories
Out[223]:
['foo', 'bar', 'baz', 'foo', 'bar']
Categories (3, object): ['bar', 'baz', 'foo']
```

If you have obtained categorical encoded data from another source, you can use the alternative `from_codes` constructor:

```
In [224]: categories = ['foo', 'bar', 'baz']
```

```
In [225]: codes = [0, 1, 2, 0, 0, 1]
```

```
In [226]: my_cats_2 = pd.Categorical.from_codes(codes, categories)
```

```
In [227]: my_cats_2
Out[227]:
['foo', 'bar', 'baz', 'foo', 'foo', 'bar']
Categories (3, object): ['foo', 'bar', 'baz']
```

Unless explicitly specified, categorical conversions assume no specific ordering of the categories. So the `categories` array may be in a different order depending on the ordering of the input data. When using `from_codes` or any of the other constructors, you can indicate that the categories have a meaningful ordering:

```
In [228]: ordered_cat = pd.Categorical.from_codes(codes, categories,
   .....:                                         ordered=True)

In [229]: ordered_cat
Out[229]:
['foo', 'bar', 'baz', 'foo', 'foo', 'bar']
Categories (3, object): ['foo' < 'bar' < 'baz']
```

The output [foo < bar < baz] indicates that 'foo' precedes 'bar' in the ordering, and so on. An unordered categorical instance can be made ordered with as_ordered:

```
In [230]: my_cats_2.as_ordered()
Out[230]:
['foo', 'bar', 'baz', 'foo', 'foo', 'bar']
Categories (3, object): ['foo' < 'bar' < 'baz']
```

As a last note, categorical data need not be strings, even though I have shown only string examples. A categorical array can consist of any immutable value types.

Computations with Categoricals

Using Categorical in pandas compared with the nonencoded version (like an array of strings) generally behaves the same way. Some parts of pandas, like the groupby function, perform better when working with categoricals. There are also some functions that can utilize the ordered flag.

Let's consider some random numeric data and use the pandas.qcut binning function. This returns pandas.Categorical; we used pandas.cut earlier in the book but glossed over the details of how categoricals work:

```
In [231]: rng = np.random.default_rng(seed=12345)

In [232]: draws = rng.standard_normal(1000)

In [233]: draws[:5]
Out[233]: array([-1.4238,  1.2637, -0.8707, -0.2592, -0.0753])
```

Let's compute a quartile binning of this data and extract some statistics:

```
In [234]: bins = pd.qcut(draws, 4)

In [235]: bins
Out[235]:
[(-3.121, -0.675], (0.687, 3.211], (-3.121, -0.675], (-0.675, 0.0134], (-0.675, 0
.0134], ..., (0.0134, 0.687], (0.0134, 0.687], (-0.675, 0.0134], (0.0134, 0.687],
 (-0.675, 0.0134]]
Length: 1000
Categories (4, interval[float64, right]): [(-3.121, -0.675] < (-0.675, 0.0134] <
(0.0134, 0.687] <
                                           (0.687, 3.211]]
```

While useful, the exact sample quartiles may be less useful for producing a report than quartile names. We can achieve this with the labels argument to qcut:

```
In [236]: bins = pd.qcut(draws, 4, labels=['Q1', 'Q2', 'Q3', 'Q4'])

In [237]: bins
Out[237]:
['Q1', 'Q4', 'Q1', 'Q2', 'Q2', ..., 'Q3', 'Q3', 'Q2', 'Q3', 'Q2']
Length: 1000
Categories (4, object): ['Q1' < 'Q2' < 'Q3' < 'Q4']

In [238]: bins.codes[:10]
Out[238]: array([0, 3, 0, 1, 1, 0, 0, 2, 2, 0], dtype=int8)
```

The labeled bins categorical does not contain information about the bin edges in the data, so we can use groupby to extract some summary statistics:

```
In [239]: bins = pd.Series(bins, name='quartile')

In [240]: results = (pd.Series(draws)
   .....:            .groupby(bins)
   .....:            .agg(['count', 'min', 'max'])
   .....:            .reset_index())

In [241]: results
Out[241]:
  quartile  count       min       max
0       Q1    250 -3.119609 -0.678494
1       Q2    250 -0.673305  0.008009
2       Q3    250  0.018753  0.686183
3       Q4    250  0.688282  3.211418
```

The 'quartile' column in the result retains the original categorical information, including ordering, from bins:

```
In [242]: results['quartile']
Out[242]:
0    Q1
1    Q2
2    Q3
3    Q4
Name: quartile, dtype: category
Categories (4, object): ['Q1' < 'Q2' < 'Q3' < 'Q4']
```

Better performance with categoricals

At the beginning of the section, I said that categorical types can improve performance and memory use, so let's look at some examples. Consider some Series with 10 million elements and a small number of distinct categories:

```
In [243]: N = 10_000_000
```

```
In [244]: labels = pd.Series(['foo', 'bar', 'baz', 'qux'] * (N // 4))
```

Now we convert `labels` to categorical:

```
In [245]: categories = labels.astype('category')
```

Now we note that `labels` uses significantly more memory than `categories`:

```
In [246]: labels.memory_usage(deep=True)
Out[246]: 600000128
```

```
In [247]: categories.memory_usage(deep=True)
Out[247]: 10000540
```

The conversion to category is not free, of course, but it is a one-time cost:

```
In [248]: %time _ = labels.astype('category')
CPU times: user 469 ms, sys: 106 ms, total: 574 ms
Wall time: 577 ms
```

GroupBy operations can be significantly faster with categoricals because the underlying algorithms use the integer-based codes array instead of an array of strings. Here we compare the performance of `value_counts()`, which internally uses the GroupBy machinery:

```
In [249]: %timeit labels.value_counts()
840 ms +- 10.9 ms per loop (mean +- std. dev. of 7 runs, 1 loop each)
```

```
In [250]: %timeit categories.value_counts()
30.1 ms +- 549 us per loop (mean +- std. dev. of 7 runs, 10 loops each)
```

Categorical Methods

Series containing categorical data have several special methods similar to the `Ser ies.str` specialized string methods. This also provides convenient access to the categories and codes. Consider the Series:

```
In [251]: s = pd.Series(['a', 'b', 'c', 'd'] * 2)
```

```
In [252]: cat_s = s.astype('category')
```

```
In [253]: cat_s
Out[253]:
0    a
1    b
2    c
3    d
4    a
5    b
6    c
7    d
```

```
dtype: category
Categories (4, object): ['a', 'b', 'c', 'd']
```

The special *accessor* attribute `cat` provides access to categorical methods:

```
In [254]: cat_s.cat.codes
Out[254]:
0    0
1    1
2    2
3    3
4    0
5    1
6    2
7    3
dtype: int8

In [255]: cat_s.cat.categories
Out[255]: Index(['a', 'b', 'c', 'd'], dtype='object')
```

Suppose that we know the actual set of categories for this data extends beyond the four values observed in the data. We can use the `set_categories` method to change them:

```
In [256]: actual_categories = ['a', 'b', 'c', 'd', 'e']

In [257]: cat_s2 = cat_s.cat.set_categories(actual_categories)

In [258]: cat_s2
Out[258]:
0    a
1    b
2    c
3    d
4    a
5    b
6    c
7    d
dtype: category
Categories (5, object): ['a', 'b', 'c', 'd', 'e']
```

While it appears that the data is unchanged, the new categories will be reflected in operations that use them. For example, `value_counts` respects the categories, if present:

```
In [259]: cat_s.value_counts()
Out[259]:
a    2
b    2
c    2
d    2
dtype: int64
```

```
In [260]: cat_s2.value_counts()
Out[260]:
a    2
b    2
c    2
d    2
e    0
dtype: int64
```

In large datasets, categoricals are often used as a convenient tool for memory savings and better performance. After you filter a large DataFrame or Series, many of the categories may not appear in the data. To help with this, we can use the remove_unused_categories method to trim unobserved categories:

```
In [261]: cat_s3 = cat_s[cat_s.isin(['a', 'b'])]

In [262]: cat_s3
Out[262]:
0    a
1    b
4    a
5    b
dtype: category
Categories (4, object): ['a', 'b', 'c', 'd']

In [263]: cat_s3.cat.remove_unused_categories()
Out[263]:
0    a
1    b
4    a
5    b
dtype: category
Categories (2, object): ['a', 'b']
```

See Table 7-7 for a listing of available categorical methods.

Table 7-7. Categorical methods for Series in pandas

Method	Description
add_categories	Append new (unused) categories at end of existing categories
as_ordered	Make categories ordered
as_unordered	Make categories unordered
remove_categories	Remove categories, setting any removed values to null
remove_unused_categories	Remove any category values that do not appear in the data
rename_categories	Replace categories with indicated set of new category names; cannot change the number of categories
reorder_categories	Behaves like rename_categories, but can also change the result to have ordered categories
set_categories	Replace the categories with the indicated set of new categories; can add or remove categories

Creating dummy variables for modeling

When you're using statistics or machine learning tools, you'll often transform categorical data into *dummy variables*, also known as *one-hot* encoding. This involves creating a DataFrame with a column for each distinct category; these columns contain 1s for occurrences of a given category and 0 otherwise.

Consider the previous example:

```
In [264]: cat_s = pd.Series(['a', 'b', 'c', 'd'] * 2, dtype='category')
```

As mentioned previously in this chapter, the `pandas.get_dummies` function converts this one-dimensional categorical data into a DataFrame containing the dummy variable:

```
In [265]: pd.get_dummies(cat_s)
Out[265]:
   a  b  c  d
0  1  0  0  0
1  0  1  0  0
2  0  0  1  0
3  0  0  0  1
4  1  0  0  0
5  0  1  0  0
6  0  0  1  0
7  0  0  0  1
```

7.6 Conclusion

Effective data preparation can significantly improve productivity by enabling you to spend more time analyzing data and less time getting it ready for analysis. We have explored a number of tools in this chapter, but the coverage here is by no means comprehensive. In the next chapter, we will explore pandas's joining and grouping functionality.

Data Wrangling: Join, Combine, and Reshape

In many applications, data may be spread across a number of files or databases, or be arranged in a form that is not convenient to analyze. This chapter focuses on tools to help combine, join, and rearrange data.

First, I introduce the concept of *hierarchical indexing* in pandas, which is used extensively in some of these operations. I then dig into the particular data manipulations. You can see various applied usages of these tools in Chapter 13.

8.1 Hierarchical Indexing

Hierarchical indexing is an important feature of pandas that enables you to have multiple (two or more) index *levels* on an axis. Another way of thinking about it is that it provides a way for you to work with higher dimensional data in a lower dimensional form. Let's start with a simple example: create a Series with a list of lists (or arrays) as the index:

```
In [11]: data = pd.Series(np.random.uniform(size=9),
   ....:                   index=[["a", "a", "a", "b", "b", "c", "c", "d", "d"],
   ....:                          [1, 2, 3, 1, 3, 1, 2, 2, 3]])

In [12]: data
Out[12]:
a  1    0.929616
   2    0.316376
   3    0.183919
b  1    0.204560
   3    0.567725
c  1    0.595545
   2    0.964515
```

```
d  2    0.653177
   3    0.748907
dtype: float64
```

What you're seeing is a prettified view of a Series with a `MultiIndex` as its index. The "gaps" in the index display mean "use the label directly above":

```
In [13]: data.index
Out[13]:
MultiIndex([('a', 1),
            ('a', 2),
            ('a', 3),
            ('b', 1),
            ('b', 3),
            ('c', 1),
            ('c', 2),
            ('d', 2),
            ('d', 3)],
           )
```

With a hierarchically indexed object, so-called *partial* indexing is possible, enabling you to concisely select subsets of the data:

```
In [14]: data["b"]
Out[14]:
1    0.204560
3    0.567725
dtype: float64

In [15]: data["b":"c"]
Out[15]:
b  1    0.204560
   3    0.567725
c  1    0.595545
   2    0.964515
dtype: float64

In [16]: data.loc[["b", "d"]]
Out[16]:
b  1    0.204560
   3    0.567725
d  2    0.653177
   3    0.748907
dtype: float64
```

Selection is even possible from an "inner" level. Here I select all of the values having the value 2 from the second index level:

```
In [17]: data.loc[:, 2]
Out[17]:
a    0.316376
c    0.964515
```

```
d    0.653177
dtype: float64
```

Hierarchical indexing plays an important role in reshaping data and in group-based operations like forming a pivot table. For example, you can rearrange this data into a DataFrame using its unstack method:

```
In [18]: data.unstack()
Out[18]:
          1         2         3
a  0.929616  0.316376  0.183919
b  0.204560       NaN  0.567725
c  0.595545  0.964515       NaN
d       NaN  0.653177  0.748907
```

The inverse operation of unstack is stack:

```
In [19]: data.unstack().stack()
Out[19]:
a  1    0.929616
   2    0.316376
   3    0.183919
b  1    0.204560
   3    0.567725
c  1    0.595545
   2    0.964515
d  2    0.653177
   3    0.748907
dtype: float64
```

stack and unstack will be explored in more detail later in Section 8.3, "Reshaping and Pivoting," on page 270.

With a DataFrame, either axis can have a hierarchical index:

```
In [20]: frame = pd.DataFrame(np.arange(12).reshape((4, 3)),
   ....:                      index=[["a", "a", "b", "b"], [1, 2, 1, 2]],
   ....:                      columns=[["Ohio", "Ohio", "Colorado"],
   ....:                               ["Green", "Red", "Green"]])

In [21]: frame
Out[21]:
      Ohio     Colorado
     Green Red    Green
a 1     0   1        2
  2     3   4        5
b 1     6   7        8
  2     9  10       11
```

The hierarchical levels can have names (as strings or any Python objects). If so, these will show up in the console output:

```
In [22]: frame.index.names = ["key1", "key2"]
```

```
In [23]: frame.columns.names = ["state", "color"]

In [24]: frame
Out[24]:
state      Ohio     Colorado
color     Green Red    Green
key1 key2
a    1        0   1        2
     2        3   4        5
b    1        6   7        8
     2        9  10       11
```

These names supersede the `name` attribute, which is used only with single-level indexes.

 Be careful to note that the index names "state" and "color" are not part of the row labels (the `frame.index` values).

You can see how many levels an index has by accessing its `nlevels` attribute:

```
In [25]: frame.index.nlevels
Out[25]: 2
```

With partial column indexing you can similarly select groups of columns:

```
In [26]: frame["Ohio"]
Out[26]:
color     Green Red
key1 key2
a    1        0   1
     2        3   4
b    1        6   7
     2        9  10
```

A `MultiIndex` can be created by itself and then reused; the columns in the preceding DataFrame with level names could also be created like this:

```
pd.MultiIndex.from_arrays([["Ohio", "Ohio", "Colorado"],
                           ["Green", "Red", "Green"]],
                          names=["state", "color"])
```

Reordering and Sorting Levels

At times you may need to rearrange the order of the levels on an axis or sort the data by the values in one specific level. The `swaplevel` method takes two level numbers or names and returns a new object with the levels interchanged (but the data is otherwise unaltered):

```
In [27]: frame.swaplevel("key1", "key2")
Out[27]:
state       Ohio      Colorado
color     Green Red     Green
key2 key1
1    a       0    1        2
2    a       3    4        5
1    b       6    7        8
2    b       9   10       11
```

sort_index by default sorts the data lexicographically using all the index levels, but you can choose to use only a single level or a subset of levels to sort by passing the level argument. For example:

```
In [28]: frame.sort_index(level=1)
Out[28]:
state       Ohio      Colorado
color     Green Red     Green
key1 key2
a    1       0    1        2
b    1       6    7        8
a    2       3    4        5
b    2       9   10       11

In [29]: frame.swaplevel(0, 1).sort_index(level=0)
Out[29]:
state       Ohio      Colorado
color     Green Red     Green
key2 key1
1    a       0    1        2
     b       6    7        8
2    a       3    4        5
     b       9   10       11
```

 Data selection performance is much better on hierarchically indexed objects if the index is lexicographically sorted starting with the outermost level—that is, the result of calling sort_index(level=0) or sort_index().

Summary Statistics by Level

Many descriptive and summary statistics on DataFrame and Series have a level option in which you can specify the level you want to aggregate by on a particular axis. Consider the above DataFrame; we can aggregate by level on either the rows or columns, like so:

```
In [30]: frame.groupby(level="key2").sum()
Out[30]:
state Ohio      Colorado
color Green Red     Green
```

```
key2
1            6   8      10
2           12  14      16

In [31]: frame.groupby(level="color", axis="columns").sum()
Out[31]:
color           Green  Red
key1 key2
a    1             2    1
     2             8    4
b    1            14    7
     2            20   10
```

We will discuss groupby in much more detail later in Chapter 10.

Indexing with a DataFrame's columns

It's not unusual to want to use one or more columns from a DataFrame as the row index; alternatively, you may wish to move the row index into the DataFrame's columns. Here's an example DataFrame:

```
In [32]: frame = pd.DataFrame({"a": range(7), "b": range(7, 0, -1),
   ....:                        "c": ["one", "one", "one", "two", "two",
   ....:                              "two", "two"],
   ....:                        "d": [0, 1, 2, 0, 1, 2, 3]})

In [33]: frame
Out[33]:
   a  b    c  d
0  0  7  one  0
1  1  6  one  1
2  2  5  one  2
3  3  4  two  0
4  4  3  two  1
5  5  2  two  2
6  6  1  two  3
```

DataFrame's set_index function will create a new DataFrame using one or more of its columns as the index:

```
In [34]: frame2 = frame.set_index(["c", "d"])

In [35]: frame2
Out[35]:
       a  b
c   d
one 0  0  7
    1  1  6
    2  2  5
two 0  3  4
    1  4  3
```

```
           2  5  2
           3  6  1
```

By default, the columns are removed from the DataFrame, though you can leave them in by passing drop=False to set_index:

```
In [36]: frame.set_index(["c", "d"], drop=False)
Out[36]:
         a  b    c  d
c   d
one 0    0  7  one  0
    1    1  6  one  1
    2    2  5  one  2
two 0    3  4  two  0
    1    4  3  two  1
    2    5  2  two  2
    3    6  1  two  3
```

reset_index, on the other hand, does the opposite of set_index; the hierarchical index levels are moved into the columns:

```
In [37]: frame2.reset_index()
Out[37]:
     c  d  a  b
0  one  0  0  7
1  one  1  1  6
2  one  2  2  5
3  two  0  3  4
4  two  1  4  3
5  two  2  5  2
6  two  3  6  1
```

8.2 Combining and Merging Datasets

Data contained in pandas objects can be combined in a number of ways:

pandas.merge
> Connect rows in DataFrames based on one or more keys. This will be familiar to users of SQL or other relational databases, as it implements database *join* operations.

pandas.concat
> Concatenate or "stack" objects together along an axis.

combine_first
> Splice together overlapping data to fill in missing values in one object with values from another.

I will address each of these and give a number of examples. They'll be utilized in examples throughout the rest of the book.

Database-Style DataFrame Joins

Merge or *join* operations combine datasets by linking rows using one or more *keys*. These operations are particularly important in relational databases (e.g., SQL-based). The pandas.merge function in pandas is the main entry point for using these algorithms on your data.

Let's start with a simple example:

```
In [38]: df1 = pd.DataFrame({"key": ["b", "b", "a", "c", "a", "a", "b"],
   ....:                      "data1": pd.Series(range(7), dtype="Int64")})

In [39]: df2 = pd.DataFrame({"key": ["a", "b", "d"],
   ....:                      "data2": pd.Series(range(3), dtype="Int64")})

In [40]: df1
Out[40]:
  key  data1
0   b      0
1   b      1
2   a      2
3   c      3
4   a      4
5   a      5
6   b      6

In [41]: df2
Out[41]:
  key  data2
0   a      0
1   b      1
2   d      2
```

Here I am using pandas's Int64 extension type for nullable integers, discussed in Section 7.3, "Extension Data Types," on page 224.

This is an example of a *many-to-one* join; the data in df1 has multiple rows labeled a and b, whereas df2 has only one row for each value in the key column. Calling pandas.merge with these objects, we obtain:

```
In [42]: pd.merge(df1, df2)
Out[42]:
  key  data1  data2
0   b      0      1
1   b      1      1
2   b      6      1
3   a      2      0
4   a      4      0
5   a      5      0
```

Note that I didn't specify which column to join on. If that information is not specified, pandas.merge uses the overlapping column names as the keys. It's a good practice to specify explicitly, though:

```
In [43]: pd.merge(df1, df2, on="key")
Out[43]:
  key  data1  data2
0   b      0      1
1   b      1      1
2   b      6      1
3   a      2      0
4   a      4      0
5   a      5      0
```

In general, the order of column output in pandas.merge operations is unspecified.

If the column names are different in each object, you can specify them separately:

```
In [44]: df3 = pd.DataFrame({"lkey": ["b", "b", "a", "c", "a", "a", "b"],
   ....:                     "data1": pd.Series(range(7), dtype="Int64")})

In [45]: df4 = pd.DataFrame({"rkey": ["a", "b", "d"],
   ....:                     "data2": pd.Series(range(3), dtype="Int64")})

In [46]: pd.merge(df3, df4, left_on="lkey", right_on="rkey")
Out[46]:
  lkey  data1 rkey  data2
0    b      0    b      1
1    b      1    b      1
2    b      6    b      1
3    a      2    a      0
4    a      4    a      0
5    a      5    a      0
```

You may notice that the "c" and "d" values and associated data are missing from the result. By default, pandas.merge does an "inner" join; the keys in the result are the intersection, or the common set found in both tables. Other possible options are "left", "right", and "outer". The outer join takes the union of the keys, combining the effect of applying both left and right joins:

```
In [47]: pd.merge(df1, df2, how="outer")
Out[47]:
  key  data1  data2
0   b      0      1
1   b      1      1
2   b      6      1
3   a      2      0
4   a      4      0
5   a      5      0
6   c      3   <NA>
7   d   <NA>      2
```

```
In [48]: pd.merge(df3, df4, left_on="lkey", right_on="rkey", how="outer")
Out[48]:
  lkey  data1 rkey  data2
0    b      0    b      1
1    b      1    b      1
2    b      6    b      1
3    a      2    a      0
4    a      4    a      0
5    a      5    a      0
6    c      3  NaN   <NA>
7  NaN   <NA>    d      2
```

In an outer join, rows from the left or right DataFrame objects that do not match on keys in the other DataFrame will appear with NA values in the other DataFrame's columns for the nonmatching rows.

See Table 8-1 for a summary of the options for how.

Table 8-1. Different join types with the how argument

Option	Behavior
how="inner"	Use only the key combinations observed in both tables
how="left"	Use all key combinations found in the left table
how="right"	Use all key combinations found in the right table
how="outer"	Use all key combinations observed in both tables together

Many-to-many merges form the Cartesian product of the matching keys. Here's an example:

```
In [49]: df1 = pd.DataFrame({"key": ["b", "b", "a", "c", "a", "b"],
   ....:                      "data1": pd.Series(range(6), dtype="Int64")})

In [50]: df2 = pd.DataFrame({"key": ["a", "b", "a", "b", "d"],
   ....:                      "data2": pd.Series(range(5), dtype="Int64")})

In [51]: df1
Out[51]:
  key  data1
0   b      0
1   b      1
2   a      2
3   c      3
4   a      4
5   b      5

In [52]: df2
Out[52]:
  key  data2
0   a      0
1   b      1
2   a      2
```

```
3   b       3
4   d       4

In [53]: pd.merge(df1, df2, on="key", how="left")
Out[53]:
    key  data1  data2
0    b      0      1
1    b      0      3
2    b      1      1
3    b      1      3
4    a      2      0
5    a      2      2
6    c      3    <NA>
7    a      4      0
8    a      4      2
9    b      5      1
10   b      5      3
```

Since there were three "b" rows in the left DataFrame and two in the right one, there are six "b" rows in the result. The join method passed to the how keyword argument affects only the distinct key values appearing in the result:

```
In [54]: pd.merge(df1, df2, how="inner")
Out[54]:
   key  data1  data2
0   b      0      1
1   b      0      3
2   b      1      1
3   b      1      3
4   b      5      1
5   b      5      3
6   a      2      0
7   a      2      2
8   a      4      0
9   a      4      2
```

To merge with multiple keys, pass a list of column names:

```
In [55]: left = pd.DataFrame({"key1": ["foo", "foo", "bar"],
   ....:                      "key2": ["one", "two", "one"],
   ....:                      "lval": pd.Series([1, 2, 3], dtype='Int64')})

In [56]: right = pd.DataFrame({"key1": ["foo", "foo", "bar", "bar"],
   ....:                       "key2": ["one", "one", "one", "two"],
   ....:                       "rval": pd.Series([4, 5, 6, 7], dtype='Int64')})

In [57]: pd.merge(left, right, on=["key1", "key2"], how="outer")
Out[57]:
   key1 key2  lval  rval
0   foo  one     1     4
1   foo  one     1     5
2   foo  two     2  <NA>
```

```
3  bar  one     3      6
4  bar  two   <NA>     7
```

To determine which key combinations will appear in the result depending on the choice of merge method, think of the multiple keys as forming an array of tuples to be used as a single join key.

 When you're joining columns on columns, the indexes on the passed DataFrame objects are discarded. If you need to preserve the index values, you can use reset_index to append the index to the columns.

A last issue to consider in merge operations is the treatment of overlapping column names. For example:

```
In [58]: pd.merge(left, right, on="key1")
Out[58]:
  key1 key2_x  lval key2_y  rval
0  foo    one     1    one     4
1  foo    one     1    one     5
2  foo    two     2    one     4
3  foo    two     2    one     5
4  bar    one     3    one     6
5  bar    one     3    two     7
```

While you can address the overlap manually (see the section "Renaming Axis Indexes" on page 214 for renaming axis labels), pandas.merge has a suffixes option for specifying strings to append to overlapping names in the left and right DataFrame objects:

```
In [59]: pd.merge(left, right, on="key1", suffixes=("_left", "_right"))
Out[59]:
  key1 key2_left  lval key2_right  rval
0  foo       one     1       one     4
1  foo       one     1       one     5
2  foo       two     2       one     4
3  foo       two     2       one     5
4  bar       one     3       one     6
5  bar       one     3       two     7
```

See Table 8-2 for an argument reference on pandas.merge. The next section covers joining using the DataFrame's row index.

Table 8-2. pandas.merge function arguments

Argument	Description
left	DataFrame to be merged on the left side.
right	DataFrame to be merged on the right side.
how	Type of join to apply: one of "inner", "outer", "left", or "right"; defaults to "inner".

Argument	Description
on	Column names to join on. Must be found in both DataFrame objects. If not specified and no other join keys given, will use the intersection of the column names in `left` and `right` as the join keys.
left_on	Columns in `left` DataFrame to use as join keys. Can be a single column name or a list of column names.
right_on	Analogous to `left_on` for `right` DataFrame.
left_index	Use row index in `left` as its join key (or keys, if a `MultiIndex`).
right_index	Analogous to `left_index`.
sort	Sort merged data lexicographically by join keys; `False` by default.
suffixes	Tuple of string values to append to column names in case of overlap; defaults to (`"_x"`, `"_y"`) (e.g., if `"data"` in both DataFrame objects, would appear as `"data_x"` and `"data_y"` in result).
copy	If `False`, avoid copying data into resulting data structure in some exceptional cases; by default always copies.
validate	Verifies if the merge is of the specified type, whether one-to-one, one-to-many, or many-to-many. See the docstring for full details on the options.
indicator	Adds a special column `_merge` that indicates the source of each row; values will be `"left_only"`, `"right_only"`, or `"both"` based on the origin of the joined data in each row.

Merging on Index

In some cases, the merge key(s) in a DataFrame will be found in its index (row labels). In this case, you can pass left_index=True or right_index=True (or both) to indicate that the index should be used as the merge key:

```
In [60]: left1 = pd.DataFrame({"key": ["a", "b", "a", "a", "b", "c"],
   ....:                        "value": pd.Series(range(6), dtype="Int64")})

In [61]: right1 = pd.DataFrame({"group_val": [3.5, 7]}, index=["a", "b"])

In [62]: left1
Out[62]:
  key  value
0   a      0
1   b      1
2   a      2
3   a      3
4   b      4
5   c      5

In [63]: right1
Out[63]:
   group_val
a        3.5
b        7.0

In [64]: pd.merge(left1, right1, left_on="key", right_index=True)
Out[64]:
  key  value  group_val
0   a      0        3.5
```

```
2   a   2        3.5
3   a   3        3.5
1   b   1        7.0
4   b   4        7.0
```

 If you look carefully here, you will see that the index values for left1 have been preserved, whereas in other examples above, the indexes of the input DataFrame objects are dropped. Because the index of right1 is unique, this "many-to-one" merge (with the default how="inner" method) can preserve the index values from left1 that correspond to rows in the output.

Since the default merge method is to intersect the join keys, you can instead form the union of them with an outer join:

```
In [65]: pd.merge(left1, right1, left_on="key", right_index=True, how="outer")
Out[65]:
  key  value  group_val
0   a      0        3.5
2   a      2        3.5
3   a      3        3.5
1   b      1        7.0
4   b      4        7.0
5   c      5        NaN
```

With hierarchically indexed data, things are more complicated, as joining on index is equivalent to a multiple-key merge:

```
In [66]: lefth = pd.DataFrame({"key1": ["Ohio", "Ohio", "Ohio",
   ....:                                "Nevada", "Nevada"],
   ....:                        "key2": [2000, 2001, 2002, 2001, 2002],
   ....:                        "data": pd.Series(range(5), dtype="Int64")})

In [67]: righth_index = pd.MultiIndex.from_arrays(
   ....:     [
   ....:         ["Nevada", "Nevada", "Ohio", "Ohio", "Ohio", "Ohio"],
   ....:         [2001, 2000, 2000, 2000, 2001, 2002]
   ....:     ]
   ....: )

In [68]: righth = pd.DataFrame({"event1": pd.Series([0, 2, 4, 6, 8, 10], dtype="Int64",
   ....:                                            index=righth_index),
   ....:                        "event2": pd.Series([1, 3, 5, 7, 9, 11], dtype="Int64",
   ....:                                            index=righth_index)})

In [69]: lefth
Out[69]:
     key1  key2  data
0    Ohio  2000     0
```

```
1    Ohio  2001    1
2    Ohio  2002    2
3  Nevada  2001    3
4  Nevada  2002    4

In [70]: righth
Out[70]:
               event1  event2
Nevada 2001         0       1
       2000         2       3
Ohio   2000         4       5
       2000         6       7
       2001         8       9
       2002        10      11
```

In this case, you have to indicate multiple columns to merge on as a list (note the handling of duplicate index values with how="outer"):

```
In [71]: pd.merge(lefth, righth, left_on=["key1", "key2"], right_index=True)
Out[71]:
     key1  key2  data  event1  event2
0    Ohio  2000     0       4       5
0    Ohio  2000     0       6       7
1    Ohio  2001     1       8       9
2    Ohio  2002     2      10      11
3  Nevada  2001     3       0       1

In [72]: pd.merge(lefth, righth, left_on=["key1", "key2"],
   ....:          right_index=True, how="outer")
Out[72]:
     key1  key2  data  event1  event2
0    Ohio  2000     0       4       5
0    Ohio  2000     0       6       7
1    Ohio  2001     1       8       9
2    Ohio  2002     2      10      11
3  Nevada  2001     3       0       1
4  Nevada  2002     4    <NA>    <NA>
4  Nevada  2000  <NA>       2       3
```

Using the indexes of both sides of the merge is also possible:

```
In [73]: left2 = pd.DataFrame([[1., 2.], [3., 4.], [5., 6.]],
   ....:                       index=["a", "c", "e"],
   ....:                       columns=["Ohio", "Nevada"]).astype("Int64")

In [74]: right2 = pd.DataFrame([[7., 8.], [9., 10.], [11., 12.], [13, 14]],
   ....:                       index=["b", "c", "d", "e"],
   ....:                       columns=["Missouri", "Alabama"]).astype("Int64")

In [75]: left2
Out[75]:
   Ohio  Nevada
a     1       2
```

```
c    3    4
e    5    6

In [76]: right2
Out[76]:
   Missouri  Alabama
b         7        8
c         9       10
d        11       12
e        13       14

In [77]: pd.merge(left2, right2, how="outer", left_index=True, right_index=True)
Out[77]:
   Ohio  Nevada  Missouri  Alabama
a     1       2      <NA>     <NA>
b  <NA>    <NA>         7        8
c     3       4         9       10
d  <NA>    <NA>        11       12
e     5       6        13       14
```

DataFrame has a `join` instance method to simplify merging by index. It can also be used to combine many DataFrame objects having the same or similar indexes but nonoverlapping columns. In the prior example, we could have written:

```
In [78]: left2.join(right2, how="outer")
Out[78]:
   Ohio  Nevada  Missouri  Alabama
a     1       2      <NA>     <NA>
b  <NA>    <NA>         7        8
c     3       4         9       10
d  <NA>    <NA>        11       12
e     5       6        13       14
```

Compared with `pandas.merge`, DataFrame's `join` method performs a left join on the join keys by default. It also supports joining the index of the passed DataFrame on one of the columns of the calling DataFrame:

```
In [79]: left1.join(right1, on="key")
Out[79]:
   key  value  group_val
0    a      0        3.5
1    b      1        7.0
2    a      2        3.5
3    a      3        3.5
4    b      4        7.0
5    c      5        NaN
```

You can think of this method as joining data "into" the object whose `join` method was called.

Lastly, for simple index-on-index merges, you can pass a list of DataFrames to `join` as an alternative to using the more general `pandas.concat` function described in the next section:

```
In [80]: another = pd.DataFrame([[7., 8.], [9., 10.], [11., 12.], [16., 17.]],
   ....:                         index=["a", "c", "e", "f"],
   ....:                         columns=["New York", "Oregon"])

In [81]: another
Out[81]:
   New York  Oregon
a       7.0     8.0
c       9.0    10.0
e      11.0    12.0
f      16.0    17.0

In [82]: left2.join([right2, another])
Out[82]:
   Ohio  Nevada  Missouri  Alabama  New York  Oregon
a     1       2      <NA>     <NA>       7.0     8.0
c     3       4         9       10       9.0    10.0
e     5       6        13       14      11.0    12.0

In [83]: left2.join([right2, another], how="outer")
Out[83]:
   Ohio  Nevada  Missouri  Alabama  New York  Oregon
a     1       2      <NA>     <NA>       7.0     8.0
c     3       4         9       10       9.0    10.0
e     5       6        13       14      11.0    12.0
b  <NA>    <NA>         7        8       NaN     NaN
d  <NA>    <NA>        11       12       NaN     NaN
f  <NA>    <NA>      <NA>     <NA>      16.0    17.0
```

Concatenating Along an Axis

Another kind of data combination operation is referred to interchangeably as *concatenation* or *stacking*. NumPy's `concatenate` function can do this with NumPy arrays:

```
In [84]: arr = np.arange(12).reshape((3, 4))

In [85]: arr
Out[85]:
array([[ 0,  1,  2,  3],
       [ 4,  5,  6,  7],
       [ 8,  9, 10, 11]])

In [86]: np.concatenate([arr, arr], axis=1)
Out[86]:
array([[ 0,  1,  2,  3,  0,  1,  2,  3],
       [ 4,  5,  6,  7,  4,  5,  6,  7],
       [ 8,  9, 10, 11,  8,  9, 10, 11]])
```

In the context of pandas objects such as Series and DataFrame, having labeled axes enable you to further generalize array concatenation. In particular, you have a number of additional concerns:

- If the objects are indexed differently on the other axes, should we combine the distinct elements in these axes or use only the values in common?
- Do the concatenated chunks of data need to be identifiable as such in the resulting object?
- Does the "concatenation axis" contain data that needs to be preserved? In many cases, the default integer labels in a DataFrame are best discarded during concatenation.

The `concat` function in pandas provides a consistent way to address each of these questions. I'll give a number of examples to illustrate how it works. Suppose we have three Series with no index overlap:

```
In [87]: s1 = pd.Series([0, 1], index=["a", "b"], dtype="Int64")

In [88]: s2 = pd.Series([2, 3, 4], index=["c", "d", "e"], dtype="Int64")

In [89]: s3 = pd.Series([5, 6], index=["f", "g"], dtype="Int64")
```

Calling `pandas.concat` with these objects in a list glues together the values and indexes:

```
In [90]: s1
Out[90]:
a    0
b    1
dtype: Int64

In [91]: s2
Out[91]:
c    2
d    3
e    4
dtype: Int64

In [92]: s3
Out[92]:
f    5
g    6
dtype: Int64

In [93]: pd.concat([s1, s2, s3])
Out[93]:
a    0
b    1
c    2
```

```
d    3
e    4
f    5
g    6
dtype: Int64
```

By default, `pandas.concat` works along `axis="index"`, producing another Series. If you pass `axis="columns"`, the result will instead be a DataFrame:

```
In [94]: pd.concat([s1, s2, s3], axis="columns")
Out[94]:
       0     1     2
a      0  <NA>  <NA>
b      1  <NA>  <NA>
c   <NA>     2  <NA>
d   <NA>     3  <NA>
e   <NA>     4  <NA>
f   <NA>  <NA>     5
g   <NA>  <NA>     6
```

In this case there is no overlap on the other axis, which as you can see is the union (the `"outer"` join) of the indexes. You can instead intersect them by passing `join="inner"`:

```
In [95]: s4 = pd.concat([s1, s3])

In [96]: s4
Out[96]:
a    0
b    1
f    5
g    6
dtype: Int64

In [97]: pd.concat([s1, s4], axis="columns")
Out[97]:
       0  1
a      0  0
b      1  1
f   <NA>  5
g   <NA>  6

In [98]: pd.concat([s1, s4], axis="columns", join="inner")
Out[98]:
   0  1
a  0  0
b  1  1
```

In this last example, the `"f"` and `"g"` labels disappeared because of the `join="inner"` option.

A potential issue is that the concatenated pieces are not identifiable in the result. Suppose instead you wanted to create a hierarchical index on the concatenation axis. To do this, use the keys argument:

```
In [99]: result = pd.concat([s1, s1, s3], keys=["one", "two", "three"])

In [100]: result
Out[100]:
one    a    0
       b    1
two    a    0
       b    1
three  f    5
       g    6
dtype: Int64

In [101]: result.unstack()
Out[101]:
          a      b      f      g
one       0      1    <NA>   <NA>
two       0      1    <NA>   <NA>
three   <NA>   <NA>    5      6
```

In the case of combining Series along axis="columns", the keys become the Data-Frame column headers:

```
In [102]: pd.concat([s1, s2, s3], axis="columns", keys=["one", "two", "three"])
Out[102]:
     one    two    three
a     0    <NA>    <NA>
b     1    <NA>    <NA>
c   <NA>     2     <NA>
d   <NA>     3     <NA>
e   <NA>     4     <NA>
f   <NA>   <NA>      5
g   <NA>   <NA>      6
```

The same logic extends to DataFrame objects:

```
In [103]: df1 = pd.DataFrame(np.arange(6).reshape(3, 2), index=["a", "b", "c"],
   .....:                    columns=["one", "two"])

In [104]: df2 = pd.DataFrame(5 + np.arange(4).reshape(2, 2), index=["a", "c"],
   .....:                    columns=["three", "four"])

In [105]: df1
Out[105]:
   one  two
a    0    1
b    2    3
c    4    5

In [106]: df2
```

```
Out[106]:
   three  four
a      5     6
c      7     8

In [107]: pd.concat([df1, df2], axis="columns", keys=["level1", "level2"])
Out[107]:
   level1      level2
   one two  three four
a    0   1    5.0  6.0
b    2   3    NaN  NaN
c    4   5    7.0  8.0
```

Here the keys argument is used to create a hierarchical index where the first level can be used to identify each of the concatenated DataFrame objects.

If you pass a dictionary of objects instead of a list, the dictionary's keys will be used for the keys option:

```
In [108]: pd.concat({"level1": df1, "level2": df2}, axis="columns")
Out[108]:
   level1      level2
   one two  three four
a    0   1    5.0  6.0
b    2   3    NaN  NaN
c    4   5    7.0  8.0
```

There are additional arguments governing how the hierarchical index is created (see Table 8-3). For example, we can name the created axis levels with the names argument:

```
In [109]: pd.concat([df1, df2], axis="columns", keys=["level1", "level2"],
    .....:           names=["upper", "lower"])
Out[109]:
upper level1      level2
lower   one two  three four
a         0   1    5.0  6.0
b         2   3    NaN  NaN
c         4   5    7.0  8.0
```

A last consideration concerns DataFrames in which the row index does not contain any relevant data:

```
In [110]: df1 = pd.DataFrame(np.random.standard_normal((3, 4)),
    .....:                    columns=["a", "b", "c", "d"])

In [111]: df2 = pd.DataFrame(np.random.standard_normal((2, 3)),
    .....:                    columns=["b", "d", "a"])

In [112]: df1
Out[112]:
          a         b         c         d
0  1.248804  0.774191 -0.319657 -0.624964
```

```
1   1.078814   0.544647   0.855588   1.343268
2  -0.267175   1.793095  -0.652929  -1.886837

In [113]: df2
Out[113]:
          b          d          a
0   1.059626   0.644448  -0.007799
1  -0.449204   2.448963   0.667226
```

In this case, you can pass `ignore_index=True`, which discards the indexes from each DataFrame and concatenates the data in the columns only, assigning a new default index:

```
In [114]: pd.concat([df1, df2], ignore_index=True)
Out[114]:
          a          b          c          d
0   1.248804   0.774191  -0.319657  -0.624964
1   1.078814   0.544647   0.855588   1.343268
2  -0.267175   1.793095  -0.652929  -1.886837
3  -0.007799   1.059626        NaN   0.644448
4   0.667226  -0.449204        NaN   2.448963
```

Table 8-3 describes the `pandas.concat` function arguments.

Table 8-3. pandas.concat function arguments

Argument	Description
objs	List or dictionary of pandas objects to be concatenated; this is the only required argument
axis	Axis to concatenate along; defaults to concatenating along rows (axis="index")
join	Either "inner" or "outer" ("outer" by default); whether to intersect (inner) or union (outer) indexes along the other axes
keys	Values to associate with objects being concatenated, forming a hierarchical index along the concatenation axis; can be a list or array of arbitrary values, an array of tuples, or a list of arrays (if multiple-level arrays passed in levels)
levels	Specific indexes to use as hierarchical index level or levels if keys passed
names	Names for created hierarchical levels if keys and/or levels passed
verify_integrity	Check new axis in concatenated object for duplicates and raise an exception if so; by default (False) allows duplicates
ignore_index	Do not preserve indexes along concatenation axis, instead produce a new range(total_length) index

Combining Data with Overlap

There is another data combination situation that can't be expressed as either a merge or concatenation operation. You may have two datasets with indexes that overlap in full or in part. As a motivating example, consider NumPy's `where` function, which performs the array-oriented equivalent of an if-else expression:

```
In [115]: a = pd.Series([np.nan, 2.5, 0.0, 3.5, 4.5, np.nan],
   .....:              index=["f", "e", "d", "c", "b", "a"])

In [116]: b = pd.Series([0., np.nan, 2., np.nan, np.nan, 5.],
   .....:              index=["a", "b", "c", "d", "e", "f"])

In [117]: a
Out[117]:
f    NaN
e    2.5
d    0.0
c    3.5
b    4.5
a    NaN
dtype: float64

In [118]: b
Out[118]:
a    0.0
b    NaN
c    2.0
d    NaN
e    NaN
f    5.0
dtype: float64

In [119]: np.where(pd.isna(a), b, a)
Out[119]: array([0. , 2.5, 0. , 3.5, 4.5, 5. ])
```

Here, whenever values in a are null, values from b are selected, otherwise the non-null values from a are selected. Using numpy.where does not check whether the index labels are aligned or not (and does not even require the objects to be the same length), so if you want to line up values by index, use the Series combine_first method:

```
In [120]: a.combine_first(b)
Out[120]:
a    0.0
b    4.5
c    3.5
d    0.0
e    2.5
f    5.0
dtype: float64
```

With DataFrames, combine_first does the same thing column by column, so you can think of it as "patching" missing data in the calling object with data from the object you pass:

```
In [121]: df1 = pd.DataFrame({"a": [1., np.nan, 5., np.nan],
   .....:                     "b": [np.nan, 2., np.nan, 6.],
   .....:                     "c": range(2, 18, 4)})
```

```
In [122]: df2 = pd.DataFrame({"a": [5., 4., np.nan, 3., 7.],
   .....:                     "b": [np.nan, 3., 4., 6., 8.]})

In [123]: df1
Out[123]:
     a    b   c
0  1.0  NaN   2
1  NaN  2.0   6
2  5.0  NaN  10
3  NaN  6.0  14

In [124]: df2
Out[124]:
     a    b
0  5.0  NaN
1  4.0  3.0
2  NaN  4.0
3  3.0  6.0
4  7.0  8.0

In [125]: df1.combine_first(df2)
Out[125]:
     a    b     c
0  1.0  NaN   2.0
1  4.0  2.0   6.0
2  5.0  4.0  10.0
3  3.0  6.0  14.0
4  7.0  8.0   NaN
```

The output of combine_first with DataFrame objects will have the union of all the column names.

8.3 Reshaping and Pivoting

There are a number of basic operations for rearranging tabular data. These are referred to as *reshape* or *pivot* operations.

Reshaping with Hierarchical Indexing

Hierarchical indexing provides a consistent way to rearrange data in a DataFrame. There are two primary actions:

stack
    This "rotates" or pivots from the columns in the data to the rows.

unstack
    This pivots from the rows into the columns.

I'll illustrate these operations through a series of examples. Consider a small Data-Frame with string arrays as row and column indexes:

```
In [126]: data = pd.DataFrame(np.arange(6).reshape((2, 3)),
    .....:                     index=pd.Index(["Ohio", "Colorado"], name="state"),
    .....:                     columns=pd.Index(["one", "two", "three"],
    .....:                     name="number"))

In [127]: data
Out[127]:
number    one  two  three
state
Ohio        0    1      2
Colorado    3    4      5
```

Using the `stack` method on this data pivots the columns into the rows, producing a Series:

```
In [128]: result = data.stack()

In [129]: result
Out[129]:
state     number
Ohio      one       0
          two       1
          three     2
Colorado  one       3
          two       4
          three     5
dtype: int64
```

From a hierarchically indexed Series, you can rearrange the data back into a Data-Frame with `unstack`:

```
In [130]: result.unstack()
Out[130]:
number    one  two  three
state
Ohio        0    1      2
Colorado    3    4      5
```

By default, the innermost level is unstacked (same with `stack`). You can unstack a different level by passing a level number or name:

```
In [131]: result.unstack(level=0)
Out[131]:
state   Ohio  Colorado
number
one        0         3
two        1         4
three      2         5

In [132]: result.unstack(level="state")
```

```
Out[132]:
state   Ohio  Colorado
number
one       0         3
two       1         4
three     2         5
```

Unstacking might introduce missing data if all of the values in the level aren't found in each subgroup:

```
In [133]: s1 = pd.Series([0, 1, 2, 3], index=["a", "b", "c", "d"], dtype="Int64")

In [134]: s2 = pd.Series([4, 5, 6], index=["c", "d", "e"], dtype="Int64")

In [135]: data2 = pd.concat([s1, s2], keys=["one", "two"])

In [136]: data2
Out[136]:
one  a   0
     b   1
     c   2
     d   3
two  c   4
     d   5
     e   6
dtype: Int64
```

Stacking filters out missing data by default, so the operation is more easily invertible:

```
In [137]: data2.unstack()
Out[137]:
        a      b    c  d     e
one     0      1    2  3   <NA>
two  <NA>   <NA>    4  5     6

In [138]: data2.unstack().stack()
Out[138]:
one  a   0
     b   1
     c   2
     d   3
two  c   4
     d   5
     e   6
dtype: Int64

In [139]: data2.unstack().stack(dropna=False)
Out[139]:
one  a      0
     b      1
     c      2
     d      3
     e   <NA>
```

```
two    a      <NA>
       b      <NA>
       c         4
       d         5
       e         6
dtype: Int64
```

When you unstack in a DataFrame, the level unstacked becomes the lowest level in
the result:

```
In [140]: df = pd.DataFrame({"left": result, "right": result + 5},
   .....:                     columns=pd.Index(["left", "right"], name="side"))

In [141]: df
Out[141]:
side          left  right
state   number
Ohio    one      0      5
        two      1      6
        three    2      7
Colorado one     3      8
        two      4      9
        three    5     10

In [142]: df.unstack(level="state")
Out[142]:
side    left           right
state   Ohio Colorado  Ohio Colorado
number
one        0        3     5        8
two        1        4     6        9
three      2        5     7       10
```

As with unstack, when calling stack we can indicate the name of the axis to stack:

```
In [143]: df.unstack(level="state").stack(level="side")
Out[143]:
state          Colorado  Ohio
number side
one     left          3     0
        right         8     5
two     left          4     1
        right         9     6
three   left          5     2
        right        10     7
```

Pivoting "Long" to "Wide" Format

A common way to store multiple time series in databases and CSV files is what
is sometimes called *long* or *stacked* format. In this format, individual values are
represented by a single row in a table rather than multiple values per row.

Let's load some example data and do a small amount of time series wrangling and other data cleaning:

```
In [144]: data = pd.read_csv("examples/macrodata.csv")

In [145]: data = data.loc[:, ["year", "quarter", "realgdp", "infl", "unemp"]]

In [146]: data.head()
Out[146]:
   year  quarter   realgdp  infl  unemp
0  1959        1  2710.349  0.00    5.8
1  1959        2  2778.801  2.34    5.1
2  1959        3  2775.488  2.74    5.3
3  1959        4  2785.204  0.27    5.6
4  1960        1  2847.699  2.31    5.2
```

First, I use pandas.PeriodIndex (which represents time intervals rather than points in time), discussed in more detail in Chapter 11, to combine the year and quarter columns to set the index to consist of datetime values at the end of each quarter:

```
In [147]: periods = pd.PeriodIndex(year=data.pop("year"),
   .....:                          quarter=data.pop("quarter"),
   .....:                          name="date")

In [148]: periods
Out[148]:
PeriodIndex(['1959Q1', '1959Q2', '1959Q3', '1959Q4', '1960Q1', '1960Q2',
             '1960Q3', '1960Q4', '1961Q1', '1961Q2',
             ...
             '2007Q2', '2007Q3', '2007Q4', '2008Q1', '2008Q2', '2008Q3',
             '2008Q4', '2009Q1', '2009Q2', '2009Q3'],
            dtype='period[Q-DEC]', name='date', length=203)

In [149]: data.index = periods.to_timestamp("D")

In [150]: data.head()
Out[150]:
             realgdp  infl  unemp
date
1959-01-01  2710.349  0.00    5.8
1959-04-01  2778.801  2.34    5.1
1959-07-01  2775.488  2.74    5.3
1959-10-01  2785.204  0.27    5.6
1960-01-01  2847.699  2.31    5.2
```

Here I used the pop method on the DataFrame, which returns a column while deleting it from the DataFrame at the same time.

Then, I select a subset of columns and give the columns index the name "item":

```
In [151]: data = data.reindex(columns=["realgdp", "infl", "unemp"])

In [152]: data.columns.name = "item"
```

```
In [153]: data.head()
Out[153]:
item          realgdp  infl  unemp
date
1959-01-01  2710.349  0.00    5.8
1959-04-01  2778.801  2.34    5.1
1959-07-01  2775.488  2.74    5.3
1959-10-01  2785.204  0.27    5.6
1960-01-01  2847.699  2.31    5.2
```

Lastly, I reshape with `stack`, turn the new index levels into columns with `reset_index`, and finally give the column containing the data values the name `"value"`:

```
In [154]: long_data = (data.stack()
   .....:              .reset_index()
   .....:              .rename(columns={0: "value"}))
```

Now, `ldata` looks like:

```
In [155]: long_data[:10]
Out[155]:
        date      item     value
0  1959-01-01  realgdp  2710.349
1  1959-01-01     infl     0.000
2  1959-01-01    unemp     5.800
3  1959-04-01  realgdp  2778.801
4  1959-04-01     infl     2.340
5  1959-04-01    unemp     5.100
6  1959-07-01  realgdp  2775.488
7  1959-07-01     infl     2.740
8  1959-07-01    unemp     5.300
9  1959-10-01  realgdp  2785.204
```

In this so-called *long* format for multiple time series, each row in the table represents a single observation.

Data is frequently stored this way in relational SQL databases, as a fixed schema (column names and data types) allows the number of distinct values in the `item` column to change as data is added to the table. In the previous example, `date` and `item` would usually be the primary keys (in relational database parlance), offering both relational integrity and easier joins. In some cases, the data may be more difficult to work with in this format; you might prefer to have a DataFrame containing one column per distinct `item` value indexed by timestamps in the `date` column. DataFrame's `pivot` method performs exactly this transformation:

```
In [156]: pivoted = long_data.pivot(index="date", columns="item",
   .....:                           values="value")

In [157]: pivoted.head()
Out[157]:
```

```
item       infl    realgdp  unemp
date
1959-01-01  0.00  2710.349    5.8
1959-04-01  2.34  2778.801    5.1
1959-07-01  2.74  2775.488    5.3
1959-10-01  0.27  2785.204    5.6
1960-01-01  2.31  2847.699    5.2
```

The first two values passed are the columns to be used, respectively, as the row and column index, then finally an optional value column to fill the DataFrame. Suppose you had two value columns that you wanted to reshape simultaneously:

```
In [158]: long_data["value2"] = np.random.standard_normal(len(long_data))
```

```
In [159]: long_data[:10]
Out[159]:
         date      item     value     value2
0  1959-01-01   realgdp  2710.349   0.802926
1  1959-01-01      infl     0.000   0.575721
2  1959-01-01     unemp     5.800   1.381918
3  1959-04-01   realgdp  2778.801   0.000992
4  1959-04-01      infl     2.340  -0.143492
5  1959-04-01     unemp     5.100  -0.206282
6  1959-07-01   realgdp  2775.488  -0.222392
7  1959-07-01      infl     2.740  -1.682403
8  1959-07-01     unemp     5.300   1.811659
9  1959-10-01   realgdp  2785.204  -0.351305
```

By omitting the last argument, you obtain a DataFrame with hierarchical columns:

```
In [160]: pivoted = long_data.pivot(index="date", columns="item")
```

```
In [161]: pivoted.head()
Out[161]:
            value                      value2
item         infl    realgdp unemp      infl    realgdp      unemp
date
1959-01-01   0.00  2710.349    5.8  0.575721   0.802926   1.381918
1959-04-01   2.34  2778.801    5.1 -0.143492   0.000992  -0.206282
1959-07-01   2.74  2775.488    5.3 -1.682403  -0.222392   1.811659
1959-10-01   0.27  2785.204    5.6  0.128317  -0.351305  -1.313554
1960-01-01   2.31  2847.699    5.2 -0.615939   0.498327   0.174072
```

```
In [162]: pivoted["value"].head()
Out[162]:
item       infl    realgdp  unemp
date
1959-01-01  0.00  2710.349    5.8
1959-04-01  2.34  2778.801    5.1
1959-07-01  2.74  2775.488    5.3
1959-10-01  0.27  2785.204    5.6
1960-01-01  2.31  2847.699    5.2
```

Note that `pivot` is equivalent to creating a hierarchical index using `set_index` followed by a call to `unstack`:

```
In [163]: unstacked = long_data.set_index(["date", "item"]).unstack(level="item")

In [164]: unstacked.head()
Out[164]:
            value                     value2
item         infl   realgdp unemp       infl   realgdp     unemp
date
1959-01-01   0.00  2710.349   5.8   0.575721  0.802926  1.381918
1959-04-01   2.34  2778.801   5.1  -0.143492  0.000992 -0.206282
1959-07-01   2.74  2775.488   5.3  -1.682403 -0.222392  1.811659
1959-10-01   0.27  2785.204   5.6   0.128317 -0.351305 -1.313554
1960-01-01   2.31  2847.699   5.2  -0.615939  0.498327  0.174072
```

Pivoting "Wide" to "Long" Format

An inverse operation to `pivot` for DataFrames is `pandas.melt`. Rather than transforming one column into many in a new DataFrame, it merges multiple columns into one, producing a DataFrame that is longer than the input. Let's look at an example:

```
In [166]: df = pd.DataFrame({"key": ["foo", "bar", "baz"],
   .....:                     "A": [1, 2, 3],
   .....:                     "B": [4, 5, 6],
   .....:                     "C": [7, 8, 9]})

In [167]: df
Out[167]:
   key  A  B  C
0  foo  1  4  7
1  bar  2  5  8
2  baz  3  6  9
```

The "key" column may be a group indicator, and the other columns are data values. When using `pandas.melt`, we must indicate which columns (if any) are group indicators. Let's use "key" as the only group indicator here:

```
In [168]: melted = pd.melt(df, id_vars="key")

In [169]: melted
Out[169]:
   key variable  value
0  foo        A      1
1  bar        A      2
2  baz        A      3
3  foo        B      4
4  bar        B      5
5  baz        B      6
6  foo        C      7
7  bar        C      8
8  baz        C      9
```

Using `pivot`, we can reshape back to the original layout:

```
In [170]: reshaped = melted.pivot(index="key", columns="variable",
    .....:                              values="value")

In [171]: reshaped
Out[171]:
variable  A  B  C
key
bar       2  5  8
baz       3  6  9
foo       1  4  7
```

Since the result of `pivot` creates an index from the column used as the row labels, we may want to use `reset_index` to move the data back into a column:

```
In [172]: reshaped.reset_index()
Out[172]:
variable  key  A  B  C
0         bar  2  5  8
1         baz  3  6  9
2         foo  1  4  7
```

You can also specify a subset of columns to use as `value` columns:

```
In [173]: pd.melt(df, id_vars="key", value_vars=["A", "B"])
Out[173]:
   key variable  value
0  foo        A      1
1  bar        A      2
2  baz        A      3
3  foo        B      4
4  bar        B      5
5  baz        B      6
```

`pandas.melt` can be used without any group identifiers, too:

```
In [174]: pd.melt(df, value_vars=["A", "B", "C"])
Out[174]:
  variable  value
0        A      1
1        A      2
2        A      3
3        B      4
4        B      5
5        B      6
6        C      7
7        C      8
8        C      9

In [175]: pd.melt(df, value_vars=["key", "A", "B"])
Out[175]:
  variable value
0      key   foo
```

```
1        key    bar
2        key    baz
3          A      1
4          A      2
5          A      3
6          B      4
7          B      5
8          B      6
```

8.4 Conclusion

Now that you have some pandas basics for data import, cleaning, and reorganization under your belt, we are ready to move on to data visualization with matplotlib. We will return to explore other areas of pandas later in the book when we discuss more advanced analytics.

Plotting and Visualization

Making informative visualizations (sometimes called *plots*) is one of the most important tasks in data analysis. It may be a part of the exploratory process—for example, to help identify outliers or needed data transformations, or as a way of generating ideas for models. For others, building an interactive visualization for the web may be the end goal. Python has many add-on libraries for making static or dynamic visualizations, but I'll be mainly focused on matplotlib (*https://matplotlib.org*) and libraries that build on top of it.

matplotlib is a desktop plotting package designed for creating plots and figures suitable for publication. The project was started by John Hunter in 2002 to enable a MATLAB-like plotting interface in Python. The matplotlib and IPython communities have collaborated to simplify interactive plotting from the IPython shell (and now, Jupyter notebook). matplotlib supports various GUI backends on all operating systems and can export visualizations to all of the common vector and raster graphics formats (PDF, SVG, JPG, PNG, BMP, GIF, etc.). With the exception of a few diagrams, nearly all of the graphics in this book were produced using matplotlib.

Over time, matplotlib has spawned a number of add-on toolkits for data visualization that use matplotlib for their underlying plotting. One of these is seaborn (*http://seaborn.pydata.org*), which we explore later in this chapter.

The simplest way to follow the code examples in the chapter is to output plots in the Jupyter notebook. To set this up, execute the following statement in a Jupyter notebook:

```
%matplotlib inline
```

Since this book's first edition in 2012, many new data visualization libraries have been created, some of which (like Bokeh and Altair) take advantage of modern web technology to create interactive visualizations that integrate well with the Jupyter notebook. Rather than use multiple visualization tools in this book, I decided to stick with matplotlib for teaching the fundamentals, in particular since pandas has good integration with matplotlib. You can adapt the principles from this chapter to learn how to use other visualization libraries as well.

9.1 A Brief matplotlib API Primer

With matplotlib, we use the following import convention:

```
In [13]: import matplotlib.pyplot as plt
```

After running %matplotlib notebook in Jupyter (or simply %matplotlib in IPython), we can try creating a simple plot. If everything is set up right, a line plot like Figure 9-1 should appear:

```
In [14]: data = np.arange(10)

In [15]: data
Out[15]: array([0, 1, 2, 3, 4, 5, 6, 7, 8, 9])

In [16]: plt.plot(data)
```

Figure 9-1. Simple line plot

While libraries like seaborn and pandas's built-in plotting functions will deal with many of the mundane details of making plots, should you wish to customize them beyond the function options provided, you will need to learn a bit about the matplotlib API.

 There is not enough room in the book to give comprehensive treatment of the breadth and depth of functionality in matplotlib. It should be enough to teach you the ropes to get up and running. The matplotlib gallery and documentation are the best resource for learning advanced features.

Figures and Subplots

Plots in matplotlib reside within a `Figure` object. You can create a new figure with `plt.figure`:

```
In [17]: fig = plt.figure()
```

In IPython, if you first run `%matplotlib` to set up the matplotlib integration, an empty plot window will appear, but in Jupyter nothing will be shown until we use a few more commands.

`plt.figure` has a number of options; notably, `figsize` will guarantee the figure has a certain size and aspect ratio if saved to disk.

You can't make a plot with a blank figure. You have to create one or more `subplots` using `add_subplot`:

```
In [18]: ax1 = fig.add_subplot(2, 2, 1)
```

This means that the figure should be 2 × 2 (so up to four plots in total), and we're selecting the first of four subplots (numbered from 1). If you create the next two subplots, you'll end up with a visualization that looks like Figure 9-2:

```
In [19]: ax2 = fig.add_subplot(2, 2, 2)
```

```
In [20]: ax3 = fig.add_subplot(2, 2, 3)
```

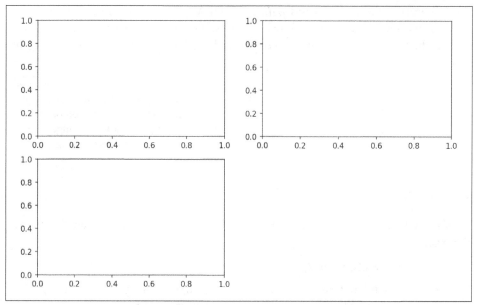

Figure 9-2. An empty matplotlib figure with three subplots

 One nuance of using Jupyter notebooks is that plots are reset after each cell is evaluated, so you must put all of the plotting commands in a single notebook cell.

Here we run all of these commands in the same cell:

```
fig = plt.figure()
ax1 = fig.add_subplot(2, 2, 1)
ax2 = fig.add_subplot(2, 2, 2)
ax3 = fig.add_subplot(2, 2, 3)
```

These plot axis objects have various methods that create different types of plots, and it is preferred to use the axis methods over the top-level plotting functions like plt.plot. For example, we could make a line plot with the plot method (see Figure 9-3):

```
In [21]: ax3.plot(np.random.standard_normal(50).cumsum(), color="black",
   ....:          linestyle="dashed")
```

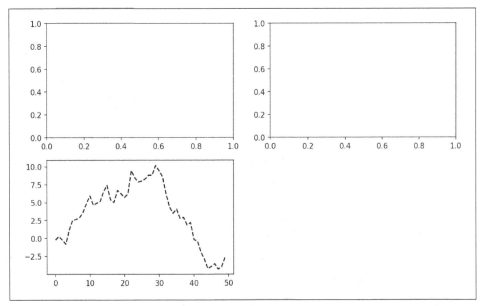

Figure 9-3. Data visualization after a single plot

You may notice output like `<matplotlib.lines.Line2D at ...>` when you run this. matplotlib returns objects that reference the plot subcomponent that was just added. A lot of the time you can safely ignore this output, or you can put a semicolon at the end of the line to suppress the output.

The additional options instruct matplotlib to plot a black dashed line. The objects returned by `fig.add_subplot` here are AxesSubplot objects, on which you can directly plot on the other empty subplots by calling each one's instance method (see Figure 9-4):

```
In [22]: ax1.hist(np.random.standard_normal(100), bins=20, color="black", alpha=0
.3);
In [23]: ax2.scatter(np.arange(30), np.arange(30) + 3 * np.random.standard_normal
(30));
```

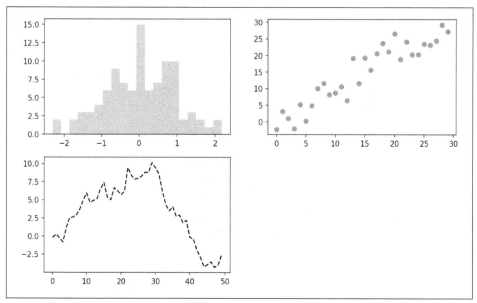

Figure 9-4. Data visualization after additional plots

The style option `alpha=0.3` sets the transparency of the overlaid plot.

You can find a comprehensive catalog of plot types in the matplotlib documentation (*https://matplotlib.org*).

To make creating a grid of subplots more convenient, matplotlib includes a `plt.sub plots` method that creates a new figure and returns a NumPy array containing the created subplot objects:

```
In [25]: fig, axes = plt.subplots(2, 3)

In [26]: axes
Out[26]:
array([[<AxesSubplot:>, <AxesSubplot:>, <AxesSubplot:>],
       [<AxesSubplot:>, <AxesSubplot:>, <AxesSubplot:>]], dtype=object)
```

The `axes` array can then be indexed like a two-dimensional array; for example, `axes[0, 1]` refers to the subplot in the top row at the center. You can also indicate that subplots should have the same x- or y-axis using `sharex` and `sharey`, respectively. This can be useful when you're comparing data on the same scale; otherwise, matplotlib autoscales plot limits independently. See Table 9-1 for more on this method.

Table 9-1. matplotlib.pyplot.subplots options

Argument	Description
nrows	Number of rows of subplots
ncols	Number of columns of subplots
sharex	All subplots should use the same x-axis ticks (adjusting the xlim will affect all subplots)
sharey	All subplots should use the same y-axis ticks (adjusting the ylim will affect all subplots)
subplot_kw	Dictionary of keywords passed to add_subplot call used to create each subplot
**fig_kw	Additional keywords to subplots are used when creating the figure, such as plt.subplots(2, 2, figsize=(8, 6))

Adjusting the spacing around subplots

By default, matplotlib leaves a certain amount of padding around the outside of the subplots and in spacing between subplots. This spacing is all specified relative to the height and width of the plot, so that if you resize the plot either programmatically or manually using the GUI window, the plot will dynamically adjust itself. You can change the spacing using the subplots_adjust method on Figure objects:

```
subplots_adjust(left=None, bottom=None, right=None, top=None,
                wspace=None, hspace=None)
```

wspace and hspace control the percent of the figure width and figure height, respectively, to use as spacing between subplots. Here is a small example you can execute in Jupyter where I shrink the spacing all the way to zero (see Figure 9-5):

```
fig, axes = plt.subplots(2, 2, sharex=True, sharey=True)
for i in range(2):
    for j in range(2):
        axes[i, j].hist(np.random.standard_normal(500), bins=50,
                        color="black", alpha=0.5)
fig.subplots_adjust(wspace=0, hspace=0)
```

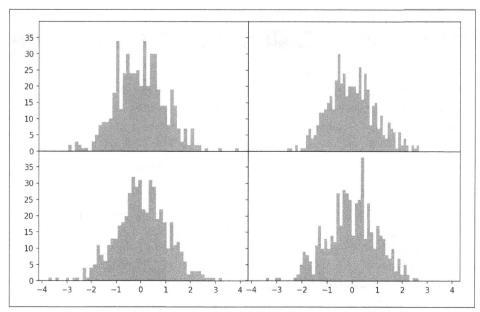

Figure 9-5. Data visualization with no inter-subplot spacing

You may notice that the axis labels overlap. matplotlib doesn't check whether the labels overlap, so in a case like this you would need to fix the labels yourself by specifying explicit tick locations and tick labels (we'll look at how to do this in the later section "Ticks, Labels, and Legends" on page 290).

Colors, Markers, and Line Styles

matplotlib's line `plot` function accepts arrays of x and y coordinates and optional color styling options. For example, to plot x versus y with green dashes, you would execute:

```
ax.plot(x, y, linestyle="--", color="green")
```

A number of color names are provided for commonly used colors, but you can use any color on the spectrum by specifying its hex code (e.g., `"#CECECE"`). You can see some of the supported line styles by looking at the docstring for `plt.plot` (use `plt.plot?` in IPython or Jupyter). A more comprehensive reference is available in the online documentation.

Line plots can additionally have *markers* to highlight the actual data points. Since matplotlib's `plot` function creates a continuous line plot, interpolating between points, it can occasionally be unclear where the points lie. The marker can be supplied as an additional styling option (see Figure 9-6):

```
In [31]: ax = fig.add_subplot()

In [32]: ax.plot(np.random.standard_normal(30).cumsum(), color="black",
   ....:         linestyle="dashed", marker="o");
```

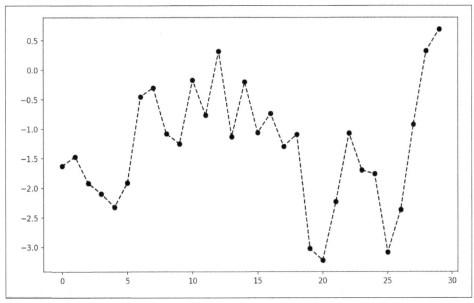

Figure 9-6. Line plot with markers

For line plots, you will notice that subsequent points are linearly interpolated by default. This can be altered with the drawstyle option (see Figure 9-7):

```
In [34]: fig = plt.figure()

In [35]: ax = fig.add_subplot()

In [36]: data = np.random.standard_normal(30).cumsum()

In [37]: ax.plot(data, color="black", linestyle="dashed", label="Default");
In [38]: ax.plot(data, color="black", linestyle="dashed",
   ....:         drawstyle="steps-post", label="steps-post");
In [39]: ax.legend()
```

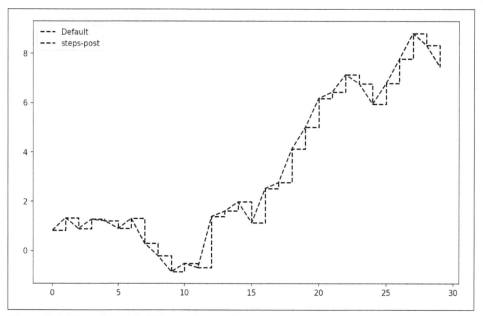

Figure 9-7. Line plot with different drawstyle options

Here, since we passed the `label` arguments to `plot`, we are able to create a plot legend to identify each line using `ax.legend`. I discuss legends more in "Ticks, Labels, and Legends" on page 290.

> You must call `ax.legend` to create the legend, whether or not you passed the `label` options when plotting the data.

Ticks, Labels, and Legends

Most kinds of plot decorations can be accessed through methods on matplotlib axes objects. This includes methods like `xlim`, `xticks`, and `xticklabels`. These control the plot range, tick locations, and tick labels, respectively. They can be used in two ways:

- Called with no arguments returns the current parameter value (e.g., `ax.xlim()` returns the current x-axis plotting range)
- Called with parameters sets the parameter value (e.g., `ax.xlim([0, 10])` sets the x-axis range to 0 to 10)

All such methods act on the active or most recently created `AxesSubplot`. Each corresponds to two methods on the subplot object itself; in the case of `xlim`, these are `ax.get_xlim` and `ax.set_xlim`.

Setting the title, axis labels, ticks, and tick labels

To illustrate customizing the axes, I'll create a simple figure and plot of a random walk (see Figure 9-8):

```
In [40]: fig, ax = plt.subplots()
```

```
In [41]: ax.plot(np.random.standard_normal(1000).cumsum());
```

Figure 9-8. Simple plot for illustrating xticks (with default labels)

To change the x-axis ticks, it's easiest to use `set_xticks` and `set_xticklabels`. The former instructs matplotlib where to place the ticks along the data range; by default these locations will also be the labels. But we can set any other values as the labels using `set_xticklabels`:

```
In [42]: ticks = ax.set_xticks([0, 250, 500, 750, 1000])
```

```
In [43]: labels = ax.set_xticklabels(["one", "two", "three", "four", "five"],
   ....:                             rotation=30, fontsize=8)
```

The `rotation` option sets the x tick labels at a 30-degree rotation. Lastly, `set_xlabel` gives a name to the x-axis, and `set_title` is the subplot title (see Figure 9-9 for the resulting figure):

```
In [44]: ax.set_xlabel("Stages")
Out[44]: Text(0.5, 6.666666666666652, 'Stages')

In [45]: ax.set_title("My first matplotlib plot")
```

Figure 9-9. Simple plot for illustrating custom xticks

Modifying the y-axis consists of the same process, substituting y for x in this example. The axes class has a `set` method that allows batch setting of plot properties. From the prior example, we could also have written:

```
ax.set(title="My first matplotlib plot", xlabel="Stages")
```

Adding legends

Legends are another critical element for identifying plot elements. There are a couple of ways to add one. The easiest is to pass the `label` argument when adding each piece of the plot:

```
In [46]: fig, ax = plt.subplots()

In [47]: ax.plot(np.random.randn(1000).cumsum(), color="black", label="one");
In [48]: ax.plot(np.random.randn(1000).cumsum(), color="black", linestyle="dashed
```

```
",
    ....:           label="two");
In [49]: ax.plot(np.random.randn(1000).cumsum(), color="black", linestyle="dotted
",
    ....:           label="three");
```

Once you've done this, you can call `ax.legend()` to automatically create a legend. The resulting plot is in Figure 9-10:

```
In [50]: ax.legend()
```

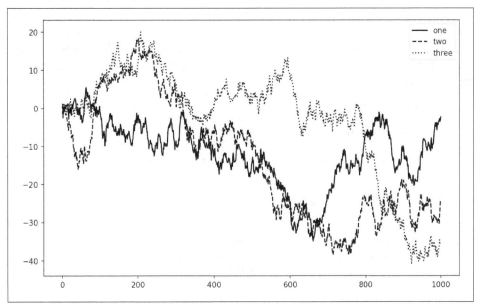

Figure 9-10. Simple plot with three lines and legend

The `legend` method has several other choices for the location `loc` argument. See the docstring (with `ax.legend?`) for more information.

The `loc` legend option tells matplotlib where to place the plot. The default is `"best"`, which tries to choose a location that is most out of the way. To exclude one or more elements from the legend, pass no label or `label="_nolegend_"`.

Annotations and Drawing on a Subplot

In addition to the standard plot types, you may wish to draw your own plot annotations, which could consist of text, arrows, or other shapes. You can add annotations and text using the text, arrow, and annotate functions. text draws text at given coordinates (x, y) on the plot with optional custom styling:

```
ax.text(x, y, "Hello world!",
        family="monospace", fontsize=10)
```

Annotations can draw both text and arrows arranged appropriately. As an example, let's plot the closing S&P 500 index price since 2007 (obtained from Yahoo! Finance) and annotate it with some of the important dates from the 2008–2009 financial crisis. You can run this code example in a single cell in a Jupyter notebook. See Figure 9-11 for the result:

```python
from datetime import datetime

fig, ax = plt.subplots()

data = pd.read_csv("examples/spx.csv", index_col=0, parse_dates=True)
spx = data["SPX"]

spx.plot(ax=ax, color="black")

crisis_data = [
    (datetime(2007, 10, 11), "Peak of bull market"),
    (datetime(2008, 3, 12), "Bear Stearns Fails"),
    (datetime(2008, 9, 15), "Lehman Bankruptcy")
]

for date, label in crisis_data:
    ax.annotate(label, xy=(date, spx.asof(date) + 75),
                xytext=(date, spx.asof(date) + 225),
                arrowprops=dict(facecolor="black", headwidth=4, width=2,
                                headlength=4),
                horizontalalignment="left", verticalalignment="top")

# Zoom in on 2007-2010
ax.set_xlim(["1/1/2007", "1/1/2011"])
ax.set_ylim([600, 1800])

ax.set_title("Important dates in the 2008-2009 financial crisis")
```

Figure 9-11. Important dates in the 2008–2009 financial crisis

There are a couple of important points to highlight in this plot. The `ax.annotate` method can draw labels at the indicated x and y coordinates. We use the `set_xlim` and `set_ylim` methods to manually set the start and end boundaries for the plot rather than using matplotlib's default. Lastly, `ax.set_title` adds a main title to the plot.

See the online matplotlib gallery for many more annotation examples to learn from.

Drawing shapes requires some more care. matplotlib has objects that represent many common shapes, referred to as *patches*. Some of these, like `Rectangle` and `Circle`, are found in `matplotlib.pyplot`, but the full set is located in `matplotlib.patches`.

To add a shape to a plot, you create the patch object and add it to a subplot `ax` by passing the patch to `ax.add_patch` (see Figure 9-12):

```
fig, ax = plt.subplots()

rect = plt.Rectangle((0.2, 0.75), 0.4, 0.15, color="black", alpha=0.3)
circ = plt.Circle((0.7, 0.2), 0.15, color="blue", alpha=0.3)
pgon = plt.Polygon([[0.15, 0.15], [0.35, 0.4], [0.2, 0.6]],
                   color="green", alpha=0.5)

ax.add_patch(rect)
ax.add_patch(circ)
ax.add_patch(pgon)
```

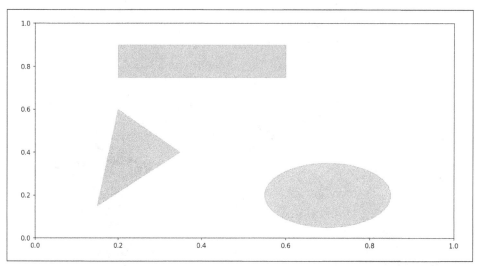

Figure 9-12. Data visualization composed from three different patches

If you look at the implementation of many familiar plot types, you will see that they are assembled from patches.

Saving Plots to File

You can save the active figure to file using the figure object's `savefig` instance method. For example, to save an SVG version of a figure, you need only type:

```
fig.savefig("figpath.svg")
```

The file type is inferred from the file extension. So if you used `.pdf` instead, you would get a PDF. One important option that I use frequently for publishing graphics is `dpi`, which controls the dots-per-inch resolution. To get the same plot as a PNG at 400 DPI, you would do:

```
fig.savefig("figpath.png", dpi=400)
```

See Table 9-2 for a list of some other options for `savefig`. For a comprehensive listing, refer to the docstring in IPython or Jupyter.

Table 9-2. Some `fig.savefig` options

Argument	Description
fname	String containing a filepath or a Python file-like object. The figure format is inferred from the file extension (e.g., `.pdf` for PDF or `.png` for PNG).
dpi	The figure resolution in dots per inch; defaults to 100 in IPython or 72 in Jupyter out of the box but can be configured.
facecolor, edgecolor	The color of the figure background outside of the subplots; "w" (white), by default.
format	The explicit file format to use ("png", "pdf", "svg", "ps", "eps", ...).

matplotlib Configuration

matplotlib comes configured with color schemes and defaults that are geared primarily toward preparing figures for publication. Fortunately, nearly all of the default behavior can be customized via global parameters governing figure size, subplot spacing, colors, font sizes, grid styles, and so on. One way to modify the configuration programmatically from Python is to use the rc method; for example, to set the global default figure size to be 10 × 10, you could enter:

```
plt.rc("figure", figsize=(10, 10))
```

All of the current configuration settings are found in the `plt.rcParams` dictionary, and they can be restored to their default values by calling the `plt.rcdefaults()` function.

The first argument to rc is the component you wish to customize, such as "figure", "axes", "xtick", "ytick", "grid", "legend", or many others. After that can follow a sequence of keyword arguments indicating the new parameters. A convenient way to write down the options in your program is as a dictionary:

```
plt.rc("font", family="monospace", weight="bold", size=8)
```

For more extensive customization and to see a list of all the options, matplotlib comes with a configuration file *matplotlibrc* in the *matplotlib/mpl-data* directory. If you customize this file and place it in your home directory titled *.matplotlibrc*, it will be loaded each time you use matplotlib.

As we'll see in the next section, the seaborn package has several built-in plot themes or *styles* that use matplotlib's configuration system internally.

9.2 Plotting with pandas and seaborn

matplotlib can be a fairly low-level tool. You assemble a plot from its base components: the data display (i.e., the type of plot: line, bar, box, scatter, contour, etc.), legend, title, tick labels, and other annotations.

In pandas, we may have multiple columns of data, along with row and column labels. pandas itself has built-in methods that simplify creating visualizations from DataFrame and Series objects. Another library is seaborn (*https://seaborn.pydata.org*), a high-level statistical graphics library built on matplotlib. seaborn simplifies creating many common visualization types.

Line Plots

Series and DataFrame have a plot attribute for making some basic plot types. By default, plot() makes line plots (see Figure 9-13):

```
In [61]: s = pd.Series(np.random.standard_normal(10).cumsum(), index=np.arange(0,
   100, 10))

In [62]: s.plot()
```

Figure 9-13. Simple Series plot

The Series object's index is passed to matplotlib for plotting on the x-axis, though you can disable this by passing use_index=False. The x-axis ticks and limits can be adjusted with the xticks and xlim options, and the y-axis respectively with yticks and ylim. See Table 9-3 for a partial listing of plot options. I'll comment on a few more of them throughout this section and leave the rest for you to explore.

Table 9-3. Series.plot method arguments

Argument	Description
label	Label for plot legend
ax	matplotlib subplot object to plot on; if nothing passed, uses active matplotlib subplot
style	Style string, like "ko--", to be passed to matplotlib
alpha	The plot fill opacity (from 0 to 1)
kind	Can be "area", "bar", "barh", "density", "hist", "kde", "line", or "pie"; defaults to "line"
figsize	Size of the figure object to create
logx	Pass True for logarithmic scaling on the x axis; pass "sym" for symmetric logarithm that permits negative values
logy	Pass True for logarithmic scaling on the y axis; pass "sym" for symmetric logarithm that permits negative values
title	Title to use for the plot
use_index	Use the object index for tick labels
rot	Rotation of tick labels (0 through 360)
xticks	Values to use for x-axis ticks
yticks	Values to use for y-axis ticks
xlim	x-axis limits (e.g., [0, 10])
ylim	y-axis limits
grid	Display axis grid (off by default)

Most of pandas's plotting methods accept an optional ax parameter, which can be a matplotlib subplot object. This gives you more flexible placement of subplots in a grid layout.

DataFrame's `plot` method plots each of its columns as a different line on the same subplot, creating a legend automatically (see Figure 9-14):

```
In [63]: df = pd.DataFrame(np.random.standard_normal((10, 4)).cumsum(0),
   ....:                    columns=["A", "B", "C", "D"],
   ....:                    index=np.arange(0, 100, 10))

In [64]: plt.style.use('grayscale')

In [65]: df.plot()
```

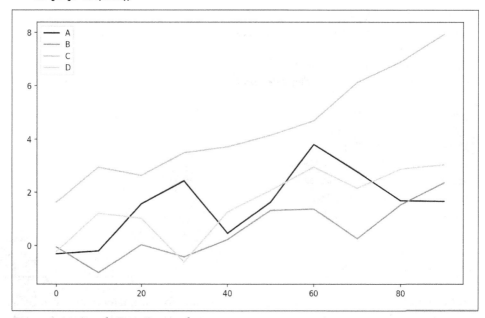

Figure 9-14. Simple DataFrame plot

Here I used `plt.style.use('grayscale')` to switch to a color scheme more suitable for black and white publication, since some readers will not be able to see the full color plots.

The `plot` attribute contains a "family" of methods for different plot types. For example, `df.plot()` is equivalent to `df.plot.line()`. We'll explore some of these methods next.

Additional keyword arguments to `plot` are passed through to the respective matplotlib plotting function, so you can further customize these plots by learning more about the matplotlib API.

DataFrame has a number of options allowing some flexibility for how the columns are handled, for example, whether to plot them all on the same subplot or to create separate subplots. See Table 9-4 for more on these.

Table 9-4. DataFrame-specific plot arguments

Argument	Description
subplots	Plot each DataFrame column in a separate subplot
layouts	2-tuple (rows, columns) providing layout of subplots
sharex	If subplots=True, share the same x-axis, linking ticks and limits
sharey	If subplots=True, share the same y-axis
legend	Add a subplot legend (True by default)
sort_columns	Plot columns in alphabetical order; by default uses existing column order

For time series plotting, see Chapter 11.

Bar Plots

The plot.bar() and plot.barh() make vertical and horizontal bar plots, respectively. In this case, the Series or DataFrame index will be used as the x (bar) or y (barh) ticks (see Figure 9-15):

```
In [66]: fig, axes = plt.subplots(2, 1)

In [67]: data = pd.Series(np.random.uniform(size=16), index=list("abcdefghijklmno
p"))

In [68]: data.plot.bar(ax=axes[0], color="black", alpha=0.7)
Out[68]: <AxesSubplot:>

In [69]: data.plot.barh(ax=axes[1], color="black", alpha=0.7)
```

Figure 9-15. Horizonal and vertical bar plot

With a DataFrame, bar plots group the values in each row in bars, side by side, for each value. See Figure 9-16:

```
In [71]: df = pd.DataFrame(np.random.uniform(size=(6, 4)),
   ....:                    index=["one", "two", "three", "four", "five", "six"],
   ....:                    columns=pd.Index(["A", "B", "C", "D"], name="Genus"))

In [72]: df
Out[72]:
Genus         A         B         C         D
one    0.370670  0.602792  0.229159  0.486744
two    0.420082  0.571653  0.049024  0.880592
three  0.814568  0.277160  0.880316  0.431326
four   0.374020  0.899420  0.460304  0.100843
five   0.433270  0.125107  0.494675  0.961825
six    0.601648  0.478576  0.205690  0.560547

In [73]: df.plot.bar()
```

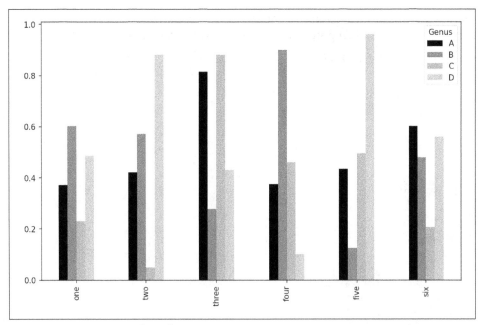

Figure 9-16. DataFrame bar plot

Note that the name "Genus" on the DataFrame's columns is used to title the legend.

We create stacked bar plots from a DataFrame by passing `stacked=True`, resulting in the value in each row being stacked together horizontally (see Figure 9-17):

```
In [75]: df.plot.barh(stacked=True, alpha=0.5)
```

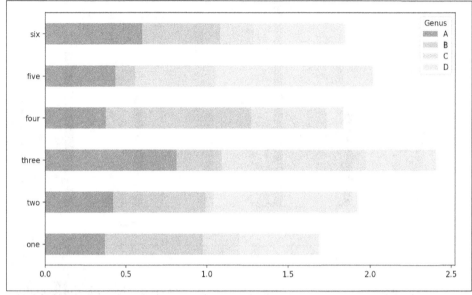

Figure 9-17. DataFrame stacked bar plot

 A useful recipe for bar plots is to visualize a Series's value frequency using `value_counts`: `s.value_counts().plot.bar()`.

Let's have a look at an example dataset about restaurant tipping. Suppose we wanted to make a stacked bar plot showing the percentage of data points for each party size for each day. I load the data using `read_csv` and make a cross-tabulation by day and party size. The `pandas.crosstab` function is a convenient way to compute a simple frequency table from two DataFrame columns:

```
In [77]: tips = pd.read_csv("examples/tips.csv")

In [78]: tips.head()
Out[78]:
   total_bill   tip smoker  day    time  size
0       16.99  1.01     No  Sun  Dinner     2
1       10.34  1.66     No  Sun  Dinner     3
2       21.01  3.50     No  Sun  Dinner     3
3       23.68  3.31     No  Sun  Dinner     2
4       24.59  3.61     No  Sun  Dinner     4
```

```
In [79]: party_counts = pd.crosstab(tips["day"], tips["size"])

In [80]: party_counts = party_counts.reindex(index=["Thur", "Fri", "Sat", "Sun"])

In [81]: party_counts
Out[81]:
size  1   2   3   4  5  6
day
Thur  1  48   4   5  1  3
Fri   1  16   1   1  0  0
Sat   2  53  18  13  1  0
Sun   0  39  15  18  3  1
```

Since there are not many one- and six-person parties, I remove them here:

```
In [82]: party_counts = party_counts.loc[:, 2:5]
```

Then, normalize so that each row sums to 1, and make the plot (see Figure 9-18):

```
# Normalize to sum to 1
In [83]: party_pcts = party_counts.div(party_counts.sum(axis="columns"),
   ....:                               axis="index")

In [84]: party_pcts
Out[84]:
size         2         3         4         5
day
Thur  0.827586  0.068966  0.086207  0.017241
Fri   0.888889  0.055556  0.055556  0.000000
Sat   0.623529  0.211765  0.152941  0.011765
Sun   0.520000  0.200000  0.240000  0.040000

In [85]: party_pcts.plot.bar(stacked=True)
```

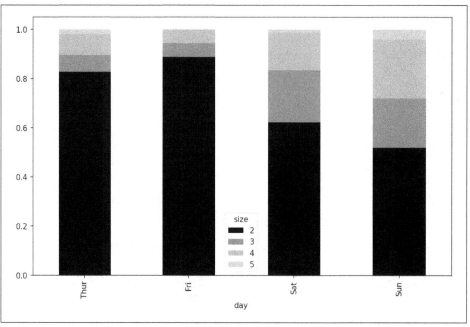

Figure 9-18. Fraction of parties by size within each day

So you can see that party sizes appear to increase on the weekend in this dataset.

With data that requires aggregation or summarization before making a plot, using the seaborn package can make things much simpler (install it with `conda install sea born`). Let's look now at the tipping percentage by day with seaborn (see Figure 9-19 for the resulting plot):

```
In [87]: import seaborn as sns

In [88]: tips["tip_pct"] = tips["tip"] / (tips["total_bill"] - tips["tip"])

In [89]: tips.head()
Out[89]:
   total_bill   tip smoker  day    time  size    tip_pct
0       16.99  1.01     No  Sun  Dinner     2   0.063204
1       10.34  1.66     No  Sun  Dinner     3   0.191244
2       21.01  3.50     No  Sun  Dinner     3   0.199886
3       23.68  3.31     No  Sun  Dinner     2   0.162494
4       24.59  3.61     No  Sun  Dinner     4   0.172069

In [90]: sns.barplot(x="tip_pct", y="day", data=tips, orient="h")
```

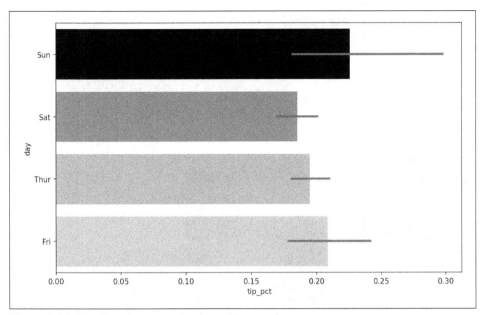

Figure 9-19. Tipping percentage by day with error bars

Plotting functions in seaborn take a `data` argument, which can be a pandas Data-Frame. The other arguments refer to column names. Because there are multiple observations for each value in the `day`, the bars are the average value of `tip_pct`. The black lines drawn on the bars represent the 95% confidence interval (this can be configured through optional arguments).

seaborn.barplot has a hue option that enables us to split by an additional categorical value (see Figure 9-20):

```
In [92]: sns.barplot(x="tip_pct", y="day", hue="time", data=tips, orient="h")
```

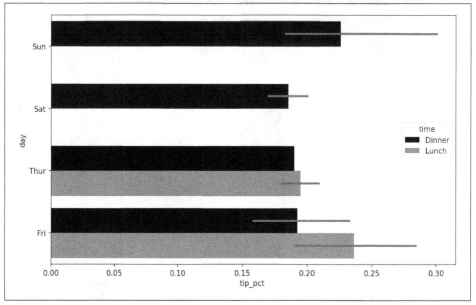

Figure 9-20. Tipping percentage by day and time

Notice that seaborn has automatically changed the aesthetics of plots: the default color palette, plot background, and grid line colors. You can switch between different plot appearances using seaborn.set_style:

```
In [94]: sns.set_style("whitegrid")
```

When producing plots for black-and-white print medium, you may find it useful to set a greyscale color palette, like so:

```
sns.set_palette("Greys_r")
```

Histograms and Density Plots

A *histogram* is a kind of bar plot that gives a discretized display of value frequency. The data points are split into discrete, evenly spaced bins, and the number of data points in each bin is plotted. Using the tipping data from before, we can make a histogram of tip percentages of the total bill using the `plot.hist` method on the Series (see Figure 9-21):

```
In [96]: tips["tip_pct"].plot.hist(bins=50)
```

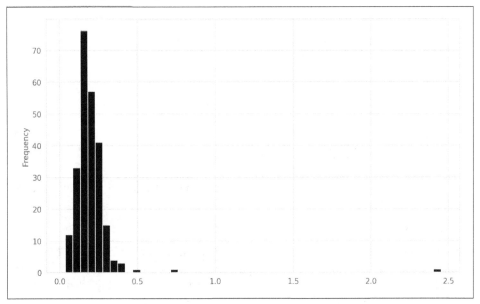

Figure 9-21. Histogram of tip percentages

A related plot type is a *density plot*, which is formed by computing an estimate of a continuous probability distribution that might have generated the observed data. The usual procedure is to approximate this distribution as a mixture of "kernels"—that is, simpler distributions like the normal distribution. Thus, density plots are also known as kernel density estimate (KDE) plots. Using `plot.density` makes a density plot using the conventional mixture-of-normals estimate (see Figure 9-22):

```
In [98]: tips["tip_pct"].plot.density()
```

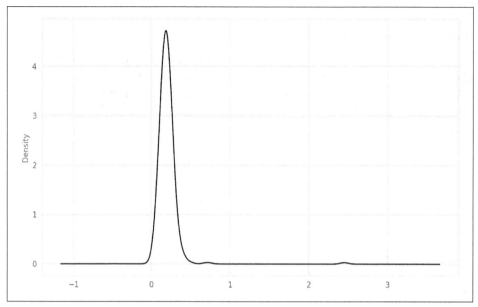

Figure 9-22. Density plot of tip percentages

This kind of plot requires SciPy, so if you do not have it installed already, you can pause and do that now:

```
conda install scipy
```

seaborn makes histograms and density plots even easier through its `histplot` method, which can plot both a histogram and a continuous density estimate simultaneously. As an example, consider a bimodal distribution consisting of draws from two different standard normal distributions (see Figure 9-23):

```
In [100]: comp1 = np.random.standard_normal(200)

In [101]: comp2 = 10 + 2 * np.random.standard_normal(200)

In [102]: values = pd.Series(np.concatenate([comp1, comp2]))

In [103]: sns.histplot(values, bins=100, color="black")
```

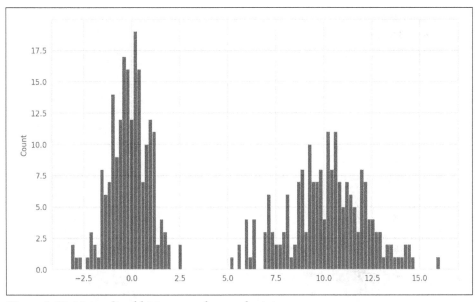

Figure 9-23. Normalized histogram of normal mixture

Scatter or Point Plots

Point plots or scatter plots can be a useful way of examining the relationship between two one-dimensional data series. For example, here we load the `macrodata` dataset from the statsmodels project, select a few variables, then compute log differences:

```
In [104]: macro = pd.read_csv("examples/macrodata.csv")

In [105]: data = macro[["cpi", "m1", "tbilrate", "unemp"]]

In [106]: trans_data = np.log(data).diff().dropna()

In [107]: trans_data.tail()
Out[107]:
          cpi        m1  tbilrate      unemp
198 -0.007904  0.045361 -0.396881  0.105361
199 -0.021979  0.066753 -2.277267  0.139762
200  0.002340  0.010286  0.606136  0.160343
201  0.008419  0.037461 -0.200671  0.127339
202  0.008894  0.012202 -0.405465  0.042560
```

We can then use seaborn's `regplot` method, which makes a scatter plot and fits a linear regression line (see Figure 9-24):

```
In [109]: ax = sns.regplot(x="m1", y="unemp", data=trans_data)
```

```
In [110]: ax.title("Changes in log(m1) versus log(unemp)")
```

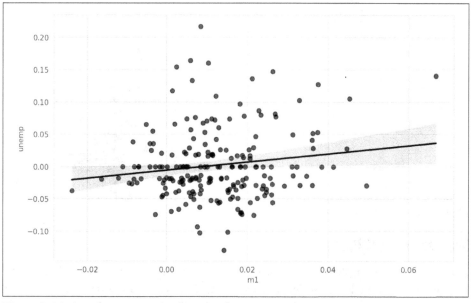

Figure 9-24. A seaborn regression/scatter plot

In exploratory data analysis, it's helpful to be able to look at all the scatter plots among a group of variables; this is known as a *pairs* plot or *scatter plot matrix*. Making such a plot from scratch is a bit of work, so seaborn has a convenient `pairplot` function that supports placing histograms or density estimates of each variable along the diagonal (see Figure 9-25 for the resulting plot):

```
In [111]: sns.pairplot(trans_data, diag_kind="kde", plot_kws={"alpha": 0.2})
```

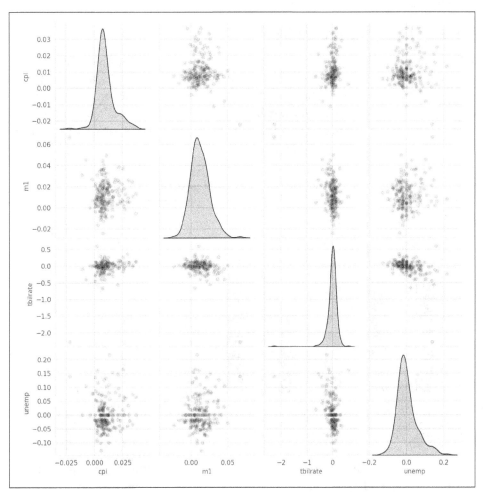

Figure 9-25. Pair plot matrix of statsmodels macro data

You may notice the `plot_kws` argument. This enables us to pass down configuration options to the individual plotting calls on the off-diagonal elements. Check out the `seaborn.pairplot` docstring for more granular configuration options.

Facet Grids and Categorical Data

What about datasets where we have additional grouping dimensions? One way to visualize data with many categorical variables is to use a *facet grid*, which is a two-dimensional layout of plots where the data is split across the plots on each axis based on the distinct values of a certain variable. seaborn has a useful built-in function `cat plot` that simplifies making many kinds of faceted plots split by categorical variables (see Figure 9-26 for the resulting plot):

```
In [112]: sns.catplot(x="day", y="tip_pct", hue="time", col="smoker",
   .....:              kind="bar", data=tips[tips.tip_pct < 1])
```

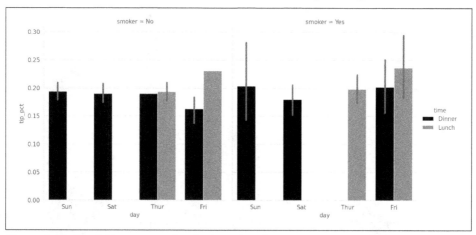

Figure 9-26. Tipping percentage by day/time/smoker

Instead of grouping by "time" by different bar colors within a facet, we can also expand the facet grid by adding one row per `time` value (see Figure 9-27):

```
In [113]: sns.catplot(x="day", y="tip_pct", row="time",
   .....:              col="smoker",
   .....:              kind="bar", data=tips[tips.tip_pct < 1])
```

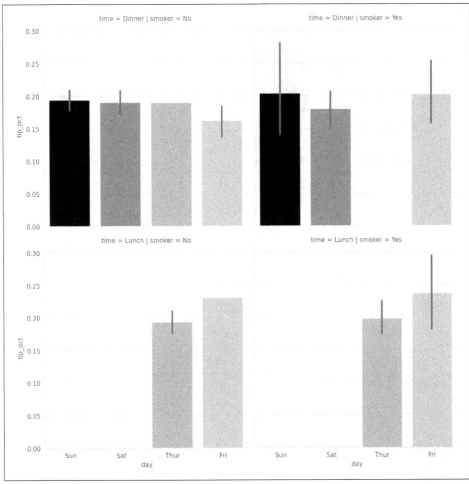

Figure 9-27. Tipping percentage by day split by time/smoker

`catplot` supports other plot types that may be useful depending on what you are trying to display. For example, *box plots* (which show the median, quartiles, and outliers) can be an effective visualization type (see Figure 9-28):

```
In [114]: sns.catplot(x="tip_pct", y="day", kind="box",
   .....:             data=tips[tips.tip_pct < 0.5])
```

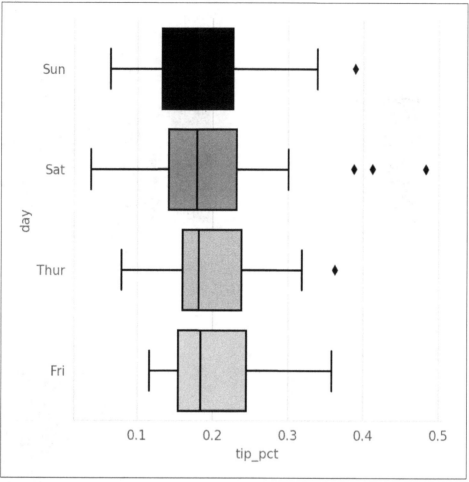

Figure 9-28. Box plot of tipping percentage by day

You can create your own facet grid plots using the more general `seaborn.FacetGrid` class. See the seaborn documentation (*https://seaborn.pydata.org/*) for more.

9.3 Other Python Visualization Tools

As is common with open source, there many options for creating graphics in Python (too many to list). Since 2010, much development effort has been focused on creating interactive graphics for publication on the web. With tools like Altair (*https://altair-viz.github.io*), Bokeh (*http://bokeh.pydata.org*), and Plotly (*https://plotly.com/python*), it's now possible to specify dynamic, interactive graphics in Python that are intended for use with web browsers.

For creating static graphics for print or web, I recommend using matplotlib and libraries that build on matplotlib, like pandas and seaborn, for your needs. For other data visualization requirements, it may be useful to learn how to use one of the other available tools. I encourage you to explore the ecosystem as it continues to evolve and innovate into the future.

An excellent book on data visualization is *Fundamentals of Data Visualization* by Claus O. Wilke (O'Reilly), which is available in print or on Claus's website at *https://clauswilke.com/dataviz*.

9.4 Conclusion

The goal of this chapter was to get your feet wet with some basic data visualization using pandas, matplotlib, and seaborn. If visually communicating the results of data analysis is important in your work, I encourage you to seek out resources to learn more about effective data visualization. It is an active field of research, and you can practice with many excellent learning resources available online and in print.

In the next chapter, we turn our attention to data aggregation and group operations with pandas.

Data Aggregation and Group Operations

Categorizing a dataset and applying a function to each group, whether an aggregation or transformation, can be a critical component of a data analysis workflow. After loading, merging, and preparing a dataset, you may need to compute group statistics or possibly *pivot tables* for reporting or visualization purposes. pandas provides a versatile groupby interface, enabling you to slice, dice, and summarize datasets in a natural way.

One reason for the popularity of relational databases and SQL (which stands for "structured query language") is the ease with which data can be joined, filtered, transformed, and aggregated. However, query languages like SQL impose certain limitations on the kinds of group operations that can be performed. As you will see, with the expressiveness of Python and pandas, we can perform quite complex group operations by expressing them as custom Python functions that manipulate the data associated with each group. In this chapter, you will learn how to:

- Split a pandas object into pieces using one or more keys (in the form of functions, arrays, or DataFrame column names)

- Calculate group summary statistics, like count, mean, or standard deviation, or a user-defined function

- Apply within-group transformations or other manipulations, like normalization, linear regression, rank, or subset selection

- Compute pivot tables and cross-tabulations

- Perform quantile analysis and other statistical group analyses

Time-based aggregation of time series data, a special use case of groupby, is referred to as *resampling* in this book and will receive separate treatment in Chapter 11.

As with the rest of the chapters, we start by importing NumPy and pandas:

```
In [12]: import numpy as np

In [13]: import pandas as pd
```

10.1 How to Think About Group Operations

Hadley Wickham, an author of many popular packages for the R programming language, coined the term *split-apply-combine* for describing group operations. In the first stage of the process, data contained in a pandas object, whether a Series, Data-Frame, or otherwise, is *split* into groups based on one or more *keys* that you provide. The splitting is performed on a particular axis of an object. For example, a DataFrame can be grouped on its rows (axis="index") or its columns (axis="columns"). Once this is done, a function is *applied* to each group, producing a new value. Finally, the results of all those function applications are *combined* into a result object. The form of the resulting object will usually depend on what's being done to the data. See Figure 10-1 for a mockup of a simple group aggregation.

Each grouping key can take many forms, and the keys do not have to be all of the same type:

- A list or array of values that is the same length as the axis being grouped
- A value indicating a column name in a DataFrame
- A dictionary or Series giving a correspondence between the values on the axis being grouped and the group names
- A function to be invoked on the axis index or the individual labels in the index

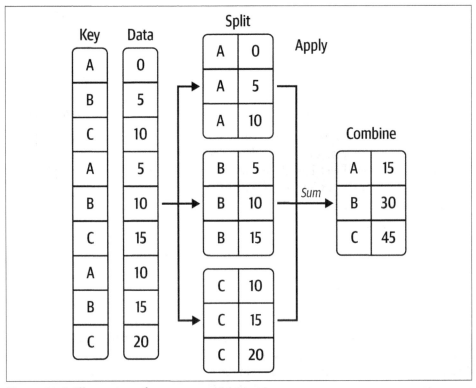

Figure 10-1. Illustration of a group aggregation

Note that the latter three methods are shortcuts for producing an array of values to be used to split up the object. Don't worry if this all seems abstract. Throughout this chapter, I will give many examples of all these methods. To get started, here is a small tabular dataset as a DataFrame:

```
In [14]: df = pd.DataFrame({"key1" : ["a", "a", None, "b", "b", "a", None],
    ....:                    "key2" : pd.Series([1, 2, 1, 2, 1, None, 1], dtype="I
nt64"),
    ....:                    "data1" : np.random.standard_normal(7),
    ....:                    "data2" : np.random.standard_normal(7)})

In [15]: df
Out[15]:
  key1 key2     data1     data2
0    a    1 -0.204708  0.281746
1    a    2  0.478943  0.769023
2 None    1 -0.519439  1.246435
3    b    2 -0.555730  1.007189
4    b    1  1.965781 -1.296221
5    a <NA>  1.393406  0.274992
6 None    1  0.092908  0.228913
```

Suppose you wanted to compute the mean of the data1 column using the labels from key1. There are a number of ways to do this. One is to access data1 and call groupby with the column (a Series) at key1:

```
In [16]: grouped = df["data1"].groupby(df["key1"])

In [17]: grouped
Out[17]: <pandas.core.groupby.generic.SeriesGroupBy object at 0x7fa9270e0a00>
```

This grouped variable is now a special *"GroupBy"* object. It has not actually computed anything yet except for some intermediate data about the group key df["key1"]. The idea is that this object has all of the information needed to then apply some operation to each of the groups. For example, to compute group means we can call the GroupBy's mean method:

```
In [18]: grouped.mean()
Out[18]:
key1
a    0.555881
b    0.705025
Name: data1, dtype: float64
```

Later in Section 10.2, "Data Aggregation," on page 329, I'll explain more about what happens when you call .mean(). The important thing here is that the data (a Series) has been aggregated by splitting the data on the group key, producing a new Series that is now indexed by the unique values in the key1 column. The result index has the name "key1" because the DataFrame column df["key1"] did.

If instead we had passed multiple arrays as a list, we'd get something different:

```
In [19]: means = df["data1"].groupby([df["key1"], df["key2"]]).mean()

In [20]: means
Out[20]:
key1  key2
a     1      -0.204708
      2       0.478943
b     1       1.965781
      2      -0.555730
Name: data1, dtype: float64
```

Here we grouped the data using two keys, and the resulting Series now has a hierarchical index consisting of the unique pairs of keys observed:

```
In [21]: means.unstack()
Out[21]:
key2         1         2
key1
a     -0.204708  0.478943
b      1.965781 -0.555730
```

In this example, the group keys are all Series, though they could be any arrays of the right length:

```
In [22]: states = np.array(["OH", "CA", "CA", "OH", "OH", "CA", "OH"])

In [23]: years = [2005, 2005, 2006, 2005, 2006, 2005, 2006]

In [24]: df["data1"].groupby([states, years]).mean()
Out[24]:
CA  2005     0.936175
    2006    -0.519439
OH  2005    -0.380219
    2006     1.029344
Name: data1, dtype: float64
```

Frequently, the grouping information is found in the same DataFrame as the data you want to work on. In that case, you can pass column names (whether those are strings, numbers, or other Python objects) as the group keys:

```
In [25]: df.groupby("key1").mean()
Out[25]:
      key2     data1     data2
key1
a      1.5  0.555881  0.441920
b      1.5  0.705025 -0.144516

In [26]: df.groupby("key2").mean()
Out[26]:
         data1     data2
key2
1     0.333636  0.115218
2    -0.038393  0.888106

In [27]: df.groupby(["key1", "key2"]).mean()
Out[27]:
              data1     data2
key1 key2
a    1    -0.204708  0.281746
     2     0.478943  0.769023
b    1     1.965781 -1.296221
     2    -0.555730  1.007189
```

You may have noticed in the second case, df.groupby("key2").mean(), that there is no key1 column in the result. Because df["key1"] is not numeric data, it is said to be a *nuisance column*, which is therefore automatically excluded from the result. By default, all of the numeric columns are aggregated, though it is possible to filter down to a subset, as you'll see soon.

Regardless of the objective in using groupby, a generally useful GroupBy method is size, which returns a Series containing group sizes:

```
In [28]: df.groupby(["key1", "key2"]).size()
Out[28]:
key1  key2
a     1       1
      2       1
b     1       1
      2       1
dtype: int64
```

Note that any missing values in a group key are excluded from the result by default. This behavior can be disabled by passing dropna=False to groupby:

```
In [29]: df.groupby("key1", dropna=False).size()
Out[29]:
key1
a      3
b      2
NaN    2
dtype: int64
```

```
In [30]: df.groupby(["key1", "key2"], dropna=False).size()
Out[30]:
key1  key2
a     1       1
      2       1
      <NA>    1
b     1       1
      2       1
NaN   1       2
dtype: int64
```

A group function similar in spirit to size is count, which computes the number of nonnull values in each group:

```
In [31]: df.groupby("key1").count()
Out[31]:
      key2  data1  data2
key1
a     2     3      3
b     2     2      2
```

Iterating over Groups

The object returned by groupby supports iteration, generating a sequence of 2-tuples containing the group name along with the chunk of data. Consider the following:

```
In [32]: for name, group in df.groupby("key1"):
   ....:     print(name)
   ....:     print(group)
   ....:
a
  key1 key2    data1     data2
0    a    1 -0.204708  0.281746
```

```
1    a     2  0.478943   0.769023
5    a  <NA>  1.393406   0.274992
b
   key1  key2     data1      data2
3    b     2 -0.555730   1.007189
4    b     1  1.965781  -1.296221
```

In the case of multiple keys, the first element in the tuple will be a tuple of key values:

```
In [33]: for (k1, k2), group in df.groupby(["key1", "key2"]):
   ....:     print((k1, k2))
   ....:     print(group)
   ....:
('a', 1)
   key1  key2     data1     data2
0    a     1 -0.204708  0.281746
('a', 2)
   key1  key2     data1     data2
1    a     2  0.478943  0.769023
('b', 1)
   key1  key2     data1      data2
4    b     1  1.965781  -1.296221
('b', 2)
   key1  key2    data1     data2
3    b     2 -0.55573  1.007189
```

Of course, you can choose to do whatever you want with the pieces of data. A recipe you may find useful is computing a dictionary of the data pieces as a one-liner:

```
In [34]: pieces = {name: group for name, group in df.groupby("key1")}
```

```
In [35]: pieces["b"]
Out[35]:
   key1  key2     data1      data2
3    b     2 -0.555730   1.007189
4    b     1  1.965781  -1.296221
```

By default groupby groups on axis="index", but you can group on any of the other axes. For example, we could group the columns of our example df here by whether they start with "key" or "data":

```
In [36]: grouped = df.groupby({"key1": "key", "key2": "key",
   ....:                       "data1": "data", "data2": "data"}, axis="columns")
```

We can print out the groups like so:

```
In [37]: for group_key, group_values in grouped:
   ....:     print(group_key)
   ....:     print(group_values)
   ....:
data
      data1     data2
0 -0.204708  0.281746
1  0.478943  0.769023
```

```
2 -0.519439  1.246435
3 -0.555730  1.007189
4  1.965781 -1.296221
5  1.393406  0.274992
6  0.092908  0.228913
key
    key1  key2
0      a     1
1      a     2
2   None     1
3      b     2
4      b     1
5      a  <NA>
6   None     1
```

Selecting a Column or Subset of Columns

Indexing a GroupBy object created from a DataFrame with a column name or array of column names has the effect of column subsetting for aggregation. This means that:

```
df.groupby("key1")["data1"]
df.groupby("key1")[["data2"]]
```

are conveniences for:

```
df["data1"].groupby(df["key1"])
df[["data2"]].groupby(df["key1"])
```

Especially for large datasets, it may be desirable to aggregate only a few columns. For example, in the preceding dataset, to compute the means for just the data2 column and get the result as a DataFrame, we could write:

```
In [38]: df.groupby(["key1", "key2"])[["data2"]].mean()
Out[38]:
              data2
key1 key2
a    1     0.281746
     2     0.769023
b    1    -1.296221
     2     1.007189
```

The object returned by this indexing operation is a grouped DataFrame if a list or array is passed, or a grouped Series if only a single column name is passed as a scalar:

```
In [39]: s_grouped = df.groupby(["key1", "key2"])["data2"]

In [40]: s_grouped
Out[40]: <pandas.core.groupby.generic.SeriesGroupBy object at 0x7fa9270e3520>

In [41]: s_grouped.mean()
Out[41]:
key1  key2
```

```
a     1       0.281746
      2       0.769023
b     1      -1.296221
      2       1.007189
Name: data2, dtype: float64
```

Grouping with Dictionaries and Series

Grouping information may exist in a form other than an array. Let's consider another example DataFrame:

```
In [42]: people = pd.DataFrame(np.random.standard_normal((5, 5)),
   ....:                       columns=["a", "b", "c", "d", "e"],
   ....:                       index=["Joe", "Steve", "Wanda", "Jill", "Trey"])

In [43]: people.iloc[2:3, [1, 2]] = np.nan # Add a few NA values

In [44]: people
Out[44]:
              a         b         c         d         e
Joe    1.352917  0.886429 -2.001637 -0.371843  1.669025
Steve -0.438570 -0.539741  0.476985  3.248944 -1.021228
Wanda -0.577087       NaN       NaN  0.523772  0.000940
Jill   1.343810 -0.713544 -0.831154 -2.370232 -1.860761
Trey  -0.860757  0.560145 -1.265934  0.119827 -1.063512
```

Now, suppose I have a group correspondence for the columns and want to sum the columns by group:

```
In [45]: mapping = {"a": "red", "b": "red", "c": "blue",
   ....:            "d": "blue", "e": "red", "f" : "orange"}
```

Now, you could construct an array from this dictionary to pass to groupby, but instead we can just pass the dictionary (I included the key "f" to highlight that unused grouping keys are OK):

```
In [46]: by_column = people.groupby(mapping, axis="columns")

In [47]: by_column.sum()
Out[47]:
           blue       red
Joe   -2.373480  3.908371
Steve  3.725929 -1.999539
Wanda  0.523772 -0.576147
Jill  -3.201385 -1.230495
Trey  -1.146107 -1.364125
```

The same functionality holds for Series, which can be viewed as a fixed-size mapping:

```
In [48]: map_series = pd.Series(mapping)

In [49]: map_series
Out[49]:
```

```
a      red
b      red
c      blue
d      blue
e      red
f      orange
dtype: object

In [50]: people.groupby(map_series, axis="columns").count()
Out[50]:
       blue  red
Joe      2    3
Steve    2    3
Wanda    1    2
Jill     2    3
Trey     2    3
```

Grouping with Functions

Using Python functions is a more generic way of defining a group mapping compared with a dictionary or Series. Any function passed as a group key will be called once per index value (or once per column value if using `axis="columns"`), with the return values being used as the group names. More concretely, consider the example DataFrame from the previous section, which has people's first names as index values. Suppose you wanted to group by name length. While you could compute an array of string lengths, it's simpler to just pass the `len` function:

```
In [51]: people.groupby(len).sum()
Out[51]:
          a          b          c          d          e
3  1.352917   0.886429  -2.001637  -0.371843   1.669025
4  0.483052  -0.153399  -2.097088  -2.250405  -2.924273
5 -1.015657  -0.539741   0.476985   3.772716  -1.020287
```

Mixing functions with arrays, dictionaries, or Series is not a problem, as everything gets converted to arrays internally:

```
In [52]: key_list = ["one", "one", "one", "two", "two"]

In [53]: people.groupby([len, key_list]).min()
Out[53]:
              a          b          c          d          e
3 one  1.352917   0.886429  -2.001637  -0.371843   1.669025
4 two -0.860757  -0.713544  -1.265934  -2.370232  -1.860761
5 one -0.577087  -0.539741   0.476985   0.523772  -1.021228
```

Grouping by Index Levels

A final convenience for hierarchically indexed datasets is the ability to aggregate using one of the levels of an axis index. Let's look at an example:

```
In [54]: columns = pd.MultiIndex.from_arrays([["US", "US", "US", "JP", "JP"],
   ....:                                      [1, 3, 5, 1, 3]],
   ....:                                      names=["cty", "tenor"])

In [55]: hier_df = pd.DataFrame(np.random.standard_normal((4, 5)), columns=column
s)

In [56]: hier_df
Out[56]:
cty           US                                JP
tenor          1         3         5         1         3
0       0.332883 -2.359419 -0.199543 -1.541996 -0.970736
1      -1.307030  0.286350  0.377984 -0.753887  0.331286
2       1.349742  0.069877  0.246674 -0.011862  1.004812
3       1.327195 -0.919262 -1.549106  0.022185  0.758363
```

To group by level, pass the level number or name using the `level` keyword:

```
In [57]: hier_df.groupby(level="cty", axis="columns").count()
Out[57]:
cty  JP  US
0     2   3
1     2   3
2     2   3
3     2   3
```

10.2 Data Aggregation

Aggregations refer to any data transformation that produces scalar values from arrays. The preceding examples have used several of them, including mean, count, min, and sum. You may wonder what is going on when you invoke mean() on a GroupBy object. Many common aggregations, such as those found in Table 10-1, have optimized implementations. However, you are not limited to only this set of methods.

Table 10-1. Optimized groupby methods

Function name	Description
any, all	Return True if any (one or more values) or all non-NA values are "truthy"
count	Number of non-NA values
cummin, cummax	Cumulative minimum and maximum of non-NA values
cumsum	Cumulative sum of non-NA values
cumprod	Cumulative product of non-NA values
first, last	First and last non-NA values
mean	Mean of non-NA values
median	Arithmetic median of non-NA values
min, max	Minimum and maximum of non-NA values
nth	Retrieve value that would appear at position n with the data in sorted order
ohlc	Compute four "open-high-low-close" statistics for time series-like data

Function name	Description
prod	Product of non-NA values
quantile	Compute sample quantile
rank	Ordinal ranks of non-NA values, like calling `Series.rank`
size	Compute group sizes, returning result as a Series
sum	Sum of non-NA values
std, var	Sample standard deviation and variance

You can use aggregations of your own devising and additionally call any method that is also defined on the object being grouped. For example, the `nsmallest` Series method selects the smallest requested number of values from the data. While `nsmallest` is not explicitly implemented for GroupBy, we can still use it with a nonoptimized implementation. Internally, GroupBy slices up the Series, calls `piece.nsmallest(n)` for each piece, and then assembles those results into the result object:

```
In [58]: df
Out[58]:
    key1 key2     data1     data2
0      a    1 -0.204708  0.281746
1      a    2  0.478943  0.769023
2   None    1 -0.519439  1.246435
3      b    2 -0.555730  1.007189
4      b    1  1.965781 -1.296221
5      a <NA>  1.393406  0.274992
6   None    1  0.092908  0.228913

In [59]: grouped = df.groupby("key1")

In [60]: grouped["data1"].nsmallest(2)
Out[60]:
key1
a     0   -0.204708
      1    0.478943
b     3   -0.555730
      4    1.965781
Name: data1, dtype: float64
```

To use your own aggregation functions, pass any function that aggregates an array to the `aggregate` method or its short alias `agg`:

```
In [61]: def peak_to_peak(arr):
    ....:     return arr.max() - arr.min()

In [62]: grouped.agg(peak_to_peak)
Out[62]:
       key2     data1     data2
key1
```

```
a        1   1.598113   0.494031
b        1   2.521511   2.303410
```

You may notice that some methods, like describe, also work, even though they are not aggregations, strictly speaking:

```
In [63]: grouped.describe()
Out[63]:
      key2                                         data1          ... \
      count mean     std  min   25%  50%  75%  max count     mean ...
key1                                                                ...
a       2.0  1.5 0.707107  1.0  1.25  1.5  1.75  2.0  3.0 0.555881 ...
b       2.0  1.5 0.707107  1.0  1.25  1.5  1.75  2.0  2.0 0.705025 ...
                         data2                                      \
           75%      max count      mean       std       min      25%
key1
a     0.936175 1.393406  3.0  0.441920  0.283299  0.274992  0.278369
b     1.335403 1.965781  2.0 -0.144516  1.628757 -1.296221 -0.720368

           50%      75%      max
key1
a     0.281746 0.525384 0.769023
b    -0.144516 0.431337 1.007189
[2 rows x 24 columns]
```

I will explain in more detail what has happened here in Section 10.3, "Apply: General split-apply-combine," on page 335.

> Custom aggregation functions are generally much slower than the optimized functions found in Table 10-1. This is because there is some extra overhead (function calls, data rearrangement) in constructing the intermediate group data chunks.

Column-Wise and Multiple Function Application

Let's return to the tipping dataset used in the last chapter. After loading it with pandas.read_csv, we add a tipping percentage column:

```
In [64]: tips = pd.read_csv("examples/tips.csv")
```

```
In [65]: tips.head()
Out[65]:
   total_bill   tip smoker  day    time  size
0       16.99  1.01     No  Sun  Dinner     2
1       10.34  1.66     No  Sun  Dinner     3
2       21.01  3.50     No  Sun  Dinner     3
3       23.68  3.31     No  Sun  Dinner     2
4       24.59  3.61     No  Sun  Dinner     4
```

Now I will add a `tip_pct` column with the tip percentage of the total bill:

```
In [66]: tips["tip_pct"] = tips["tip"] / tips["total_bill"]

In [67]: tips.head()
Out[67]:
   total_bill  tip smoker  day    time  size   tip_pct
0       16.99 1.01     No  Sun  Dinner     2  0.059447
1       10.34 1.66     No  Sun  Dinner     3  0.160542
2       21.01 3.50     No  Sun  Dinner     3  0.166587
3       23.68 3.31     No  Sun  Dinner     2  0.139780
4       24.59 3.61     No  Sun  Dinner     4  0.146808
```

As you've already seen, aggregating a Series or all of the columns of a DataFrame is a matter of using `aggregate` (or `agg`) with the desired function or calling a method like `mean` or `std`. However, you may want to aggregate using a different function, depending on the column, or multiple functions at once. Fortunately, this is possible to do, which I'll illustrate through a number of examples. First, I'll group the `tips` by `day` and `smoker`:

```
In [68]: grouped = tips.groupby(["day", "smoker"])
```

Note that for descriptive statistics like those in Table 10-1, you can pass the name of the function as a string:

```
In [69]: grouped_pct = grouped["tip_pct"]

In [70]: grouped_pct.agg("mean")
Out[70]:
day   smoker
Fri   No        0.151650
      Yes       0.174783
Sat   No        0.158048
      Yes       0.147906
Sun   No        0.160113
      Yes       0.187250
Thur  No        0.160298
      Yes       0.163863
Name: tip_pct, dtype: float64
```

If you pass a list of functions or function names instead, you get back a DataFrame with column names taken from the functions:

```
In [71]: grouped_pct.agg(["mean", "std", peak_to_peak])
Out[71]:
                  mean       std  peak_to_peak
day   smoker
Fri   No      0.151650  0.028123      0.067349
      Yes     0.174783  0.051293      0.159925
Sat   No      0.158048  0.039767      0.235193
      Yes     0.147906  0.061375      0.290095
Sun   No      0.160113  0.042347      0.193226
```

```
       Yes      0.187250  0.154134     0.644685
Thur   No       0.160298  0.038774     0.193350
       Yes      0.163863  0.039389     0.151240
```

Here we passed a list of aggregation functions to agg to evaluate independently on the data groups.

You don't need to accept the names that GroupBy gives to the columns; notably, lambda functions have the name "<lambda>", which makes them hard to identify (you can see for yourself by looking at a function's __name__ attribute). Thus, if you pass a list of (name, function) tuples, the first element of each tuple will be used as the DataFrame column names (you can think of a list of 2-tuples as an ordered mapping):

```
In [72]: grouped_pct.agg([("average", "mean"), ("stdev", np.std)])
Out[72]:
                  average     stdev
day   smoker
Fri   No         0.151650  0.028123
      Yes        0.174783  0.051293
Sat   No         0.158048  0.039767
      Yes        0.147906  0.061375
Sun   No         0.160113  0.042347
      Yes        0.187250  0.154134
Thur  No         0.160298  0.038774
      Yes        0.163863  0.039389
```

With a DataFrame you have more options, as you can specify a list of functions to apply to all of the columns or different functions per column. To start, suppose we wanted to compute the same three statistics for the tip_pct and total_bill columns:

```
In [73]: functions = ["count", "mean", "max"]

In [74]: result = grouped[["tip_pct", "total_bill"]].agg(functions)

In [75]: result
Out[75]:
                 tip_pct                        total_bill
                 count      mean       max      count       mean       max
day   smoker
Fri   No         4     0.151650  0.187735      4     18.420000  22.75
      Yes        15    0.174783  0.263480      15    16.813333  40.17
Sat   No         45    0.158048  0.291990      45    19.661778  48.33
      Yes        42    0.147906  0.325733      42    21.276667  50.81
Sun   No         57    0.160113  0.252672      57    20.506667  48.17
      Yes        19    0.187250  0.710345      19    24.120000  45.35
Thur  No         45    0.160298  0.266312      45    17.113111  41.19
      Yes        17    0.163863  0.241255      17    19.190588  43.11
```

As you can see, the resulting DataFrame has hierarchical columns, the same as you would get aggregating each column separately and using concat to glue the results together using the column names as the keys argument:

```
In [76]: result["tip_pct"]
Out[76]:
            count     mean       max
day  smoker
Fri  No         4  0.151650  0.187735
     Yes       15  0.174783  0.263480
Sat  No        45  0.158048  0.291990
     Yes       42  0.147906  0.325733
Sun  No        57  0.160113  0.252672
     Yes       19  0.187250  0.710345
Thur No        45  0.160298  0.266312
     Yes       17  0.163863  0.241255
```

As before, a list of tuples with custom names can be passed:

```
In [77]: ftuples = [("Average", "mean"), ("Variance", np.var)]

In [78]: grouped[["tip_pct", "total_bill"]].agg(ftuples)
Out[78]:
              tip_pct             total_bill
            Average  Variance     Average    Variance
day  smoker
Fri  No     0.151650  0.000791  18.420000    25.596333
     Yes    0.174783  0.002631  16.813333    82.562438
Sat  No     0.158048  0.001581  19.661778    79.908965
     Yes    0.147906  0.003767  21.276667   101.387535
Sun  No     0.160113  0.001793  20.506667    66.099980
     Yes    0.187250  0.023757  24.120000   109.046044
Thur No     0.160298  0.001503  17.113111    59.625081
     Yes    0.163863  0.001551  19.190588    69.808518
```

Now, suppose you wanted to apply potentially different functions to one or more of the columns. To do this, pass a dictionary to agg that contains a mapping of column names to any of the function specifications listed so far:

```
In [79]: grouped.agg({"tip" : np.max, "size" : "sum"})
Out[79]:
             tip  size
day  smoker
Fri  No     3.50     9
     Yes    4.73    31
Sat  No     9.00   115
     Yes   10.00   104
Sun  No     6.00   167
     Yes    6.50    49
Thur No     6.70   112
     Yes    5.00    40

In [80]: grouped.agg({"tip_pct" : ["min", "max", "mean", "std"],
```

```
        ....:                   "size" : "sum"})
Out[80]:
                    tip_pct                                  size
                        min       max      mean       std    sum
day    smoker
Fri    No         0.120385  0.187735  0.151650  0.028123      9
       Yes        0.103555  0.263480  0.174783  0.051293     31
Sat    No         0.056797  0.291990  0.158048  0.039767    115
       Yes        0.035638  0.325733  0.147906  0.061375    104
Sun    No         0.059447  0.252672  0.160113  0.042347    167
       Yes        0.065660  0.710345  0.187250  0.154134     49
Thur   No         0.072961  0.266312  0.160298  0.038774    112
       Yes        0.090014  0.241255  0.163863  0.039389     40
```

A DataFrame will have hierarchical columns only if multiple functions are applied to at least one column.

Returning Aggregated Data Without Row Indexes

In all of the examples up until now, the aggregated data comes back with an index, potentially hierarchical, composed from the unique group key combinations. Since this isn't always desirable, you can disable this behavior in most cases by passing as_index=False to groupby:

```
In [81]: tips.groupby(["day", "smoker"], as_index=False).mean()
Out[81]:
    day smoker  total_bill       tip      size    tip_pct
0   Fri     No   18.420000  2.812500  2.250000   0.151650
1   Fri    Yes   16.813333  2.714000  2.066667   0.174783
2   Sat     No   19.661778  3.102889  2.555556   0.158048
3   Sat    Yes   21.276667  2.875476  2.476190   0.147906
4   Sun     No   20.506667  3.167895  2.929825   0.160113
5   Sun    Yes   24.120000  3.516842  2.578947   0.187250
6  Thur     No   17.113111  2.673778  2.488889   0.160298
7  Thur    Yes   19.190588  3.030000  2.352941   0.163863
```

Of course, it's always possible to obtain the result in this format by calling reset_index on the result. Using the as_index=False argument avoids some unnecessary computations.

10.3 Apply: General split-apply-combine

The most general-purpose GroupBy method is apply, which is the subject of this section. apply splits the object being manipulated into pieces, invokes the passed function on each piece, and then attempts to concatenate the pieces.

Returning to the tipping dataset from before, suppose you wanted to select the top five tip_pct values by group. First, write a function that selects the rows with the largest values in a particular column:

```
In [82]: def top(df, n=5, column="tip_pct"):
   ....:     return df.sort_values(column, ascending=False)[:n]

In [83]: top(tips, n=6)
Out[83]:
     total_bill   tip smoker  day    time  size   tip_pct
172        7.25  5.15    Yes  Sun  Dinner     2  0.710345
178        9.60  4.00    Yes  Sun  Dinner     2  0.416667
67         3.07  1.00    Yes  Sat  Dinner     1  0.325733
232       11.61  3.39     No  Sat  Dinner     2  0.291990
183       23.17  6.50    Yes  Sun  Dinner     4  0.280535
109       14.31  4.00    Yes  Sat  Dinner     2  0.279525
```

Now, if we group by smoker, say, and call apply with this function, we get the following:

```
In [84]: tips.groupby("smoker").apply(top)
Out[84]:
            total_bill   tip smoker   day    time  size   tip_pct
smoker
No     232       11.61  3.39     No   Sat  Dinner     2  0.291990
       149        7.51  2.00     No  Thur   Lunch     2  0.266312
       51        10.29  2.60     No   Sun  Dinner     2  0.252672
       185       20.69  5.00     No   Sun  Dinner     5  0.241663
       88        24.71  5.85     No  Thur   Lunch     2  0.236746
Yes    172        7.25  5.15    Yes   Sun  Dinner     2  0.710345
       178        9.60  4.00    Yes   Sun  Dinner     2  0.416667
       67         3.07  1.00    Yes   Sat  Dinner     1  0.325733
       183       23.17  6.50    Yes   Sun  Dinner     4  0.280535
       109       14.31  4.00    Yes   Sat  Dinner     2  0.279525
```

What has happened here? First, the tips DataFrame is split into groups based on the value of smoker. Then the top function is called on each group, and the results of each function call are glued together using pandas.concat, labeling the pieces with the group names. The result therefore has a hierarchical index with an inner level that contains index values from the original DataFrame.

If you pass a function to apply that takes other arguments or keywords, you can pass these after the function:

```
In [85]: tips.groupby(["smoker", "day"]).apply(top, n=1, column="total_bill")
Out[85]:
                total_bill   tip smoker   day    time  size   tip_pct
smoker day
No     Fri  94       22.75  3.25     No   Fri  Dinner     2  0.142857
       Sat  212      48.33  9.00     No   Sat  Dinner     4  0.186220
       Sun  156      48.17  5.00     No   Sun  Dinner     6  0.103799
       Thur 142      41.19  5.00     No  Thur   Lunch     5  0.121389
Yes    Fri  95       40.17  4.73    Yes   Fri  Dinner     4  0.117750
       Sat  170      50.81 10.00    Yes   Sat  Dinner     3  0.196812
       Sun  182      45.35  3.50    Yes   Sun  Dinner     3  0.077178
       Thur 197      43.11  5.00    Yes  Thur   Lunch     4  0.115982
```

Beyond these basic usage mechanics, getting the most out of apply may require some creativity. What occurs inside the function passed is up to you; it must either return a pandas object or a scalar value. The rest of this chapter will consist mainly of examples showing you how to solve various problems using groupby.

For example, you may recall that I earlier called describe on a GroupBy object:

```
In [86]: result = tips.groupby("smoker")["tip_pct"].describe()

In [87]: result
Out[87]:
         count      mean       std       min       25%       50%       75%  \
smoker
No       151.0  0.159328  0.039910  0.056797  0.136906  0.155625  0.185014
Yes       93.0  0.163196  0.085119  0.035638  0.106771  0.153846  0.195059

              max
smoker
No       0.291990
Yes      0.710345

In [88]: result.unstack("smoker")
Out[88]:
        smoker
count   No       151.000000
        Yes       93.000000
mean    No         0.159328
        Yes        0.163196
std     No         0.039910
        Yes        0.085119
min     No         0.056797
        Yes        0.035638
25%     No         0.136906
        Yes        0.106771
50%     No         0.155625
        Yes        0.153846
75%     No         0.185014
        Yes        0.195059
max     No         0.291990
        Yes        0.710345
dtype: float64
```

Inside GroupBy, when you invoke a method like describe, it is actually just a shortcut for:

```
def f(group):
    return group.describe()

grouped.apply(f)
```

Suppressing the Group Keys

In the preceding examples, you see that the resulting object has a hierarchical index formed from the group keys, along with the indexes of each piece of the original object. You can disable this by passing group_keys=False to groupby:

```
In [89]: tips.groupby("smoker", group_keys=False).apply(top)
Out[89]:
     total_bill   tip smoker   day    time  size    tip_pct
232       11.61  3.39     No   Sat  Dinner     2   0.291990
149        7.51  2.00     No  Thur   Lunch     2   0.266312
51        10.29  2.60     No   Sun  Dinner     2   0.252672
185       20.69  5.00     No   Sun  Dinner     5   0.241663
88        24.71  5.85     No  Thur   Lunch     2   0.236746
172        7.25  5.15    Yes   Sun  Dinner     2   0.710345
178        9.60  4.00    Yes   Sun  Dinner     2   0.416667
67         3.07  1.00    Yes   Sat  Dinner     1   0.325733
183       23.17  6.50    Yes   Sun  Dinner     4   0.280535
109       14.31  4.00    Yes   Sat  Dinner     2   0.279525
```

Quantile and Bucket Analysis

As you may recall from Chapter 8, pandas has some tools, in particular pandas.cut and pandas.qcut, for slicing data up into buckets with bins of your choosing, or by sample quantiles. Combining these functions with groupby makes it convenient to perform bucket or quantile analysis on a dataset. Consider a simple random dataset and an equal-length bucket categorization using pandas.cut:

```
In [90]: frame = pd.DataFrame({"data1": np.random.standard_normal(1000),
   ....:                       "data2": np.random.standard_normal(1000)})

In [91]: frame.head()
Out[91]:
      data1     data2
0 -0.660524 -0.612905
1  0.862580  0.316447
2 -0.010032  0.838295
3  0.050009 -1.034423
4  0.670216  0.434304

In [92]: quartiles = pd.cut(frame["data1"], 4)

In [93]: quartiles.head(10)
Out[93]:
0    (-1.23, 0.489]
1    (0.489, 2.208]
2    (-1.23, 0.489]
3    (-1.23, 0.489]
4    (0.489, 2.208]
5    (0.489, 2.208]
6    (-1.23, 0.489]
```

```
7     (-1.23, 0.489]
8     (-2.956, -1.23]
9     (-1.23, 0.489]
Name: data1, dtype: category
Categories (4, interval[float64, right]): [(-2.956, -1.23] < (-1.23, 0.489] < (0.
489, 2.208] <

                                          (2.208, 3.928]]
```

The Categorical object returned by cut can be passed directly to groupby. So we could compute a set of group statistics for the quartiles, like so:

```
In [94]: def get_stats(group):
   ....:     return pd.DataFrame(
   ....:         {"min": group.min(), "max": group.max(),
   ....:          "count": group.count(), "mean": group.mean()}
   ....:     )

In [95]: grouped = frame.groupby(quartiles)

In [96]: grouped.apply(get_stats)
Out[96]:
                            min        max  count       mean
data1
(-2.956, -1.23] data1 -2.949343  -1.230179     94  -1.658818
                data2 -3.399312   1.670835     94  -0.033333
(-1.23, 0.489]  data1 -1.228918   0.488675    598  -0.329524
                data2 -2.989741   3.260383    598  -0.002622
(0.489, 2.208]  data1  0.489965   2.200997    298   1.065727
                data2 -3.745356   2.954439    298   0.078249
(2.208, 3.928]  data1  2.212303   3.927528     10   2.644253
                data2 -1.929776   1.765640     10   0.024750
```

Keep in mind the same result could have been computed more simply with:

```
In [97]: grouped.agg(["min", "max", "count", "mean"])
Out[97]:
                     data1                               data2                      \
                       min        max count       mean        min        max count
data1
(-2.956, -1.23] -2.949343  -1.230179    94  -1.658818  -3.399312   1.670835    94
(-1.23, 0.489]  -1.228918   0.488675   598  -0.329524  -2.989741   3.260383   598
(0.489, 2.208]   0.489965   2.200997   298   1.065727  -3.745356   2.954439   298
(2.208, 3.928]   2.212303   3.927528    10   2.644253  -1.929776   1.765640    10


                      mean
data1
(-2.956, -1.23] -0.033333
(-1.23, 0.489]  -0.002622
(0.489, 2.208]   0.078249
(2.208, 3.928]   0.024750
```

These were equal-length buckets; to compute equal-size buckets based on sample quantiles, use pandas.qcut. We can pass 4 as the number of bucket compute sample quartiles, and pass `labels=False` to obtain just the quartile indices instead of intervals:

```
In [98]: quartiles_samp = pd.qcut(frame["data1"], 4, labels=False)

In [99]: quartiles_samp.head()
Out[99]:
0    1
1    3
2    2
3    2
4    3
Name: data1, dtype: int64

In [100]: grouped = frame.groupby(quartiles_samp)

In [101]: grouped.apply(get_stats)
Out[101]:
                    min       max  count       mean
data1
0       data1 -2.949343 -0.685484    250  -1.212173
        data2 -3.399312  2.628441    250  -0.027045
1       data1 -0.683066 -0.030280    250  -0.368334
        data2 -2.630247  3.260383    250  -0.027845
2       data1 -0.027734  0.618965    250   0.295812
        data2 -3.056990  2.458842    250   0.014450
3       data1  0.623587  3.927528    250   1.248875
        data2 -3.745356  2.954439    250   0.115899
```

Example: Filling Missing Values with Group-Specific Values

When cleaning up missing data, in some cases you will remove data observations using `dropna`, but in others you may want to fill in the null (NA) values using a fixed value or some value derived from the data. `fillna` is the right tool to use; for example, here I fill in the null values with the mean:

```
In [102]: s = pd.Series(np.random.standard_normal(6))

In [103]: s[::2] = np.nan

In [104]: s
Out[104]:
0         NaN
1    0.227290
2         NaN
3   -2.153545
4         NaN
5   -0.375842
dtype: float64

In [105]: s.fillna(s.mean())
```

```
Out[105]:
0    -0.767366
1     0.227290
2    -0.767366
3    -2.153545
4    -0.767366
5    -0.375842
dtype: float64
```

Suppose you need the fill value to vary by group. One way to do this is to group the data and use `apply` with a function that calls `fillna` on each data chunk. Here is some sample data on US states divided into eastern and western regions:

```
In [106]: states = ["Ohio", "New York", "Vermont", "Florida",
   .....:           "Oregon", "Nevada", "California", "Idaho"]

In [107]: group_key = ["East", "East", "East", "East",
   .....:              "West", "West", "West", "West"]

In [108]: data = pd.Series(np.random.standard_normal(8), index=states)

In [109]: data
Out[109]:
Ohio          0.329939
New York      0.981994
Vermont       1.105913
Florida      -1.613716
Oregon        1.561587
Nevada        0.406510
California    0.359244
Idaho        -0.614436
dtype: float64
```

Let's set some values in the data to be missing:

```
In [110]: data[["Vermont", "Nevada", "Idaho"]] = np.nan

In [111]: data
Out[111]:
Ohio          0.329939
New York      0.981994
Vermont            NaN
Florida      -1.613716
Oregon        1.561587
Nevada             NaN
California    0.359244
Idaho              NaN
dtype: float64

In [112]: data.groupby(group_key).size()
Out[112]:
East    4
West    4
```

```
dtype: int64

In [113]: data.groupby(group_key).count()
Out[113]:
East    3
West    2
dtype: int64

In [114]: data.groupby(group_key).mean()
Out[114]:
East   -0.100594
West    0.960416
dtype: float64
```

We can fill the NA values using the group means, like so:

```
In [115]: def fill_mean(group):
   .....:     return group.fillna(group.mean())

In [116]: data.groupby(group_key).apply(fill_mean)
Out[116]:
Ohio          0.329939
New York      0.981994
Vermont      -0.100594
Florida      -1.613716
Oregon        1.561587
Nevada        0.960416
California    0.359244
Idaho         0.960416
dtype: float64
```

In another case, you might have predefined fill values in your code that vary by group. Since the groups have a name attribute set internally, we can use that:

```
In [117]: fill_values = {"East": 0.5, "West": -1}

In [118]: def fill_func(group):
   .....:     return group.fillna(fill_values[group.name])

In [119]: data.groupby(group_key).apply(fill_func)
Out[119]:
Ohio          0.329939
New York      0.981994
Vermont       0.500000
Florida      -1.613716
Oregon        1.561587
Nevada       -1.000000
California    0.359244
Idaho        -1.000000
dtype: float64
```

Example: Random Sampling and Permutation

Suppose you wanted to draw a random sample (with or without replacement) from a large dataset for Monte Carlo simulation purposes or some other application. There are a number of ways to perform the "draws"; here we use the `sample` method for Series.

To demonstrate, here's a way to construct a deck of English-style playing cards:

```
suits = ["H", "S", "C", "D"]  # Hearts, Spades, Clubs, Diamonds
card_val = (list(range(1, 11)) + [10] * 3) * 4
base_names = ["A"] + list(range(2, 11)) + ["J", "K", "Q"]
cards = []
for suit in suits:
    cards.extend(str(num) + suit for num in base_names)

deck = pd.Series(card_val, index=cards)
```

Now we have a Series of length 52 whose index contains card names, and values are the ones used in blackjack and other games (to keep things simple, I let the ace "A" be 1):

```
In [121]: deck.head(13)
Out[121]:
AH      1
2H      2
3H      3
4H      4
5H      5
6H      6
7H      7
8H      8
9H      9
10H     10
JH      10
KH      10
QH      10
dtype: int64
```

Now, based on what I said before, drawing a hand of five cards from the deck could be written as:

```
In [122]: def draw(deck, n=5):
    .....:     return deck.sample(n)

In [123]: draw(deck)
Out[123]:
4D      4
QH      10
8S      8
7D      7
```

```
9C     9
dtype: int64
```

Suppose you wanted two random cards from each suit. Because the suit is the last character of each card name, we can group based on this and use `apply`:

```
In [124]: def get_suit(card):
   .....:      # last letter is suit
   .....:      return card[-1]

In [125]: deck.groupby(get_suit).apply(draw, n=2)
Out[125]:
C  6C     6
   KC    10
D  7D     7
   3D     3
H  7H     7
   9H     9
S  2S     2
   QS    10
dtype: int64
```

Alternatively, we could pass `group_keys=False` to drop the outer suit index, leaving in just the selected cards:

```
In [126]: deck.groupby(get_suit, group_keys=False).apply(draw, n=2)
Out[126]:
AC     1
3C     3
5D     5
4D     4
10H   10
7H     7
QS    10
7S     7
dtype: int64
```

Example: Group Weighted Average and Correlation

Under the split-apply-combine paradigm of `groupby`, operations between columns in a DataFrame or two Series, such as a group weighted average, are possible. As an example, take this dataset containing group keys, values, and some weights:

```
In [127]: df = pd.DataFrame({"category": ["a", "a", "a", "a",
   .....:                                 "b", "b", "b", "b"],
   .....:                    "data": np.random.standard_normal(8),
   .....:                    "weights": np.random.uniform(size=8)})

In [128]: df
Out[128]:
  category      data   weights
0        a -1.691656  0.955905
```

```
1        a  0.511622  0.012745
2        a -0.401675  0.137009
3        a  0.968578  0.763037
4        b -1.818215  0.492472
5        b  0.279963  0.832908
6        b -0.200819  0.658331
7        b -0.217221  0.612009
```

The weighted average by `category` would then be:

```
In [129]: grouped = df.groupby("category")

In [130]: def get_wavg(group):
   .....:     return np.average(group["data"], weights=group["weights"])

In [131]: grouped.apply(get_wavg)
Out[131]:
category
a   -0.495807
b   -0.357273
dtype: float64
```

As another example, consider a financial dataset originally obtained from Yahoo! Finance containing end-of-day prices for a few stocks and the S&P 500 index (the SPX symbol):

```
In [132]: close_px = pd.read_csv("examples/stock_px.csv", parse_dates=True,
   .....:                        index_col=0)

In [133]: close_px.info()
<class 'pandas.core.frame.DataFrame'>
DatetimeIndex: 2214 entries, 2003-01-02 to 2011-10-14
Data columns (total 4 columns):
 #   Column  Non-Null Count  Dtype
---  ------  --------------  -----
 0   AAPL    2214 non-null   float64
 1   MSFT    2214 non-null   float64
 2   XOM     2214 non-null   float64
 3   SPX     2214 non-null   float64
dtypes: float64(4)
memory usage: 86.5 KB

In [134]: close_px.tail(4)
Out[134]:
              AAPL    MSFT    XOM      SPX
2011-10-11  400.29   27.00  76.27  1195.54
2011-10-12  402.19   26.96  77.16  1207.25
2011-10-13  408.43   27.18  76.37  1203.66
2011-10-14  422.00   27.27  78.11  1224.58
```

The DataFrame `info()` method here is a convenient way to get an overview of the contents of a DataFrame.

One task of interest might be to compute a DataFrame consisting of the yearly correlations of daily returns (computed from percent changes) with SPX. As one way to do this, we first create a function that computes the pair-wise correlation of each column with the "SPX" column:

```
In [135]: def spx_corr(group):
   .....:        return group.corrwith(group["SPX"])
```

Next, we compute percent change on close_px using pct_change:

```
In [136]: rets = close_px.pct_change().dropna()
```

Lastly, we group these percent changes by year, which can be extracted from each row label with a one-line function that returns the year attribute of each datetime label:

```
In [137]: def get_year(x):
   .....:        return x.year

In [138]: by_year = rets.groupby(get_year)

In [139]: by_year.apply(spx_corr)
Out[139]:
          AAPL      MSFT       XOM  SPX
2003  0.541124  0.745174  0.661265  1.0
2004  0.374283  0.588531  0.557742  1.0
2005  0.467540  0.562374  0.631010  1.0
2006  0.428267  0.406126  0.518514  1.0
2007  0.508118  0.658770  0.786264  1.0
2008  0.681434  0.804626  0.828303  1.0
2009  0.707103  0.654902  0.797921  1.0
2010  0.710105  0.730118  0.839057  1.0
2011  0.691931  0.800996  0.859975  1.0
```

You could also compute intercolumn correlations. Here we compute the annual correlation between Apple and Microsoft:

```
In [140]: def corr_aapl_msft(group):
   .....:        return group["AAPL"].corr(group["MSFT"])

In [141]: by_year.apply(corr_aapl_msft)
Out[141]:
2003    0.480868
2004    0.259024
2005    0.300093
2006    0.161735
2007    0.417738
2008    0.611901
2009    0.432738
2010    0.571946
2011    0.581987
dtype: float64
```

Example: Group-Wise Linear Regression

In the same theme as the previous example, you can use groupby to perform more complex group-wise statistical analysis, as long as the function returns a pandas object or scalar value. For example, I can define the following regress function (using the statsmodels econometrics library), which executes an ordinary least squares (OLS) regression on each chunk of data:

```
import statsmodels.api as sm
def regress(data, yvar=None, xvars=None):
    Y = data[yvar]
    X = data[xvars]
    X["intercept"] = 1.
    result = sm.OLS(Y, X).fit()
    return result.params
```

You can install statsmodels with conda if you don't have it already:

```
conda install statsmodels
```

Now, to run a yearly linear regression of AAPL on SPX returns, execute:

```
In [143]: by_year.apply(regress, yvar="AAPL", xvars=["SPX"])
Out[143]:
           SPX  intercept
2003  1.195406   0.000710
2004  1.363463   0.004201
2005  1.766415   0.003246
2006  1.645496   0.000080
2007  1.198761   0.003438
2008  0.968016  -0.001110
2009  0.879103   0.002954
2010  1.052608   0.001261
2011  0.806605   0.001514
```

10.4 Group Transforms and "Unwrapped" GroupBys

In Section 10.3, "Apply: General split-apply-combine," on page 335, we looked at the apply method in grouped operations for performing transformations. There is another built-in method called transform, which is similar to apply but imposes more constraints on the kind of function you can use:

- It can produce a scalar value to be broadcast to the shape of the group.
- It can produce an object of the same shape as the input group.
- It must not mutate its input.

Let's consider a simple example for illustration:

```
In [144]: df = pd.DataFrame({'key': ['a', 'b', 'c'] * 4,
   .....:                     'value': np.arange(12.)})

In [145]: df
Out[145]:
   key  value
0    a    0.0
1    b    1.0
2    c    2.0
3    a    3.0
4    b    4.0
5    c    5.0
6    a    6.0
7    b    7.0
8    c    8.0
9    a    9.0
10   b   10.0
11   c   11.0
```

Here are the group means by key:

```
In [146]: g = df.groupby('key')['value']

In [147]: g.mean()
Out[147]:
key
a    4.5
b    5.5
c    6.5
Name: value, dtype: float64
```

Suppose instead we wanted to produce a Series of the same shape as df['value'] but with values replaced by the average grouped by 'key'. We can pass a function that computes the mean of a single group to transform:

```
In [148]: def get_mean(group):
   .....:     return group.mean()

In [149]: g.transform(get_mean)
Out[149]:
0     4.5
1     5.5
2     6.5
3     4.5
4     5.5
5     6.5
6     4.5
7     5.5
8     6.5
9     4.5
10    5.5
11    6.5
Name: value, dtype: float64
```

For built-in aggregation functions, we can pass a string alias as with the GroupBy agg method:

```
In [150]: g.transform('mean')
Out[150]:
0      4.5
1      5.5
2      6.5
3      4.5
4      5.5
5      6.5
6      4.5
7      5.5
8      6.5          .
9      4.5
10     5.5
11     6.5
Name: value, dtype: float64
```

Like apply, transform works with functions that return Series, but the result must be the same size as the input. For example, we can multiply each group by 2 using a helper function:

```
In [151]: def times_two(group):
   .....:     return group * 2

In [152]: g.transform(times_two)
Out[152]:
0       0.0
1       2.0
2       4.0
3       6.0
4       8.0
5      10.0
6      12.0
7      14.0
8      16.0
9      18.0
10     20.0
11     22.0
Name: value, dtype: float64
```

As a more complicated example, we can compute the ranks in descending order for each group:

```
In [153]: def get_ranks(group):
   .....:     return group.rank(ascending=False)

In [154]: g.transform(get_ranks)
Out[154]:
0       4.0
1       4.0
2       4.0
```

```
3     3.0
4     3.0
5     3.0
6     2.0
7     2.0
8     2.0
9     1.0
10    1.0
11    1.0
Name: value, dtype: float64
```

Consider a group transformation function composed from simple aggregations:

```
In [155]: def normalize(x):
   .....:     return (x - x.mean()) / x.std()
```

We can obtain equivalent results in this case using either transform or apply:

```
In [156]: g.transform(normalize)
Out[156]:
0     -1.161895
1     -1.161895
2     -1.161895
3     -0.387298
4     -0.387298
5     -0.387298
6      0.387298
7      0.387298
8      0.387298
9      1.161895
10     1.161895
11     1.161895
Name: value, dtype: float64

In [157]: g.apply(normalize)
Out[157]:
0     -1.161895
1     -1.161895
2     -1.161895
3     -0.387298
4     -0.387298
5     -0.387298
6      0.387298
7      0.387298
8      0.387298
9      1.161895
10     1.161895
11     1.161895
Name: value, dtype: float64
```

Built-in aggregate functions like 'mean' or 'sum' are often much faster than a general apply function. These also have a "fast path" when used with transform. This allows us to perform what is called an *unwrapped* group operation:

```
In [158]: g.transform('mean')
Out[158]:
0     4.5
1     5.5
2     6.5
3     4.5
4     5.5
5     6.5
6     4.5
7     5.5
8     6.5
9     4.5
10    5.5
11    6.5
Name: value, dtype: float64

In [159]: normalized = (df['value'] - g.transform('mean')) / g.transform('std')

In [160]: normalized
Out[160]:
0    -1.161895
1    -1.161895
2    -1.161895
3    -0.387298
4    -0.387298
5    -0.387298
6     0.387298
7     0.387298
8     0.387298
9     1.161895
10    1.161895
11    1.161895
Name: value, dtype: float64
```

Here, we are doing arithmetic between the outputs of multiple GroupBy operations instead of writing a function and passing it to `groupby(...).apply`. That is what is meant by "unwrapped."

While an unwrapped group operation may involve multiple group aggregations, the overall benefit of vectorized operations often outweighs this.

10.5 Pivot Tables and Cross-Tabulation

A *pivot table* is a data summarization tool frequently found in spreadsheet programs and other data analysis software. It aggregates a table of data by one or more keys, arranging the data in a rectangle with some of the group keys along the rows and some along the columns. Pivot tables in Python with pandas are made possible through the `groupby` facility described in this chapter, combined with reshape operations utilizing hierarchical indexing. DataFrame also has a `pivot_table` method, and there is also a top-level pandas.pivot_table function. In addition to providing a convenience interface to groupby, pivot_table can add partial totals, also known as *margins*.

Returning to the tipping dataset, suppose you wanted to compute a table of group means (the default pivot_table aggregation type) arranged by day and smoker on the rows:

```
In [161]: tips.head()
Out[161]:
   total_bill   tip smoker  day    time  size    tip_pct
0       16.99  1.01     No  Sun  Dinner     2   0.059447
1       10.34  1.66     No  Sun  Dinner     3   0.160542
2       21.01  3.50     No  Sun  Dinner     3   0.166587
3       23.68  3.31     No  Sun  Dinner     2   0.139780
4       24.59  3.61     No  Sun  Dinner     4   0.146808

In [162]: tips.pivot_table(index=["day", "smoker"])
Out[162]:
                 size       tip   tip_pct  total_bill
day  smoker
Fri  No      2.250000  2.812500  0.151650   18.420000
     Yes     2.066667  2.714000  0.174783   16.813333
Sat  No      2.555556  3.102889  0.158048   19.661778
     Yes     2.476190  2.875476  0.147906   21.276667
Sun  No      2.929825  3.167895  0.160113   20.506667
     Yes     2.578947  3.516842  0.187250   24.120000
Thur No      2.488889  2.673778  0.160298   17.113111
     Yes     2.352941  3.030000  0.163863   19.190588
```

This could have been produced with groupby directly, using tips.groupby(["day", "smoker"]).mean(). Now, suppose we want to take the average of only tip_pct and size, and additionally group by time. I'll put smoker in the table columns and time and day in the rows:

```
In [163]: tips.pivot_table(index=["time", "day"], columns="smoker",
   .....:                   values=["tip_pct", "size"])
Out[163]:
                  size              tip_pct
smoker              No       Yes        No       Yes
time   day
Dinner Fri    2.000000  2.222222  0.139622  0.165347
       Sat    2.555556  2.476190  0.158048  0.147906
       Sun    2.929825  2.578947  0.160113  0.187250
       Thur   2.000000       NaN  0.159744       NaN
Lunch  Fri    3.000000  1.833333  0.187735  0.188937
       Thur   2.500000  2.352941  0.160311  0.163863
```

We could augment this table to include partial totals by passing margins=True. This has the effect of adding All row and column labels, with corresponding values being the group statistics for all the data within a single tier:

```
In [164]: tips.pivot_table(index=["time", "day"], columns="smoker",
   .....:                  values=["tip_pct", "size"], margins=True)
Out[164]:
                    size                          tip_pct
smoker                No       Yes       All          No       Yes       All
time   day
Dinner Fri     2.000000  2.222222  2.166667    0.139622  0.165347  0.158916
       Sat     2.555556  2.476190  2.517241    0.158048  0.147906  0.153152
       Sun     2.929825  2.578947  2.842105    0.160113  0.187250  0.166897
       Thur    2.000000       NaN  2.000000    0.159744       NaN  0.159744
Lunch  Fri     3.000000  1.833333  2.000000    0.187735  0.188937  0.188765
       Thur    2.500000  2.352941  2.459016    0.160311  0.163863  0.161301
All            2.668874  2.408602  2.569672    0.159328  0.163196  0.160803
```

Here, the All values are means without taking into account smoker versus non-smoker (the All columns) or any of the two levels of grouping on the rows (the All row).

To use an aggregation function other than mean, pass it to the aggfunc keyword argument. For example, "count" or len will give you a cross-tabulation (count or frequency) of group sizes (though "count" will exclude null values from the count within data groups, while len will not):

```
In [165]: tips.pivot_table(index=["time", "smoker"], columns="day",
   .....:                  values="tip_pct", aggfunc=len, margins=True)
Out[165]:
day            Fri   Sat   Sun  Thur  All
time   smoker
Dinner No      3.0  45.0  57.0   1.0  106
       Yes     9.0  42.0  19.0   NaN   70
Lunch  No      1.0   NaN   NaN  44.0   45
       Yes     6.0   NaN   NaN  17.0   23
All           19.0  87.0  76.0  62.0  244
```

If some combinations are empty (or otherwise NA), you may wish to pass a fill_value:

```
In [166]: tips.pivot_table(index=["time", "size", "smoker"], columns="day",
   .....:                  values="tip_pct", fill_value=0)
Out[166]:
day                      Fri       Sat       Sun      Thur
time   size smoker
Dinner 1    No      0.000000  0.137931  0.000000  0.000000
            Yes     0.000000  0.325733  0.000000  0.000000
       2    No      0.139622  0.162705  0.168859  0.159744
            Yes     0.171297  0.148668  0.207893  0.000000
       3    No      0.000000  0.154661  0.152663  0.000000
...                      ...       ...       ...       ...
Lunch  3    Yes     0.000000  0.000000  0.000000  0.204952
       4    No      0.000000  0.000000  0.000000  0.138919
            Yes     0.000000  0.000000  0.000000  0.155410
       5    No      0.000000  0.000000  0.000000  0.121389
```

```
    6    No      0.000000   0.000000   0.000000   0.173706
[21 rows x 4 columns]
```

See Table 10-2 for a summary of `pivot_table` options.

Table 10-2. pivot_table options

Argument	Description
`values`	Column name or names to aggregate; by default, aggregates all numeric columns
`index`	Column names or other group keys to group on the rows of the resulting pivot table
`columns`	Column names or other group keys to group on the columns of the resulting pivot table
`aggfunc`	Aggregation function or list of functions (`"mean"` by default); can be any function valid in a `groupby` context
`fill_value`	Replace missing values in the result table
`dropna`	If `True`, do not include columns whose entries are all NA
`margins`	Add row/column subtotals and grand total (`False` by default)
`margins_name`	Name to use for the margin row/column labels when passing `margins=True`; defaults to `"All"`
`observed`	With Categorical group keys, if `True`, show only the observed category values in the keys rather than all categories

Cross-Tabulations: Crosstab

A *cross-tabulation* (or *crosstab* for short) is a special case of a pivot table that computes group frequencies. Here is an example:

```
In [167]: from io import StringIO

In [168]: data = """Sample  Nationality  Handedness
    ....: 1   USA  Right-handed
    ....: 2   Japan    Left-handed
    ....: 3   USA  Right-handed
    ....: 4   Japan    Right-handed
    ....: 5   Japan    Left-handed
    ....: 6   Japan    Right-handed
    ....: 7   USA  Right-handed
    ....: 8   USA  Left-handed
    ....: 9   Japan    Right-handed
    ....: 10  USA  Right-handed"""
    ....:

In [169]: data = pd.read_table(StringIO(data), sep="\s+")

In [170]: data
Out[170]:
    Sample Nationality   Handedness
0     1           USA  Right-handed
1     2         Japan   Left-handed
2     3           USA  Right-handed
3     4         Japan  Right-handed
4     5         Japan   Left-handed
```

```
5      6        Japan  Right-handed
6      7          USA  Right-handed
7      8          USA   Left-handed
8      9        Japan  Right-handed
9     10          USA  Right-handed
```

As part of some survey analysis, we might want to summarize this data by nationality and handedness. You could use `pivot_table` to do this, but the `pandas.crosstab` function can be more convenient:

```
In [171]: pd.crosstab(data["Nationality"], data["Handedness"], margins=True)
Out[171]:
Handedness   Left-handed  Right-handed  All
Nationality
Japan                  2             3    5
USA                    1             4    5
All                    3             7   10
```

The first two arguments to `crosstab` can each be an array or Series or a list of arrays. As in the tips data:

```
In [172]: pd.crosstab([tips["time"], tips["day"]], tips["smoker"], margins=True)
Out[172]:
smoker         No  Yes  All
time   day
Dinner Fri      3    9   12
       Sat     45   42   87
       Sun     57   19   76
       Thur     1    0    1
Lunch  Fri      1    6    7
       Thur    44   17   61
All           151   93  244
```

10.6 Conclusion

Mastering pandas's data grouping tools can help with data cleaning and modeling or statistical analysis work. In Chapter 13 we will look at several more example use cases for groupby on real data.

In the next chapter, we turn our attention to time series data.

Time Series

Time series data is an important form of structured data in many different fields, such as finance, economics, ecology, neuroscience, and physics. Anything that is recorded repeatedly at many points in time forms a time series. Many time series are *fixed frequency*, which is to say that data points occur at regular intervals according to some rule, such as every 15 seconds, every 5 minutes, or once per month. Time series can also be *irregular* without a fixed unit of time or offset between units. How you mark and refer to time series data depends on the application, and you may have one of the following:

Timestamps
    Specific instants in time.

Fixed periods
    Such as the whole month of January 2017, or the whole year 2020.

Intervals of time
    Indicated by a start and end timestamp. Periods can be thought of as special cases of intervals.

Experiment or elapsed time
    Each timestamp is a measure of time relative to a particular start time (e.g., the diameter of a cookie baking each second since being placed in the oven), starting from 0.

In this chapter, I am mainly concerned with time series in the first three categories, though many of the techniques can be applied to experimental time series where the index may be an integer or floating-point number indicating elapsed time from the start of the experiment. The simplest kind of time series is indexed by timestamp.

pandas also supports indexes based on timedeltas, which can be a useful way of representing experiment or elapsed time. We do not explore timedelta indexes in this book, but you can learn more in the pandas documentation (*https://pandas.pydata.org*).

pandas provides many built-in time series tools and algorithms. You can efficiently work with large time series, and slice and dice, aggregate, and resample irregular- and fixed-frequency time series. Some of these tools are useful for financial and economics applications, but you could certainly use them to analyze server log data, too.

As with the rest of the chapters, we start by importing NumPy and pandas:

```
In [12]: import numpy as np

In [13]: import pandas as pd
```

11.1 Date and Time Data Types and Tools

The Python standard library includes data types for date and time data, as well as calendar-related functionality. The datetime, time, and calendar modules are the main places to start. The datetime.datetime type, or simply datetime, is widely used:

```
In [14]: from datetime import datetime

In [15]: now = datetime.now()

In [16]: now
Out[16]: datetime.datetime(2022, 8, 12, 14, 9, 11, 337033)

In [17]: now.year, now.month, now.day
Out[17]: (2022, 8, 12)
```

datetime stores both the date and time down to the microsecond. datetime.time delta, or simply timedelta, represents the temporal difference between two date time objects:

```
In [18]: delta = datetime(2011, 1, 7) - datetime(2008, 6, 24, 8, 15)

In [19]: delta
Out[19]: datetime.timedelta(days=926, seconds=56700)

In [20]: delta.days
Out[20]: 926

In [21]: delta.seconds
Out[21]: 56700
```

You can add (or subtract) a `timedelta` or multiple thereof to a `datetime` object to yield a new shifted object:

```
In [22]: from datetime import timedelta

In [23]: start = datetime(2011, 1, 7)

In [24]: start + timedelta(12)
Out[24]: datetime.datetime(2011, 1, 19, 0, 0)

In [25]: start - 2 * timedelta(12)
Out[25]: datetime.datetime(2010, 12, 14, 0, 0)
```

Table 11-1 summarizes the data types in the `datetime` module. While this chapter is mainly concerned with the data types in pandas and higher-level time series manipulation, you may encounter the `datetime`-based types in many other places in Python in the wild.

Table 11-1. Types in the datetime module

Type	Description
date	Store calendar date (year, month, day) using the Gregorian calendar
time	Store time of day as hours, minutes, seconds, and microseconds
datetime	Store both date and time
timedelta	The difference between two `datetime` values (as days, seconds, and microseconds)
tzinfo	Base type for storing time zone information

Converting Between String and Datetime

You can format `datetime` objects and pandas `Timestamp` objects, which I'll introduce later, as strings using `str` or the `strftime` method, passing a format specification:

```
In [26]: stamp = datetime(2011, 1, 3)

In [27]: str(stamp)
Out[27]: '2011-01-03 00:00:00'

In [28]: stamp.strftime("%Y-%m-%d")
Out[28]: '2011-01-03'
```

See Table 11-2 for a complete list of the format codes.

Table 11-2. datetime format specification (ISO C89 compatible)

Type	Description
%Y	Four-digit year
%y	Two-digit year
%m	Two-digit month [01, 12]

Type	Description
%d	Two-digit day [01, 31]
%H	Hour (24-hour clock) [00, 23]
%I	Hour (12-hour clock) [01, 12]
%M	Two-digit minute [00, 59]
%S	Second [00, 61] (seconds 60, 61 account for leap seconds)
%f	Microsecond as an integer, zero-padded (from 000000 to 999999)
%j	Day of the year as a zero-padded integer (from 001 to 336)
%w	Weekday as an integer [0 (Sunday), 6]
%u	Weekday as an integer starting from 1, where 1 is Monday.
%U	Week number of the year [00, 53]; Sunday is considered the first day of the week, and days before the first Sunday of the year are "week 0"
%W	Week number of the year [00, 53]; Monday is considered the first day of the week, and days before the first Monday of the year are "week 0"
%z	UTC time zone offset as +HHMM or -HHMM; empty if time zone naive
%Z	Time zone name as a string, or empty string if no time zone
%F	Shortcut for %Y-%m-%d (e.g., 2012-4-18)
%D	Shortcut for %m/%d/%y (e.g., 04/18/12)

You can use many of the same format codes to convert strings to dates using date time.strptime (but some codes, like %F, cannot be used):

```
In [29]: value = "2011-01-03"

In [30]: datetime.strptime(value, "%Y-%m-%d")
Out[30]: datetime.datetime(2011, 1, 3, 0, 0)

In [31]: datestrs = ["7/6/2011", "8/6/2011"]

In [32]: [datetime.strptime(x, "%m/%d/%Y") for x in datestrs]
Out[32]:
[datetime.datetime(2011, 7, 6, 0, 0),
 datetime.datetime(2011, 8, 6, 0, 0)]
```

datetime.strptime is one way to parse a date with a known format.

pandas is generally oriented toward working with arrays of dates, whether used as an axis index or a column in a DataFrame. The pandas.to_datetime method parses many different kinds of date representations. Standard date formats like ISO 8601 can be parsed quickly:

```
In [33]: datestrs = ["2011-07-06 12:00:00", "2011-08-06 00:00:00"]

In [34]: pd.to_datetime(datestrs)
Out[34]: DatetimeIndex(['2011-07-06 12:00:00', '2011-08-06 00:00:00'], dtype='dat
etime64[ns]', freq=None)
```

It also handles values that should be considered missing (None, empty string, etc.):

```
In [35]: idx = pd.to_datetime(datestrs + [None])

In [36]: idx
Out[36]: DatetimeIndex(['2011-07-06 12:00:00', '2011-08-06 00:00:00', 'NaT'], dty
pe='datetime64[ns]', freq=None)

In [37]: idx[2]
Out[37]: NaT

In [38]: pd.isna(idx)
Out[38]: array([False, False,  True])
```

NaT (Not a Time) is pandas's null value for timestamp data.

> dateutil.parser is a useful but imperfect tool. Notably, it will recognize some strings as dates that you might prefer that it didn't; for example, "42" will be parsed as the year 2042 with today's calendar date.

datetime objects also have a number of locale-specific formatting options for systems in other countries or languages. For example, the abbreviated month names will be different on German or French systems compared with English systems. See Table 11-3 for a listing.

Table 11-3. Locale-specific date formatting

Type	Description
%a	Abbreviated weekday name
%A	Full weekday name
%b	Abbreviated month name
%B	Full month name
%c	Full date and time (e.g., 'Tue 01 May 2012 04:20:57 PM')
%p	Locale equivalent of AM or PM
%x	Locale-appropriate formatted date (e.g., in the United States, May 1, 2012 yields '05/01/2012')
%X	Locale-appropriate time (e.g., '04:24:12 PM')

11.2 Time Series Basics

A basic kind of time series object in pandas is a Series indexed by timestamps, which is often represented outside of pandas as Python strings or datetime objects:

```
In [39]: dates = [datetime(2011, 1, 2), datetime(2011, 1, 5),
   ....:          datetime(2011, 1, 7), datetime(2011, 1, 8),
   ....:          datetime(2011, 1, 10), datetime(2011, 1, 12)]
```

```
In [40]: ts = pd.Series(np.random.standard_normal(6), index=dates)

In [41]: ts
Out[41]:
2011-01-02    -0.204708
2011-01-05     0.478943
2011-01-07    -0.519439
2011-01-08    -0.555730
2011-01-10     1.965781
2011-01-12     1.393406
dtype: float64
```

Under the hood, these `datetime` objects have been put in a `DatetimeIndex`:

```
In [42]: ts.index
Out[42]:
DatetimeIndex(['2011-01-02', '2011-01-05', '2011-01-07', '2011-01-08',
               '2011-01-10', '2011-01-12'],
              dtype='datetime64[ns]', freq=None)
```

Like other Series, arithmetic operations between differently indexed time series automatically align on the dates:

```
In [43]: ts + ts[::2]
Out[43]:
2011-01-02    -0.409415
2011-01-05          NaN
2011-01-07    -1.038877
2011-01-08          NaN
2011-01-10     3.931561
2011-01-12          NaN
dtype: float64
```

Recall that `ts[::2]` selects every second element in `ts`.

pandas stores timestamps using NumPy's `datetime64` data type at the nanosecond resolution:

```
In [44]: ts.index.dtype
Out[44]: dtype('<M8[ns]')
```

Scalar values from a `DatetimeIndex` are pandas `Timestamp` objects:

```
In [45]: stamp = ts.index[0]

In [46]: stamp
Out[46]: Timestamp('2011-01-02 00:00:00')
```

A `pandas.Timestamp` can be substituted most places where you would use a `datetime` object. The reverse is not true, however, because `pandas.Timestamp` can store nanosecond precision data, while `datetime` stores only up to microseconds. Additionally, `pandas.Timestamp` can store frequency information (if any) and understands how to do time zone conversions and other kinds of manipulations. More on both of these things later in Section 11.4, "Time Zone Handling," on page 374.

Indexing, Selection, Subsetting

Time series behaves like any other Series when you are indexing and selecting data based on the label:

```
In [47]: stamp = ts.index[2]

In [48]: ts[stamp]
Out[48]: -0.5194387150567381
```

As a convenience, you can also pass a string that is interpretable as a date:

```
In [49]: ts["2011-01-10"]
Out[49]: 1.9657805725027142
```

For longer time series, a year or only a year and month can be passed to easily select slices of data (pandas.date_range is discussed in more detail in "Generating Date Ranges" on page 367):

```
In [50]: longer_ts = pd.Series(np.random.standard_normal(1000),
   ....:                       index=pd.date_range("2000-01-01", periods=1000))

In [51]: longer_ts
Out[51]:
2000-01-01    0.092908
2000-01-02    0.281746
2000-01-03    0.769023
2000-01-04    1.246435
2000-01-05    1.007189
                ...
2002-09-22    0.930944
2002-09-23   -0.811676
2002-09-24   -1.830156
2002-09-25   -0.138730
2002-09-26    0.334088
Freq: D, Length: 1000, dtype: float64

In [52]: longer_ts["2001"]
Out[52]:
2001-01-01    1.599534
2001-01-02    0.474071
2001-01-03    0.151326
2001-01-04   -0.542173
2001-01-05   -0.475496
                ...
2001-12-27    0.057874
2001-12-28   -0.433739
2001-12-29    0.092698
2001-12-30   -1.397820
```

```
2001-12-31    1.457823
Freq: D, Length: 365, dtype: float64
```

Here, the string `"2001"` is interpreted as a year and selects that time period. This also works if you specify the month:

```
In [53]: longer_ts["2001-05"]
Out[53]:
2001-05-01    -0.622547
2001-05-02     0.936289
2001-05-03     0.750018
2001-05-04    -0.056715
2001-05-05     2.300675
                 ...
2001-05-27     0.235477
2001-05-28     0.111835
2001-05-29    -1.251504
2001-05-30    -2.949343
2001-05-31     0.634634
Freq: D, Length: 31, dtype: float64
```

Slicing with `datetime` objects works as well:

```
In [54]: ts[datetime(2011, 1, 7):]
Out[54]:
2011-01-07    -0.519439
2011-01-08    -0.555730
2011-01-10     1.965781
2011-01-12     1.393406
dtype: float64

In [55]: ts[datetime(2011, 1, 7):datetime(2011, 1, 10)]
Out[55]:
2011-01-07    -0.519439
2011-01-08    -0.555730
2011-01-10     1.965781
dtype: float64
```

Because most time series data is ordered chronologically, you can slice with time-stamps not contained in a time series to perform a range query:

```
In [56]: ts
Out[56]:
2011-01-02    -0.204708
2011-01-05     0.478943
2011-01-07    -0.519439
2011-01-08    -0.555730
2011-01-10     1.965781
2011-01-12     1.393406
dtype: float64

In [57]: ts["2011-01-06":"2011-01-11"]
Out[57]:
2011-01-07    -0.519439
```

```
2011-01-08    -0.555730
2011-01-10     1.965781
dtype: float64
```

As before, you can pass a string date, datetime, or timestamp. Remember that slicing in this manner produces views on the source time series, like slicing NumPy arrays. This means that no data is copied, and modifications on the slice will be reflected in the original data.

There is an equivalent instance method, truncate, that slices a Series between two dates:

```
In [58]: ts.truncate(after="2011-01-09")
Out[58]:
2011-01-02    -0.204708
2011-01-05     0.478943
2011-01-07    -0.519439
2011-01-08    -0.555730
dtype: float64
```

All of this holds true for DataFrame as well, indexing on its rows:

```
In [59]: dates = pd.date_range("2000-01-01", periods=100, freq="W-WED")

In [60]: long_df = pd.DataFrame(np.random.standard_normal((100, 4)),
   ....:                        index=dates,
   ....:                        columns=["Colorado", "Texas",
   ....:                                 "New York", "Ohio"])

In [61]: long_df.loc["2001-05"]
Out[61]:
            Colorado     Texas  New York      Ohio
2001-05-02 -0.006045  0.490094 -0.277186 -0.707213
2001-05-09 -0.560107  2.735527  0.927335  1.513906
2001-05-16  0.538600  1.273768  0.667876 -0.969206
2001-05-23  1.676091 -0.817649  0.050188  1.951312
2001-05-30  3.260383  0.963301  1.201206 -1.852001
```

Time Series with Duplicate Indices

In some applications, there may be multiple data observations falling on a particular timestamp. Here is an example:

```
In [62]: dates = pd.DatetimeIndex(["2000-01-01", "2000-01-02", "2000-01-02",
   ....:                           "2000-01-02", "2000-01-03"])

In [63]: dup_ts = pd.Series(np.arange(5), index=dates)

In [64]: dup_ts
Out[64]:
2000-01-01    0
2000-01-02    1
```

```
2000-01-02    2
2000-01-02    3
2000-01-03    4
dtype: int64
```

We can tell that the index is not unique by checking its `is_unique` property:

```
In [65]: dup_ts.index.is_unique
Out[65]: False
```

Indexing into this time series will now either produce scalar values or slices, depending on whether a timestamp is duplicated:

```
In [66]: dup_ts["2000-01-03"]  # not duplicated
Out[66]: 4

In [67]: dup_ts["2000-01-02"]  # duplicated
Out[67]:
2000-01-02    1
2000-01-02    2
2000-01-02    3
dtype: int64
```

Suppose you wanted to aggregate the data having nonunique timestamps. One way to do this is to use `groupby` and pass `level=0` (the one and only level):

```
In [68]: grouped = dup_ts.groupby(level=0)

In [69]: grouped.mean()
Out[69]:
2000-01-01    0.0
2000-01-02    2.0
2000-01-03    4.0
dtype: float64

In [70]: grouped.count()
Out[70]:
2000-01-01    1
2000-01-02    3
2000-01-03    1
dtype: int64
```

11.3 Date Ranges, Frequencies, and Shifting

Generic time series in pandas are assumed to be irregular; that is, they have no fixed frequency. For many applications this is sufficient. However, it's often desirable to work relative to a fixed frequency, such as daily, monthly, or every 15 minutes, even if that means introducing missing values into a time series. Fortunately, pandas has a full suite of standard time series frequencies and tools for resampling (discussed in more detail later in Section 11.6, "Resampling and Frequency Conversion," on page

387), inferring frequencies, and generating fixed-frequency date ranges. For example, you can convert the sample time series to fixed daily frequency by calling `resample`:

```
In [71]: ts
Out[71]:
2011-01-02   -0.204708
2011-01-05    0.478943
2011-01-07   -0.519439
2011-01-08   -0.555730
2011-01-10    1.965781
2011-01-12    1.393406
dtype: float64

In [72]: resampler = ts.resample("D")

In [73]: resampler
Out[73]: <pandas.core.resample.DatetimeIndexResampler object at 0x7febd896bc40>
```

The string "D" is interpreted as daily frequency.

Conversion between frequencies or *resampling* is a big enough topic to have its own section later (Section 11.6, "Resampling and Frequency Conversion," on page 387). Here, I'll show you how to use the base frequencies and multiples thereof.

Generating Date Ranges

While I used it previously without explanation, `pandas.date_range` is responsible for generating a `DatetimeIndex` with an indicated length according to a particular frequency:

```
In [74]: index = pd.date_range("2012-04-01", "2012-06-01")

In [75]: index
Out[75]:
DatetimeIndex(['2012-04-01', '2012-04-02', '2012-04-03', '2012-04-04',
               '2012-04-05', '2012-04-06', '2012-04-07', '2012-04-08',
               '2012-04-09', '2012-04-10', '2012-04-11', '2012-04-12',
               '2012-04-13', '2012-04-14', '2012-04-15', '2012-04-16',
               '2012-04-17', '2012-04-18', '2012-04-19', '2012-04-20',
               '2012-04-21', '2012-04-22', '2012-04-23', '2012-04-24',
               '2012-04-25', '2012-04-26', '2012-04-27', '2012-04-28',
               '2012-04-29', '2012-04-30', '2012-05-01', '2012-05-02',
               '2012-05-03', '2012-05-04', '2012-05-05', '2012-05-06',
               '2012-05-07', '2012-05-08', '2012-05-09', '2012-05-10',
               '2012-05-11', '2012-05-12', '2012-05-13', '2012-05-14',
               '2012-05-15', '2012-05-16', '2012-05-17', '2012-05-18',
               '2012-05-19', '2012-05-20', '2012-05-21', '2012-05-22',
               '2012-05-23', '2012-05-24', '2012-05-25', '2012-05-26',
               '2012-05-27', '2012-05-28', '2012-05-29', '2012-05-30',
               '2012-05-31', '2012-06-01'],
              dtype='datetime64[ns]', freq='D')
```

By default, pandas.date_range generates daily timestamps. If you pass only a start or end date, you must pass a number of periods to generate:

```
In [76]: pd.date_range(start="2012-04-01", periods=20)
Out[76]:
DatetimeIndex(['2012-04-01', '2012-04-02', '2012-04-03', '2012-04-04',
               '2012-04-05', '2012-04-06', '2012-04-07', '2012-04-08',
               '2012-04-09', '2012-04-10', '2012-04-11', '2012-04-12',
               '2012-04-13', '2012-04-14', '2012-04-15', '2012-04-16',
               '2012-04-17', '2012-04-18', '2012-04-19', '2012-04-20'],
              dtype='datetime64[ns]', freq='D')

In [77]: pd.date_range(end="2012-06-01", periods=20)
Out[77]:
DatetimeIndex(['2012-05-13', '2012-05-14', '2012-05-15', '2012-05-16',
               '2012-05-17', '2012-05-18', '2012-05-19', '2012-05-20',
               '2012-05-21', '2012-05-22', '2012-05-23', '2012-05-24',
               '2012-05-25', '2012-05-26', '2012-05-27', '2012-05-28',
               '2012-05-29', '2012-05-30', '2012-05-31', '2012-06-01'],
              dtype='datetime64[ns]', freq='D')
```

The start and end dates define strict boundaries for the generated date index. For example, if you wanted a date index containing the last business day of each month, you would pass the "BM" frequency (business end of month; see a more complete listing of frequencies in Table 11-4), and only dates falling on or inside the date interval will be included:

```
In [78]: pd.date_range("2000-01-01", "2000-12-01", freq="BM")
Out[78]:
DatetimeIndex(['2000-01-31', '2000-02-29', '2000-03-31', '2000-04-28',
               '2000-05-31', '2000-06-30', '2000-07-31', '2000-08-31',
               '2000-09-29', '2000-10-31', '2000-11-30'],
              dtype='datetime64[ns]', freq='BM')
```

Table 11-4. Base time series frequencies (not comprehensive)

Alias	Offset type	Description
D	Day	Calendar daily
B	BusinessDay	Business daily
H	Hour	Hourly
T or min	Minute	Once a minute
S	Second	Once a second
L or ms	Milli	Millisecond (1/1,000 of 1 second)
U	Micro	Microsecond (1/1,000,000 of 1 second)
M	MonthEnd	Last calendar day of month
BM	BusinessMonthEnd	Last business day (weekday) of month
MS	MonthBegin	First calendar day of month
BMS	BusinessMonthBegin	First weekday of month

Alias	Offset type	Description
W-MON, W-TUE, ...	Week	Weekly on given day of week (MON, TUE, WED, THU, FRI, SAT, or SUN)
WOM-1MON, WOM-2MON, ...	WeekOfMonth	Generate weekly dates in the first, second, third, or fourth week of the month (e.g., WOM-3FRI for the third Friday of each month)
Q-JAN, Q-FEB, ...	QuarterEnd	Quarterly dates anchored on last calendar day of each month, for year ending in indicated month (JAN, FEB, MAR, APR, MAY, JUN, JUL, AUG, SEP, OCT, NOV, or DEC)
BQ-JAN, BQ-FEB, ...	BusinessQuarterEnd	Quarterly dates anchored on last weekday day of each month, for year ending in indicated month
QS-JAN, QS-FEB, ...	QuarterBegin	Quarterly dates anchored on first calendar day of each month, for year ending in indicated month
BQS-JAN, BQS-FEB, ...	BusinessQuarterBegin	Quarterly dates anchored on first weekday day of each month, for year ending in indicated month
A-JAN, A-FEB, ...	YearEnd	Annual dates anchored on last calendar day of given month (JAN, FEB, MAR, APR, MAY, JUN, JUL, AUG, SEP, OCT, NOV, or DEC)
BA-JAN, BA-FEB, ...	BusinessYearEnd	Annual dates anchored on last weekday of given month
AS-JAN, AS-FEB, ...	YearBegin	Annual dates anchored on first day of given month
BAS-JAN, BAS-FEB, ...	BusinessYearBegin	Annual dates anchored on first weekday of given month

pandas.date_range by default preserves the time (if any) of the start or end time-stamp:

```
In [79]: pd.date_range("2012-05-02 12:56:31", periods=5)
Out[79]:
DatetimeIndex(['2012-05-02 12:56:31', '2012-05-03 12:56:31',
               '2012-05-04 12:56:31', '2012-05-05 12:56:31',
               '2012-05-06 12:56:31'],
              dtype='datetime64[ns]', freq='D')
```

Sometimes you will have start or end dates with time information but want to generate a set of timestamps *normalized* to midnight as a convention. To do this, there is a normalize option:

```
In [80]: pd.date_range("2012-05-02 12:56:31", periods=5, normalize=True)
Out[80]:
DatetimeIndex(['2012-05-02', '2012-05-03', '2012-05-04', '2012-05-05',
               '2012-05-06'],
              dtype='datetime64[ns]', freq='D')
```

Frequencies and Date Offsets

Frequencies in pandas are composed of a *base frequency* and a multiplier. Base frequencies are typically referred to by a string alias, like "M" for monthly or "H" for hourly. For each base frequency, there is an object referred to as a *date offset*. For example, hourly frequency can be represented with the Hour class:

```
In [81]: from pandas.tseries.offsets import Hour, Minute
```

```
In [82]: hour = Hour()
```

```
In [83]: hour
Out[83]: <Hour>
```

You can define a multiple of an offset by passing an integer:

```
In [84]: four_hours = Hour(4)
```

```
In [85]: four_hours
Out[85]: <4 * Hours>
```

In most applications, you would never need to explicitly create one of these objects; instead you'd use a string alias like "H" or "4H". Putting an integer before the base frequency creates a multiple:

```
In [86]: pd.date_range("2000-01-01", "2000-01-03 23:59", freq="4H")
Out[86]:
DatetimeIndex(['2000-01-01 00:00:00', '2000-01-01 04:00:00',
               '2000-01-01 08:00:00', '2000-01-01 12:00:00',
               '2000-01-01 16:00:00', '2000-01-01 20:00:00',
               '2000-01-02 00:00:00', '2000-01-02 04:00:00',
               '2000-01-02 08:00:00', '2000-01-02 12:00:00',
               '2000-01-02 16:00:00', '2000-01-02 20:00:00',
               '2000-01-03 00:00:00', '2000-01-03 04:00:00',
               '2000-01-03 08:00:00', '2000-01-03 12:00:00',
               '2000-01-03 16:00:00', '2000-01-03 20:00:00'],
              dtype='datetime64[ns]', freq='4H')
```

Many offsets can be combined by addition:

```
In [87]: Hour(2) + Minute(30)
Out[87]: <150 * Minutes>
```

Similarly, you can pass frequency strings, like "1h30min", that will effectively be parsed to the same expression:

```
In [88]: pd.date_range("2000-01-01", periods=10, freq="1h30min")
Out[88]:
DatetimeIndex(['2000-01-01 00:00:00', '2000-01-01 01:30:00',
               '2000-01-01 03:00:00', '2000-01-01 04:30:00',
               '2000-01-01 06:00:00', '2000-01-01 07:30:00',
               '2000-01-01 09:00:00', '2000-01-01 10:30:00',
```

```
                '2000-01-01 12:00:00', '2000-01-01 13:30:00'],
               dtype='datetime64[ns]', freq='90T')
```

Some frequencies describe points in time that are not evenly spaced. For example, "M" (calendar month end) and "BM" (last business/weekday of month) depend on the number of days in a month and, in the latter case, whether the month ends on a weekend or not. We refer to these as *anchored* offsets.

Refer to Table 11-4 for a listing of frequency codes and date offset classes available in pandas.

 Users can define their own custom frequency classes to provide date logic not available in pandas, though the full details of that are outside the scope of this book.

Week of month dates

One useful frequency class is "week of month," starting with WOM. This enables you to get dates like the third Friday of each month:

```
In [89]: monthly_dates = pd.date_range("2012-01-01", "2012-09-01", freq="WOM-3FRI
")

In [90]: list(monthly_dates)
Out[90]:
[Timestamp('2012-01-20 00:00:00', freq='WOM-3FRI'),
 Timestamp('2012-02-17 00:00:00', freq='WOM-3FRI'),
 Timestamp('2012-03-16 00:00:00', freq='WOM-3FRI'),
 Timestamp('2012-04-20 00:00:00', freq='WOM-3FRI'),
 Timestamp('2012-05-18 00:00:00', freq='WOM-3FRI'),
 Timestamp('2012-06-15 00:00:00', freq='WOM-3FRI'),
 Timestamp('2012-07-20 00:00:00', freq='WOM-3FRI'),
 Timestamp('2012-08-17 00:00:00', freq='WOM-3FRI')]
```

Shifting (Leading and Lagging) Data

Shifting refers to moving data backward and forward through time. Both Series and DataFrame have a shift method for doing naive shifts forward or backward, leaving the index unmodified:

```
In [91]: ts = pd.Series(np.random.standard_normal(4),
   ....:                 index=pd.date_range("2000-01-01", periods=4, freq="M"))

In [92]: ts
Out[92]:
2000-01-31   -0.066748
2000-02-29    0.838639
2000-03-31   -0.117388
```

```
2000-04-30   -0.517795
Freq: M, dtype: float64

In [93]: ts.shift(2)
Out[93]:
2000-01-31         NaN
2000-02-29         NaN
2000-03-31   -0.066748
2000-04-30    0.838639
Freq: M, dtype: float64

In [94]: ts.shift(-2)
Out[94]:
2000-01-31   -0.117388
2000-02-29   -0.517795
2000-03-31         NaN
2000-04-30         NaN
Freq: M, dtype: float64
```

When we shift like this, missing data is introduced either at the start or the end of the time series.

A common use of shift is computing consecutive percent changes in a time series or multiple time series as DataFrame columns. This is expressed as:

```
ts / ts.shift(1) - 1
```

Because naive shifts leave the index unmodified, some data is discarded. Thus if the frequency is known, it can be passed to shift to advance the timestamps instead of simply the data:

```
In [95]: ts.shift(2, freq="M")
Out[95]:
2000-03-31   -0.066748
2000-04-30    0.838639
2000-05-31   -0.117388
2000-06-30   -0.517795
Freq: M, dtype: float64
```

Other frequencies can be passed, too, giving you some flexibility in how to lead and lag the data:

```
In [96]: ts.shift(3, freq="D")
Out[96]:
2000-02-03   -0.066748
2000-03-03    0.838639
2000-04-03   -0.117388
2000-05-03   -0.517795
dtype: float64

In [97]: ts.shift(1, freq="90T")
Out[97]:
2000-01-31 01:30:00   -0.066748
```

```
2000-02-29 01:30:00     0.838639
2000-03-31 01:30:00    -0.117388
2000-04-30 01:30:00    -0.517795
dtype: float64
```

The T here stands for minutes. Note that the freq parameter here indicates the offset to apply to the timestamps, but it does not change the underlying frequency of the data, if any.

Shifting dates with offsets

The pandas date offsets can also be used with datetime or Timestamp objects:

```
In [98]: from pandas.tseries.offsets import Day, MonthEnd

In [99]: now = datetime(2011, 11, 17)

In [100]: now + 3 * Day()
Out[100]: Timestamp('2011-11-20 00:00:00')
```

If you add an anchored offset like MonthEnd, the first increment will "roll forward" a date to the next date according to the frequency rule:

```
In [101]: now + MonthEnd()
Out[101]: Timestamp('2011-11-30 00:00:00')

In [102]: now + MonthEnd(2)
Out[102]: Timestamp('2011-12-31 00:00:00')
```

Anchored offsets can explicitly "roll" dates forward or backward by simply using their rollforward and rollback methods, respectively:

```
In [103]: offset = MonthEnd()

In [104]: offset.rollforward(now)
Out[104]: Timestamp('2011-11-30 00:00:00')

In [105]: offset.rollback(now)
Out[105]: Timestamp('2011-10-31 00:00:00')
```

A creative use of date offsets is to use these methods with groupby:

```
In [106]: ts = pd.Series(np.random.standard_normal(20),
   .....:                 index=pd.date_range("2000-01-15", periods=20, freq="4D")
)

In [107]: ts
Out[107]:
2000-01-15   -0.116696
2000-01-19    2.389645
2000-01-23   -0.932454
2000-01-27   -0.229331
2000-01-31   -1.140330
```

```
2000-02-04    0.439920
2000-02-08   -0.823758
2000-02-12   -0.520930
2000-02-16    0.350282
2000-02-20    0.204395
2000-02-24    0.133445
2000-02-28    0.327905
2000-03-03    0.072153
2000-03-07    0.131678
2000-03-11   -1.297459
2000-03-15    0.997747
2000-03-19    0.870955
2000-03-23   -0.991253
2000-03-27    0.151699
2000-03-31    1.266151
Freq: 4D, dtype: float64

In [108]: ts.groupby(MonthEnd().rollforward).mean()
Out[108]:
2000-01-31   -0.005833
2000-02-29    0.015894
2000-03-31    0.150209
dtype: float64
```

Of course, an easier and faster way to do this is with `resample` (we'll discuss this in much more depth in Section 11.6, "Resampling and Frequency Conversion," on page 387):

```
In [109]: ts.resample("M").mean()
Out[109]:
2000-01-31   -0.005833
2000-02-29    0.015894
2000-03-31    0.150209
Freq: M, dtype: float64
```

11.4 Time Zone Handling

Working with time zones can be one of the most unpleasant parts of time series manipulation. As a result, many time series users choose to work with time series in *coordinated universal time* or *UTC*, which is the geography-independent international standard. Time zones are expressed as offsets from UTC; for example, New York is four hours behind UTC during daylight saving time (DST) and five hours behind the rest of the year.

In Python, time zone information comes from the third-party `pytz` library (installable with pip or conda), which exposes the *Olson database*, a compilation of world time zone information. This is especially important for historical data because the DST transition dates (and even UTC offsets) have been changed numerous times depending on the regional laws. In the United States, the DST transition times have been changed many times since 1900!

For detailed information about the pytz library, you'll need to look at that library's documentation. As far as this book is concerned, pandas wraps pytz's functionality so you can ignore its API outside of the time zone names. Since pandas has a hard dependency on pytz, it isn't necessary to install it separately. Time zone names can be found interactively and in the docs:

```
In [110]: import pytz
```

```
In [111]: pytz.common_timezones[-5:]
Out[111]: ['US/Eastern', 'US/Hawaii', 'US/Mountain', 'US/Pacific', 'UTC']
```

To get a time zone object from pytz, use pytz.timezone:

```
In [112]: tz = pytz.timezone("America/New_York")
```

```
In [113]: tz
Out[113]: <DstTzInfo 'America/New_York' LMT-1 day, 19:04:00 STD>
```

Methods in pandas will accept either time zone names or these objects.

Time Zone Localization and Conversion

By default, time series in pandas are *time zone naive*. For example, consider the following time series:

```
In [114]: dates = pd.date_range("2012-03-09 09:30", periods=6)
```

```
In [115]: ts = pd.Series(np.random.standard_normal(len(dates)), index=dates)
```

```
In [116]: ts
Out[116]:
2012-03-09 09:30:00   -0.202469
2012-03-10 09:30:00    0.050718
2012-03-11 09:30:00    0.639869
2012-03-12 09:30:00    0.597594
2012-03-13 09:30:00   -0.797246
2012-03-14 09:30:00    0.472879
Freq: D, dtype: float64
```

The index's tz field is None:

```
In [117]: print(ts.index.tz)
None
```

Date ranges can be generated with a time zone set:

```
In [118]: pd.date_range("2012-03-09 09:30", periods=10, tz="UTC")
Out[118]:
DatetimeIndex(['2012-03-09 09:30:00+00:00', '2012-03-10 09:30:00+00:00',
               '2012-03-11 09:30:00+00:00', '2012-03-12 09:30:00+00:00',
```

```
                    '2012-03-13 09:30:00+00:00', '2012-03-14 09:30:00+00:00',
                    '2012-03-15 09:30:00+00:00', '2012-03-16 09:30:00+00:00',
                    '2012-03-17 09:30:00+00:00', '2012-03-18 09:30:00+00:00'],
                  dtype='datetime64[ns, UTC]', freq='D')
```

Conversion from naive to *localized* (reinterpreted as having been observed in a particular time zone) is handled by the `tz_localize` method:

```
In [119]: ts
Out[119]:
2012-03-09 09:30:00    -0.202469
2012-03-10 09:30:00     0.050718
2012-03-11 09:30:00     0.639869
2012-03-12 09:30:00     0.597594
2012-03-13 09:30:00    -0.797246
2012-03-14 09:30:00     0.472879
Freq: D, dtype: float64

In [120]: ts_utc = ts.tz_localize("UTC")

In [121]: ts_utc
Out[121]:
2012-03-09 09:30:00+00:00    -0.202469
2012-03-10 09:30:00+00:00     0.050718
2012-03-11 09:30:00+00:00     0.639869
2012-03-12 09:30:00+00:00     0.597594
2012-03-13 09:30:00+00:00    -0.797246
2012-03-14 09:30:00+00:00     0.472879
Freq: D, dtype: float64

In [122]: ts_utc.index
Out[122]:
DatetimeIndex(['2012-03-09 09:30:00+00:00', '2012-03-10 09:30:00+00:00',
               '2012-03-11 09:30:00+00:00', '2012-03-12 09:30:00+00:00',
               '2012-03-13 09:30:00+00:00', '2012-03-14 09:30:00+00:00'],
              dtype='datetime64[ns, UTC]', freq='D')
```

Once a time series has been localized to a particular time zone, it can be converted to another time zone with `tz_convert`:

```
In [123]: ts_utc.tz_convert("America/New_York")
Out[123]:
2012-03-09 04:30:00-05:00    -0.202469
2012-03-10 04:30:00-05:00     0.050718
2012-03-11 05:30:00-04:00     0.639869
2012-03-12 05:30:00-04:00     0.597594
2012-03-13 05:30:00-04:00    -0.797246
2012-03-14 05:30:00-04:00     0.472879
Freq: D, dtype: float64
```

In the case of the preceding time series, which straddles a DST transition in the America/New_York time zone, we could localize to US Eastern time and convert to, say, UTC or Berlin time:

```
In [124]: ts_eastern = ts.tz_localize("America/New_York")

In [125]: ts_eastern.tz_convert("UTC")
Out[125]:
2012-03-09 14:30:00+00:00   -0.202469
2012-03-10 14:30:00+00:00    0.050718
2012-03-11 13:30:00+00:00    0.639869
2012-03-12 13:30:00+00:00    0.597594
2012-03-13 13:30:00+00:00   -0.797246
2012-03-14 13:30:00+00:00    0.472879
dtype: float64

In [126]: ts_eastern.tz_convert("Europe/Berlin")
Out[126]:
2012-03-09 15:30:00+01:00   -0.202469
2012-03-10 15:30:00+01:00    0.050718
2012-03-11 14:30:00+01:00    0.639869
2012-03-12 14:30:00+01:00    0.597594
2012-03-13 14:30:00+01:00   -0.797246
2012-03-14 14:30:00+01:00    0.472879
dtype: float64
```

`tz_localize` and `tz_convert` are also instance methods on `DatetimeIndex`:

```
In [127]: ts.index.tz_localize("Asia/Shanghai")
Out[127]:
DatetimeIndex(['2012-03-09 09:30:00+08:00', '2012-03-10 09:30:00+08:00',
               '2012-03-11 09:30:00+08:00', '2012-03-12 09:30:00+08:00',
               '2012-03-13 09:30:00+08:00', '2012-03-14 09:30:00+08:00'],
              dtype='datetime64[ns, Asia/Shanghai]', freq=None)
```

Localizing naive timestamps also checks for ambiguous or non-existent times around daylight saving time transitions.

Operations with Time Zone-Aware Timestamp Objects

Similar to time series and date ranges, individual `Timestamp` objects similarly can be localized from naive to time zone-aware and converted from one time zone to another:

```
In [128]: stamp = pd.Timestamp("2011-03-12 04:00")

In [129]: stamp_utc = stamp.tz_localize("utc")

In [130]: stamp_utc.tz_convert("America/New_York")
Out[130]: Timestamp('2011-03-11 23:00:00-0500', tz='America/New_York')
```

You can also pass a time zone when creating the `Timestamp`:

```
In [131]: stamp_moscow = pd.Timestamp("2011-03-12 04:00", tz="Europe/Moscow")

In [132]: stamp_moscow
Out[132]: Timestamp('2011-03-12 04:00:00+0300', tz='Europe/Moscow')
```

Time zone-aware `Timestamp` objects internally store a UTC timestamp value as nano-seconds since the Unix epoch (January 1, 1970), so changing the time zone does not alter the internal UTC value:

```
In [133]: stamp_utc.value
Out[133]: 1299902400000000000

In [134]: stamp_utc.tz_convert("America/New_York").value
Out[134]: 1299902400000000000
```

When performing time arithmetic using pandas's `DateOffset` objects, pandas respects daylight saving time transitions where possible. Here we construct time-stamps that occur right before DST transitions (forward and backward). First, 30 minutes before transitioning to DST:

```
In [135]: stamp = pd.Timestamp("2012-03-11 01:30", tz="US/Eastern")

In [136]: stamp
Out[136]: Timestamp('2012-03-11 01:30:00-0500', tz='US/Eastern')

In [137]: stamp + Hour()
Out[137]: Timestamp('2012-03-11 03:30:00-0400', tz='US/Eastern')
```

Then, 90 minutes before transitioning out of DST:

```
In [138]: stamp = pd.Timestamp("2012-11-04 00:30", tz="US/Eastern")

In [139]: stamp
Out[139]: Timestamp('2012-11-04 00:30:00-0400', tz='US/Eastern')

In [140]: stamp + 2 * Hour()
Out[140]: Timestamp('2012-11-04 01:30:00-0500', tz='US/Eastern')
```

Operations Between Different Time Zones

If two time series with different time zones are combined, the result will be UTC. Since the timestamps are stored under the hood in UTC, this is a straightforward operation and requires no conversion:

```
In [141]: dates = pd.date_range("2012-03-07 09:30", periods=10, freq="B")

In [142]: ts = pd.Series(np.random.standard_normal(len(dates)), index=dates)

In [143]: ts
Out[143]:
```

```
2012-03-07 09:30:00     0.522356
2012-03-08 09:30:00    -0.546348
2012-03-09 09:30:00    -0.733537
2012-03-12 09:30:00     1.302736
2012-03-13 09:30:00     0.022199
2012-03-14 09:30:00     0.364287
2012-03-15 09:30:00    -0.922839
2012-03-16 09:30:00     0.312656
2012-03-19 09:30:00    -1.128497
2012-03-20 09:30:00    -0.333488
Freq: B, dtype: float64

In [144]: ts1 = ts[:7].tz_localize("Europe/London")

In [145]: ts2 = ts1[2:].tz_convert("Europe/Moscow")

In [146]: result = ts1 + ts2

In [147]: result.index
Out[147]:
DatetimeIndex(['2012-03-07 09:30:00+00:00', '2012-03-08 09:30:00+00:00',
               '2012-03-09 09:30:00+00:00', '2012-03-12 09:30:00+00:00',
               '2012-03-13 09:30:00+00:00', '2012-03-14 09:30:00+00:00',
               '2012-03-15 09:30:00+00:00'],
              dtype='datetime64[ns, UTC]', freq=None)
```

Operations between time zone-naive and time zone-aware data are not supported and will raise an exception.

11.5 Periods and Period Arithmetic

Periods represent time spans, like days, months, quarters, or years. The pan das.Period class represents this data type, requiring a string or integer and a supported frequency from Table 11-4:

```
In [148]: p = pd.Period("2011", freq="A-DEC")

In [149]: p
Out[149]: Period('2011', 'A-DEC')
```

In this case, the Period object represents the full time span from January 1, 2011, to December 31, 2011, inclusive. Conveniently, adding and subtracting integers from periods has the effect of shifting their frequency:

```
In [150]: p + 5
Out[150]: Period('2016', 'A-DEC')

In [151]: p - 2
Out[151]: Period('2009', 'A-DEC')
```

If two periods have the same frequency, their difference is the number of units between them as a date offset:

```
In [152]: pd.Period("2014", freq="A-DEC") - p
Out[152]: <3 * YearEnds: month=12>
```

Regular ranges of periods can be constructed with the `period_range` function:

```
In [153]: periods = pd.period_range("2000-01-01", "2000-06-30", freq="M")

In [154]: periods
Out[154]: PeriodIndex(['2000-01', '2000-02', '2000-03', '2000-04', '2000-05', '20
00-06'], dtype='period[M]')
```

The `PeriodIndex` class stores a sequence of periods and can serve as an axis index in any pandas data structure:

```
In [155]: pd.Series(np.random.standard_normal(6), index=periods)
Out[155]:
2000-01   -0.514551
2000-02   -0.559782
2000-03   -0.783408
2000-04   -1.797685
2000-05   -0.172670
2000-06    0.680215
Freq: M, dtype: float64
```

If you have an array of strings, you can also use the `PeriodIndex` class, where all of its values are periods:

```
In [156]: values = ["2001Q3", "2002Q2", "2003Q1"]

In [157]: index = pd.PeriodIndex(values, freq="Q-DEC")

In [158]: index
Out[158]: PeriodIndex(['2001Q3', '2002Q2', '2003Q1'], dtype='period[Q-DEC]')
```

Period Frequency Conversion

Periods and `PeriodIndex` objects can be converted to another frequency with their `asfreq` method. As an example, suppose we had an annual period and wanted to convert it into a monthly period either at the start or end of the year. This can be done like so:

```
In [159]: p = pd.Period("2011", freq="A-DEC")

In [160]: p
Out[160]: Period('2011', 'A-DEC')

In [161]: p.asfreq("M", how="start")
Out[161]: Period('2011-01', 'M')

In [162]: p.asfreq("M", how="end")
```

```
Out[162]: Period('2011-12', 'M')

In [163]: p.asfreq("M")
Out[163]: Period('2011-12', 'M')
```

You can think of Period("2011", "A-DEC") as being a sort of cursor pointing to a span of time, subdivided by monthly periods. See Figure 11-1 for an illustration of this. For a *fiscal year* ending on a month other than December, the corresponding monthly subperiods are different:

```
In [164]: p = pd.Period("2011", freq="A-JUN")

In [165]: p
Out[165]: Period('2011', 'A-JUN')

In [166]: p.asfreq("M", how="start")
Out[166]: Period('2010-07', 'M')

In [167]: p.asfreq("M", how="end")
Out[167]: Period('2011-06', 'M')
```

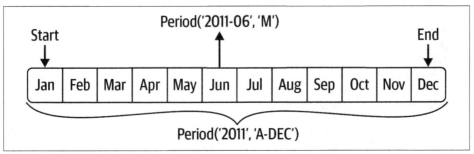

Figure 11-1. Period frequency conversion illustration

When you are converting from high to low frequency, pandas determines the superperiod, depending on where the superperiod "belongs." For example, in A-JUN frequency, the month Aug-2011 is actually part of the 2012 period:

```
In [168]: p = pd.Period("Aug-2011", "M")

In [169]: p.asfreq("A-JUN")
Out[169]: Period('2012', 'A-JUN')
```

Whole PeriodIndex objects or time series can be similarly converted with the same semantics:

```
In [170]: periods = pd.period_range("2006", "2009", freq="A-DEC")

In [171]: ts = pd.Series(np.random.standard_normal(len(periods)), index=periods)

In [172]: ts
Out[172]:
```

```
2006     1.607578
2007     0.200381
2008    -0.834068
2009    -0.302988
Freq: A-DEC, dtype: float64

In [173]: ts.asfreq("M", how="start")
Out[173]:
2006-01     1.607578
2007-01     0.200381
2008-01    -0.834068
2009-01    -0.302988
Freq: M, dtype: float64
```

Here, the annual periods are replaced with monthly periods corresponding to the first month falling within each annual period. If we instead wanted the last business day of each year, we can use the "B" frequency and indicate that we want the end of the period:

```
In [174]: ts.asfreq("B", how="end")
Out[174]:
2006-12-29     1.607578
2007-12-31     0.200381
2008-12-31    -0.834068
2009-12-31    -0.302988
Freq: B, dtype: float64
```

Quarterly Period Frequencies

Quarterly data is standard in accounting, finance, and other fields. Much quarterly data is reported relative to a *fiscal year end*, typically the last calendar or business day of one of the 12 months of the year. Thus, the period 2012Q4 has a different meaning depending on fiscal year end. pandas supports all 12 possible quarterly frequencies as Q-JAN through Q-DEC:

```
In [175]: p = pd.Period("2012Q4", freq="Q-JAN")

In [176]: p
Out[176]: Period('2012Q4', 'Q-JAN')
```

In the case of a fiscal year ending in January, 2012Q4 runs from November 2011 through January 2012, which you can check by converting to daily frequency:

```
In [177]: p.asfreq("D", how="start")
Out[177]: Period('2011-11-01', 'D')

In [178]: p.asfreq("D", how="end")
Out[178]: Period('2012-01-31', 'D')
```

See Figure 11-2 for an illustration.

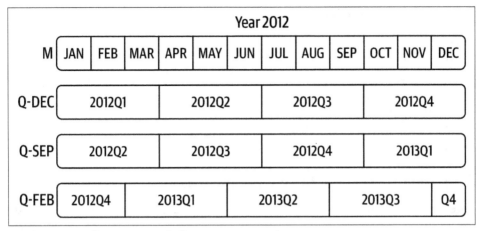

Figure 11-2. Different quarterly frequency conventions

Thus, it's possible to do convenient period arithmetic; for example, to get the time-stamp at 4 P.M. on the second-to-last business day of the quarter, you could do:

```
In [179]: p4pm = (p.asfreq("B", how="end") - 1).asfreq("T", how="start") + 16 * 6
0

In [180]: p4pm
Out[180]: Period('2012-01-30 16:00', 'T')

In [181]: p4pm.to_timestamp()
Out[181]: Timestamp('2012-01-30 16:00:00')
```

The to_timestamp method returns the Timestamp at the start of the period by default.

You can generate quarterly ranges using pandas.period_range. The arithmetic is identical, too:

```
In [182]: periods = pd.period_range("2011Q3", "2012Q4", freq="Q-JAN")

In [183]: ts = pd.Series(np.arange(len(periods)), index=periods)

In [184]: ts
Out[184]:
2011Q3    0
2011Q4    1
2012Q1    2
2012Q2    3
2012Q3    4
2012Q4    5
Freq: Q-JAN, dtype: int64

In [185]: new_periods = (periods.asfreq("B", "end") - 1).asfreq("H", "start") + 1
6
```

```
In [186]: ts.index = new_periods.to_timestamp()

In [187]: ts
Out[187]:
2010-10-28 16:00:00    0
2011-01-28 16:00:00    1
2011-04-28 16:00:00    2
2011-07-28 16:00:00    3
2011-10-28 16:00:00    4
2012-01-30 16:00:00    5
dtype: int64
```

Converting Timestamps to Periods (and Back)

Series and DataFrame objects indexed by timestamps can be converted to periods with the to_period method:

```
In [188]: dates = pd.date_range("2000-01-01", periods=3, freq="M")

In [189]: ts = pd.Series(np.random.standard_normal(3), index=dates)

In [190]: ts
Out[190]:
2000-01-31    1.663261
2000-02-29   -0.996206
2000-03-31    1.521760
Freq: M, dtype: float64

In [191]: pts = ts.to_period()

In [192]: pts
Out[192]:
2000-01    1.663261
2000-02   -0.996206
2000-03    1.521760
Freq: M, dtype: float64
```

Since periods refer to nonoverlapping time spans, a timestamp can only belong to a single period for a given frequency. While the frequency of the new PeriodIndex is inferred from the timestamps by default, you can specify any supported frequency (most of those listed in Table 11-4 are supported). There is also no problem with having duplicate periods in the result:

```
In [193]: dates = pd.date_range("2000-01-29", periods=6)

In [194]: ts2 = pd.Series(np.random.standard_normal(6), index=dates)

In [195]: ts2
Out[195]:
2000-01-29    0.244175
2000-01-30    0.423331
2000-01-31   -0.654040
```

```
2000-02-01      2.089154
2000-02-02     -0.060220
2000-02-03     -0.167933
Freq: D, dtype: float64

In [196]: ts2.to_period("M")
Out[196]:
2000-01      0.244175
2000-01      0.423331
2000-01     -0.654040
2000-02      2.089154
2000-02     -0.060220
2000-02     -0.167933
Freq: M, dtype: float64
```

To convert back to timestamps, use the to_timestamp method, which returns a DatetimeIndex:

```
In [197]: pts = ts2.to_period()

In [198]: pts
Out[198]:
2000-01-29      0.244175
2000-01-30      0.423331
2000-01-31     -0.654040
2000-02-01      2.089154
2000-02-02     -0.060220
2000-02-03     -0.167933
Freq: D, dtype: float64

In [199]: pts.to_timestamp(how="end")
Out[199]:
2000-01-29 23:59:59.999999999      0.244175
2000-01-30 23:59:59.999999999      0.423331
2000-01-31 23:59:59.999999999     -0.654040
2000-02-01 23:59:59.999999999      2.089154
2000-02-02 23:59:59.999999999     -0.060220
2000-02-03 23:59:59.999999999     -0.167933
Freq: D, dtype: float64
```

Creating a PeriodIndex from Arrays

Fixed frequency datasets are sometimes stored with time span information spread across multiple columns. For example, in this macroeconomic dataset, the year and quarter are in different columns:

```
In [200]: data = pd.read_csv("examples/macrodata.csv")

In [201]: data.head(5)
Out[201]:
   year  quarter    realgdp  realcons  realinv  realgovt  realdpi    cpi  \
0  1959        1   2710.349    1707.4  286.898   470.045   1886.9  28.98
```

```
1  1959       2  2778.801   1733.7  310.859   481.301   1919.7  29.15
2  1959       3  2775.488   1751.8  289.226   491.260   1916.4  29.35
3  1959       4  2785.204   1753.7  299.356   484.052   1931.3  29.37
4  1960       1  2847.699   1770.5  331.722   462.199   1955.5  29.54
      m1  tbilrate  unemp       pop  infl  realint
0  139.7      2.82    5.8  177.146  0.00     0.00
1  141.7      3.08    5.1  177.830  2.34     0.74
2  140.5      3.82    5.3  178.657  2.74     1.09
3  140.0      4.33    5.6  179.386  0.27     4.06
4  139.6      3.50    5.2  180.007  2.31     1.19

In [202]: data["year"]
Out[202]:
0      1959
1      1959
2      1959
3      1959
4      1960
       ...
198    2008
199    2008
200    2009
201    2009
202    2009
Name: year, Length: 203, dtype: int64

In [203]: data["quarter"]
Out[203]:
0      1
1      2
2      3
3      4
4      1
      ..
198    3
199    4
200    1
201    2
202    3
Name: quarter, Length: 203, dtype: int64
```

By passing these arrays to `PeriodIndex` with a frequency, you can combine them to form an index for the DataFrame:

```
In [204]: index = pd.PeriodIndex(year=data["year"], quarter=data["quarter"],
   .....:                        freq="Q-DEC")

In [205]: index
Out[205]:
PeriodIndex(['1959Q1', '1959Q2', '1959Q3', '1959Q4', '1960Q1', '1960Q2',
             '1960Q3', '1960Q4', '1961Q1', '1961Q2',
             ...
             '2007Q2', '2007Q3', '2007Q4', '2008Q1', '2008Q2', '2008Q3',
```

```
            '2008Q4', '2009Q1', '2009Q2', '2009Q3'],
           dtype='period[Q-DEC]', length=203)

In [206]: data.index = index

In [207]: data["infl"]
Out[207]:
1959Q1    0.00
1959Q2    2.34
1959Q3    2.74
1959Q4    0.27
1960Q1    2.31
          ...
2008Q3   -3.16
2008Q4   -8.79
2009Q1    0.94
2009Q2    3.37
2009Q3    3.56
Freq: Q-DEC, Name: infl, Length: 203, dtype: float64
```

11.6 Resampling and Frequency Conversion

Resampling refers to the process of converting a time series from one frequency to another. Aggregating higher frequency data to lower frequency is called *downsampling*, while converting lower frequency to higher frequency is called *upsampling*. Not all resampling falls into either of these categories; for example, converting W-WED (weekly on Wednesday) to W-FRI is neither upsampling nor downsampling.

pandas objects are equipped with a resample method, which is the workhorse function for all frequency conversion. resample has a similar API to groupby; you call resample to group the data, then call an aggregation function:

```
In [208]: dates = pd.date_range("2000-01-01", periods=100)

In [209]: ts = pd.Series(np.random.standard_normal(len(dates)), index=dates)

In [210]: ts
Out[210]:
2000-01-01    0.631634
2000-01-02   -1.594313
2000-01-03   -1.519937
2000-01-04    1.108752
2000-01-05    1.255853
                ...
2000-04-05   -0.423776
2000-04-06    0.789740
2000-04-07    0.937568
2000-04-08   -2.253294
2000-04-09   -1.772919
Freq: D, Length: 100, dtype: float64
```

```
In [211]: ts.resample("M").mean()
Out[211]:
2000-01-31    -0.165893
2000-02-29     0.078606
2000-03-31     0.223811
2000-04-30    -0.063643
Freq: M, dtype: float64

In [212]: ts.resample("M", kind="period").mean()
Out[212]:
2000-01    -0.165893
2000-02     0.078606
2000-03     0.223811
2000-04    -0.063643
Freq: M, dtype: float64
```

resample is a flexible method that can be used to process large time series. The examples in the following sections illustrate its semantics and use. Table 11-5 summarizes some of its options.

Table 11-5. resample method arguments

Argument	Description
rule	String, DateOffset, or timedelta indicating desired resampled frequency (for example, 'M', '5min', or Second(15))
axis	Axis to resample on; default axis=0
fill_method	How to interpolate when upsampling, as in "ffill" or "bfill"; by default does no interpolation
closed	In downsampling, which end of each interval is closed (inclusive), "right" or "left"
label	In downsampling, how to label the aggregated result, with the "right" or "left" bin edge (e.g., the 9:30 to 9:35 five-minute interval could be labeled 9:30 or 9:35)
limit	When forward or backward filling, the maximum number of periods to fill
kind	Aggregate to periods ("period") or timestamps ("timestamp"); defaults to the type of index the time series has
convention	When resampling periods, the convention ("start" or "end") for converting the low-frequency period to high frequency; defaults to "start"
origin	The "base" timestamp from which to determine the resampling bin edges; can also be one of "epoch", "start", "start_day", "end", or "end_day"; see the resample docstring for full details
offset	An offset timedelta added to the origin; defaults to None

Downsampling

Downsampling is aggregating data to a regular, lower frequency. The data you're aggregating doesn't need to be fixed frequently; the desired frequency defines *bin edges* that are used to slice the time series into pieces to aggregate. For example, to convert to monthly, "M" or "BM", you need to chop up the data into one-month intervals. Each interval is said to be *half-open*; a data point can belong only to one interval, and the union of the intervals must make up the whole time frame. There are a couple things to think about when using `resample` to downsample data:

- Which side of each interval is *closed*
- How to label each aggregated bin, either with the start of the interval or the end

To illustrate, let's look at some one-minute frequency data:

```
In [213]: dates = pd.date_range("2000-01-01", periods=12, freq="T")

In [214]: ts = pd.Series(np.arange(len(dates)), index=dates)

In [215]: ts
Out[215]:
2000-01-01 00:00:00     0
2000-01-01 00:01:00     1
2000-01-01 00:02:00     2
2000-01-01 00:03:00     3
2000-01-01 00:04:00     4
2000-01-01 00:05:00     5
2000-01-01 00:06:00     6
2000-01-01 00:07:00     7
2000-01-01 00:08:00     8
2000-01-01 00:09:00     9
2000-01-01 00:10:00    10
2000-01-01 00:11:00    11
Freq: T, dtype: int64
```

Suppose you wanted to aggregate this data into five-minute chunks or *bars* by taking the sum of each group:

```
In [216]: ts.resample("5min").sum()
Out[216]:
2000-01-01 00:00:00    10
2000-01-01 00:05:00    35
2000-01-01 00:10:00    21
Freq: 5T, dtype: int64
```

The frequency you pass defines bin edges in five-minute increments. For this frequency, by default the *left* bin edge is inclusive, so the `00:00` value is included in the `00:00` to `00:05` interval, and the `00:05` value is excluded from that interval.[1]

```
In [217]: ts.resample("5min", closed="right").sum()
Out[217]:
1999-12-31 23:55:00     0
```

---

[1] The choice of the default values for `closed` and `label` might seem a bit odd to some users. The default is `closed="left"` for all but a specific set ("M", "A", "Q", "BM", "BQ", and "W") for which the default is `closed="right"`. The defaults were chosen to make the results more intuitive, but it is worth knowing that the default is not always one or the other.

```
2000-01-01 00:00:00    15
2000-01-01 00:05:00    40
2000-01-01 00:10:00    11
Freq: 5T, dtype: int64
```

The resulting time series is labeled by the timestamps from the left side of each bin. By passing label="right" you can label them with the right bin edge:

```
In [218]: ts.resample("5min", closed="right", label="right").sum()
Out[218]:
2000-01-01 00:00:00     0
2000-01-01 00:05:00    15
2000-01-01 00:10:00    40
2000-01-01 00:15:00    11
Freq: 5T, dtype: int64
```

See Figure 11-3 for an illustration of minute frequency data being resampled to five-minute frequency.

Figure 11-3. Five-minute resampling illustration of closed, label conventions

Lastly, you might want to shift the result index by some amount, say subtracting one second from the right edge to make it more clear which interval the timestamp refers to. To do this, add an offset to the resulting index:

```
In [219]: from pandas.tseries.frequencies import to_offset

In [220]: result = ts.resample("5min", closed="right", label="right").sum()

In [221]: result.index = result.index + to_offset("-1s")

In [222]: result
Out[222]:
1999-12-31 23:59:59     0
2000-01-01 00:04:59    15
2000-01-01 00:09:59    40
2000-01-01 00:14:59    11
Freq: 5T, dtype: int64
```

Open-high-low-close (OHLC) resampling

In finance, a popular way to aggregate a time series is to compute four values for each bucket: the first (open), last (close), maximum (high), and minimal (low) values. By using the ohlc aggregate function, you will obtain a DataFrame having columns containing these four aggregates, which are efficiently computed in a single function call:

```
In [223]: ts = pd.Series(np.random.permutation(np.arange(len(dates))), index=date
s)

In [224]: ts.resample("5min").ohlc()
Out[224]:
                     open  high  low  close
2000-01-01 00:00:00     8     8    1      5
2000-01-01 00:05:00     6    11    2      2
2000-01-01 00:10:00     0     7    0      7
```

Upsampling and Interpolation

Upsampling is converting from a lower frequency to a higher frequency, where no aggregation is needed. Let's consider a DataFrame with some weekly data:

```
In [225]: frame = pd.DataFrame(np.random.standard_normal((2, 4)),
   .....:                      index=pd.date_range("2000-01-01", periods=2,
   .....:                                          freq="W-WED"),
   .....:                      columns=["Colorado", "Texas", "New York", "Ohio"])

In [226]: frame
Out[226]:
            Colorado     Texas  New York      Ohio
2000-01-05 -0.896431  0.927238  0.482284 -0.867130
2000-01-12  0.493841 -0.155434  1.397286  1.507055
```

When you are using an aggregation function with this data, there is only one value per group, and missing values result in the gaps. We use the asfreq method to convert to the higher frequency without any aggregation:

```
In [227]: df_daily = frame.resample("D").asfreq()

In [228]: df_daily
Out[228]:
            Colorado     Texas  New York      Ohio
2000-01-05 -0.896431  0.927238  0.482284 -0.867130
2000-01-06       NaN       NaN       NaN       NaN
2000-01-07       NaN       NaN       NaN       NaN
2000-01-08       NaN       NaN       NaN       NaN
2000-01-09       NaN       NaN       NaN       NaN
2000-01-10       NaN       NaN       NaN       NaN
2000-01-11       NaN       NaN       NaN       NaN
2000-01-12  0.493841 -0.155434  1.397286  1.507055
```

Suppose you wanted to fill forward each weekly value on the non-Wednesdays. The same filling or interpolation methods available in the `fillna` and `reindex` methods are available for resampling:

```
In [229]: frame.resample("D").ffill()
Out[229]:
            Colorado     Texas  New York      Ohio
2000-01-05 -0.896431  0.927238  0.482284 -0.867130
2000-01-06 -0.896431  0.927238  0.482284 -0.867130
2000-01-07 -0.896431  0.927238  0.482284 -0.867130
2000-01-08 -0.896431  0.927238  0.482284 -0.867130
2000-01-09 -0.896431  0.927238  0.482284 -0.867130
2000-01-10 -0.896431  0.927238  0.482284 -0.867130
2000-01-11 -0.896431  0.927238  0.482284 -0.867130
2000-01-12  0.493841 -0.155434  1.397286  1.507055
```

You can similarly choose to only fill a certain number of periods forward to limit how far to continue using an observed value:

```
In [230]: frame.resample("D").ffill(limit=2)
Out[230]:
            Colorado     Texas  New York      Ohio
2000-01-05 -0.896431  0.927238  0.482284 -0.867130
2000-01-06 -0.896431  0.927238  0.482284 -0.867130
2000-01-07 -0.896431  0.927238  0.482284 -0.867130
2000-01-08       NaN       NaN       NaN       NaN
2000-01-09       NaN       NaN       NaN       NaN
2000-01-10       NaN       NaN       NaN       NaN
2000-01-11       NaN       NaN       NaN       NaN
2000-01-12  0.493841 -0.155434  1.397286  1.507055
```

Notably, the new date index need not coincide with the old one at all:

```
In [231]: frame.resample("W-THU").ffill()
Out[231]:
            Colorado     Texas  New York      Ohio
2000-01-06 -0.896431  0.927238  0.482284 -0.867130
2000-01-13  0.493841 -0.155434  1.397286  1.507055
```

Resampling with Periods

Resampling data indexed by periods is similar to timestamps:

```
In [232]: frame = pd.DataFrame(np.random.standard_normal((24, 4)),
   .....:                      index=pd.period_range("1-2000", "12-2001",
   .....:                                            freq="M"),
   .....:                      columns=["Colorado", "Texas", "New York", "Ohio"])

In [233]: frame.head()
Out[233]:
         Colorado     Texas  New York      Ohio
2000-01 -1.179442  0.443171  1.395676 -0.529658
2000-02  0.787358  0.248845  0.743239  1.267746
```

```
2000-03   1.302395 -0.272154 -0.051532 -0.467740
2000-04  -1.040816  0.426419  0.312945 -1.115689
2000-05   1.234297 -1.893094 -1.661605 -0.005477

In [234]: annual_frame = frame.resample("A-DEC").mean()

In [235]: annual_frame
Out[235]:
      Colorado    Texas  New York      Ohio
2000  0.487329  0.104466  0.020495 -0.273945
2001  0.203125  0.162429  0.056146 -0.103794
```

Upsampling is more nuanced, as before resampling you must make a decision about which end of the time span in the new frequency to place the values. The convention argument defaults to "start" but can also be "end":

```
# Q-DEC: Quarterly, year ending in December
In [236]: annual_frame.resample("Q-DEC").ffill()
Out[236]:
        Colorado    Texas  New York      Ohio
2000Q1  0.487329  0.104466  0.020495 -0.273945
2000Q2  0.487329  0.104466  0.020495 -0.273945
2000Q3  0.487329  0.104466  0.020495 -0.273945
2000Q4  0.487329  0.104466  0.020495 -0.273945
2001Q1  0.203125  0.162429  0.056146 -0.103794
2001Q2  0.203125  0.162429  0.056146 -0.103794
2001Q3  0.203125  0.162429  0.056146 -0.103794
2001Q4  0.203125  0.162429  0.056146 -0.103794

In [237]: annual_frame.resample("Q-DEC", convention="end").asfreq()
Out[237]:
        Colorado    Texas  New York      Ohio
2000Q4  0.487329  0.104466  0.020495 -0.273945
2001Q1       NaN       NaN       NaN       NaN
2001Q2       NaN       NaN       NaN       NaN
2001Q3       NaN       NaN       NaN       NaN
2001Q4  0.203125  0.162429  0.056146 -0.103794
```

Since periods refer to time spans, the rules about upsampling and downsampling are more rigid:

- In downsampling, the target frequency must be a *subperiod* of the source frequency.

- In upsampling, the target frequency must be a *superperiod* of the source frequency.

If these rules are not satisfied, an exception will be raised. This mainly affects the quarterly, annual, and weekly frequencies; for example, the time spans defined by Q-MAR only line up with A-MAR, A-JUN, A-SEP, and A-DEC:

```
In [238]: annual_frame.resample("Q-MAR").ffill()
Out[238]:
        Colorado    Texas  New York      Ohio
2000Q4  0.487329  0.104466  0.020495 -0.273945
2001Q1  0.487329  0.104466  0.020495 -0.273945
2001Q2  0.487329  0.104466  0.020495 -0.273945
2001Q3  0.487329  0.104466  0.020495 -0.273945
2001Q4  0.203125  0.162429  0.056146 -0.103794
2002Q1  0.203125  0.162429  0.056146 -0.103794
2002Q2  0.203125  0.162429  0.056146 -0.103794
2002Q3  0.203125  0.162429  0.056146 -0.103794
```

Grouped Time Resampling

For time series data, the resample method is semantically a group operation based on a time intervalization. Here's a small example table:

```
In [239]: N = 15

In [240]: times = pd.date_range("2017-05-20 00:00", freq="1min", periods=N)

In [241]: df = pd.DataFrame({"time": times,
   .....:                    "value": np.arange(N)})

In [242]: df
Out[242]:
                  time  value
0  2017-05-20 00:00:00      0
1  2017-05-20 00:01:00      1
2  2017-05-20 00:02:00      2
3  2017-05-20 00:03:00      3
4  2017-05-20 00:04:00      4
5  2017-05-20 00:05:00      5
6  2017-05-20 00:06:00      6
7  2017-05-20 00:07:00      7
8  2017-05-20 00:08:00      8
9  2017-05-20 00:09:00      9
10 2017-05-20 00:10:00     10
11 2017-05-20 00:11:00     11
12 2017-05-20 00:12:00     12
13 2017-05-20 00:13:00     13
14 2017-05-20 00:14:00     14
```

Here, we can index by `"time"` and then resample:

```
In [243]: df.set_index("time").resample("5min").count()
Out[243]:
                     value
time
2017-05-20 00:00:00      5
2017-05-20 00:05:00      5
2017-05-20 00:10:00      5
```

Suppose that a DataFrame contains multiple time series, marked by an additional group key column:

```
In [244]: df2 = pd.DataFrame({"time": times.repeat(3),
   .....:                     "key": np.tile(["a", "b", "c"], N),
   .....:                     "value": np.arange(N * 3.)})

In [245]: df2.head(7)
Out[245]:
                 time key  value
0 2017-05-20 00:00:00   a    0.0
1 2017-05-20 00:00:00   b    1.0
2 2017-05-20 00:00:00   c    2.0
3 2017-05-20 00:01:00   a    3.0
4 2017-05-20 00:01:00   b    4.0
5 2017-05-20 00:01:00   c    5.0
6 2017-05-20 00:02:00   a    6.0
```

To do the same resampling for each value of `"key"`, we introduce the `pandas.Grouper` object:

```
In [246]: time_key = pd.Grouper(freq="5min")
```

We can then set the time index, group by `"key"` and `time_key`, and aggregate:

```
In [247]: resampled = (df2.set_index("time")
   .....:              .groupby(["key", time_key])
   .....:              .sum())

In [248]: resampled
Out[248]:
                         value
key time
a   2017-05-20 00:00:00   30.0
    2017-05-20 00:05:00  105.0
    2017-05-20 00:10:00  180.0
b   2017-05-20 00:00:00   35.0
    2017-05-20 00:05:00  110.0
    2017-05-20 00:10:00  185.0
c   2017-05-20 00:00:00   40.0
    2017-05-20 00:05:00  115.0
    2017-05-20 00:10:00  190.0

In [249]: resampled.reset_index()
```

```
Out[249]:
  key                time  value
0   a 2017-05-20 00:00:00   30.0
1   a 2017-05-20 00:05:00  105.0
2   a 2017-05-20 00:10:00  180.0
3   b 2017-05-20 00:00:00   35.0
4   b 2017-05-20 00:05:00  110.0
5   b 2017-05-20 00:10:00  185.0
6   c 2017-05-20 00:00:00   40.0
7   c 2017-05-20 00:05:00  115.0
8   c 2017-05-20 00:10:00  190.0
```

One constraint with using pandas.Grouper is that the time must be the index of the Series or DataFrame.

11.7 Moving Window Functions

An important class of array transformations used for time series operations are statistics and other functions evaluated over a sliding window or with exponentially decaying weights. This can be useful for smoothing noisy or gappy data. I call these *moving window functions*, even though they include functions without a fixed-length window like exponentially weighted moving average. Like other statistical functions, these also automatically exclude missing data.

Before digging in, we can load up some time series data and resample it to business day frequency:

```
In [250]: close_px_all = pd.read_csv("examples/stock_px.csv",
   .....:                            parse_dates=True, index_col=0)

In [251]: close_px = close_px_all[["AAPL", "MSFT", "XOM"]]

In [252]: close_px = close_px.resample("B").ffill()
```

I now introduce the rolling operator, which behaves similarly to resample and groupby. It can be called on a Series or DataFrame along with a window (expressed as a number of periods; see Figure 11-4 for the plot created):

```
In [253]: close_px["AAPL"].plot()
Out[253]: <AxesSubplot:>

In [254]: close_px["AAPL"].rolling(250).mean().plot()
```

Figure 11-4. Apple price with 250-day moving average

The expression rolling(250) is similar in behavior to groupby, but instead of grouping, it creates an object that enables grouping over a 250-day sliding window. So here we have the 250-day moving window average of Apple's stock price.

By default, rolling functions require all of the values in the window to be non-NA. This behavior can be changed to account for missing data and, in particular, the fact that you will have fewer than window periods of data at the beginning of the time series (see Figure 11-5):

```
In [255]: plt.figure()
Out[255]: <Figure size 1000x600 with 0 Axes>

In [256]: std250 = close_px["AAPL"].pct_change().rolling(250, min_periods=10).std
()

In [257]: std250[5:12]
Out[257]:
2003-01-09         NaN
2003-01-10         NaN
2003-01-13         NaN
2003-01-14         NaN
2003-01-15         NaN
2003-01-16    0.009628
2003-01-17    0.013818
Freq: B, Name: AAPL, dtype: float64

In [258]: std250.plot()
```

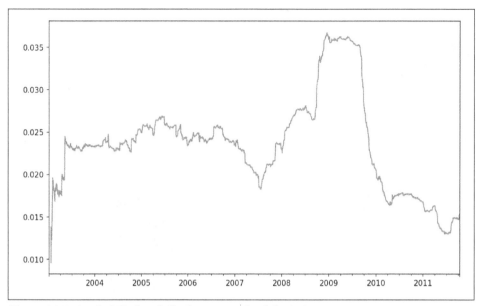

Figure 11-5. Apple 250-day daily return standard deviation

To compute an *expanding window mean*, use the `expanding` operator instead of `rolling`. The expanding mean starts the time window from the same point as the rolling window and increases the size of the window until it encompasses the whole series. An expanding window mean on the `std250` time series looks like this:

```
In [259]: expanding_mean = std250.expanding().mean()
```

Calling a moving window function on a DataFrame applies the transformation to each column (see Figure 11-6):

```
In [261]: plt.style.use('grayscale')
```

```
In [262]: close_px.rolling(60).mean().plot(logy=True)
```

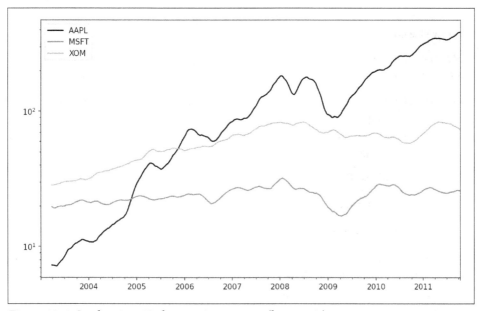

Figure 11-6. Stock prices 60-day moving average (log y-axis)

The rolling function also accepts a string indicating a fixed-size time offset rolling() in moving window functions rather than a set number of periods. Using this notation can be useful for irregular time series. These are the same strings that you can pass to resample. For example, we could compute a 20-day rolling mean like so:

```
In [263]: close_px.rolling("20D").mean()
Out[263]:
                  AAPL        MSFT        XOM
2003-01-02     7.400000   21.110000   29.220000
2003-01-03     7.425000   21.125000   29.230000
2003-01-06     7.433333   21.256667   29.473333
2003-01-07     7.432500   21.425000   29.342500
2003-01-08     7.402000   21.402000   29.240000
...                 ...         ...         ...
2011-10-10   389.351429   25.602143   72.527857
2011-10-11   388.505000   25.674286   72.835000
2011-10-12   388.531429   25.810000   73.400714
2011-10-13   388.826429   25.961429   73.905000
2011-10-14   391.038000   26.048667   74.185333
[2292 rows x 3 columns]
```

Exponentially Weighted Functions

An alternative to using a fixed window size with equally weighted observations is to specify a constant *decay factor* to give more weight to more recent observations. There are a couple of ways to specify the decay factor. A popular one is using a *span*, which makes the result comparable to a simple moving window function with window size equal to the span.

Since an exponentially weighted statistic places more weight on more recent observations, it "adapts" faster to changes compared with the equal-weighted version.

pandas has the `ewm` operator (which stands for exponentially weighted moving) to go along with `rolling` and `expanding`. Here's an example comparing a 30-day moving average of Apple's stock price with an exponentially weighted (EW) moving average with `span=60` (see Figure 11-7):

```
In [265]: aapl_px = close_px["AAPL"]["2006":"2007"]

In [266]: ma30 = aapl_px.rolling(30, min_periods=20).mean()

In [267]: ewma30 = aapl_px.ewm(span=30).mean()

In [268]: aapl_px.plot(style="k-", label="Price")
Out[268]: <AxesSubplot:>

In [269]: ma30.plot(style="k--", label="Simple Moving Avg")
Out[269]: <AxesSubplot:>

In [270]: ewma30.plot(style="k-", label="EW MA")
Out[270]: <AxesSubplot:>

In [271]: plt.legend()
```

Figure 11-7. Simple moving average versus exponentially weighted

Binary Moving Window Functions

Some statistical operators, like correlation and covariance, need to operate on two time series. As an example, financial analysts are often interested in a stock's correlation to a benchmark index like the S&P 500. To have a look at this, we first compute the percent change for all of our time series of interest:

```
In [273]: spx_px = close_px_all["SPX"]

In [274]: spx_rets = spx_px.pct_change()

In [275]: returns = close_px.pct_change()
```

After we call `rolling`, the `corr` aggregation function can then compute the rolling correlation with `spx_rets` (see Figure 11-8 for the resulting plot):

```
In [276]: corr = returns["AAPL"].rolling(125, min_periods=100).corr(spx_rets)

In [277]: corr.plot()
```

Figure 11-8. Six-month AAPL return correlation to S&P 500

Suppose you wanted to compute the rolling correlation of the S&P 500 index with many stocks at once. You could write a loop computing this for each stock like we did for Apple above, but if each stock is a column in a single DataFrame, we can compute all of the rolling correlations in one shot by calling `rolling` on the DataFrame and passing the `spx_rets` Series.

See Figure 11-9 for the plot of the result:

```
In [279]: corr = returns.rolling(125, min_periods=100).corr(spx_rets)
```

```
In [280]: corr.plot()
```

Figure 11-9. Six-month return correlations to S&P 500

User-Defined Moving Window Functions

The `apply` method on `rolling` and related methods provides a way to apply an array function of your own creation over a moving window. The only requirement is that the function produce a single value (a reduction) from each piece of the array. For example, while we can compute sample quantiles using `rolling(...).quantile(q)`, we might be interested in the percentile rank of a particular value over the sample. The `scipy.stats.percentileofscore` function does just this (see Figure 11-10 for the resulting plot):

```
In [282]: from scipy.stats import percentileofscore
```

```
In [283]: def score_at_2percent(x):
    .....:     return percentileofscore(x, 0.02)
```

```
In [284]: result = returns["AAPL"].rolling(250).apply(score_at_2percent)
```

```
In [285]: result.plot()
```

Figure 11-10. Percentile rank of 2% AAPL return over one-year window

If you don't have SciPy installed already, you can install it with conda or pip:

```
conda install scipy
```

11.8 Conclusion

Time series data calls for different types of analysis and data transformation tools than the other types of data we have explored in previous chapters.

In the following chapter, we will show how to start using modeling libraries like statsmodels and scikit-learn.

CHAPTER 12

Introduction to Modeling Libraries in Python

In this book, I have focused on providing a programming foundation for doing data analysis in Python. Since data analysts and scientists often report spending a disproportionate amount of time with data wrangling and preparation, the book's structure reflects the importance of mastering these techniques.

Which library you use for developing models will depend on the application. Many statistical problems can be solved by simpler techniques like ordinary least squares regression, while other problems may call for more advanced machine learning methods. Fortunately, Python has become one of the languages of choice for implementing analytical methods, so there are many tools you can explore after completing this book.

In this chapter, I will review some features of pandas that may be helpful when you're crossing back and forth between data wrangling with pandas and model fitting and scoring. I will then give short introductions to two popular modeling toolkits, statsmodels (*http://statsmodels.org*) and scikit-learn (*http://scikit-learn.org*). Since each of these projects is large enough to warrant its own dedicated book, I make no effort to be comprehensive and instead direct you to both projects' online documentation along with some other Python-based books on data science, statistics, and machine learning.

12.1 Interfacing Between pandas and Model Code

A common workflow for model development is to use pandas for data loading and cleaning before switching over to a modeling library to build the model itself. An important part of the model development process is called *feature engineering* in machine learning. This can describe any data transformation or analytics that extract information from a raw dataset that may be useful in a modeling context. The data aggregation and GroupBy tools we have explored in this book are used often in a feature engineering context.

While details of "good" feature engineering are out of scope for this book, I will show some methods to make switching between data manipulation with pandas and modeling as painless as possible.

The point of contact between pandas and other analysis libraries is usually NumPy arrays. To turn a DataFrame into a NumPy array, use the to_numpy method:

```
In [12]: data = pd.DataFrame({
   ....:     'x0': [1, 2, 3, 4, 5],
   ....:     'x1': [0.01, -0.01, 0.25, -4.1, 0.],
   ....:     'y': [-1.5, 0., 3.6, 1.3, -2.]})

In [13]: data
Out[13]:
   x0    x1    y
0   1  0.01 -1.5
1   2 -0.01  0.0
2   3  0.25  3.6
3   4 -4.10  1.3
4   5  0.00 -2.0

In [14]: data.columns
Out[14]: Index(['x0', 'x1', 'y'], dtype='object')

In [15]: data.to_numpy()
Out[15]:
array([[ 1.  ,  0.01, -1.5 ],
       [ 2.  , -0.01,  0.  ],
       [ 3.  ,  0.25,  3.6 ],
       [ 4.  , -4.1 ,  1.3 ],
       [ 5.  ,  0.  , -2.  ]])
```

To convert back to a DataFrame, as you may recall from earlier chapters, you can pass a two-dimensional ndarray with optional column names:

```
In [16]: df2 = pd.DataFrame(data.to_numpy(), columns=['one', 'two', 'three'])

In [17]: df2
Out[17]:
   one   two  three
0  1.0  0.01   -1.5
1  2.0 -0.01    0.0
2  3.0  0.25    3.6
3  4.0 -4.10    1.3
4  5.0  0.00   -2.0
```

The to_numpy method is intended to be used when your data is homogeneous—for example, all numeric types. If you have heterogeneous data, the result will be an ndarray of Python objects:

```
In [18]: df3 = data.copy()

In [19]: df3['strings'] = ['a', 'b', 'c', 'd', 'e']

In [20]: df3
Out[20]:
   x0    x1    y strings
0   1  0.01 -1.5       a
1   2 -0.01  0.0       b
2   3  0.25  3.6       c
3   4 -4.10  1.3       d
4   5  0.00 -2.0       e

In [21]: df3.to_numpy()
Out[21]:
array([[1, 0.01, -1.5, 'a'],
       [2, -0.01, 0.0, 'b'],
       [3, 0.25, 3.6, 'c'],
       [4, -4.1, 1.3, 'd'],
       [5, 0.0, -2.0, 'e']], dtype=object)
```

For some models, you may wish to use only a subset of the columns. I recommend using loc indexing with to_numpy:

```
In [22]: model_cols = ['x0', 'x1']

In [23]: data.loc[:, model_cols].to_numpy()
Out[23]:
array([[ 1.  ,  0.01],
       [ 2.  , -0.01],
       [ 3.  ,  0.25],
       [ 4.  , -4.1 ],
       [ 5.  ,  0.  ]])
```

Some libraries have native support for pandas and do some of this work for you automatically: converting to NumPy from DataFrame and attaching model parameter names to the columns of output tables or Series. In other cases, you will have to perform this "metadata management" manually.

In Section 7.5, "Categorical Data," on page 235, we looked at pandas's Categorical type and the pandas.get_dummies function. Suppose we had a nonnumeric column in our example dataset:

```
In [24]: data['category'] = pd.Categorical(['a', 'b', 'a', 'a', 'b'],
   ....:                                    categories=['a', 'b'])

In [25]: data
Out[25]:
```

```
      x0    x1     y category
0     1   0.01  -1.5        a
1     2  -0.01   0.0        b
2     3   0.25   3.6        a
3     4  -4.10   1.3        a
4     5   0.00  -2.0        b
```

If we wanted to replace the `'category'` column with dummy variables, we create dummy variables, drop the `'category'` column, and then join the result:

```
In [26]: dummies = pd.get_dummies(data.category, prefix='category')

In [27]: data_with_dummies = data.drop('category', axis=1).join(dummies)

In [28]: data_with_dummies
Out[28]:
      x0    x1     y  category_a  category_b
0     1   0.01  -1.5           1           0
1     2  -0.01   0.0           0           1
2     3   0.25   3.6           1           0
3     4  -4.10   1.3           1           0
4     5   0.00  -2.0           0           1
```

There are some nuances to fitting certain statistical models with dummy variables. It may be simpler and less error-prone to use Patsy (the subject of the next section) when you have more than simple numeric columns.

12.2 Creating Model Descriptions with Patsy

Patsy (*https://patsy.readthedocs.io/*) is a Python library for describing statistical models (especially linear models) with a string-based "formula syntax," which is inspired by (but not exactly the same as) the formula syntax used by the R and S statistical programming languages. It is installed automatically when you install statsmodels:

```
conda install statsmodels
```

Patsy is well supported for specifying linear models in statsmodels, so I will focus on some of the main features to help you get up and running. Patsy's *formulas* are a special string syntax that looks like:

```
y ~ x0 + x1
```

The syntax a + b does not mean to add a to b, but rather that these are *terms* in the *design matrix* created for the model. The `patsy.dmatrices` function takes a formula string along with a dataset (which can be a DataFrame or a dictionary of arrays) and produces design matrices for a linear model:

```
In [29]: data = pd.DataFrame({
   ....:     'x0': [1, 2, 3, 4, 5],
   ....:     'x1': [0.01, -0.01, 0.25, -4.1, 0.],
   ....:     'y': [-1.5, 0., 3.6, 1.3, -2.]})
```

```
In [30]: data
Out[30]:
   x0    x1    y
0   1   0.01 -1.5
1   2  -0.01  0.0
2   3   0.25  3.6
3   4  -4.10  1.3
4   5   0.00 -2.0

In [31]: import patsy

In [32]: y, X = patsy.dmatrices('y ~ x0 + x1', data)
```

Now we have:

```
In [33]: y
Out[33]:
DesignMatrix with shape (5, 1)
     y
  -1.5
   0.0
   3.6
   1.3
  -2.0
  Terms:
    'y' (column 0)

In [34]: X
Out[34]:
DesignMatrix with shape (5, 3)
  Intercept  x0     x1
          1   1   0.01
          1   2  -0.01
          1   3   0.25
          1   4  -4.10
          1   5   0.00
  Terms:
    'Intercept' (column 0)
    'x0' (column 1)
    'x1' (column 2)
```

These Patsy `DesignMatrix` instances are NumPy ndarrays with additional metadata:

```
In [35]: np.asarray(y)
Out[35]:
array([[-1.5],
       [ 0. ],
       [ 3.6],
       [ 1.3],
       [-2. ]])

In [36]: np.asarray(X)
```

```
Out[36]:
array([[ 1.  , 1.  ,  0.01],
       [ 1.  , 2.  , -0.01],
       [ 1.  , 3.  ,  0.25],
       [ 1.  , 4.  , -4.1 ],
       [ 1.  , 5.  ,  0.  ]])
```

You might wonder where the Intercept term came from. This is a convention for linear models like ordinary least squares (OLS) regression. You can suppress the intercept by adding the term + 0 to the model:

```
In [37]: patsy.dmatrices('y ~ x0 + x1 + 0', data)[1]
Out[37]:
DesignMatrix with shape (5, 2)
  x0    x1
   1   0.01
   2  -0.01
   3   0.25
   4  -4.10
   5   0.00
  Terms:
    'x0' (column 0)
    'x1' (column 1)
```

The Patsy objects can be passed directly into algorithms like numpy.linalg.lstsq, which performs an ordinary least squares regression:

```
In [38]: coef, resid, _, _ = np.linalg.lstsq(X, y)
```

The model metadata is retained in the design_info attribute, so you can reattach the model column names to the fitted coefficients to obtain a Series, for example:

```
In [39]: coef
Out[39]:
array([[ 0.3129],
       [-0.0791],
       [-0.2655]])

In [40]: coef = pd.Series(coef.squeeze(), index=X.design_info.column_names)

In [41]: coef
Out[41]:
Intercept    0.312910
x0          -0.079106
x1          -0.265464
dtype: float64
```

Data Transformations in Patsy Formulas

You can mix Python code into your Patsy formulas; when evaluating the formula, the library will try to find the functions you use in the enclosing scope:

```
In [42]: y, X = patsy.dmatrices('y ~ x0 + np.log(np.abs(x1) + 1)', data)

In [43]: X
Out[43]:
DesignMatrix with shape (5, 3)
  Intercept  x0  np.log(np.abs(x1) + 1)
          1   1                 0.00995
          1   2                 0.00995
          1   3                 0.22314
          1   4                 1.62924
          1   5                 0.00000
  Terms:
    'Intercept' (column 0)
    'x0' (column 1)
    'np.log(np.abs(x1) + 1)' (column 2)
```

Some commonly used variable transformations include *standardizing* (to mean 0 and variance 1) and *centering* (subtracting the mean). Patsy has built-in functions for this purpose:

```
In [44]: y, X = patsy.dmatrices('y ~ standardize(x0) + center(x1)', data)

In [45]: X
Out[45]:
DesignMatrix with shape (5, 3)
  Intercept  standardize(x0)  center(x1)
          1         -1.41421        0.78
          1         -0.70711        0.76
          1          0.00000        1.02
          1          0.70711       -3.33
          1          1.41421        0.77
  Terms:
    'Intercept' (column 0)
    'standardize(x0)' (column 1)
    'center(x1)' (column 2)
```

As part of a modeling process, you may fit a model on one dataset, then evaluate the model based on another. This might be a *hold-out* portion or new data that is observed later. When applying transformations like center and standardize, you should be careful when using the model to form predications based on new data. These are called *stateful* transformations, because you must use statistics like the mean or standard deviation of the original dataset when transforming a new dataset.

The patsy.build_design_matrices function can apply transformations to new *out-of-sample* data using the saved information from the original *in-sample* dataset:

```
In [46]: new_data = pd.DataFrame({
   ....:     'x0': [6, 7, 8, 9],
   ....:     'x1': [3.1, -0.5, 0, 2.3],
   ....:     'y': [1, 2, 3, 4]})

In [47]: new_X = patsy.build_design_matrices([X.design_info], new_data)
```

```
In [48]: new_X
Out[48]:
[DesignMatrix with shape (4, 3)
   Intercept  standardize(x0)  center(x1)
           1          2.12132        3.87
           1          2.82843        0.27
           1          3.53553        0.77
           1          4.24264        3.07
  Terms:
    'Intercept' (column 0)
    'standardize(x0)' (column 1)
    'center(x1)' (column 2)]
```

Because the plus symbol (+) in the context of Patsy formulas does not mean addition, when you want to add columns from a dataset by name, you must wrap them in the special I function:

```
In [49]: y, X = patsy.dmatrices('y ~ I(x0 + x1)', data)

In [50]: X
Out[50]:
DesignMatrix with shape (5, 2)
  Intercept  I(x0 + x1)
          1        1.01
          1        1.99
          1        3.25
          1       -0.10
          1        5.00
  Terms:
    'Intercept' (column 0)
    'I(x0 + x1)' (column 1)
```

Patsy has several other built-in transforms in the `patsy.builtins` module. See the online documentation for more.

Categorical data has a special class of transformations, which I explain next.

Categorical Data and Patsy

Nonnumeric data can be transformed for a model design matrix in many different ways. A complete treatment of this topic is outside the scope of this book and would be studied best along with a course in statistics.

When you use nonnumeric terms in a Patsy formula, they are converted to dummy variables by default. If there is an intercept, one of the levels will be left out to avoid collinearity:

```
In [51]: data = pd.DataFrame({
   ....:        'key1': ['a', 'a', 'b', 'b', 'a', 'b', 'a', 'b'],
   ....:        'key2': [0, 1, 0, 1, 0, 1, 0, 0],
   ....:        'v1': [1, 2, 3, 4, 5, 6, 7, 8],
```

```
    ....:        'v2': [-1, 0, 2.5, -0.5, 4.0, -1.2, 0.2, -1.7]
    ....: })

In [52]: y, X = patsy.dmatrices('v2 ~ key1', data)

In [53]: X
Out[53]:
DesignMatrix with shape (8, 2)
  Intercept  key1[T.b]
          1          0
          1          0
          1          1
          1          1
          1          0
          1          1
          1          0
          1          1
  Terms:
    'Intercept' (column 0)
    'key1' (column 1)
```

If you omit the intercept from the model, then columns for each category value will be included in the model design matrix:

```
In [54]: y, X = patsy.dmatrices('v2 ~ key1 + 0', data)

In [55]: X
Out[55]:
DesignMatrix with shape (8, 2)
  key1[a]  key1[b]
        1        0
        1        0
        0        1
        0        1
        1        0
        0        1
        1        0
        0        1
  Terms:
    'key1' (columns 0:2)
```

Numeric columns can be interpreted as categorical with the C function:

```
In [56]: y, X = patsy.dmatrices('v2 ~ C(key2)', data)

In [57]: X
Out[57]:
DesignMatrix with shape (8, 2)
  Intercept  C(key2)[T.1]
          1             0
          1             1
          1             0
          1             1
```

```
               1              0
               1              1
               1              0
               1              0
    Terms:
       'Intercept' (column 0)
       'C(key2)' (column 1)
```

When you're using multiple categorical terms in a model, things can be more complicated, as you can include interaction terms of the form key1:key2, which can be
used, for example, in analysis of variance (ANOVA) models:

```
In [58]: data['key2'] = data['key2'].map({0: 'zero', 1: 'one'})

In [59]: data
Out[59]:
  key1 key2  v1   v2
0    a zero   1 -1.0
1    a  one   2  0.0
2    b zero   3  2.5
3    b  one   4 -0.5
4    a zero   5  4.0
5    b  one   6 -1.2
6    a zero   7  0.2
7    b zero   8 -1.7

In [60]: y, X = patsy.dmatrices('v2 ~ key1 + key2', data)

In [61]: X
Out[61]:
DesignMatrix with shape (8, 3)
  Intercept  key1[T.b]  key2[T.zero]
          1          0             1
          1          0             0
          1          1             1
          1          1             0
          1          0             1
          1          1             0
          1          0             1
          1          1             1
    Terms:
       'Intercept' (column 0)
       'key1' (column 1)
       'key2' (column 2)

In [62]: y, X = patsy.dmatrices('v2 ~ key1 + key2 + key1:key2', data)

In [63]: X
Out[63]:
DesignMatrix with shape (8, 4)
  Intercept  key1[T.b]  key2[T.zero]  key1[T.b]:key2[T.zero]
          1          0             1                       0
```

```
1          0          0          0
1          1          1          1
1          1          0          0
1          0          1          0
1          1          0          0
1          0          1          0
1          1          1          1
Terms:
    'Intercept' (column 0)
    'key1' (column 1)
    'key2' (column 2)
    'key1:key2' (column 3)
```

Patsy provides for other ways to transform categorical data, including transformations for terms with a particular ordering. See the online documentation for more.

12.3 Introduction to statsmodels

statsmodels (*http://www.statsmodels.org*) is a Python library for fitting many kinds of statistical models, performing statistical tests, and data exploration and visualization. statsmodels contains more "classical" frequentist statistical methods, while Bayesian methods and machine learning models are found in other libraries.

Some kinds of models found in statsmodels include:

- Linear models, generalized linear models, and robust linear models
- Linear mixed effects models
- Analysis of variance (ANOVA) methods
- Time series processes and state space models
- Generalized method of moments

In the next few pages, we will use a few basic tools in statsmodels and explore how to use the modeling interfaces with Patsy formulas and pandas DataFrame objects. If you didn't install statsmodels in the Patsy discussion earlier, you can install it now with:

```
conda install statsmodels
```

Estimating Linear Models

There are several kinds of linear regression models in statsmodels, from the more basic (e.g., ordinary least squares) to more complex (e.g., iteratively reweighted least squares).

Linear models in statsmodels have two different main interfaces: array based and formula based. These are accessed through these API module imports:

```
import statsmodels.api as sm
import statsmodels.formula.api as smf
```

To show how to use these, we generate a linear model from some random data. Run the following code in a Jupyter cell:

```
# To make the example reproducible
rng = np.random.default_rng(seed=12345)

def dnorm(mean, variance, size=1):
    if isinstance(size, int):
        size = size,
    return mean + np.sqrt(variance) * rng.standard_normal(*size)

N = 100
X = np.c_[dnorm(0, 0.4, size=N),
          dnorm(0, 0.6, size=N),
          dnorm(0, 0.2, size=N)]
eps = dnorm(0, 0.1, size=N)
beta = [0.1, 0.3, 0.5]

y = np.dot(X, beta) + eps
```

Here, I wrote down the "true" model with known parameters beta. In this case, dnorm is a helper function for generating normally distributed data with a particular mean and variance. So now we have:

```
In [66]: X[:5]
Out[66]:
array([[-0.9005, -0.1894, -1.0279],
       [ 0.7993, -1.546 , -0.3274],
       [-0.5507, -0.1203,  0.3294],
       [-0.1639,  0.824 ,  0.2083],
       [-0.0477, -0.2131, -0.0482]])

In [67]: y[:5]
Out[67]: array([-0.5995, -0.5885,  0.1856, -0.0075, -0.0154])
```

A linear model is generally fitted with an intercept term, as we saw before with Patsy. The sm.add_constant function can add an intercept column to an existing matrix:

```
In [68]: X_model = sm.add_constant(X)

In [69]: X_model[:5]
Out[69]:
array([[ 1.    , -0.9005, -0.1894, -1.0279],
       [ 1.    ,  0.7993, -1.546 , -0.3274],
       [ 1.    , -0.5507, -0.1203,  0.3294],
       [ 1.    , -0.1639,  0.824 ,  0.2083],
       [ 1.    , -0.0477, -0.2131, -0.0482]])
```

The sm.OLS class can fit an ordinary least squares linear regression:

```
In [70]: model = sm.OLS(y, X)
```

The model's `fit` method returns a regression results object containing estimated model parameters and other diagnostics:

```
In [71]: results = model.fit()

In [72]: results.params
Out[72]: array([0.0668, 0.268 , 0.4505])
```

The `summary` method on `results` can print a model detailing diagnostic output of the model:

```
In [73]: print(results.summary())
OLS Regression Results
===========================================================================
======
Dep. Variable:                       y   R-squared (uncentered):
 0.469
Model:                             OLS   Adj. R-squared (uncentered):
 0.452
Method:                  Least Squares   F-statistic:
 28.51
Date:                 Fri, 12 Aug 2022   Prob (F-statistic):                2.
66e-13
Time:                         14:09:18   Log-Likelihood:                      -
25.611
No. Observations:                  100   AIC:
 57.22
Df Residuals:                       97   BIC:
 65.04
Df Model:                            3

Covariance Type:             nonrobust

===========================================================================
                 coef    std err          t      P>|t|      [0.025      0.975]
---------------------------------------------------------------------------
x1             0.0668      0.054      1.243      0.217     -0.040      0.174
x2             0.2680      0.042      6.313      0.000      0.184      0.352
x3             0.4505      0.068      6.605      0.000      0.315      0.586
===========================================================================
Omnibus:                         0.435   Durbin-Watson:                   1.869
Prob(Omnibus):                   0.805   Jarque-Bera (JB):                0.301
Skew:                            0.134   Prob(JB):                        0.860
Kurtosis:                        2.995   Cond. No.                        1.64
===========================================================================

Notes:
[1] R² is computed without centering (uncentered) since the model does not contai
n a constant.
[2] Standard Errors assume that the covariance matrix of the errors is correctly
specified.
```

The parameter names here have been given the generic names x1, x2, and so on. Suppose instead that all of the model parameters are in a DataFrame:

```
In [74]: data = pd.DataFrame(X, columns=['col0', 'col1', 'col2'])

In [75]: data['y'] = y

In [76]: data[:5]
Out[76]:
        col0      col1      col2         y
0 -0.900506 -0.189430 -1.027870 -0.599527
1  0.799252 -1.545984 -0.327397 -0.588454
2 -0.550655 -0.120254  0.329359  0.185634
3 -0.163916  0.824040  0.208275 -0.007477
4 -0.047651 -0.213147 -0.048244 -0.015374
```

Now we can use the statsmodels formula API and Patsy formula strings:

```
In [77]: results = smf.ols('y ~ col0 + col1 + col2', data=data).fit()

In [78]: results.params
Out[78]:
Intercept   -0.020799
col0         0.065813
col1         0.268970
col2         0.449419
dtype: float64

In [79]: results.tvalues
Out[79]:
Intercept   -0.652501
col0         1.219768
col1         6.312369
col2         6.567428
dtype: float64
```

Observe how statsmodels has returned results as Series with the DataFrame column names attached. We also do not need to use add_constant when using formulas and pandas objects.

Given new out-of-sample data, you can compute predicted values given the estimated model parameters:

```
In [80]: results.predict(data[:5])
Out[80]:
0   -0.592959
1   -0.531160
2    0.058636
3    0.283658
4   -0.102947
dtype: float64
```

There are many additional tools for analysis, diagnostics, and visualization of linear model results in statsmodels that you can explore. There are also other kinds of linear models beyond ordinary least squares.

Estimating Time Series Processes

Another class of models in statsmodels is for time series analysis. Among these are autoregressive processes, Kalman filtering and other state space models, and multivariate autoregressive models.

Let's simulate some time series data with an autoregressive structure and noise. Run the following in Jupyter:

```
init_x = 4

values = [init_x, init_x]
N = 1000

b0 = 0.8
b1 = -0.4
noise = dnorm(0, 0.1, N)
for i in range(N):
    new_x = values[-1] * b0 + values[-2] * b1 + noise[i]
    values.append(new_x)
```

This data has an AR(2) structure (two *lags*) with parameters 0.8 and -0.4. When you fit an AR model, you may not know the number of lagged terms to include, so you can fit the model with some larger number of lags:

```
In [82]: from statsmodels.tsa.ar_model import AutoReg

In [83]: MAXLAGS = 5

In [84]: model = AutoReg(values, MAXLAGS)

In [85]: results = model.fit()
```

The estimated parameters in the results have the intercept first, and the estimates for the first two lags next:

```
In [86]: results.params
Out[86]: array([ 0.0235,  0.8097, -0.4287, -0.0334,  0.0427, -0.0567])
```

Deeper details of these models and how to interpret their results are beyond what I can cover in this book, but there's plenty more to discover in the statsmodels documentation.

12.4 Introduction to scikit-learn

scikit-learn (*http://scikit-learn.org*) is one of the most widely used and trusted general-purpose Python machine learning toolkits. It contains a broad selection of standard supervised and unsupervised machine learning methods, with tools for model selection and evaluation, data transformation, data loading, and model persistence. These models can be used for classification, clustering, prediction, and other common tasks. You can install scikit-learn from conda like so:

```
conda install scikit-learn
```

There are excellent online and print resources for learning about machine learning and how to apply libraries like scikit-learn to solve real-world problems. In this section, I will give a brief flavor of the scikit-learn API style.

pandas integration in scikit-learn has improved significantly in recent years, and by the time you are reading this it may have improved even more. I encourage you to check out the latest project documentation.

As an example for this chapter, I use a now-classic dataset from a Kaggle competition (*https://www.kaggle.com/c/titanic*) about passenger survival rates on the *Titanic* in 1912. We load the training and test datasets using pandas:

```
In [87]: train = pd.read_csv('datasets/titanic/train.csv')

In [88]: test = pd.read_csv('datasets/titanic/test.csv')

In [89]: train.head(4)
Out[89]:
   PassengerId  Survived  Pclass  \
0            1         0       3
1            2         1       1
2            3         1       3
3            4         1       1

                                                 Name     Sex   Age  SibSp  \
0                              Braund, Mr. Owen Harris    male  22.0      1
1  Cumings, Mrs. John Bradley (Florence Briggs Thayer)  female  38.0      1
2                               Heikkinen, Miss. Laina  female  26.0      0
3         Futrelle, Mrs. Jacques Heath (Lily May Peel)  female  35.0      1
   Parch            Ticket     Fare Cabin Embarked
0      0         A/5 21171   7.2500   NaN        S
1      0          PC 17599  71.2833   C85        C
2      0  STON/O2. 3101282   7.9250   NaN        S
3      0            113803  53.1000  C123        S
```

Libraries like statsmodels and scikit-learn generally cannot be fed missing data, so we look at the columns to see if there are any that contain missing data:

```
In [90]: train.isna().sum()
Out[90]:
PassengerId      0
```

```
Survived       0
Pclass         0
Name           0
Sex            0
Age          177
SibSp          0
Parch          0
Ticket         0
Fare           0
Cabin        687
Embarked       2
dtype: int64

In [91]: test.isna().sum()
Out[91]:
PassengerId    0
Pclass         0
Name           0
Sex            0
Age           86
SibSp          0
Parch          0
Ticket         0
Fare           1
Cabin        327
Embarked       0
dtype: int64
```

In statistics and machine learning examples like this one, a typical task is to predict whether a passenger would survive based on features in the data. A model is fitted on a *training* dataset and then evaluated on an out-of-sample *testing* dataset.

I would like to use Age as a predictor, but it has missing data. There are a number of ways to do missing data imputation, but I will do a simple one and use the median of the training dataset to fill the nulls in both tables:

```
In [92]: impute_value = train['Age'].median()
```

```
In [93]: train['Age'] = train['Age'].fillna(impute_value)
```

```
In [94]: test['Age'] = test['Age'].fillna(impute_value)
```

Now we need to specify our models. I add a column IsFemale as an encoded version of the 'Sex' column:

```
In [95]: train['IsFemale'] = (train['Sex'] == 'female').astype(int)
```

```
In [96]: test['IsFemale'] = (test['Sex'] == 'female').astype(int)
```

Then we decide on some model variables and create NumPy arrays:

```
In [97]: predictors = ['Pclass', 'IsFemale', 'Age']
```

```
In [98]: X_train = train[predictors].to_numpy()

In [99]: X_test = test[predictors].to_numpy()

In [100]: y_train = train['Survived'].to_numpy()

In [101]: X_train[:5]
Out[101]:
array([[ 3.,  0., 22.],
       [ 1.,  1., 38.],
       [ 3.,  1., 26.],
       [ 1.,  1., 35.],
       [ 3.,  0., 35.]])

In [102]: y_train[:5]
Out[102]: array([0, 1, 1, 1, 0])
```

I make no claims that this is a good model or that these features are engineered properly. We use the `LogisticRegression` model from scikit-learn and create a model instance:

```
In [103]: from sklearn.linear_model import LogisticRegression

In [104]: model = LogisticRegression()
```

We can fit this model to the training data using the model's `fit` method:

```
In [105]: model.fit(X_train, y_train)
Out[105]: LogisticRegression()
```

Now, we can form predictions for the test dataset using `model.predict`:

```
In [106]: y_predict = model.predict(X_test)

In [107]: y_predict[:10]
Out[107]: array([0, 0, 0, 0, 1, 0, 1, 0, 1, 0])
```

If you had the true values for the test dataset, you could compute an accuracy percentage or some other error metric:

```
(y_true == y_predict).mean()
```

In practice, there are often many additional layers of complexity in model training. Many models have parameters that can be tuned, and there are techniques such as *cross-validation* that can be used for parameter tuning to avoid overfitting to the training data. This can often yield better predictive performance or robustness on new data.

Cross-validation works by splitting the training data to simulate out-of-sample prediction. Based on a model accuracy score like mean squared error, you can perform a grid search on model parameters. Some models, like logistic regression, have estimator classes with built-in cross-validation. For example, the `LogisticRegressionCV` class can be used with a parameter indicating how fine-grained of a grid search to do on the model regularization parameter C:

```
In [108]: from sklearn.linear_model import LogisticRegressionCV

In [109]: model_cv = LogisticRegressionCV(Cs=10)

In [110]: model_cv.fit(X_train, y_train)
Out[110]: LogisticRegressionCV()
```

To do cross-validation by hand, you can use the `cross_val_score` helper function, which handles the data splitting process. For example, to cross-validate our model with four nonoverlapping splits of the training data, we can do:

```
In [111]: from sklearn.model_selection import cross_val_score

In [112]: model = LogisticRegression(C=10)

In [113]: scores = cross_val_score(model, X_train, y_train, cv=4)

In [114]: scores
Out[114]: array([0.7758, 0.7982, 0.7758, 0.7883])
```

The default scoring metric is model dependent, but it is possible to choose an explicit scoring function. Cross-validated models take longer to train but can often yield better model performance.

12.5 Conclusion

While I have only skimmed the surface of some Python modeling libraries, there are more and more frameworks for various kinds of statistics and machine learning either implemented in Python or with a Python user interface.

This book is focused especially on data wrangling, but there are many others dedicated to modeling and data science tools. Some excellent ones are:

- *Introduction to Machine Learning with Python* by Andreas Müller and Sarah Guido (O'Reilly)
- *Python Data Science Handbook* by Jake VanderPlas (O'Reilly)
- *Data Science from Scratch: First Principles with Python* by Joel Grus (O'Reilly)
- *Python Machine Learning* by Sebastian Raschka and Vahid Mirjalili (Packt Publishing)
- *Hands-On Machine Learning with Scikit-Learn, Keras, and TensorFlow* by Aurélien Géron (O'Reilly)

While books can be valuable resources for learning, they can sometimes grow out of date when the underlying open source software changes. It's a good idea to be familiar with the documentation for the various statistics or machine learning frameworks to stay up to date on the latest features and API.

Data Analysis Examples

Now that we've reached the final chapter of this book, we're going to take a look at a number of real-world datasets. For each dataset, we'll use the techniques presented in this book to extract meaning from the raw data. The demonstrated techniques can be applied to all manner of other datasets. This chapter contains a collection of miscellaneous example datasets that you can use for practice with the tools in this book.

The example datasets are found in the book's accompanying GitHub repository (*http://github.com/wesm/pydata-book*). If you are unable to access GitHub, you can also get them from the repository mirror on Gitee (*https://gitee.com/wesmckinn/pydata-book*).

13.1 Bitly Data from 1.USA.gov

In 2011, the URL shortening service Bitly (*https://bitly.com*) partnered with the US government website USA.gov (*https://www.usa.gov*) to provide a feed of anonymous data gathered from users who shorten links ending with *.gov* or *.mil*. In 2011, a live feed as well as hourly snapshots were available as downloadable text files. This service is shut down at the time of this writing (2022), but we preserved one of the data files for the book's examples.

In the case of the hourly snapshots, each line in each file contains a common form of web data known as JSON, which stands for JavaScript Object Notation. For example, if we read just the first line of a file, we may see something like this:

```
In [5]: path = "datasets/bitly_usagov/example.txt"

In [6]: with open(path) as f:
   ...:     print(f.readline())
   ...:
```

{ "a": "Mozilla\\/5.0 (Windows NT 6.1; WOW64) AppleWebKit\\/535.11
(KHTML, like Gecko) Chrome\\/17.0.963.78 Safari\\/535.11", "c": "US", "nk": 1,
"tz": "America\\/New_York", "gr": "MA", "g": "A6qOVH", "h": "wfLQtf", "l":
"orofrog", "al": "en-US,en;q=0.8", "hh": "1.usa.gov", "r":
"http:\\/\\/www.facebook.com\\/l\\/7AQEFzjSi\\/1.usa.gov\\/wfLQtf", "u":
"http:\\/\\/www.ncbi.nlm.nih.gov\\/pubmed\\/22415991", "t": 1331923247, "hc":
1331822918, "cy": "Danvers", "ll": [42.576698, -70.954903] }

Python has both built-in and third-party libraries for converting a JSON string into a
Python dictionary. Here we'll use the json module and its loads function invoked on
each line in the sample file we downloaded:

```
import json
with open(path) as f:
    records = [json.loads(line) for line in f]
```

The resulting object records is now a list of Python dictionaries:

```
In [18]: records[0]
Out[18]:
{'a': 'Mozilla/5.0 (Windows NT 6.1; WOW64) AppleWebKit/535.11 (KHTML, like Gecko)
Chrome/17.0.963.78 Safari/535.11',
 'al': 'en-US,en;q=0.8',
 'c': 'US',
 'cy': 'Danvers',
 'g': 'A6qOVH',
 'gr': 'MA',
 'h': 'wfLQtf',
 'hc': 1331822918,
 'hh': '1.usa.gov',
 'l': 'orofrog',
 'll': [42.576698, -70.954903],
 'nk': 1,
 'r': 'http://www.facebook.com/l/7AQEFzjSi/1.usa.gov/wfLQtf',
 't': 1331923247,
 'tz': 'America/New_York',
 'u': 'http://www.ncbi.nlm.nih.gov/pubmed/22415991'}
```

Counting Time Zones in Pure Python

Suppose we were interested in finding the time zones that occur most often in the
dataset (the tz field). There are many ways we could do this. First, let's extract a list of
time zones again using a list comprehension:

```
In [15]: time_zones = [rec["tz"] for rec in records]
---------------------------------------------------------------------------
KeyError                                  Traceback (most recent call last)
<ipython-input-15-abdeba901c13> in <module>
----> 1 time_zones = [rec["tz"] for rec in records]
<ipython-input-15-abdeba901c13> in <listcomp>(.0)
----> 1 time_zones = [rec["tz"] for rec in records]
KeyError: 'tz'
```

Oops! Turns out that not all of the records have a time zone field. We can handle this by adding the check `if "tz" in rec` at the end of the list comprehension:

```
In [16]: time_zones = [rec["tz"] for rec in records if "tz" in rec]
```

```
In [17]: time_zones[:10]
Out[17]:
['America/New_York',
 'America/Denver',
 'America/New_York',
 'America/Sao_Paulo',
 'America/New_York',
 'America/New_York',
 'Europe/Warsaw',
 '',
 '',
 '']
```

Just looking at the first 10 time zones, we see that some of them are unknown (empty string). You can filter these out also, but I'll leave them in for now. Next, to produce counts by time zone, I'll show two approaches: a harder way (using just the Python standard library) and a simpler way (using pandas). One way to do the counting is to use a dictionary to store counts while we iterate through the time zones:

```python
def get_counts(sequence):
    counts = {}
    for x in sequence:
        if x in counts:
            counts[x] += 1
        else:
            counts[x] = 1
    return counts
```

Using more advanced tools in the Python standard library, you can write the same thing more briefly:

```python
from collections import defaultdict

def get_counts2(sequence):
    counts = defaultdict(int) # values will initialize to 0
    for x in sequence:
        counts[x] += 1
    return counts
```

I put this logic in a function just to make it more reusable. To use it on the time zones, just pass the `time_zones` list:

```
In [20]: counts = get_counts(time_zones)
```

```
In [21]: counts["America/New_York"]
Out[21]: 1251
```

```
In [22]: len(time_zones)
Out[22]: 3440
```

If we wanted the top 10 time zones and their counts, we can make a list of tuples by (count, timezone) and sort it:

```
def top_counts(count_dict, n=10):
    value_key_pairs = [(count, tz) for tz, count in count_dict.items()]
    value_key_pairs.sort()
    return value_key_pairs[-n:]
```

We have then:

```
In [24]: top_counts(counts)
Out[24]:
[(33, 'America/Sao_Paulo'),
 (35, 'Europe/Madrid'),
 (36, 'Pacific/Honolulu'),
 (37, 'Asia/Tokyo'),
 (74, 'Europe/London'),
 (191, 'America/Denver'),
 (382, 'America/Los_Angeles'),
 (400, 'America/Chicago'),
 (521, ''),
 (1251, 'America/New_York')]
```

If you search the Python standard library, you may find the collections.Counter class, which makes this task even simpler:

```
In [25]: from collections import Counter

In [26]: counts = Counter(time_zones)

In [27]: counts.most_common(10)
Out[27]:
[('America/New_York', 1251),
 ('', 521),
 ('America/Chicago', 400),
 ('America/Los_Angeles', 382),
 ('America/Denver', 191),
 ('Europe/London', 74),
 ('Asia/Tokyo', 37),
 ('Pacific/Honolulu', 36),
 ('Europe/Madrid', 35),
 ('America/Sao_Paulo', 33)]
```

Counting Time Zones with pandas

You can create a DataFrame from the original set of records by passing the list of records to pandas.DataFrame:

```
In [28]: frame = pd.DataFrame(records)
```

We can look at some basic information about this new DataFrame, such as column names, inferred column types, or number of missing values, using frame.info():

```
In [29]: frame.info()
<class 'pandas.core.frame.DataFrame'>
RangeIndex: 3560 entries, 0 to 3559
Data columns (total 18 columns):
 #   Column      Non-Null Count  Dtype
---  ------      --------------  -----
 0   a           3440 non-null   object
 1   c           2919 non-null   object
 2   nk          3440 non-null   float64
 3   tz          3440 non-null   object
 4   gr          2919 non-null   object
 5   g           3440 non-null   object
 6   h           3440 non-null   object
 7   l           3440 non-null   object
 8   al          3094 non-null   object
 9   hh          3440 non-null   object
 10  r           3440 non-null   object
 11  u           3440 non-null   object
 12  t           3440 non-null   float64
 13  hc          3440 non-null   float64
 14  cy          2919 non-null   object
 15  ll          2919 non-null   object
 16  _heartbeat_ 120 non-null    float64
 17  kw          93 non-null     object
dtypes: float64(4), object(14)
memory usage: 500.8+ KB

In [30]: frame["tz"].head()
Out[30]:
0     America/New_York
1       America/Denver
2     America/New_York
3    America/Sao_Paulo
4     America/New_York
Name: tz, dtype: object
```

The output shown for the frame is the *summary view*, shown for large DataFrame objects. We can then use the value_counts method for the Series:

```
In [31]: tz_counts = frame["tz"].value_counts()

In [32]: tz_counts.head()
Out[32]:
America/New_York       1251
                        521
America/Chicago         400
America/Los_Angeles     382
America/Denver          191
Name: tz, dtype: int64
```

We can visualize this data using matplotlib. We can make the plots a bit nicer by filling in a substitute value for unknown or missing time zone data in the records. We replace the missing values with the `fillna` method and use Boolean array indexing for the empty strings:

```
In [33]: clean_tz = frame["tz"].fillna("Missing")

In [34]: clean_tz[clean_tz == ""] = "Unknown"

In [35]: tz_counts = clean_tz.value_counts()

In [36]: tz_counts.head()
Out[36]:
America/New_York       1251
Unknown                 521
America/Chicago         400
America/Los_Angeles     382
America/Denver          191
Name: tz, dtype: int64
```

At this point, we can use the seaborn package (*http://seaborn.pydata.org*) to make a horizontal bar plot (see Figure 13-1 for the resulting visualization):

```
In [38]: import seaborn as sns

In [39]: subset = tz_counts.head()

In [40]: sns.barplot(y=subset.index, x=subset.to_numpy())
```

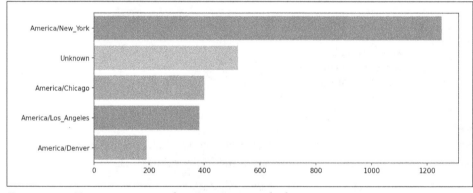

Figure 13-1. Top time zones in the 1.usa.gov sample data

The a field contains information about the browser, device, or application used to perform the URL shortening:

```
In [41]: frame["a"][1]
Out[41]: 'GoogleMaps/RochesterNY'

In [42]: frame["a"][50]
```

```
Out[42]: 'Mozilla/5.0 (Windows NT 5.1; rv:10.0.2) Gecko/20100101 Firefox/10.0.2'

In [43]: frame["a"][51][:50]  # long line
Out[43]: 'Mozilla/5.0 (Linux; U; Android 2.2.2; en-us; LG-P9'
```

Parsing all of the interesting information in these "agent" strings may seem like a daunting task. One possible strategy is to split off the first token in the string (corresponding roughly to the browser capability) and make another summary of the user behavior:

```
In [44]: results = pd.Series([x.split()[0] for x in frame["a"].dropna()])

In [45]: results.head(5)
Out[45]:
0             Mozilla/5.0
1    GoogleMaps/RochesterNY
2             Mozilla/4.0
3             Mozilla/5.0
4             Mozilla/5.0
dtype: object

In [46]: results.value_counts().head(8)
Out[46]:
Mozilla/5.0                 2594
Mozilla/4.0                  601
GoogleMaps/RochesterNY       121
Opera/9.80                    34
TEST_INTERNET_AGENT           24
GoogleProducer                21
Mozilla/6.0                    5
BlackBerry8520/5.0.0.681       4
dtype: int64
```

Now, suppose you wanted to decompose the top time zones into Windows and non-Windows users. As a simplification, let's say that a user is on Windows if the string "Windows" is in the agent string. Since some of the agents are missing, we'll exclude these from the data:

```
In [47]: cframe = frame[frame["a"].notna()].copy()
```

We want to then compute a value for whether or not each row is Windows:

```
In [48]: cframe["os"] = np.where(cframe["a"].str.contains("Windows"),
   ....:                         "Windows", "Not Windows")

In [49]: cframe["os"].head(5)
Out[49]:
0        Windows
1    Not Windows
2        Windows
3    Not Windows
4        Windows
Name: os, dtype: object
```

Then, you can group the data by its time zone column and this new list of operating systems:

```
In [50]: by_tz_os = cframe.groupby(["tz", "os"])
```

The group counts, analogous to the value_counts function, can be computed with size. This result is then reshaped into a table with unstack:

```
In [51]: agg_counts = by_tz_os.size().unstack().fillna(0)
```

```
In [52]: agg_counts.head()
Out[52]:
os                   Not Windows  Windows
tz
                          245.0    276.0
Africa/Cairo                0.0      3.0
Africa/Casablanca           0.0      1.0
Africa/Ceuta                0.0      2.0
Africa/Johannesburg         0.0      1.0
```

Finally, let's select the top overall time zones. To do so, I construct an indirect index array from the row counts in agg_counts. After computing the row counts with agg_counts.sum("columns"), I can call argsort() to obtain an index array that can be used to sort in ascending order:

```
In [53]: indexer = agg_counts.sum("columns").argsort()
```

```
In [54]: indexer.values[:10]
Out[54]: array([24, 20, 21, 92, 87, 53, 54, 57, 26, 55])
```

I use take to select the rows in that order, then slice off the last 10 rows (largest values):

```
In [55]: count_subset = agg_counts.take(indexer[-10:])
```

```
In [56]: count_subset
Out[56]:
os                   Not Windows  Windows
tz
America/Sao_Paulo           13.0     20.0
Europe/Madrid               16.0     19.0
Pacific/Honolulu             0.0     36.0
Asia/Tokyo                   2.0     35.0
Europe/London               43.0     31.0
America/Denver             132.0     59.0
America/Los_Angeles        130.0    252.0
America/Chicago            115.0    285.0
                           245.0    276.0
America/New_York           339.0    912.0
```

pandas has a convenience method called `nlargest` that does the same thing:

```
In [57]: agg_counts.sum(axis="columns").nlargest(10)
Out[57]:
tz
America/New_York        1251.0
                         521.0
America/Chicago          400.0
America/Los_Angeles      382.0
America/Denver           191.0
Europe/London             74.0
Asia/Tokyo                37.0
Pacific/Honolulu          36.0
Europe/Madrid             35.0
America/Sao_Paulo         33.0
dtype: float64
```

Then, this can be plotted in a grouped bar plot comparing the number of Windows and non-Windows users, using seaborn's `barplot` function (see Figure 13-2). I first call `count_subset.stack()` and reset the index to rearrange the data for better compatibility with seaborn:

```
In [59]: count_subset = count_subset.stack()

In [60]: count_subset.name = "total"

In [61]: count_subset = count_subset.reset_index()

In [62]: count_subset.head(10)
Out[62]:
                tz           os   total
0  America/Sao_Paulo  Not Windows   13.0
1  America/Sao_Paulo      Windows   20.0
2     Europe/Madrid   Not Windows   16.0
3     Europe/Madrid       Windows   19.0
4  Pacific/Honolulu   Not Windows    0.0
5  Pacific/Honolulu       Windows   36.0
6       Asia/Tokyo    Not Windows    2.0
7       Asia/Tokyo        Windows   35.0
8    Europe/London    Not Windows   43.0
9    Europe/London        Windows   31.0

In [63]: sns.barplot(x="total", y="tz", hue="os",  data=count_subset)
```

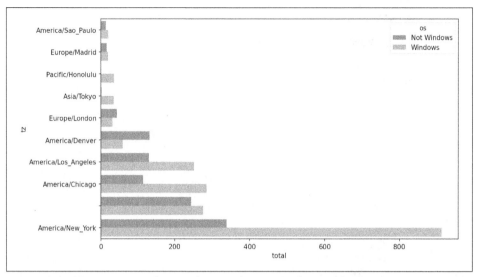

Figure 13-2. Top time zones by Windows and non-Windows users

It is a bit difficult to see the relative percentage of Windows users in the smaller groups, so let's normalize the group percentages to sum to 1:

```
def norm_total(group):
    group["normed_total"] = group["total"] / group["total"].sum()
    return group

results = count_subset.groupby("tz").apply(norm_total)
```

Then plot this in Figure 13-3:

```
In [66]: sns.barplot(x="normed_total", y="tz", hue="os", data=results)
```

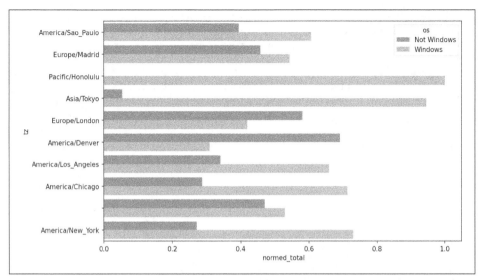

Figure 13-3. Percentage Windows and non-Windows users in top occurring time zones

We could have computed the normalized sum more efficiently by using the `trans form` method with `groupby`:

```
In [67]: g = count_subset.groupby("tz")

In [68]: results2 = count_subset["total"] / g["total"].transform("sum")
```

13.2 MovieLens 1M Dataset

GroupLens Research (*https://grouplens.org/datasets/movielens*) provides a number of collections of movie ratings data collected from users of MovieLens in the late 1990s and early 2000s. The data provides movie ratings, movie metadata (genres and year), and demographic data about the users (age, zip code, gender identification, and occupation). Such data is often of interest in the development of recommendation systems based on machine learning algorithms. While we do not explore machine learning techniques in detail in this book, I will show you how to slice and dice datasets like these into the exact form you need.

The MovieLens 1M dataset contains one million ratings collected from six thousand users on four thousand movies. It's spread across three tables: ratings, user information, and movie information. We can load each table into a pandas DataFrame object using `pandas.read_table`. Run the following code in a Jupyter cell:

```
unames = ["user_id", "gender", "age", "occupation", "zip"]
users = pd.read_table("datasets/movielens/users.dat", sep="::",
                      header=None, names=unames, engine="python")
```

```
rnames = ["user_id", "movie_id", "rating", "timestamp"]
ratings = pd.read_table("datasets/movielens/ratings.dat", sep="::",
                        header=None, names=rnames, engine="python")

mnames = ["movie_id", "title", "genres"]
movies = pd.read_table("datasets/movielens/movies.dat", sep="::",
                       header=None, names=mnames, engine="python")
```

You can verify that everything succeeded by looking at each DataFrame:

```
In [70]: users.head(5)
Out[70]:
   user_id gender  age  occupation    zip
0        1      F    1          10  48067
1        2      M   56          16  70072
2        3      M   25          15  55117
3        4      M   45           7  02460
4        5      M   25          20  55455

In [71]: ratings.head(5)
Out[71]:
   user_id  movie_id  rating   timestamp
0        1      1193       5   978300760
1        1       661       3   978302109
2        1       914       3   978301968
3        1      3408       4   978300275
4        1      2355       5   978824291

In [72]: movies.head(5)
Out[72]:
   movie_id                               title                         genres
0         1                    Toy Story (1995)    Animation|Children's|Comedy
1         2                      Jumanji (1995)   Adventure|Children's|Fantasy
2         3             Grumpier Old Men (1995)                 Comedy|Romance
3         4            Waiting to Exhale (1995)                   Comedy|Drama
4         5  Father of the Bride Part II (1995)                         Comedy

In [73]: ratings
Out[73]:
         user_id  movie_id  rating   timestamp
0              1      1193       5   978300760
1              1       661       3   978302109
2              1       914       3   978301968
3              1      3408       4   978300275
4              1      2355       5   978824291
...          ...       ...     ...         ...
1000204     6040      1091       1   956716541
1000205     6040      1094       5   956704887
1000206     6040       562       5   956704746
1000207     6040      1096       4   956715648
1000208     6040      1097       4   956715569
[1000209 rows x 4 columns]
```

Note that ages and occupations are coded as integers indicating groups described in the dataset's *README* file. Analyzing the data spread across three tables is not a simple task; for example, suppose you wanted to compute mean ratings for a particular movie by gender identity and age. As you will see, this is more convenient to do with all of the data merged together into a single table. Using pandas's `merge` function, we first merge `ratings` with `users` and then merge that result with the `movies` data. pandas infers which columns to use as the merge (or *join*) keys based on overlapping names:

```
In [74]: data = pd.merge(pd.merge(ratings, users), movies)
```

```
In [75]: data
Out[75]:
         user_id  movie_id  rating   timestamp gender  age  occupation    zip \
0              1      1193       5  978300760      F    1          10  48067
1              2      1193       5  978298413      M   56          16  70072
2             12      1193       4  978220179      M   25          12  32793
3             15      1193       4  978199279      M   25           7  22903
4             17      1193       5  978158471      M   50           1  95350
...          ...       ...     ...        ...    ...  ...         ...    ...
1000204     5949      2198       5  958846401      M   18          17  47901
1000205     5675      2703       3  976029116      M   35          14  30030
1000206     5780      2845       1  958153068      M   18          17  92886
1000207     5851      3607       5  957756608      F   18          20  55410
1000208     5938      2909       4  957273353      M   25           1  35401
                                              title                genres
0                   One Flew Over the Cuckoo's Nest (1975)               Drama
1                   One Flew Over the Cuckoo's Nest (1975)               Drama
2                   One Flew Over the Cuckoo's Nest (1975)               Drama
3                   One Flew Over the Cuckoo's Nest (1975)               Drama
4                   One Flew Over the Cuckoo's Nest (1975)               Drama
...                                             ...                   ...
1000204                          Modulations (1998)           Documentary
1000205                       Broken Vessels (1998)                 Drama
1000206                          White Boys (1999)                 Drama
1000207                    One Little Indian (1973)  Comedy|Drama|Western
1000208  Five Wives, Three Secretaries and Me (1998)           Documentary
[1000209 rows x 10 columns]
```

```
In [76]: data.iloc[0]
Out[76]:
user_id                                          1
movie_id                                      1193
rating                                           5
timestamp                                978300760
gender                                           F
age                                              1
occupation                                      10
zip                                          48067
title          One Flew Over the Cuckoo's Nest (1975)
```

```
genres                                    Drama
Name: 0, dtype: object
```

To get mean movie ratings for each film grouped by gender, we can use the
`pivot_table` method:

```
In [77]: mean_ratings = data.pivot_table("rating", index="title",
   ....:                                  columns="gender", aggfunc="mean")

In [78]: mean_ratings.head(5)
Out[78]:
gender                            F         M
title
$1,000,000 Duck (1971)       3.375000  2.761905
'Night Mother (1986)         3.388889  3.352941
'Til There Was You (1997)    2.675676  2.733333
'burbs, The (1989)           2.793478  2.962085
...And Justice for All (1979) 3.828571  3.689024
```

This produced another DataFrame containing mean ratings with movie titles as row
labels (the "index") and gender as column labels. I first filter down to movies that
received at least 250 ratings (an arbitrary number); to do this, I group the data by
title, and use `size()` to get a Series of group sizes for each title:

```
In [79]: ratings_by_title = data.groupby("title").size()

In [80]: ratings_by_title.head()
Out[80]:
title
$1,000,000 Duck (1971)        37
'Night Mother (1986)          70
'Til There Was You (1997)     52
'burbs, The (1989)           303
...And Justice for All (1979) 199
dtype: int64

In [81]: active_titles = ratings_by_title.index[ratings_by_title >= 250]

In [82]: active_titles
Out[82]:
Index([''burbs, The (1989)', '10 Things I Hate About You (1999)',
       '101 Dalmatians (1961)', '101 Dalmatians (1996)', '12 Angry Men (1957)',
       '13th Warrior, The (1999)', '2 Days in the Valley (1996)',
       '20,000 Leagues Under the Sea (1954)', '2001: A Space Odyssey (1968)',
       '2010 (1984)',
       ...
       'X-Men (2000)', 'Year of Living Dangerously (1982)',
       'Yellow Submarine (1968)', 'You've Got Mail (1998)',
       'Young Frankenstein (1974)', 'Young Guns (1988)',
       'Young Guns II (1990)', 'Young Sherlock Holmes (1985)',
       'Zero Effect (1998)', 'eXistenZ (1999)'],
      dtype='object', name='title', length=1216)
```

The index of titles receiving at least 250 ratings can then be used to select rows from mean_ratings using .loc:

```
In [83]: mean_ratings = mean_ratings.loc[active_titles]

In [84]: mean_ratings
Out[84]:
gender                                      F         M
title
'burbs, The (1989)                   2.793478  2.962085
10 Things I Hate About You (1999)    3.646552  3.311966
101 Dalmatians (1961)                3.791444  3.500000
101 Dalmatians (1996)                3.240000  2.911215
12 Angry Men (1957)                  4.184397  4.328421
...                                       ...       ...
Young Guns (1988)                    3.371795  3.425620
Young Guns II (1990)                 2.934783  2.904025
Young Sherlock Holmes (1985)         3.514706  3.363344
Zero Effect (1998)                   3.864407  3.723140
eXistenZ (1999)                      3.098592  3.289086
[1216 rows x 2 columns]
```

To see the top films among female viewers, we can sort by the F column in descending order:

```
In [86]: top_female_ratings = mean_ratings.sort_values("F", ascending=False)

In [87]: top_female_ratings.head()
Out[87]:
gender                                                      F         M
title
Close Shave, A (1995)                               4.644444  4.473795
Wrong Trousers, The (1993)                          4.588235  4.478261
Sunset Blvd. (a.k.a. Sunset Boulevard) (1950)       4.572650  4.464589
Wallace & Gromit: The Best of Aardman Animation (1996)  4.563107  4.385075
Schindler's List (1993)                             4.562602  4.491415
```

Measuring Rating Disagreement

Suppose you wanted to find the movies that are most divisive between male and female viewers. One way is to add a column to mean_ratings containing the difference in means, then sort by that:

```
In [88]: mean_ratings["diff"] = mean_ratings["M"] - mean_ratings["F"]
```

Sorting by "diff" yields the movies with the greatest rating difference so that we can see which ones were preferred by women:

```
In [89]: sorted_by_diff = mean_ratings.sort_values("diff")

In [90]: sorted_by_diff.head()
Out[90]:
```

```
gender                                   F         M       diff
title
Dirty Dancing (1987)              3.790378  2.959596 -0.830782
Jumpin' Jack Flash (1986)         3.254717  2.578358 -0.676359
Grease (1978)                     3.975265  3.367041 -0.608224
Little Women (1994)               3.870588  3.321739 -0.548849
Steel Magnolias (1989)            3.901734  3.365957 -0.535777
```

Reversing the order of the rows and again slicing off the top 10 rows, we get the movies preferred by men that women didn't rate as highly:

```
In [91]: sorted_by_diff[::-1].head()
Out[91]:
gender                                            F         M       diff
title
Good, The Bad and The Ugly, The (1966)     3.494949  4.221300  0.726351
Kentucky Fried Movie, The (1977)           2.878788  3.555147  0.676359
Dumb & Dumber (1994)                       2.697987  3.336595  0.638608
Longest Day, The (1962)                    3.411765  4.031447  0.619682
Cable Guy, The (1996)                      2.250000  2.863787  0.613787
```

Suppose instead you wanted the movies that elicited the most disagreement among viewers, independent of gender identification. Disagreement can be measured by the variance or standard deviation of the ratings. To get this, we first compute the rating standard deviation by title and then filter down to the active titles:

```
In [92]: rating_std_by_title = data.groupby("title")["rating"].std()

In [93]: rating_std_by_title = rating_std_by_title.loc[active_titles]

In [94]: rating_std_by_title.head()
Out[94]:
title
'burbs, The (1989)                1.107760
10 Things I Hate About You (1999) 0.989815
101 Dalmatians (1961)             0.982103
101 Dalmatians (1996)             1.098717
12 Angry Men (1957)               0.812731
Name: rating, dtype: float64
```

Then, we sort in descending order and select the first 10 rows, which are roughly the 10 most divisively rated movies:

```
In [95]: rating_std_by_title.sort_values(ascending=False)[:10]
Out[95]:
title
Dumb & Dumber (1994)                     1.321333
Blair Witch Project, The (1999)          1.316368
Natural Born Killers (1994)              1.307198
Tank Girl (1995)                         1.277695
Rocky Horror Picture Show, The (1975)    1.260177
Eyes Wide Shut (1999)                    1.259624
Evita (1996)                             1.253631
```

```
Billy Madison (1995)                    1.249970
Fear and Loathing in Las Vegas (1998)   1.246408
Bicentennial Man (1999)                 1.245533
Name: rating, dtype: float64
```

You may have noticed that movie genres are given as a pipe-separated (|) string, since a single movie can belong to multiple genres. To help us group the ratings data by genre, we can use the explode method on DataFrame. Let's take a look at how this works. First, we can split the genres string into a list of genres using the str.split method on the Series:

```
In [96]: movies["genres"].head()
Out[96]:
0      Animation|Children's|Comedy
1      Adventure|Children's|Fantasy
2                   Comedy|Romance
3                    Comedy|Drama
4                          Comedy
Name: genres, dtype: object

In [97]: movies["genres"].head().str.split("|")
Out[97]:
0      [Animation, Children's, Comedy]
1      [Adventure, Children's, Fantasy]
2                    [Comedy, Romance]
3                      [Comedy, Drama]
4                           [Comedy]
Name: genres, dtype: object

In [98]: movies["genre"] = movies.pop("genres").str.split("|")

In [99]: movies.head()
Out[99]:
   movie_id                             title  \
0         1                   Toy Story (1995)
1         2                     Jumanji (1995)
2         3            Grumpier Old Men (1995)
3         4           Waiting to Exhale (1995)
4         5  Father of the Bride Part II (1995)
                                     genre
0      [Animation, Children's, Comedy]
1      [Adventure, Children's, Fantasy]
2                    [Comedy, Romance]
3                      [Comedy, Drama]
4                           [Comedy]
```

Now, calling movies.explode("genre") generates a new DataFrame with one row for each "inner" element in each list of movie genres. For example, if a movie is classified as both a comedy and a romance, then there will be two rows in the result, one with just "Comedy" and the other with just "Romance":

```
In [100]: movies_exploded = movies.explode("genre")

In [101]: movies_exploded[:10]
Out[101]:
   movie_id                   title       genre
0         1         Toy Story (1995)   Animation
0         1         Toy Story (1995)  Children's
0         1         Toy Story (1995)      Comedy
1         2           Jumanji (1995)   Adventure
1         2           Jumanji (1995)  Children's
1         2           Jumanji (1995)     Fantasy
2         3   Grumpier Old Men (1995)      Comedy
2         3   Grumpier Old Men (1995)     Romance
3         4  Waiting to Exhale (1995)      Comedy
3         4  Waiting to Exhale (1995)       Drama
```

Now, we can merge all three tables together and group by genre:

```
In [102]: ratings_with_genre = pd.merge(pd.merge(movies_exploded, ratings), users
)

In [103]: ratings_with_genre.iloc[0]
Out[103]:
movie_id                       1
title          Toy Story (1995)
genre                 Animation
user_id                        1
rating                         5
timestamp              978824268
gender                         F
age                            1
occupation                    10
zip                        48067
Name: 0, dtype: object

In [104]: genre_ratings = (ratings_with_genre.groupby(["genre", "age"])
   .....:                  ["rating"].mean()
   .....:                  .unstack("age"))

In [105]: genre_ratings[:10]
Out[105]:
age                 1        18        25        35        45        50  \
genre
Action       3.506385  3.447097  3.453358  3.538107  3.528543  3.611333
Adventure    3.449975  3.408525  3.443163  3.515291  3.528963  3.628163
Animation    3.476113  3.624014  3.701228  3.740545  3.734856  3.780020
Children's   3.241642  3.294257  3.426873  3.518423  3.527593  3.556555
Comedy       3.497491  3.460417  3.490385  3.561984  3.591789  3.646868
Crime        3.710170  3.668054  3.680321  3.733736  3.750661  3.810688
Documentary  3.730769  3.865865  3.946690  3.953747  3.966521  3.908108
Drama        3.794735  3.721930  3.726428  3.782512  3.784356  3.878415
Fantasy      3.317647  3.353778  3.452484  3.482301  3.532468  3.581570
Film-Noir    4.145455  3.997368  4.058725  4.064910  4.105376  4.175401
```

```
age               56
genre
Action       3.610709
Adventure    3.649064
Animation    3.756233
Children's   3.621822
Comedy       3.650949
Crime        3.832549
Documentary  3.961538
Drama        3.933465
Fantasy      3.532700
Film-Noir    4.125932
```

13.3 US Baby Names 1880–2010

The United States Social Security Administration (SSA) has made available data on the frequency of baby names from 1880 through the present. Hadley Wickham, an author of several popular R packages, has this dataset in illustrating data manipulation in R.

We need to do some data wrangling to load this dataset, but once we do that we will have a DataFrame that looks like this:

```
In [4]: names.head(10)
Out[4]:
        name sex  births  year
0       Mary   F    7065  1880
1       Anna   F    2604  1880
2       Emma   F    2003  1880
3  Elizabeth   F    1939  1880
4     Minnie   F    1746  1880
5   Margaret   F    1578  1880
6        Ida   F    1472  1880
7      Alice   F    1414  1880
8     Bertha   F    1320  1880
9      Sarah   F    1288  1880
```

There are many things you might want to do with the dataset:

- Visualize the proportion of babies given a particular name (your own, or another name) over time
- Determine the relative rank of a name
- Determine the most popular names in each year or the names whose popularity has advanced or declined the most
- Analyze trends in names: vowels, consonants, length, overall diversity, changes in spelling, first and last letters
- Analyze external sources of trends: biblical names, celebrities, demographics

With the tools in this book, many of these kinds of analyses are within reach, so I will walk you through some of them.

As of this writing, the US Social Security Administration makes available data files, one per year, containing the total number of births for each sex/name combination. You can download the raw archive (*http://www.ssa.gov/oact/babynames/limits.html*) of these files.

If this page has been moved by the time you're reading this, it can most likely be located again with an internet search. After downloading the "National data" file *names.zip* and unzipping it, you will have a directory containing a series of files like *yob1880.txt*. I use the Unix `head` command to look at the first 10 lines of one of the files (on Windows, you can use the `more` command or open it in a text editor):

```
In [106]: !head -n 10 datasets/babynames/yob1880.txt
Mary,F,7065
Anna,F,2604
Emma,F,2003
Elizabeth,F,1939
Minnie,F,1746
Margaret,F,1578
Ida,F,1472
Alice,F,1414
Bertha,F,1320
Sarah,F,1288
```

As this is already in comma-separated form, it can be loaded into a DataFrame with `pandas.read_csv`:

```
In [107]: names1880 = pd.read_csv("datasets/babynames/yob1880.txt",
   .....:                          names=["name", "sex", "births"])

In [108]: names1880
Out[108]:
           name sex  births
0          Mary   F    7065
1          Anna   F    2604
2          Emma   F    2003
3     Elizabeth   F    1939
4        Minnie   F    1746
...         ...  ..     ...
1995     Woodie   M       5
1996     Worthy   M       5
1997     Wright   M       5
1998       York   M       5
1999  Zachariah   M       5
[2000 rows x 3 columns]
```

These files only contain names with at least five occurrences in each year, so for simplicity's sake we can use the sum of the births column by sex as the total number of births in that year:

```
In [109]: names1880.groupby("sex")["births"].sum()
Out[109]:
sex
F     90993
M    110493
Name: births, dtype: int64
```

Since the dataset is split into files by year, one of the first things to do is to assemble all of the data into a single DataFrame and further add a year field. You can do this using pandas.concat. Run the following in a Jupyter cell:

```
pieces = []
for year in range(1880, 2011):
    path = f"datasets/babynames/yob{year}.txt"
    frame = pd.read_csv(path, names=["name", "sex", "births"])

    # Add a column for the year
    frame["year"] = year
    pieces.append(frame)

# Concatenate everything into a single DataFrame
names = pd.concat(pieces, ignore_index=True)
```

There are a couple things to note here. First, remember that concat combines the DataFrame objects by row by default. Second, you have to pass ignore_index=True because we're not interested in preserving the original row numbers returned from pandas.read_csv. So we now have a single DataFrame containing all of the names data across all years:

```
In [111]: names
Out[111]:
              name sex  births  year
0             Mary   F    7065  1880
1             Anna   F    2604  1880
2             Emma   F    2003  1880
3        Elizabeth   F    1939  1880
4           Minnie   F    1746  1880
...            ...  ..     ...   ...
1690779     Zymaire  M       5  2010
1690780      Zyonne  M       5  2010
1690781   Zyquarius  M       5  2010
1690782       Zyran  M       5  2010
1690783       Zzyzx  M       5  2010
[1690784 rows x 4 columns]
```

With this data in hand, we can already start aggregating the data at the year and sex level using groupby or pivot_table (see Figure 13-4):

```
In [112]: total_births = names.pivot_table("births", index="year",
     .....:                                 columns="sex", aggfunc=sum)

In [113]: total_births.tail()
Out[113]:
sex         F       M
year
2006    1896468  2050234
2007    1916888  2069242
2008    1883645  2032310
2009    1827643  1973359
2010    1759010  1898382

In [114]: total_births.plot(title="Total births by sex and year")
```

Figure 13-4. Total births by sex and year

Next, let's insert a column prop with the fraction of babies given each name relative to the total number of births. A prop value of 0.02 would indicate that 2 out of every 100 babies were given a particular name. Thus, we group the data by year and sex, then add the new column to each group:

```
def add_prop(group):
    group["prop"] = group["births"] / group["births"].sum()
```

```
        return group
names = names.groupby(["year", "sex"]).apply(add_prop)
```

The resulting complete dataset now has the following columns:

```
In [116]: names
Out[116]:
              name sex  births  year      prop
0             Mary  F     7065  1880  0.077643
1             Anna  F     2604  1880  0.028618
2             Emma  F     2003  1880  0.022013
3        Elizabeth  F     1939  1880  0.021309
4           Minnie  F     1746  1880  0.019188
...            ...  ..     ...   ...       ...
1690779    Zymaire  M        5  2010  0.000003
1690780     Zyonne  M        5  2010  0.000003
1690781   Zyquarius  M       5  2010  0.000003
1690782      Zyran  M        5  2010  0.000003
1690783      Zzyzx  M        5  2010  0.000003
[1690784 rows x 5 columns]
```

When performing a group operation like this, it's often valuable to do a sanity check, like verifying that the prop column sums to 1 within all the groups:

```
In [117]: names.groupby(["year", "sex"])["prop"].sum()
Out[117]:
year  sex
1880  F      1.0
      M      1.0
1881  F      1.0
      M      1.0
1882  F      1.0
             ...
2008  M      1.0
2009  F      1.0
      M      1.0
2010  F      1.0
      M      1.0
Name: prop, Length: 262, dtype: float64
```

Now that this is done, I'm going to extract a subset of the data to facilitate further analysis: the top 1,000 names for each sex/year combination. This is yet another group operation:

```
In [118]: def get_top1000(group):
   .....:     return group.sort_values("births", ascending=False)[:1000]

In [119]: grouped = names.groupby(["year", "sex"])

In [120]: top1000 = grouped.apply(get_top1000)

In [121]: top1000.head()
Out[121]:
```

```
          name sex  births  year      prop
year sex
1880 F 0        Mary   F    7065  1880  0.077643
       1        Anna   F    2604  1880  0.028618
       2        Emma   F    2003  1880  0.022013
       3   Elizabeth   F    1939  1880  0.021309
       4      Minnie   F    1746  1880  0.019188
```

We can drop the group index since we don't need it for our analysis:

```
In [122]: top1000 = top1000.reset_index(drop=True)
```

The resulting dataset is now quite a bit smaller:

```
In [123]: top1000.head()
Out[123]:
        name sex  births  year      prop
0       Mary   F    7065  1880  0.077643
1       Anna   F    2604  1880  0.028618
2       Emma   F    2003  1880  0.022013
3  Elizabeth   F    1939  1880  0.021309
4     Minnie   F    1746  1880  0.019188
```

We'll use this top one thousand dataset in the following investigations into the data.

Analyzing Naming Trends

With the full dataset and the top one thousand dataset in hand, we can start analyzing various naming trends of interest. First, we can split the top one thousand names into the boy and girl portions:

```
In [124]: boys = top1000[top1000["sex"] == "M"]
```

```
In [125]: girls = top1000[top1000["sex"] == "F"]
```

Simple time series, like the number of Johns or Marys for each year, can be plotted but require some manipulation to be more useful. Let's form a pivot table of the total number of births by year and name:

```
In [126]: total_births = top1000.pivot_table("births", index="year",
    .....:                                   columns="name",
    .....:                                   aggfunc=sum)
```

Now, this can be plotted for a handful of names with DataFrame's plot method (Figure 13-5 shows the result):

```
In [127]: total_births.info()
<class 'pandas.core.frame.DataFrame'>
Int64Index: 131 entries, 1880 to 2010
Columns: 6868 entries, Aaden to Zuri
dtypes: float64(6868)
memory usage: 6.9 MB

In [128]: subset = total_births[["John", "Harry", "Mary", "Marilyn"]]
```

```
In [129]: subset.plot(subplots=True, figsize=(12, 10),
    .....:             title="Number of births per year")
```

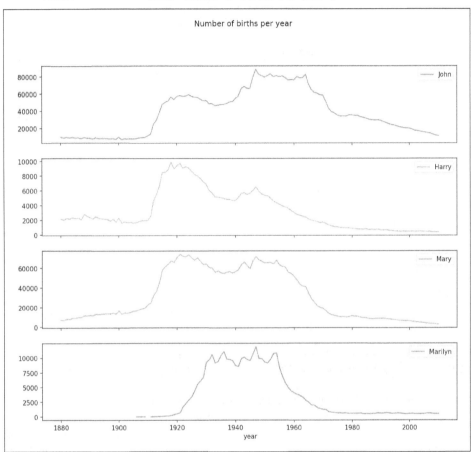

Figure 13-5. A few boy and girl names over time

On looking at this, you might conclude that these names have grown out of favor with the American population. But the story is actually more complicated than that, as will be explored in the next section.

Measuring the increase in naming diversity

One explanation for the decrease in plots is that fewer parents are choosing common names for their children. This hypothesis can be explored and confirmed in the data. One measure is the proportion of births represented by the top 1,000 most popular names, which I aggregate and plot by year and sex (Figure 13-6 shows the resulting plot):

```
In [131]: table = top1000.pivot_table("prop", index="year",
   .....:                              columns="sex", aggfunc=sum)

In [132]: table.plot(title="Sum of table1000.prop by year and sex",
   .....:            yticks=np.linspace(0, 1.2, 13))
```

Figure 13-6. Proportion of births represented in top one thousand names by sex

You can see that, indeed, there appears to be increasing name diversity (decreasing total proportion in the top one thousand). Another interesting metric is the number of distinct names, taken in order of popularity from highest to lowest, in the top 50% of births. This number is trickier to compute. Let's consider just the boy names from 2010:

```
In [133]: df = boys[boys["year"] == 2010]

In [134]: df
Out[134]:
          name sex  births  year      prop
260877   Jacob   M   21875  2010  0.011523
260878   Ethan   M   17866  2010  0.009411
260879 Michael   M   17133  2010  0.009025
260880  Jayden   M   17030  2010  0.008971
260881 William   M   16870  2010  0.008887
...        ...  ..     ...   ...       ...
261872  Camilo   M     194  2010  0.000102
261873  Destin   M     194  2010  0.000102
261874  Jaquan   M     194  2010  0.000102
```

```
261875   Jaydan   M     194  2010  0.000102
261876   Maxton   M     193  2010  0.000102
[1000 rows x 5 columns]
```

After sorting prop in descending order, we want to know how many of the most popular names it takes to reach 50%. You could write a for loop to do this, but a vectorized NumPy way is more computationally efficient. Taking the cumulative sum, cumsum, of prop and then calling the method searchsorted returns the position in the cumulative sum at which 0.5 would need to be inserted to keep it in sorted order:

```
In [135]: prop_cumsum = df["prop"].sort_values(ascending=False).cumsum()

In [136]: prop_cumsum[:10]
Out[136]:
260877   0.011523
260878   0.020934
260879   0.029959
260880   0.038930
260881   0.047817
260882   0.056579
260883   0.065155
260884   0.073414
260885   0.081528
260886   0.089621
Name: prop, dtype: float64

In [137]: prop_cumsum.searchsorted(0.5)
Out[137]: 116
```

Since arrays are zero-indexed, adding 1 to this result gives you a result of 117. By contrast, in 1900 this number was much smaller:

```
In [138]: df = boys[boys.year == 1900]

In [139]: in1900 = df.sort_values("prop", ascending=False).prop.cumsum()

In [140]: in1900.searchsorted(0.5) + 1
Out[140]: 25
```

You can now apply this operation to each year/sex combination, groupby those fields, and apply a function returning the count for each group:

```
def get_quantile_count(group, q=0.5):
    group = group.sort_values("prop", ascending=False)
    return group.prop.cumsum().searchsorted(q) + 1

diversity = top1000.groupby(["year", "sex"]).apply(get_quantile_count)
diversity = diversity.unstack()
```

This resulting DataFrame diversity now has two time series, one for each sex, indexed by year. This can be inspected and plotted as before (see Figure 13-7):

```
In [143]: diversity.head()
Out[143]:
sex     F    M
year
1880    38   14
1881    38   14
1882    38   15
1883    39   15
1884    39   16
```

```
In [144]: diversity.plot(title="Number of popular names in top 50%")
```

Figure 13-7. Plot of diversity metric by year

As you can see, girl names have always been more diverse than boy names, and they have only become more so over time. Further analysis of what exactly is driving the diversity, like the increase of alternative spellings, is left to the reader.

The "last letter" revolution

In 2007, baby name researcher Laura Wattenberg pointed out that the distribution of boy names by final letter has changed significantly over the last 100 years. To see this, we first aggregate all of the births in the full dataset by year, sex, and final letter:

```
def get_last_letter(x):
    return x[-1]

last_letters = names["name"].map(get_last_letter)
```

```
last_letters.name = "last_letter"

table = names.pivot_table("births", index=last_letters,
                          columns=["sex", "year"], aggfunc=sum)
```

Then we select three representative years spanning the history and print the first few rows:

```
In [146]: subtable = table.reindex(columns=[1910, 1960, 2010], level="year")

In [147]: subtable.head()
Out[147]:
sex                 F                              M
year             1910      1960      2010      1910      1960      2010
last_letter
a            108376.0  691247.0  670605.0     977.0    5204.0   28438.0
b                 NaN     694.0     450.0     411.0    3912.0   38859.0
c                 5.0      49.0     946.0     482.0   15476.0   23125.0
d              6750.0    3729.0    2607.0   22111.0  262112.0   44398.0
e            133569.0  435013.0  313833.0   28655.0  178823.0  129012.0
```

Next, normalize the table by total births to compute a new table containing the proportion of total births for each sex ending in each letter:

```
In [148]: subtable.sum()
Out[148]:
sex  year
F    1910     396416.0
     1960    2022062.0
     2010    1759010.0
M    1910     194198.0
     1960    2132588.0
     2010    1898382.0
dtype: float64

In [149]: letter_prop = subtable / subtable.sum()

In [150]: letter_prop
Out[150]:
sex                 F                              M
year             1910      1960      2010      1910      1960      2010
last_letter
a            0.273390  0.341853  0.381240  0.005031  0.002440  0.014980
b                 NaN  0.000343  0.000256  0.002116  0.001834  0.020470
c            0.000013  0.000024  0.000538  0.002482  0.007257  0.012181
d            0.017028  0.001844  0.001482  0.113858  0.122908  0.023387
e            0.336941  0.215133  0.178415  0.147556  0.083853  0.067959
...               ...       ...       ...       ...       ...       ...
v                 NaN  0.000060  0.000117  0.000113  0.000037  0.001434
w            0.000020  0.000031  0.001182  0.006329  0.007711  0.016148
x            0.000015  0.000037  0.000727  0.003965  0.001851  0.008614
y            0.110972  0.152569  0.116828  0.077349  0.160987  0.058168
```

```
z          0.002439  0.000659  0.000704  0.000170  0.000184  0.001831
[26 rows x 6 columns]
```

With the letter proportions now in hand, we can make bar plots for each sex, broken down by year (see Figure 13-8):

```
import matplotlib.pyplot as plt

fig, axes = plt.subplots(2, 1, figsize=(10, 8))
letter_prop["M"].plot(kind="bar", rot=0, ax=axes[0], title="Male")
letter_prop["F"].plot(kind="bar", rot=0, ax=axes[1], title="Female",
                      legend=False)
```

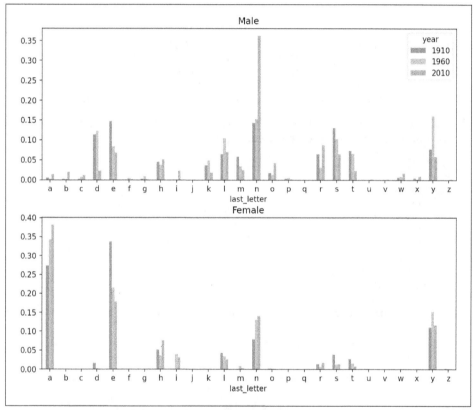

Figure 13-8. Proportion of boy and girl names ending in each letter

As you can see, boy names ending in *n* have experienced significant growth since the 1960s. Going back to the full table created before, I again normalize by year and sex and select a subset of letters for the boy names, finally transposing to make each column a time series:

```
In [153]: letter_prop = table / table.sum()
```

```
In [154]: dny_ts = letter_prop.loc[["d", "n", "y"], "M"].T
```

```
In [155]: dny_ts.head()
Out[155]:
last_letter          d          n          y
year
1880          0.083055   0.153213   0.075760
1881          0.083247   0.153214   0.077451
1882          0.085340   0.149560   0.077537
1883          0.084066   0.151646   0.079144
1884          0.086120   0.149915   0.080405
```

With this DataFrame of time series in hand, I can make a plot of the trends over time again with its plot method (see Figure 13-9):

```
In [158]: dny_ts.plot()
```

Figure 13-9. Proportion of boys born with names ending in d/n/y over time

Boy names that became girl names (and vice versa)

Another fun trend is looking at names that were more popular with one gender earlier in the sample but have become preferred as a name for the other gender over time. One example is the name Lesley or Leslie. Going back to the top1000 DataFrame, I compute a list of names occurring in the dataset starting with "Lesl":

```
In [159]: all_names = pd.Series(top1000["name"].unique())
```

```
In [160]: lesley_like = all_names[all_names.str.contains("Lesl")]
```

```
In [161]: lesley_like
Out[161]:
632      Leslie
2294     Lesley
4262     Leslee
4728      Lesli
6103      Lesly
dtype: object
```

From there, we can filter down to just those names and sum births grouped by name to see the relative frequencies:

```
In [162]: filtered = top1000[top1000["name"].isin(lesley_like)]

In [163]: filtered.groupby("name")["births"].sum()
Out[163]:
name
Leslee      1082
Lesley     35022
Lesli        929
Leslie    370429
Lesly      10067
Name: births, dtype: int64
```

Next, let's aggregate by sex and year, and normalize within year:

```
In [164]: table = filtered.pivot_table("births", index="year",
   .....:                               columns="sex", aggfunc="sum")

In [165]: table = table.div(table.sum(axis="columns"), axis="index")

In [166]: table.tail()
Out[166]:
sex     F    M
year
2006  1.0  NaN
2007  1.0  NaN
2008  1.0  NaN
2009  1.0  NaN
2010  1.0  NaN
```

Lastly, it's now possible to make a plot of the breakdown by sex over time (see Figure 13-10):

```
In [168]: table.plot(style={"M": "k-", "F": "k--"})
```

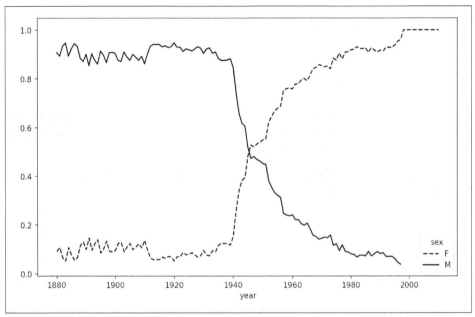

Figure 13-10. Proportion of male/female Lesley-like names over time

13.4 USDA Food Database

The US Department of Agriculture (USDA) makes available a database of food nutrient information. Programmer Ashley Williams created a version of this database in JSON format. The records look like this:

```
{
  "id": 21441,
  "description": "KENTUCKY FRIED CHICKEN, Fried Chicken, EXTRA CRISPY,
Wing, meat and skin with breading",
  "tags": ["KFC"],
  "manufacturer": "Kentucky Fried Chicken",
  "group": "Fast Foods",
  "portions": [
    {
      "amount": 1,
      "unit": "wing, with skin",
      "grams": 68.0
    },

    ...
  ],
  "nutrients": [
    {
      "value": 20.8,
      "units": "g",
```

```
        "description": "Protein",
        "group": "Composition"
    },

    ...
  ]
}
```

Each food has a number of identifying attributes along with two lists of nutrients and portion sizes. Data in this form is not particularly amenable to analysis, so we need to do some work to wrangle the data into a better form.

You can load this file into Python with any JSON library of your choosing. I'll use the built-in Python `json` module:

```
In [169]: import json

In [170]: db = json.load(open("datasets/usda_food/database.json"))

In [171]: len(db)
Out[171]: 6636
```

Each entry in db is a dictionary containing all the data for a single food. The `"nutrients"` field is a list of dictionaries, one for each nutrient:

```
In [172]: db[0].keys()
Out[172]: dict_keys(['id', 'description', 'tags', 'manufacturer', 'group', 'porti
ons', 'nutrients'])

In [173]: db[0]["nutrients"][0]
Out[173]:
{'value': 25.18,
 'units': 'g',
 'description': 'Protein',
 'group': 'Composition'}

In [174]: nutrients = pd.DataFrame(db[0]["nutrients"])

In [175]: nutrients.head(7)
Out[175]:
    value units                  description       group
0   25.18     g                      Protein  Composition
1   29.20     g              Total lipid (fat)  Composition
2    3.06     g  Carbohydrate, by difference  Composition
3    3.28     g                          Ash        Other
4  376.00  kcal                       Energy       Energy
5   39.28     g                        Water  Composition
6 1573.00    kJ                       Energy       Energy
```

When converting a list of dictionaries to a DataFrame, we can specify a list of fields to extract. We'll take the food names, group, ID, and manufacturer:

```
In [176]: info_keys = ["description", "group", "id", "manufacturer"]

In [177]: info = pd.DataFrame(db, columns=info_keys)

In [178]: info.head()
Out[178]:
                          description                   group    id  \
0                     Cheese, caraway  Dairy and Egg Products  1008
1                     Cheese, cheddar  Dairy and Egg Products  1009
2                        Cheese, edam  Dairy and Egg Products  1018
3                        Cheese, feta  Dairy and Egg Products  1019
4  Cheese, mozzarella, part skim milk  Dairy and Egg Products  1028
  manufacturer
0
1
2
3
4

In [179]: info.info()
<class 'pandas.core.frame.DataFrame'>
RangeIndex: 6636 entries, 0 to 6635
Data columns (total 4 columns):
 #   Column        Non-Null Count  Dtype
---  ------        --------------  -----
 0   description   6636 non-null   object
 1   group         6636 non-null   object
 2   id            6636 non-null   int64
 3   manufacturer  5195 non-null   object
dtypes: int64(1), object(3)
memory usage: 207.5+ KB
```

From the output of `info.info()`, we can see that there is missing data in the `manufac`turer column.

You can see the distribution of food groups with `value_counts`:

```
In [180]: pd.value_counts(info["group"])[:10]
Out[180]:
Vegetables and Vegetable Products    812
Beef Products                        618
Baked Products                       496
Breakfast Cereals                    403
Legumes and Legume Products          365
Fast Foods                           365
Lamb, Veal, and Game Products        345
Sweets                               341
Fruits and Fruit Juices              328
Pork Products                        328
Name: group, dtype: int64
```

Now, to do some analysis on all of the nutrient data, it's easiest to assemble the nutrients for each food into a single large table. To do so, we need to take several steps. First, I'll convert each list of food nutrients to a DataFrame, add a column for the food id, and append the DataFrame to a list. Then, these can be concatenated with concat. Run the following code in a Jupyter cell:

```
nutrients = []

for rec in db:
    fnuts = pd.DataFrame(rec["nutrients"])
    fnuts["id"] = rec["id"]
    nutrients.append(fnuts)

nutrients = pd.concat(nutrients, ignore_index=True)
```

If all goes well, nutrients should look like this:

```
In [182]: nutrients
Out[182]:
          value units                          description       group     id
0        25.180     g                              Protein  Composition   1008
1        29.200     g                    Total lipid (fat)  Composition   1008
2         3.060     g         Carbohydrate, by difference  Composition   1008
3         3.280     g                                  Ash        Other   1008
4       376.000  kcal                               Energy       Energy   1008
...         ...   ...                                  ...          ...    ...
389350    0.000   mcg                 Vitamin B-12, added     Vitamins  43546
389351    0.000    mg                          Cholesterol        Other  43546
389352    0.072     g          Fatty acids, total saturated       Other  43546
389353    0.028     g  Fatty acids, total monounsaturated       Other  43546
389354    0.041     g  Fatty acids, total polyunsaturated       Other  43546
[389355 rows x 5 columns]
```

I noticed that there are duplicates in this DataFrame, so it makes things easier to drop them:

```
In [183]: nutrients.duplicated().sum()  # number of duplicates
Out[183]: 14179

In [184]: nutrients = nutrients.drop_duplicates()
```

Since "group" and "description" are in both DataFrame objects, we can rename for clarity:

```
In [185]: col_mapping = {"description" : "food",
   .....:                      "group"       : "fgroup"}

In [186]: info = info.rename(columns=col_mapping, copy=False)

In [187]: info.info()
<class 'pandas.core.frame.DataFrame'>
RangeIndex: 6636 entries, 0 to 6635
Data columns (total 4 columns):
 #   Column        Non-Null Count  Dtype
---  ------        --------------  -----
```

```
0   food         6636 non-null   object
1   fgroup       6636 non-null   object
2   id           6636 non-null   int64
3   manufacturer 5195 non-null   object
dtypes: int64(1), object(3)
memory usage: 207.5+ KB

In [188]: col_mapping = {"description" : "nutrient",
   .....:                "group" : "nutgroup"}

In [189]: nutrients = nutrients.rename(columns=col_mapping, copy=False)

In [190]: nutrients
Out[190]:
         value units                           nutrient      nutgroup     id
0       25.180     g                            Protein   Composition   1008
1       29.200     g                   Total lipid (fat)   Composition   1008
2        3.060     g          Carbohydrate, by difference   Composition   1008
3        3.280     g                                Ash         Other   1008
4      376.000  kcal                             Energy        Energy   1008
...        ...   ...                                ...           ...    ...
389350   0.000   mcg                Vitamin B-12, added      Vitamins  43546
389351   0.000    mg                        Cholesterol         Other  43546
389352   0.072     g          Fatty acids, total saturated       Other  43546
389353   0.028     g    Fatty acids, total monounsaturated       Other  43546
389354   0.041     g    Fatty acids, total polyunsaturated       Other  43546
[375176 rows x 5 columns]
```

With all of this done, we're ready to merge info with nutrients:

```
In [191]: ndata = pd.merge(nutrients, info, on="id")

In [192]: ndata.info()
<class 'pandas.core.frame.DataFrame'>
Int64Index: 375176 entries, 0 to 375175
Data columns (total 8 columns):
 #   Column       Non-Null Count    Dtype
---  ------       --------------    -----
 0   value        375176 non-null   float64
 1   units        375176 non-null   object
 2   nutrient     375176 non-null   object
 3   nutgroup     375176 non-null   object
 4   id           375176 non-null   int64
 5   food         375176 non-null   object
 6   fgroup       375176 non-null   object
 7   manufacturer 293054 non-null   object
dtypes: float64(1), int64(1), object(6)
memory usage: 25.8+ MB

In [193]: ndata.iloc[30000]
Out[193]:
value                                         0.04
units                                            g
```

```
nutrient                                          Glycine
nutgroup                                      Amino Acids
id                                                   6158
food             Soup, tomato bisque, canned, condensed
fgroup                      Soups, Sauces, and Gravies
manufacturer
Name: 30000, dtype: object
```

We could now make a plot of median values by food group and nutrient type (see Figure 13-11):

```
In [195]: result = ndata.groupby(["nutrient", "fgroup"])["value"].quantile(0.5)

In [196]: result["Zinc, Zn"].sort_values().plot(kind="barh")
```

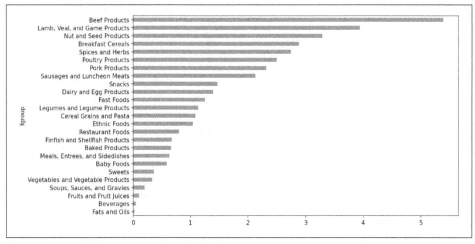

Figure 13-11. Median zinc values by food group

Using the `idxmax` or `argmax` Series methods, you can find which food is most dense in each nutrient. Run the following in a Jupyter cell:

```
by_nutrient = ndata.groupby(["nutgroup", "nutrient"])

def get_maximum(x):
    return x.loc[x.value.idxmax()]

max_foods = by_nutrient.apply(get_maximum)[["value", "food"]]

# make the food a little smaller
max_foods["food"] = max_foods["food"].str[:50]
```

The resulting DataFrame is a bit too large to display in the book; here is only the `"Amino Acids"` nutrient group:

```
In [198]: max_foods.loc["Amino Acids"]["food"]
Out[198]:
```

```
nutrient
Alanine                    Gelatins, dry powder, unsweetened
Arginine                       Seeds, sesame flour, low-fat
Aspartic acid                          Soy protein isolate
Cystine             Seeds, cottonseed flour, low fat (glandless)
Glutamic acid                          Soy protein isolate
Glycine                    Gelatins, dry powder, unsweetened
Histidine             Whale, beluga, meat, dried (Alaska Native)
Hydroxyproline    KENTUCKY FRIED CHICKEN, Fried Chicken, ORIGINAL RE
Isoleucine        Soy protein isolate, PROTEIN TECHNOLOGIES INTERNAT
Leucine           Soy protein isolate, PROTEIN TECHNOLOGIES INTERNAT
Lysine            Seal, bearded (Oogruk), meat, dried (Alaska Native
Methionine                 Fish, cod, Atlantic, dried and salted
Phenylalanine     Soy protein isolate, PROTEIN TECHNOLOGIES INTERNAT
Proline                    Gelatins, dry powder, unsweetened
Serine            Soy protein isolate, PROTEIN TECHNOLOGIES INTERNAT
Threonine         Soy protein isolate, PROTEIN TECHNOLOGIES INTERNAT
Tryptophan          Sea lion, Steller, meat with fat (Alaska Native)
Tyrosine          Soy protein isolate, PROTEIN TECHNOLOGIES INTERNAT
Valine            Soy protein isolate, PROTEIN TECHNOLOGIES INTERNAT
Name: food, dtype: object
```

13.5 2012 Federal Election Commission Database

The US Federal Election Commission (FEC) publishes data on contributions to political campaigns. This includes contributor names, occupation and employer, address, and contribution amount. The contribution data from the 2012 US presidential election was available as a single 150-megabyte CSV file *P00000001-ALL.csv* (see the book's data repository), which can be loaded with pandas.read_csv:

```
In [199]: fec = pd.read_csv("datasets/fec/P00000001-ALL.csv", low_memory=False)
```

```
In [200]: fec.info()
<class 'pandas.core.frame.DataFrame'>
RangeIndex: 1001731 entries, 0 to 1001730
Data columns (total 16 columns):
 #   Column             Non-Null Count      Dtype
---  ------             --------------      -----
 0   cmte_id            1001731 non-null    object
 1   cand_id            1001731 non-null    object
 2   cand_nm            1001731 non-null    object
 3   contbr_nm          1001731 non-null    object
 4   contbr_city        1001712 non-null    object
 5   contbr_st          1001727 non-null    object
 6   contbr_zip         1001620 non-null    object
 7   contbr_employer    988002 non-null     object
 8   contbr_occupation  993301 non-null     object
 9   contb_receipt_amt  1001731 non-null    float64
 10  contb_receipt_dt   1001731 non-null    object
 11  receipt_desc       14166 non-null      object
 12  memo_cd            92482 non-null      object
```

```
13  memo_text           97770 non-null    object
14  form_tp             1001731 non-null  object
15  file_num            1001731 non-null  int64
dtypes: float64(1), int64(1), object(14)
memory usage: 122.3+ MB
```

 Several people asked me to update the dataset from the 2012 election to the 2016 or 2020 elections. Unfortunately, the more recent datasets provided by the FEC have become larger and more complex, and I decided that working with them here would be a distraction from the analysis techniques that I wanted to illustrate.

A sample record in the DataFrame looks like this:

```
In [201]: fec.iloc[123456]
Out[201]:
cmte_id                         C00431445
cand_id                         P80003338
cand_nm                      Obama, Barack
contbr_nm                      ELLMAN, IRA
contbr_city                          TEMPE
contbr_st                               AZ
contbr_zip                       852816719
contbr_employer     ARIZONA STATE UNIVERSITY
contbr_occupation               PROFESSOR
contb_receipt_amt                     50.0
contb_receipt_dt                 01-DEC-11
receipt_desc                          NaN
memo_cd                               NaN
memo_text                             NaN
form_tp                              SA17A
file_num                            772372
Name: 123456, dtype: object
```

You may think of some ways to start slicing and dicing this data to extract informative statistics about donors and patterns in the campaign contributions. I'll show you a number of different analyses that apply the techniques in this book.

You can see that there are no political party affiliations in the data, so this would be useful to add. You can get a list of all the unique political candidates using unique:

```
In [202]: unique_cands = fec["cand_nm"].unique()

In [203]: unique_cands
Out[203]:
array(['Bachmann, Michelle', 'Romney, Mitt', 'Obama, Barack',
       "Roemer, Charles E. 'Buddy' III", 'Pawlenty, Timothy',
       'Johnson, Gary Earl', 'Paul, Ron', 'Santorum, Rick',
       'Cain, Herman', 'Gingrich, Newt', 'McCotter, Thaddeus G',
       'Huntsman, Jon', 'Perry, Rick'], dtype=object)
```

```
In [204]: unique_cands[2]
Out[204]: 'Obama, Barack'
```

One way to indicate party affiliation is using a dictionary:[1]

```
parties = {"Bachmann, Michelle": "Republican",
           "Cain, Herman": "Republican",
           "Gingrich, Newt": "Republican",
           "Huntsman, Jon": "Republican",
           "Johnson, Gary Earl": "Republican",
           "McCotter, Thaddeus G": "Republican",
           "Obama, Barack": "Democrat",
           "Paul, Ron": "Republican",
           "Pawlenty, Timothy": "Republican",
           "Perry, Rick": "Republican",
           "Roemer, Charles E. 'Buddy' III": "Republican",
           "Romney, Mitt": "Republican",
           "Santorum, Rick": "Republican"}
```

Now, using this mapping and the map method on Series objects, you can compute an array of political parties from the candidate names:

```
In [206]: fec["cand_nm"][123456:123461]
Out[206]:
123456    Obama, Barack
123457    Obama, Barack
123458    Obama, Barack
123459    Obama, Barack
123460    Obama, Barack
Name: cand_nm, dtype: object

In [207]: fec["cand_nm"][123456:123461].map(parties)
Out[207]:
123456    Democrat
123457    Democrat
123458    Democrat
123459    Democrat
123460    Democrat
Name: cand_nm, dtype: object

# Add it as a column
In [208]: fec["party"] = fec["cand_nm"].map(parties)

In [209]: fec["party"].value_counts()
Out[209]:
Democrat      593746
Republican    407985
Name: party, dtype: int64
```

---

1 This makes the simplifying assumption that Gary Johnson is a Republican even though he later became the Libertarian party candidate.

A couple of data preparation points. First, this data includes both contributions and refunds (negative contribution amount):

```
In [210]: (fec["contb_receipt_amt"] > 0).value_counts()
Out[210]:
True     991475
False     10256
Name: contb_receipt_amt, dtype: int64
```

To simplify the analysis, I'll restrict the dataset to positive contributions:

```
In [211]: fec = fec[fec["contb_receipt_amt"] > 0]
```

Since Barack Obama and Mitt Romney were the main two candidates, I'll also prepare a subset that just has contributions to their campaigns:

```
In [212]: fec_mrbo = fec[fec["cand_nm"].isin(["Obama, Barack", "Romney, Mitt"])]
```

Donation Statistics by Occupation and Employer

Donations by occupation is another oft-studied statistic. For example, attorneys tend to donate more money to Democrats, while business executives tend to donate more to Republicans. You have no reason to believe me; you can see for yourself in the data. First, the total number of donations by occupation can be computed with value_counts:

```
In [213]: fec["contbr_occupation"].value_counts()[:10]
Out[213]:
RETIRED                                  233990
INFORMATION REQUESTED                     35107
ATTORNEY                                  34286
HOMEMAKER                                 29931
PHYSICIAN                                 23432
INFORMATION REQUESTED PER BEST EFFORTS    21138
ENGINEER                                  14334
TEACHER                                   13990
CONSULTANT                                13273
PROFESSOR                                 12555
Name: contbr_occupation, dtype: int64
```

You will notice by looking at the occupations that many refer to the same basic job type, or there are several variants of the same thing. The following code snippet illustrates a technique for cleaning up a few of them by mapping from one occupation to another; note the "trick" of using dict.get to allow occupations with no mapping to "pass through":

```
occ_mapping = {
   "INFORMATION REQUESTED PER BEST EFFORTS" : "NOT PROVIDED",
   "INFORMATION REQUESTED" : "NOT PROVIDED",
   "INFORMATION REQUESTED (BEST EFFORTS)" : "NOT PROVIDED",
   "C.E.O.": "CEO"
}
```

```
def get_occ(x):
    # If no mapping provided, return x
    return occ_mapping.get(x, x)

fec["contbr_occupation"] = fec["contbr_occupation"].map(get_occ)
```

I'll also do the same thing for employers:

```
emp_mapping = {
    "INFORMATION REQUESTED PER BEST EFFORTS" : "NOT PROVIDED",
    "INFORMATION REQUESTED" : "NOT PROVIDED",
    "SELF" : "SELF-EMPLOYED",
    "SELF EMPLOYED" : "SELF-EMPLOYED",
}

def get_emp(x):
    # If no mapping provided, return x
    return emp_mapping.get(x, x)

fec["contbr_employer"] = fec["contbr_employer"].map(f)
```

Now, you can use `pivot_table` to aggregate the data by party and occupation, then filter down to the subset that donated at least $2 million overall:

```
In [216]: by_occupation = fec.pivot_table("contb_receipt_amt",
   .....:                                  index="contbr_occupation",
   .....:                                  columns="party", aggfunc="sum")

In [217]: over_2mm = by_occupation[by_occupation.sum(axis="columns") > 2000000]

In [218]: over_2mm
Out[218]:
party                   Democrat    Republican
contbr_occupation
ATTORNEY             11141982.97    7477194.43
CEO                   2074974.79    4211040.52
CONSULTANT            2459912.71    2544725.45
ENGINEER              951525.55     1818373.70
EXECUTIVE            1355161.05     4138850.09
HOMEMAKER            4248875.80    13634275.78
INVESTOR              884133.00     2431768.92
LAWYER               3160478.87      391224.32
MANAGER               762883.22     1444532.37
NOT PROVIDED         4866973.96    20565473.01
OWNER                1001567.36     2408286.92
PHYSICIAN            3735124.94     3594320.24
PRESIDENT            1878509.95     4720923.76
PROFESSOR            2165071.08      296702.73
REAL ESTATE           528902.09     1625902.25
RETIRED             25305116.38    23561244.49
SELF-EMPLOYED         672393.40     1640252.54
```

It can be easier to look at this data graphically as a bar plot ("barh" means horizontal bar plot; see Figure 13-12):

```
In [220]: over_2mm.plot(kind="barh")
```

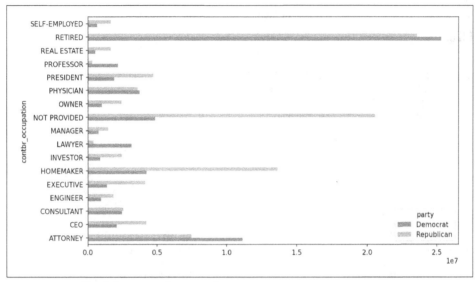

Figure 13-12. Total donations by party for top occupations

You might be interested in the top donor occupations or top companies that donated to Obama and Romney. To do this, you can group by candidate name and use a variant of the top method from earlier in the chapter:

```
def get_top_amounts(group, key, n=5):
    totals = group.groupby(key)["contb_receipt_amt"].sum()
    return totals.nlargest(n)
```

Then aggregate by occupation and employer:

```
In [222]: grouped = fec_mrbo.groupby("cand_nm")

In [223]: grouped.apply(get_top_amounts, "contbr_occupation", n=7)
Out[223]:
cand_nm          contbr_occupation
Obama, Barack    RETIRED                                25305116.38
                 ATTORNEY                               11141982.97
                 INFORMATION REQUESTED                   4866973.96
                 HOMEMAKER                               4248875.80
                 PHYSICIAN                               3735124.94
                 LAWYER                                  3160478.87
                 CONSULTANT                              2459912.71
Romney, Mitt     RETIRED                                11508473.59
                 INFORMATION REQUESTED PER BEST EFFORTS 11396894.84
                 HOMEMAKER                               8147446.22
```

```
                    ATTORNEY                                      5364718.82
                    PRESIDENT                                     2491244.89
                    EXECUTIVE                                     2300947.03
                    C.E.O.                                        1968386.11
        Name: contb_receipt_amt, dtype: float64

        In [224]: grouped.apply(get_top_amounts, "contbr_employer", n=10)
        Out[224]:
        cand_nm         contbr_employer
        Obama, Barack   RETIRED                                  22694358.85
                        SELF-EMPLOYED                            17080985.96
                        NOT EMPLOYED                              8586308.70
                        INFORMATION REQUESTED                     5053480.37
                        HOMEMAKER                                 2605408.54
                        SELF                                      1076531.20
                        SELF EMPLOYED                              469290.00
                        STUDENT                                    318831.45
                        VOLUNTEER                                  257104.00
                        MICROSOFT                                  215585.36
        Romney, Mitt    INFORMATION REQUESTED PER BEST EFFORTS   12059527.24
                        RETIRED                                  11506225.71
                        HOMEMAKER                                 8147196.22
                        SELF-EMPLOYED                             7409860.98
                        STUDENT                                    496490.94
                        CREDIT SUISSE                              281150.00
                        MORGAN STANLEY                             267266.00
                        GOLDMAN SACH & CO.                         238250.00
                        BARCLAYS CAPITAL                           162750.00
                        H.I.G. CAPITAL                             139500.00
        Name: contb_receipt_amt, dtype: float64
```

Bucketing Donation Amounts

A useful way to analyze this data is to use the cut function to discretize the contributor amounts into buckets by contribution size:

```
In [225]: bins = np.array([0, 1, 10, 100, 1000, 10000,
   .....:                   100_000, 1_000_000, 10_000_000])

In [226]: labels = pd.cut(fec_mrbo["contb_receipt_amt"], bins)

In [227]: labels
Out[227]:
411        (10, 100]
412      (100, 1000]
413      (100, 1000]
414        (10, 100]
415        (10, 100]
             ...
701381     (10, 100]
701382   (100, 1000]
701383       (1, 10]
```

```
701384      (10, 100]
701385     (100, 1000]
Name: contb_receipt_amt, Length: 694282, dtype: category
Categories (8, interval[int64, right]): [(0, 1] < (1, 10] < (10, 100] < (100, 100
0] <
                                        (1000, 10000] < (10000, 100000] < (10000
0, 1000000] <
                                        (1000000, 10000000]]
```

We can then group the data for Obama and Romney by name and bin label to get a histogram by donation size:

```
In [228]: grouped = fec_mrbo.groupby(["cand_nm", labels])

In [229]: grouped.size().unstack(level=0)
Out[229]:
cand_nm               Obama, Barack  Romney, Mitt
contb_receipt_amt
(0, 1]                          493            77
(1, 10]                       40070          3681
(10, 100]                    372280         31853
(100, 1000]                  153991         43357
(1000, 10000]                 22284         26186
(10000, 100000]                   2             1
(100000, 1000000]                 3             0
(1000000, 10000000]               4             0
```

This data shows that Obama received a significantly larger number of small donations than Romney. You can also sum the contribution amounts and normalize within buckets to visualize the percentage of total donations of each size by candidate (Figure 13-13 shows the resulting plot):

```
In [231]: bucket_sums = grouped["contb_receipt_amt"].sum().unstack(level=0)

In [232]: normed_sums = bucket_sums.div(bucket_sums.sum(axis="columns"),
   .....:                               axis="index")

In [233]: normed_sums
Out[233]:
cand_nm               Obama, Barack  Romney, Mitt
contb_receipt_amt
(0, 1]                     0.805182      0.194818
(1, 10]                    0.918767      0.081233
(10, 100]                  0.910769      0.089231
(100, 1000]                0.710176      0.289824
(1000, 10000]              0.447326      0.552674
(10000, 100000]            0.823120      0.176880
(100000, 1000000]          1.000000      0.000000
(1000000, 10000000]        1.000000      0.000000

In [234]: normed_sums[:-2].plot(kind="barh")
```

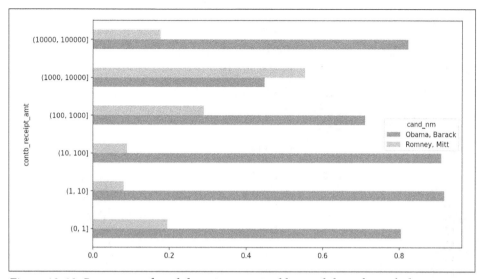

Figure 13-13. Percentage of total donations received by candidates for each donation size

I excluded the two largest bins, as these are not donations by individuals.

This analysis can be refined and improved in many ways. For example, you could aggregate donations by donor name and zip code to adjust for donors who gave many small amounts versus one or more large donations. I encourage you to explore the dataset yourself.

Donation Statistics by State

We can start by aggregating the data by candidate and state:

```
In [235]: grouped = fec_mrbo.groupby(["cand_nm", "contbr_st"])

In [236]: totals = grouped["contb_receipt_amt"].sum().unstack(level=0).fillna(0)

In [237]: totals = totals[totals.sum(axis="columns") > 100000]

In [238]: totals.head(10)
Out[238]:
cand_nm     Obama, Barack  Romney, Mitt
contbr_st
AK             281840.15      86204.24
AL             543123.48     527303.51
AR             359247.28     105556.00
AZ            1506476.98    1888436.23
CA           23824984.24   11237636.60
CO            2132429.49    1506714.12
CT            2068291.26    3499475.45
DC            4373538.80    1025137.50
```

```
DE               336669.14       82712.00
FL              7318178.58     8338458.81
```

If you divide each row by the total contribution amount, you get the relative percentage of total donations by state for each candidate:

```
In [239]: percent = totals.div(totals.sum(axis="columns"), axis="index")

In [240]: percent.head(10)
Out[240]:
cand_nm    Obama, Barack  Romney, Mitt
contbr_st
AK              0.765778      0.234222
AL              0.507390      0.492610
AR              0.772902      0.227098
AZ              0.443745      0.556255
CA              0.679498      0.320502
CO              0.585970      0.414030
CT              0.371476      0.628524
DC              0.810113      0.189887
DE              0.802776      0.197224
FL              0.467417      0.532583
```

13.6 Conclusion

We've reached the end of this book. I have included some additional content you may find useful in the appendixes.

In the 10 years since the first edition of this book was published, Python has become a popular and widespread language for data analysis. The programming skills you have developed here will stay relevant for a long time into the future. I hope the programming tools and libraries we've explored will serve you well.

Advanced NumPy

In this appendix, I will go deeper into the NumPy library for array computing. This will include more internal details about the ndarray type and more advanced array manipulations and algorithms.

This appendix contains miscellaneous topics and does not necessarily need to be read linearly. Throughout the chapters, I will generate random data for many examples that will use the default random number generator in the numpy.random module:

```
In [11]: rng = np.random.default_rng(seed=12345)
```

A.1 ndarray Object Internals

The NumPy ndarray provides a way to interpret a block of homogeneously typed data (either contiguous or strided) as a multidimensional array object. The data type, or *dtype*, determines how the data is interpreted as being floating point, integer, Boolean, or any of the other types we've been looking at.

Part of what makes ndarray flexible is that every array object is a *strided* view on a block of data. You might wonder, for example, how the array view arr[::2, ::-1] does not copy any data. The reason is that the ndarray is more than just a chunk of memory and a data type; it also has *striding* information that enables the array to move through memory with varying step sizes. More precisely, the ndarray internally consists of the following:

- A *pointer to data*—that is, a block of data in RAM or in a memory-mapped file
- The *data type* or dtype describing fixed-size value cells in the array
- A tuple indicating the array's *shape*

- A tuple of *strides*—integers indicating the number of bytes to "step" in order to advance one element along a dimension

See Figure A-1 for a simple mock-up of the ndarray innards.

Figure A-1. The NumPy ndarray object

For example, a 10 × 5 array would have the shape (10, 5):

```
In [12]: np.ones((10, 5)).shape
Out[12]: (10, 5)
```

A typical (C order) 3 × 4 × 5 array of float64 (8-byte) values has the strides (160, 40, 8) (knowing about the strides can be useful because, in general, the larger the strides on a particular axis, the more costly it is to perform computation along that axis):

```
In [13]: np.ones((3, 4, 5), dtype=np.float64).strides
Out[13]: (160, 40, 8)
```

While it is rare that a typical NumPy user would be interested in the array strides, they are needed to construct "zero-copy" array views. Strides can even be negative, which enables an array to move "backward" through memory (this would be the case, for example, in a slice like obj[::-1] or obj[:, ::-1]).

NumPy Data Type Hierarchy

You may occasionally have code that needs to check whether an array contains integers, floating-point numbers, strings, or Python objects. Because there are multiple types of floating-point numbers (float16 through float128), checking that the data type is among a list of types would be very verbose. Fortunately, the data types have superclasses, such as np.integer and np.floating, which can be used with the np.issubdtype function:

```
In [14]: ints = np.ones(10, dtype=np.uint16)

In [15]: floats = np.ones(10, dtype=np.float32)

In [16]: np.issubdtype(ints.dtype, np.integer)
Out[16]: True
```

```
In [17]: np.issubdtype(floats.dtype, np.floating)
Out[17]: True
```

You can see all of the parent classes of a specific data type by calling the type's `mro` method:

```
In [18]: np.float64.mro()
Out[18]:
[numpy.float64,
 numpy.floating,
 numpy.inexact,
 numpy.number,
 numpy.generic,
 float,
 object]
```

Therefore, we also have:

```
In [19]: np.issubdtype(ints.dtype, np.number)
Out[19]: True
```

Most NumPy users will never have to know about this, but it is occasionally useful. See Figure A-2 for a graph of the data type hierarchy and parent–subclass relationships.[1]

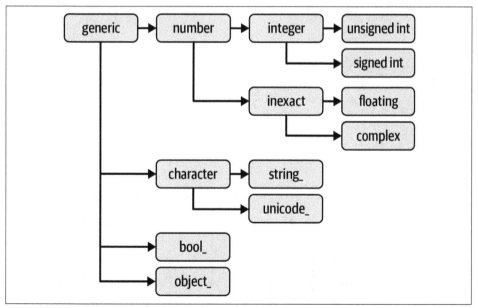

Figure A-2. The NumPy data type class hierarchy

---

1 Some of the data types have trailing underscores in their names. These are there to avoid variable name conflicts between the NumPy-specific types and the Python built-in ones.

A.2 Advanced Array Manipulation

There are many ways to work with arrays beyond fancy indexing, slicing, and Boolean subsetting. While much of the heavy lifting for data analysis applications is handled by higher-level functions in pandas, you may at some point need to write a data algorithm that is not found in one of the existing libraries.

Reshaping Arrays

In many cases, you can convert an array from one shape to another without copying any data. To do this, pass a tuple indicating the new shape to the reshape array instance method. For example, suppose we had a one-dimensional array of values that we wished to rearrange into a matrix (this is illustrated in Figure A-3):

```
In [20]: arr = np.arange(8)

In [21]: arr
Out[21]: array([0, 1, 2, 3, 4, 5, 6, 7])

In [22]: arr.reshape((4, 2))
Out[22]:
array([[0, 1],
       [2, 3],
       [4, 5],
       [6, 7]])
```

Figure A-3. Reshaping in C (row major) or FORTRAN (column major) order

A multidimensional array can also be reshaped:

```
In [23]: arr.reshape((4, 2)).reshape((2, 4))
Out[23]:
array([[0, 1, 2, 3],
       [4, 5, 6, 7]])
```

One of the passed shape dimensions can be –1, in which case the value used for that dimension will be inferred from the data:

```
In [24]: arr = np.arange(15)

In [25]: arr.reshape((5, -1))
Out[25]:
array([[ 0,  1,  2],
       [ 3,  4,  5],
       [ 6,  7,  8],
       [ 9, 10, 11],
       [12, 13, 14]])
```

Since an array's shape attribute is a tuple, it can be passed to reshape, too:

```
In [26]: other_arr = np.ones((3, 5))

In [27]: other_arr.shape
Out[27]: (3, 5)

In [28]: arr.reshape(other_arr.shape)
Out[28]:
array([[ 0,  1,  2,  3,  4],
       [ 5,  6,  7,  8,  9],
       [10, 11, 12, 13, 14]])
```

The opposite operation of reshape from one-dimensional to a higher dimension is typically known as *flattening* or *raveling*:

```
In [29]: arr = np.arange(15).reshape((5, 3))

In [30]: arr
Out[30]:
array([[ 0,  1,  2],
       [ 3,  4,  5],
       [ 6,  7,  8],
       [ 9, 10, 11],
       [12, 13, 14]])

In [31]: arr.ravel()
Out[31]: array([ 0,  1,  2,  3,  4,  5,  6,  7,  8,  9, 10, 11, 12, 13, 14])
```

ravel does not produce a copy of the underlying values if the values in the result were contiguous in the original array.

The `flatten` method behaves like `ravel` except it always returns a copy of the data:

```
In [32]: arr.flatten()
Out[32]: array([ 0,  1,  2,  3,  4,  5,  6,  7,  8,  9, 10, 11, 12, 13, 14])
```

The data can be reshaped or raveled in different orders. This is a slightly nuanced topic for new NumPy users and is therefore the next subtopic.

C Versus FORTRAN Order

NumPy is able to adapt to many different layouts of your data in memory. By default, NumPy arrays are created in *row major* order. Spatially this means that if you have a two-dimensional array of data, the items in each row of the array are stored in adjacent memory locations. The alternative to row major ordering is *column major* order, which means that values within each column of data are stored in adjacent memory locations.

For historical reasons, row and column major order are also known as C and FORTRAN order, respectively. In the FORTRAN 77 language, matrices are all column major.

Functions like `reshape` and `ravel` accept an `order` argument indicating the order to use the data in the array. This is usually set to `'C'` or `'F'` in most cases (there are also less commonly used options `'A'` and `'K'`; see the NumPy documentation, and refer back to Figure A-3 for an illustration of these options):

```
In [33]: arr = np.arange(12).reshape((3, 4))

In [34]: arr
Out[34]:
array([[ 0,  1,  2,  3],
       [ 4,  5,  6,  7],
       [ 8,  9, 10, 11]])

In [35]: arr.ravel()
Out[35]: array([ 0,  1,  2,  3,  4,  5,  6,  7,  8,  9, 10, 11])

In [36]: arr.ravel('F')
Out[36]: array([ 0,  4,  8,  1,  5,  9,  2,  6, 10,  3,  7, 11])
```

Reshaping arrays with more than two dimensions can be a bit mind-bending (see Figure A-3). The key difference between C and FORTRAN order is the way in which the dimensions are walked:

C/row major order
  Traverse higher dimensions *first* (e.g., axis 1 before advancing on axis 0).

FORTRAN/column major order
  Traverse higher dimensions *last* (e.g., axis 0 before advancing on axis 1).

Concatenating and Splitting Arrays

`numpy.concatenate` takes a sequence (tuple, list, etc.) of arrays and joins them in order along the input axis:

```
In [37]: arr1 = np.array([[1, 2, 3], [4, 5, 6]])

In [38]: arr2 = np.array([[7, 8, 9], [10, 11, 12]])

In [39]: np.concatenate([arr1, arr2], axis=0)
Out[39]:
array([[ 1,  2,  3],
       [ 4,  5,  6],
       [ 7,  8,  9],
       [10, 11, 12]])

In [40]: np.concatenate([arr1, arr2], axis=1)
Out[40]:
array([[ 1,  2,  3,  7,  8,  9],
       [ 4,  5,  6, 10, 11, 12]])
```

There are some convenience functions, like `vstack` and `hstack`, for common kinds of concatenation. The preceding operations could have been expressed as:

```
In [41]: np.vstack((arr1, arr2))
Out[41]:
array([[ 1,  2,  3],
       [ 4,  5,  6],
       [ 7,  8,  9],
       [10, 11, 12]])

In [42]: np.hstack((arr1, arr2))
Out[42]:
array([[ 1,  2,  3,  7,  8,  9],
       [ 4,  5,  6, 10, 11, 12]])
```

`split`, on the other hand, slices an array into multiple arrays along an axis:

```
In [43]: arr = rng.standard_normal((5, 2))

In [44]: arr
Out[44]:
array([[-1.4238,  1.2637],
       [-0.8707, -0.2592],
       [-0.0753, -0.7409],
       [-1.3678,  0.6489],
       [ 0.3611, -1.9529]])

In [45]: first, second, third = np.split(arr, [1, 3])

In [46]: first
Out[46]: array([[-1.4238,  1.2637]])
```

```
In [47]: second
Out[47]:
array([[-0.8707, -0.2592],
       [-0.0753, -0.7409]])

In [48]: third
Out[48]:
array([[-1.3678,  0.6489],
       [ 0.3611, -1.9529]])
```

The value [1, 3] passed to np.split indicates the indices at which to split the array into pieces.

See Table A-1 for a list of all relevant concatenation and splitting functions, some of which are provided only as a convenience of the very general-purpose concatenate.

Table A-1. Array concatenation functions

Function	Description
concatenate	Most general function, concatenate collection of arrays along one axis
vstack, row_stack	Stack arrays by rows (along axis 0)
hstack	Stack arrays by columns (along axis 1)
column_stack	Like hstack, but convert 1D arrays to 2D column vectors first
dstack	Stack arrays by "depth" (along axis 2)
split	Split array at passed locations along a particular axis
hsplit/vsplit	Convenience functions for splitting on axis 0 and 1, respectively

Stacking helpers: r_ and c_

There are two special objects in the NumPy namespace, r_ and c_, that make stacking arrays more concise:

```
In [49]: arr = np.arange(6)

In [50]: arr1 = arr.reshape((3, 2))

In [51]: arr2 = rng.standard_normal((3, 2))

In [52]: np.r_[arr1, arr2]
Out[52]:
array([[ 0.    ,  1.    ],
       [ 2.    ,  3.    ],
       [ 4.    ,  5.    ],
       [ 2.3474,  0.9685],
       [-0.7594,  0.9022],
       [-0.467 , -0.0607]])

In [53]: np.c_[np.r_[arr1, arr2], arr]
Out[53]:
array([[ 0.    ,  1.    ,  0.    ],
```

```
       [ 2.    ,  3.    ,  1.    ],
       [ 4.    ,  5.    ,  2.    ],
       [ 2.3474,  0.9685,  3.    ],
       [-0.7594,  0.9022,  4.    ],
       [-0.467 , -0.0607,  5.    ]])
```

These additionally can translate slices to arrays:

```
In [54]: np.c_[1:6, -10:-5]
Out[54]:
array([[  1, -10],
       [  2,  -9],
       [  3,  -8],
       [  4,  -7],
       [  5,  -6]])
```

See the docstring for more on what you can do with c_ and r_.

Repeating Elements: tile and repeat

Two useful tools for repeating or replicating arrays to produce larger arrays are the repeat and tile functions. repeat replicates each element in an array some number of times, producing a larger array:

```
In [55]: arr = np.arange(3)

In [56]: arr
Out[56]: array([0, 1, 2])

In [57]: arr.repeat(3)
Out[57]: array([0, 0, 0, 1, 1, 1, 2, 2, 2])
```

> The need to replicate or repeat arrays can be less common with NumPy than it is with other array programming frameworks like MATLAB. One reason for this is that *broadcasting* often fills this need better, which is the subject of the next section.

By default, if you pass an integer, each element will be repeated that number of times. If you pass an array of integers, each element can be repeated a different number of times:

```
In [58]: arr.repeat([2, 3, 4])
Out[58]: array([0, 0, 1, 1, 1, 2, 2, 2, 2])
```

Multidimensional arrays can have their elements repeated along a particular axis:

```
In [59]: arr = rng.standard_normal((2, 2))

In [60]: arr
Out[60]:
array([[ 0.7888, -1.2567],
```

```
       [ 0.5759,  1.399 ]])

In [61]: arr.repeat(2, axis=0)
Out[61]:
array([[ 0.7888, -1.2567],
       [ 0.7888, -1.2567],
       [ 0.5759,  1.399 ],
       [ 0.5759,  1.399 ]])
```

Note that if no axis is passed, the array will be flattened first, which is likely not what you want. Similarly, you can pass an array of integers when repeating a multidimensional array to repeat a given slice a different number of times:

```
In [62]: arr.repeat([2, 3], axis=0)
Out[62]:
array([[ 0.7888, -1.2567],
       [ 0.7888, -1.2567],
       [ 0.5759,  1.399 ],
       [ 0.5759,  1.399 ],
       [ 0.5759,  1.399 ]])

In [63]: arr.repeat([2, 3], axis=1)
Out[63]:
array([[ 0.7888,  0.7888, -1.2567, -1.2567, -1.2567],
       [ 0.5759,  0.5759,  1.399 ,  1.399 ,  1.399 ]])
```

tile, on the other hand, is a shortcut for stacking copies of an array along an axis. Visually you can think of it as being akin to "laying down tiles":

```
In [64]: arr
Out[64]:
array([[ 0.7888, -1.2567],
       [ 0.5759,  1.399 ]])

In [65]: np.tile(arr, 2)
Out[65]:
array([[ 0.7888, -1.2567,  0.7888, -1.2567],
       [ 0.5759,  1.399 ,  0.5759,  1.399 ]])
```

The second argument is the number of tiles; with a scalar, the tiling is made row by row, rather than column by column. The second argument to tile can be a tuple indicating the layout of the "tiling":

```
In [66]: arr
Out[66]:
array([[ 0.7888, -1.2567],
       [ 0.5759,  1.399 ]])

In [67]: np.tile(arr, (2, 1))
Out[67]:
array([[ 0.7888, -1.2567],
       [ 0.5759,  1.399 ],
       [ 0.7888, -1.2567],
```

```
              [ 0.5759,  1.399 ]])

In [68]: np.tile(arr, (3, 2))
Out[68]:
array([[ 0.7888, -1.2567,  0.7888, -1.2567],
       [ 0.5759,  1.399 ,  0.5759,  1.399 ],
       [ 0.7888, -1.2567,  0.7888, -1.2567],
       [ 0.5759,  1.399 ,  0.5759,  1.399 ],
       [ 0.7888, -1.2567,  0.7888, -1.2567],
       [ 0.5759,  1.399 ,  0.5759,  1.399 ]])
```

Fancy Indexing Equivalents: take and put

As you may recall from Chapter 4, one way to get and set subsets of arrays is by *fancy* indexing using integer arrays:

```
In [69]: arr = np.arange(10) * 100

In [70]: inds = [7, 1, 2, 6]

In [71]: arr[inds]
Out[71]: array([700, 100, 200, 600])
```

There are alternative ndarray methods that are useful in the special case of making a selection only on a single axis:

```
In [72]: arr.take(inds)
Out[72]: array([700, 100, 200, 600])

In [73]: arr.put(inds, 42)

In [74]: arr
Out[74]: array([  0,  42,  42, 300, 400, 500,  42,  42, 800, 900])

In [75]: arr.put(inds, [40, 41, 42, 43])

In [76]: arr
Out[76]: array([  0,  41,  42, 300, 400, 500,  43,  40, 800, 900])
```

To use take along other axes, you can pass the axis keyword:

```
In [77]: inds = [2, 0, 2, 1]

In [78]: arr = rng.standard_normal((2, 4))

In [79]: arr
Out[79]:
array([[ 1.3223, -0.2997,  0.9029, -1.6216],
       [-0.1582,  0.4495, -1.3436, -0.0817]])

In [80]: arr.take(inds, axis=1)
Out[80]:
```

```
array([[ 0.9029,  1.3223,  0.9029, -0.2997],
       [-1.3436, -0.1582, -1.3436,  0.4495]])
```

put does not accept an `axis` argument but rather indexes into the flattened (one-dimensional, C order) version of the array. Thus, when you need to set elements using an index array on other axes, it is best to use [ ]-based indexing.

A.3 Broadcasting

Broadcasting governs how operations work between arrays of different shapes. It can be a powerful feature, but it can cause confusion, even for experienced users. The simplest example of broadcasting occurs when combining a scalar value with an array:

```
In [81]: arr = np.arange(5)

In [82]: arr
Out[82]: array([0, 1, 2, 3, 4])

In [83]: arr * 4
Out[83]: array([ 0,  4,  8, 12, 16])
```

Here we say that the scalar value 4 has been *broadcast* to all of the other elements in the multiplication operation.

For example, we can demean each column of an array by subtracting the column means. In this case, it is necessary only to subtract an array containing the mean of each column:

```
In [84]: arr = rng.standard_normal((4, 3))

In [85]: arr.mean(0)
Out[85]: array([0.1206, 0.243 , 0.1444])

In [86]: demeaned = arr - arr.mean(0)

In [87]: demeaned
Out[87]:
array([[ 1.6042,  2.3751,  0.633 ],
       [ 0.7081, -1.202 , -1.3538],
       [-1.5329,  0.2985,  0.6076],
       [-0.7793, -1.4717,  0.1132]])

In [88]: demeaned.mean(0)
Out[88]: array([ 0., -0.,  0.])
```

See Figure A-4 for an illustration of this operation. Demeaning the rows as a broadcast operation requires a bit more care. Fortunately, broadcasting potentially lower dimensional values across any dimension of an array (like subtracting the row means from each column of a two-dimensional array) is possible as long as you follow the rules.

This brings us to the broadcasting rule.

The Broadcasting Rule

Two arrays are compatible for broadcasting if for each *trailing dimension* (i.e., starting from the end) the axis lengths match or if either of the lengths is 1. Broadcasting is then performed over the missing or length 1 dimensions.

Figure A-4. *Broadcasting over axis 0 with a 1D array*

Even as an experienced NumPy user, I often find myself having to pause and draw a diagram as I think about the broadcasting rule. Consider the last example and suppose we wished instead to subtract the mean value from each row. Since arr.mean(0) has length 3, it is compatible for broadcasting across axis 0 because the trailing dimension in arr is 3 and therefore matches. According to the rules, to subtract over axis 1 (i.e., subtract the row mean from each row), the smaller array must have the shape (4, 1):

```
In [89]: arr
Out[89]:
array([[ 1.7247,  2.6182,  0.7774],
       [ 0.8286, -0.959 , -1.2094],
       [-1.4123,  0.5415,  0.7519],
       [-0.6588, -1.2287,  0.2576]])

In [90]: row_means = arr.mean(1)
```

```
In [91]: row_means.shape
Out[91]: (4,)

In [92]: row_means.reshape((4, 1))
Out[92]:
array([[ 1.7068],
       [-0.4466],
       [-0.0396],
       [-0.5433]])

In [93]: demeaned = arr - row_means.reshape((4, 1))

In [94]: demeaned.mean(1)
Out[94]: array([-0.,  0.,  0.,  0.])
```

See Figure A-5 for an illustration of this operation.

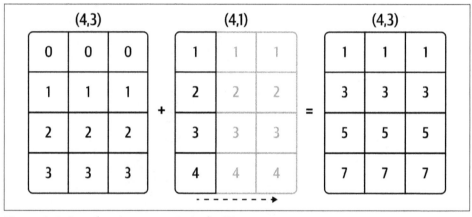

Figure A-5. Broadcasting over axis 1 of a 2D array

See Figure A-6 for another illustration, this time adding a two-dimensional array to a three-dimensional one across axis 0.

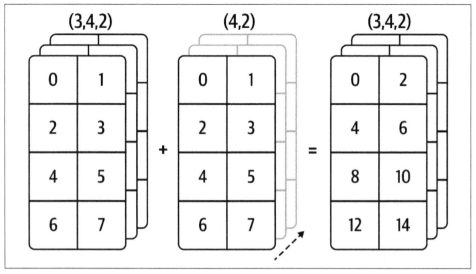

Figure A-6. Broadcasting over axis 0 of a 3D array

Broadcasting over Other Axes

Broadcasting with higher dimensional arrays can seem even more mind-bending, but it is really a matter of following the rules. If you don't, you'll get an error like this:

```
In [95]: arr - arr.mean(1)
---------------------------------------------------------------
ValueError                          Traceback (most recent call last)
<ipython-input-95-8b8ada26fac0> in <module>
----> 1 arr - arr.mean(1)
ValueError: operands could not be broadcast together with shapes (4,3) (4,)
```

It's quite common to want to perform an arithmetic operation with a lower dimensional array across axes other than axis 0. According to the broadcasting rule, the "broadcast dimensions" must be 1 in the smaller array. In the example of row demeaning shown here, this means reshaping the row to be shape (4, 1) instead of (4,):

```
In [96]: arr - arr.mean(1).reshape((4, 1))
Out[96]:
array([[ 0.018 ,  0.9114, -0.9294],
       [ 1.2752, -0.5124, -0.7628],
       [-1.3727,  0.5811,  0.7915],
       [-0.1155, -0.6854,  0.8009]])
```

In the three-dimensional case, broadcasting over any of the three dimensions is only a matter of reshaping the data to be shape compatible. Figure A-7 nicely visualizes the shapes required to broadcast over each axis of a three-dimensional array.

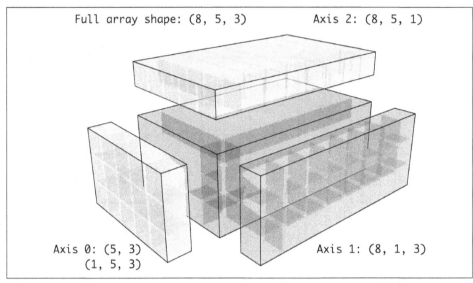

Figure A-7. Compatible 2D array shapes for broadcasting over a 3D array

A common problem, therefore, is needing to add a new axis with length 1 specifically for broadcasting purposes. Using reshape is one option, but inserting an axis requires constructing a tuple indicating the new shape. This often can be a tedious exercise. Thus, NumPy arrays offer a special syntax for inserting new axes by indexing. We use the special np.newaxis attribute along with "full" slices to insert the new axis:

```
In [97]: arr = np.zeros((4, 4))

In [98]: arr_3d = arr[:, np.newaxis, :]

In [99]: arr_3d.shape
Out[99]: (4, 1, 4)

In [100]: arr_1d = rng.standard_normal(3)

In [101]: arr_1d[:, np.newaxis]
Out[101]:
array([[ 0.3129],
       [-0.1308],
       [ 1.27  ]])

In [102]: arr_1d[np.newaxis, :]
Out[102]: array([[ 0.3129, -0.1308,  1.27  ]])
```

Thus, if we had a three-dimensional array and wanted to demean axis 2, we would need to write:

```
In [103]: arr = rng.standard_normal((3, 4, 5))

In [104]: depth_means = arr.mean(2)

In [105]: depth_means
Out[105]:
array([[ 0.0431,  0.2747, -0.1885, -0.2014],
       [-0.5732, -0.5467,  0.1183, -0.6301],
       [ 0.0972,  0.5954,  0.0331, -0.6002]])

In [106]: depth_means.shape
Out[106]: (3, 4)

In [107]: demeaned = arr - depth_means[:, :, np.newaxis]

In [108]: demeaned.mean(2)
Out[108]:
array([[ 0., -0.,  0., -0.],
       [ 0., -0., -0., -0.],
       [ 0.,  0.,  0.,  0.]])
```

You might be wondering if there's a way to generalize demeaning over an axis without sacrificing performance. There is, but it requires some indexing gymnastics:

```
def demean_axis(arr, axis=0):
    means = arr.mean(axis)

    # This generalizes things like [:, :, np.newaxis] to N dimensions
    indexer = [slice(None)] * arr.ndim
    indexer[axis] = np.newaxis
    return arr - means[indexer]
```

Setting Array Values by Broadcasting

The same broadcasting rule governing arithmetic operations also applies to setting values via array indexing. In a simple case, we can do things like:

```
In [109]: arr = np.zeros((4, 3))

In [110]: arr[:] = 5

In [111]: arr
Out[111]:
array([[5., 5., 5.],
       [5., 5., 5.],
       [5., 5., 5.],
       [5., 5., 5.]])
```

However, if we had a one-dimensional array of values we wanted to set into the columns of the array, we can do that as long as the shape is compatible:

```
In [112]: col = np.array([1.28, -0.42, 0.44, 1.6])
```

```
In [113]: arr[:] = col[:, np.newaxis]

In [114]: arr
Out[114]:
array([[ 1.28,  1.28,  1.28],
       [-0.42, -0.42, -0.42],
       [ 0.44,  0.44,  0.44],
       [ 1.6 ,  1.6 ,  1.6 ]])

In [115]: arr[:2] = [[-1.37], [0.509]]

In [116]: arr
Out[116]:
array([[-1.37 , -1.37 , -1.37 ],
       [ 0.509,  0.509,  0.509],
       [ 0.44 ,  0.44 ,  0.44 ],
       [ 1.6  ,  1.6  ,  1.6  ]])
```

A.4 Advanced ufunc Usage

While many NumPy users will only use the fast element-wise operations provided by the universal functions, a number of additional features occasionally can help you write more concise code without explicit loops.

ufunc Instance Methods

Each of NumPy's binary ufuncs has special methods for performing certain kinds of special vectorized operations. These are summarized in Table A-2, but I'll give a few concrete examples to illustrate how they work.

reduce takes a single array and aggregates its values, optionally along an axis, by performing a sequence of binary operations. For example, an alternative way to sum elements in an array is to use np.add.reduce:

```
In [117]: arr = np.arange(10)

In [118]: np.add.reduce(arr)
Out[118]: 45

In [119]: arr.sum()
Out[119]: 45
```

The starting value (for example, 0 for add) depends on the ufunc. If an axis is passed, the reduction is performed along that axis. This allows you to answer certain kinds of questions in a concise way. As a less mundane example, we can use np.logical_and to check whether the values in each row of an array are sorted:

```
In [120]: my_rng = np.random.default_rng(12346)  # for reproducibility

In [121]: arr = my_rng.standard_normal((5, 5))
```

```
In [122]: arr
Out[122]:
array([[-0.9039,  0.1571,  0.8976, -0.7622, -0.1763],
       [ 0.053 , -1.6284, -0.1775,  1.9636,  1.7813],
       [-0.8797, -1.6985, -1.8189,  0.119 , -0.4441],
       [ 0.7691, -0.0343,  0.3925,  0.7589, -0.0705],
       [ 1.0498,  1.0297, -0.4201,  0.7863,  0.9612]])

In [123]: arr[::2].sort(1) # sort a few rows

In [124]: arr[:, :-1] < arr[:, 1:]
Out[124]:
array([[ True,  True,  True,  True],
       [False,  True,  True, False],
       [ True,  True,  True,  True],
       [False,  True,  True, False],
       [ True,  True,  True,  True]])

In [125]: np.logical_and.reduce(arr[:, :-1] < arr[:, 1:], axis=1)
Out[125]: array([ True, False,  True, False,  True])
```

Note that logical_and.reduce is equivalent to the all method.

The accumulate ufunc method is related to reduce, like cumsum is related to sum. It produces an array of the same size with the intermediate "accumulated" values:

```
In [126]: arr = np.arange(15).reshape((3, 5))

In [127]: np.add.accumulate(arr, axis=1)
Out[127]:
array([[ 0,  1,  3,  6, 10],
       [ 5, 11, 18, 26, 35],
       [10, 21, 33, 46, 60]])
```

outer performs a pair-wise cross product between two arrays:

```
In [128]: arr = np.arange(3).repeat([1, 2, 2])

In [129]: arr
Out[129]: array([0, 1, 1, 2, 2])

In [130]: np.multiply.outer(arr, np.arange(5))
Out[130]:
array([[0, 0, 0, 0, 0],
       [0, 1, 2, 3, 4],
       [0, 1, 2, 3, 4],
       [0, 2, 4, 6, 8],
       [0, 2, 4, 6, 8]])
```

The output of outer will have a dimension that is the concatenation of the dimensions of the inputs:

```
In [131]: x, y = rng.standard_normal((3, 4)), rng.standard_normal(5)

In [132]: result = np.subtract.outer(x, y)

In [133]: result.shape
Out[133]: (3, 4, 5)
```

The last method, reduceat, performs a "local reduce," in essence an array "group by" operation in which slices of the array are aggregated together. It accepts a sequence of "bin edges" that indicate how to split and aggregate the values:

```
In [134]: arr = np.arange(10)

In [135]: np.add.reduceat(arr, [0, 5, 8])
Out[135]: array([10, 18, 17])
```

The results are the reductions (here, sums) performed over arr[0:5], arr[5:8], and arr[8:]. As with the other methods, you can pass an axis argument:

```
In [136]: arr = np.multiply.outer(np.arange(4), np.arange(5))

In [137]: arr
Out[137]:
array([[ 0,  0,  0,  0,  0],
       [ 0,  1,  2,  3,  4],
       [ 0,  2,  4,  6,  8],
       [ 0,  3,  6,  9, 12]])

In [138]: np.add.reduceat(arr, [0, 2, 4], axis=1)
Out[138]:
array([[ 0,  0,  0],
       [ 1,  5,  4],
       [ 2, 10,  8],
       [ 3, 15, 12]])
```

See Table A-2 for a partial listing of ufunc methods.

Table A-2. ufunc methods

Method	Description
accumulate(x)	Aggregate values, preserving all partial aggregates.
at(x, indices, b=None)	Perform operation in place on x at the specified indices. The argument b is the second input to ufuncs that requires two array inputs.
reduce(x)	Aggregate values by successive applications of the operation.
reduceat(x, bins)	"Local" reduce or "group by"; reduce contiguous slices of data to produce an aggregated array.
outer(x, y)	Apply operation to all pairs of elements in x and y; the resulting array has shape x.shape + y.shape.

Writing New ufuncs in Python

There are a number of ways to create your own NumPy ufuncs. The most general is to use the NumPy C API, but that is beyond the scope of this book. In this section, we will look at pure Python ufuncs.

numpy.frompyfunc accepts a Python function along with a specification for the number of inputs and outputs. For example, a simple function that adds element-wise would be specified as:

```
In [139]: def add_elements(x, y):
   .....:     return x + y

In [140]: add_them = np.frompyfunc(add_elements, 2, 1)

In [141]: add_them(np.arange(8), np.arange(8))
Out[141]: array([0, 2, 4, 6, 8, 10, 12, 14], dtype=object)
```

Functions created using frompyfunc always return arrays of Python objects, which can be inconvenient. Fortunately, there is an alternative (but slightly less feature rich) function, numpy.vectorize, that allows you to specify the output type:

```
In [142]: add_them = np.vectorize(add_elements, otypes=[np.float64])

In [143]: add_them(np.arange(8), np.arange(8))
Out[143]: array([ 0.,  2.,  4.,  6.,  8., 10., 12., 14.])
```

These functions provide a way to create ufunc-like functions, but they are very slow because they require a Python function call to compute each element, which is a lot slower than NumPy's C-based ufunc loops:

```
In [144]: arr = rng.standard_normal(10000)

In [145]: %timeit add_them(arr, arr)
2.43 ms +- 30.5 us per loop (mean +- std. dev. of 7 runs, 100 loops each)

In [146]: %timeit np.add(arr, arr)
2.88 us +- 47.9 ns per loop (mean +- std. dev. of 7 runs, 100000 loops each)
```

Later in this appendix we'll show how to create fast ufuncs in Python using the Numba library (*http://numba.pydata.org*).

A.5 Structured and Record Arrays

You may have noticed up until now that ndarray is a *homogeneous* data container; that is, it represents a block of memory in which each element takes up the same number of bytes, as determined by the data type. On the surface, this would appear to not allow you to represent heterogeneous or tabular data. A *structured* array is an ndarray in which each element can be thought of as representing a *struct* in C (hence the "structured" name) or a row in a SQL table with multiple named fields:

```
In [147]: dtype = [('x', np.float64), ('y', np.int32)]

In [148]: sarr = np.array([(1.5, 6), (np.pi, -2)], dtype=dtype)

In [149]: sarr
Out[149]: array([(1.5   , 6), (3.1416, -2)], dtype=[('x', '<f8'), ('y', '<i4')])
```

There are several ways to specify a structured data type (see the online NumPy documentation). One typical way is as a list of tuples with (field_name, field_data_type). Now, the elements of the array are tuple-like objects whose elements can be accessed like a dictionary:

```
In [150]: sarr[0]
Out[150]: (1.5, 6)

In [151]: sarr[0]['y']
Out[151]: 6
```

The field names are stored in the dtype.names attribute. When you access a field on the structured array, a strided view on the data is returned, thus copying nothing:

```
In [152]: sarr['x']
Out[152]: array([1.5   , 3.1416])
```

Nested Data Types and Multidimensional Fields

When specifying a structured data type, you can additionally pass a shape (as an int or tuple):

```
In [153]: dtype = [('x', np.int64, 3), ('y', np.int32)]

In [154]: arr = np.zeros(4, dtype=dtype)

In [155]: arr
Out[155]:
array([([0, 0, 0], 0), ([0, 0, 0], 0), ([0, 0, 0], 0), ([0, 0, 0], 0)],
      dtype=[('x', '<i8', (3,)), ('y', '<i4')])
```

In this case, the x field now refers to an array of length 3 for each record:

```
In [156]: arr[0]['x']
Out[156]: array([0, 0, 0])
```

Conveniently, accessing arr['x'] then returns a two-dimensional array instead of a one-dimensional array as in prior examples:

```
In [157]: arr['x']
Out[157]:
array([[0, 0, 0],
       [0, 0, 0],
       [0, 0, 0],
       [0, 0, 0]])
```

This enables you to express more complicated, nested structures as a single block of memory in an array. You can also nest data types to make more complex structures. Here is an example:

```
In [158]: dtype = [('x', [('a', 'f8'), ('b', 'f4')]), ('y', np.int32)]

In [159]: data = np.array([((1, 2), 5), ((3, 4), 6)], dtype=dtype)

In [160]: data['x']
Out[160]: array([(1., 2.), (3., 4.)], dtype=[('a', '<f8'), ('b', '<f4')])

In [161]: data['y']
Out[161]: array([5, 6], dtype=int32)

In [162]: data['x']['a']
Out[162]: array([1., 3.])
```

pandas DataFrame does not support this feature in the same way, though it is similar to hierarchical indexing.

Why Use Structured Arrays?

Compared with a pandas DataFrame, NumPy structured arrays are a lower level tool. They provide a means to interpret a block of memory as a tabular structure with nested columns. Since each element in the array is represented in memory as a fixed number of bytes, structured arrays provide an efficient way of writing data to and from disk (including memory maps), transporting it over the network, and other such uses. The memory layout of each value in a structured array is based on the binary representation of struct data types in the C programming language.

As another common use for structured arrays, writing data files as fixed-length record byte streams is a common way to serialize data in C and C++ code, which is sometimes found in legacy systems in industry. As long as the format of the file is known (the size of each record and the order, byte size, and data type of each element), the data can be read into memory with np.fromfile. Specialized uses like this are beyond the scope of this book, but it's worth knowing that such things are possible.

A.6 More About Sorting

Like Python's built-in list, the ndarray sort instance method is an *in-place* sort, meaning that the array contents are rearranged without producing a new array:

```
In [163]: arr = rng.standard_normal(6)

In [164]: arr.sort()
```

```
In [165]: arr
Out[165]: array([-1.1553, -0.9319, -0.5218, -0.4745, -0.1649,  0.03  ])
```

When sorting arrays in place, remember that if the array is a view on a different ndarray, the original array will be modified:

```
In [166]: arr = rng.standard_normal((3, 5))

In [167]: arr
Out[167]:
array([[-1.1956,  0.4691, -0.3598,  1.0359,  0.2267],
       [-0.7448, -0.5931, -1.055 , -0.0683,  0.458 ],
       [-0.07  ,  0.1462, -0.9944,  1.1436,  0.5026]])

In [168]: arr[:, 0].sort()  # Sort first column values in place

In [169]: arr
Out[169]:
array([[-1.1956,  0.4691, -0.3598,  1.0359,  0.2267],
       [-0.7448, -0.5931, -1.055 , -0.0683,  0.458 ],
       [-0.07  ,  0.1462, -0.9944,  1.1436,  0.5026]])
```

On the other hand, numpy.sort creates a new, sorted copy of an array. Otherwise, it accepts the same arguments (such as kind) as ndarray's sort method:

```
In [170]: arr = rng.standard_normal(5)

In [171]: arr
Out[171]: array([ 0.8981, -1.1704, -0.2686, -0.796 ,  1.4522])

In [172]: np.sort(arr)
Out[172]: array([-1.1704, -0.796 , -0.2686,  0.8981,  1.4522])

In [173]: arr
Out[173]: array([ 0.8981, -1.1704, -0.2686, -0.796 ,  1.4522])
```

All of these sort methods take an axis argument for independently sorting the sections of data along the passed axis:

```
In [174]: arr = rng.standard_normal((3, 5))

In [175]: arr
Out[175]:
array([[-0.2535,  2.1183,  0.3634, -0.6245,  1.1279],
       [ 1.6164, -0.2287, -0.6201, -0.1143, -1.2067],
       [-1.0872, -2.1518, -0.6287, -1.3199,  0.083 ]])

In [176]: arr.sort(axis=1)

In [177]: arr
Out[177]:
array([[-0.6245, -0.2535,  0.3634,  1.1279,  2.1183],
```

```
       [-1.2067, -0.6201, -0.2287, -0.1143,  1.6164],
       [-2.1518, -1.3199, -1.0872, -0.6287,  0.083 ]])
```

You may notice that none of the sort methods have an option to sort in descending order. This is a problem in practice because array slicing produces views, thus not producing a copy or requiring any computational work. Many Python users are familiar with the "trick" that for a list of values, values[::-1] returns a list in reverse order. The same is true for ndarrays:

```
In [178]: arr[:, ::-1]
Out[178]:
array([[ 2.1183,  1.1279,  0.3634, -0.2535, -0.6245],
       [ 1.6164, -0.1143, -0.2287, -0.6201, -1.2067],
       [ 0.083 , -0.6287, -1.0872, -1.3199, -2.1518]])
```

Indirect Sorts: argsort and lexsort

In data analysis you may need to reorder datasets by one or more keys. For example, a table of data about some students might need to be sorted by last name, then by first name. This is an example of an *indirect* sort, and if you've read the pandas-related chapters, you have already seen many higher-level examples. Given a key or keys (an array of values or multiple arrays of values), you wish to obtain an array of integer *indices* (I refer to them colloquially as *indexers*) that tells you how to reorder the data to be in sorted order. Two methods for this are argsort and numpy.lexsort. As an example:

```
In [179]: values = np.array([5, 0, 1, 3, 2])

In [180]: indexer = values.argsort()

In [181]: indexer
Out[181]: array([1, 2, 4, 3, 0])

In [182]: values[indexer]
Out[182]: array([0, 1, 2, 3, 5])
```

As a more complicated example, this code reorders a two-dimensional array by its first row:

```
In [183]: arr = rng.standard_normal((3, 5))

In [184]: arr[0] = values

In [185]: arr
Out[185]:
array([[ 5.    ,  0.    ,  1.    ,  3.    ,  2.    ],
       [-0.7503, -2.1268, -1.391 , -0.4922,  0.4505],
       [ 0.8926, -1.0479,  0.9553,  0.2936,  0.5379]])

In [186]: arr[:, arr[0].argsort()]
Out[186]:
```

```
array([[ 0.    ,  1.    ,  2.    ,  3.    ,  5.    ],
       [-2.1268, -1.391 ,  0.4505, -0.4922, -0.7503],
       [-1.0479,  0.9553,  0.5379,  0.2936,  0.8926]])
```

lexsort is similar to argsort, but it performs an indirect *lexicographical* sort on multiple key arrays. Suppose we wanted to sort some data identified by first and last names:

```
In [187]: first_name = np.array(['Bob', 'Jane', 'Steve', 'Bill', 'Barbara'])

In [188]: last_name = np.array(['Jones', 'Arnold', 'Arnold', 'Jones', 'Walters'])

In [189]: sorter = np.lexsort((first_name, last_name))

In [190]: sorter
Out[190]: array([1, 2, 3, 0, 4])

In [191]: list(zip(last_name[sorter], first_name[sorter]))
Out[191]:
[('Arnold', 'Jane'),
 ('Arnold', 'Steve'),
 ('Jones', 'Bill'),
 ('Jones', 'Bob'),
 ('Walters', 'Barbara')]
```

lexsort can be a bit confusing the first time you use it, because the order in which the keys are used to order the data starts with the *last* array passed. Here, last_name was used before first_name.

Alternative Sort Algorithms

A *stable* sorting algorithm preserves the relative position of equal elements. This can be especially important in indirect sorts where the relative ordering is meaningful:

```
In [192]: values = np.array(['2:first', '2:second', '1:first', '1:second',
     .....:                   '1:third'])

In [193]: key = np.array([2, 2, 1, 1, 1])

In [194]: indexer = key.argsort(kind='mergesort')

In [195]: indexer
Out[195]: array([2, 3, 4, 0, 1])

In [196]: values.take(indexer)
Out[196]:
array(['1:first', '1:second', '1:third', '2:first', '2:second'],
      dtype='<U8')
```

The only stable sort available is *mergesort*, which has guaranteed O(n log n) performance, but its performance is on average worse than the default quicksort method.

See Table A-3 for a summary of available methods and their relative performance (and performance guarantees). This is not something that most users will ever have to think about, but it's useful to know that it's there.

Table A-3. Array sorting methods

Kind	Speed	Stable	Work space	Worst case
'quicksort'	1	No	0	O(n^2)
'mergesort'	2	Yes	n / 2	O(n log n)
'heapsort'	3	No	0	O(n log n)

Partially Sorting Arrays

One of the goals of sorting can be to determine the largest or smallest elements in an array. NumPy has fast methods, numpy.partition and np.argpartition, for partitioning an array around the k-th smallest element:

```
In [197]: rng = np.random.default_rng(12345)

In [198]: arr = rng.standard_normal(20)

In [199]: arr
Out[199]:
array([-1.4238,  1.2637, -0.8707, -0.2592, -0.0753, -0.7409, -1.3678,
        0.6489,  0.3611, -1.9529,  2.3474,  0.9685, -0.7594,  0.9022,
       -0.467 , -0.0607,  0.7888, -1.2567,  0.5759,  1.399 ])

In [200]: np.partition(arr, 3)
Out[200]:
array([-1.9529, -1.4238, -1.3678, -1.2567, -0.8707, -0.7594, -0.7409,
       -0.0607,  0.3611, -0.0753, -0.2592, -0.467 ,  0.5759,  0.9022,
        0.9685,  0.6489,  0.7888,  1.2637,  1.399 ,  2.3474])
```

After you call partition(arr, 3), the first three elements in the result are the smallest three values in no particular order. numpy.argpartition, similar to numpy.arg sort, returns the indices that rearrange the data into the equivalent order:

```
In [201]: indices = np.argpartition(arr, 3)

In [202]: indices
Out[202]:
array([ 9,  0,  6, 17,  2, 12,  5, 15,  8,  4,  3, 14, 18, 13, 11,  7, 16,
        1, 19, 10])

In [203]: arr.take(indices)
Out[203]:
array([-1.9529, -1.4238, -1.3678, -1.2567, -0.8707, -0.7594, -0.7409,
       -0.0607,  0.3611, -0.0753, -0.2592, -0.467 ,  0.5759,  0.9022,
        0.9685,  0.6489,  0.7888,  1.2637,  1.399 ,  2.3474])
```

numpy.searchsorted: Finding Elements in a Sorted Array

`searchsorted` is an array method that performs a binary search on a sorted array, returning the location in the array where the value would need to be inserted to maintain sortedness:

```
In [204]: arr = np.array([0, 1, 7, 12, 15])

In [205]: arr.searchsorted(9)
Out[205]: 3
```

You can also pass an array of values to get an array of indices back:

```
In [206]: arr.searchsorted([0, 8, 11, 16])
Out[206]: array([0, 3, 3, 5])
```

You might have noticed that `searchsorted` returned 0 for the 0 element. This is because the default behavior is to return the index at the left side of a group of equal values:

```
In [207]: arr = np.array([0, 0, 0, 1, 1, 1, 1])

In [208]: arr.searchsorted([0, 1])
Out[208]: array([0, 3])

In [209]: arr.searchsorted([0, 1], side='right')
Out[209]: array([3, 7])
```

As another application of `searchsorted`, suppose we had an array of values between 0 and 10,000, and a separate array of "bucket edges" that we wanted to use to bin the data:

```
In [210]: data = np.floor(rng.uniform(0, 10000, size=50))

In [211]: bins = np.array([0, 100, 1000, 5000, 10000])

In [212]: data
Out[212]:
array([ 815., 1598., 3401., 4651., 2664., 8157., 1932., 1294.,  916.,
       5985., 8547., 6016., 9319., 7247., 8605., 9293., 5461., 9376.,
       4949., 2737., 4517., 6650., 3308., 9034., 2570., 3398., 2588.,
       3554.,   50., 6286., 2823.,  680., 6168., 1763., 3043., 4408.,
       1502., 2179., 4743., 4763., 2552., 2975., 2790., 2605., 4827.,
       2119., 4956., 2462., 8384., 1801.])
```

To then get a labeling to which interval each data point belongs (where 1 would mean the bucket [0, 100)), we can simply use `searchsorted`:

```
In [213]: labels = bins.searchsorted(data)

In [214]: labels
Out[214]:
array([2, 3, 3, 3, 3, 4, 3, 3, 2, 4, 4, 4, 4, 4, 4, 4, 4, 4, 3, 3, 3, 4,
```

```
3, 4, 3, 3, 3, 3, 1, 4, 3, 2, 4, 3, 3, 3, 3, 3, 3, 3, 3, 3, 3, 3,
3, 3, 3, 3, 4, 3])
```

This, combined with pandas's `groupby`, can be used to bin data:

```
In [215]: pd.Series(data).groupby(labels).mean()
Out[215]:
1      50.000000
2     803.666667
3    3079.741935
4    7635.200000
dtype: float64
```

A.7 Writing Fast NumPy Functions with Numba

Numba (*http://numba.pydata.org*) is an open source project that creates fast functions
for NumPy-like data using CPUs, GPUs, or other hardware. It uses the LLVM Project
(*http://llvm.org/*) to translate Python code into compiled machine code.

To introduce Numba, let's consider a pure Python function that computes the expression `(x - y).mean()` using a `for` loop:

```
import numpy as np

def mean_distance(x, y):
    nx = len(x)
    result = 0.0
    count = 0
    for i in range(nx):
        result += x[i] - y[i]
        count += 1
    return result / count
```

This function is slow:

```
In [209]: x = rng.standard_normal(10_000_000)

In [210]: y = rng.standard_normal(10_000_000)

In [211]: %timeit mean_distance(x, y)
1 loop, best of 3: 2 s per loop

In [212]: %timeit (x - y).mean()
100 loops, best of 3: 14.7 ms per loop
```

The NumPy version is over 100 times faster. We can turn this function into a
compiled Numba function using the `numba.jit` function:

```
In [213]: import numba as nb

In [214]: numba_mean_distance = nb.jit(mean_distance)
```

We also could have written this as a decorator:

```
@nb.jit
def numba_mean_distance(x, y):
    nx = len(x)
    result = 0.0
    count = 0
    for i in range(nx):
        result += x[i] - y[i]
        count += 1
    return result / count
```

The resulting function is actually faster than the vectorized NumPy version:

```
In [215]: %timeit numba_mean_distance(x, y)
100 loops, best of 3: 10.3 ms per loop
```

Numba cannot compile all pure Python code, but it supports a significant subset of Python that is most useful for writing numerical algorithms.

Numba is a deep library, supporting different kinds of hardware, modes of compilation, and user extensions. It is also able to compile a substantial subset of the NumPy Python API without explicit for loops. Numba is able to recognize constructs that can be compiled to machine code, while substituting calls to the CPython API for functions that it does not know how to compile. Numba's jit function option, nopython=True, restricts allowed code to Python code that can be compiled to LLVM without any Python C API calls. jit(nopython=True) has a shorter alias, numba.njit.

In the previous example, we could have written:

```
from numba import float64, njit

@njit(float64(float64[:], float64[:]))
def mean_distance(x, y):
    return (x - y).mean()
```

I encourage you to learn more by reading the online documentation for Numba (*http://numba.pydata.org/*). The next section shows an example of creating custom NumPy ufunc objects.

Creating Custom numpy.ufunc Objects with Numba

The numba.vectorize function creates compiled NumPy ufuncs, which behave like built-in ufuncs. Let's consider a Python implementation of numpy.add:

```
from numba import vectorize

@vectorize
def nb_add(x, y):
    return x + y
```

Now we have:

```
In [13]: x = np.arange(10)

In [14]: nb_add(x, x)
Out[14]: array([  0.,   2.,   4.,   6.,   8.,  10.,  12.,  14.,  16.,  18.])

In [15]: nb_add.accumulate(x, 0)
Out[15]: array([  0.,   1.,   3.,   6.,  10.,  15.,  21.,  28.,  36.,  45.])
```

A.8 Advanced Array Input and Output

In Chapter 4, we became acquainted with `np.save` and `np.load` for storing arrays in binary format on disk. There are a number of additional options to consider for more sophisticated use. In particular, memory maps have the additional benefit of enabling you to do certain operations with datasets that do not fit into RAM.

Memory-Mapped Files

A *memory-mapped* file is a method for interacting with binary data on disk as though it is stored in an in-memory array. NumPy implements a `memmap` object that is ndarray-like, enabling small segments of a large file to be read and written without reading the whole array into memory. Additionally, a `memmap` has the same methods as an in-memory array and thus can be substituted into many algorithms where an ndarray would be expected.

To create a new memory map, use the function `np.memmap` and pass a file path, data type, shape, and file mode:

```
In [217]: mmap = np.memmap('mymmap', dtype='float64', mode='w+',
   .....:                  shape=(10000, 10000))

In [218]: mmap
Out[218]:
memmap([[0., 0., 0., ..., 0., 0., 0.],
        [0., 0., 0., ..., 0., 0., 0.],
        [0., 0., 0., ..., 0., 0., 0.],
        ...,
        [0., 0., 0., ..., 0., 0., 0.],
        [0., 0., 0., ..., 0., 0., 0.],
        [0., 0., 0., ..., 0., 0., 0.]])
```

Slicing a `memmap` returns views on the data on disk:

```
In [219]: section = mmap[:5]
```

If you assign data to these, it will be buffered in memory, which means that the changes will not be immediately reflected in the on-disk file if you were to read the file in a different application. Any modifications can be synchronized to disk by calling `flush`:

```
In [220]: section[:] = rng.standard_normal((5, 10000))
```

```
In [221]: mmap.flush()
```

```
In [222]: mmap
Out[222]:
memmap([[-0.9074, -1.0954,  0.0071, ...,  0.2753, -1.1641,  0.8521],
        [-0.0103, -0.0646, -1.0615, ..., -1.1003,  0.2505,  0.5832],
        [ 0.4583,  1.2992,  1.7137, ...,  0.8691, -0.7889, -0.2431],
        ...,
        [ 0.    ,  0.    ,  0.    , ...,  0.    ,  0.    ,  0.    ],
        [ 0.    ,  0.    ,  0.    , ...,  0.    ,  0.    ,  0.    ],
        [ 0.    ,  0.    ,  0.    , ...,  0.    ,  0.    ,  0.    ]])
```

```
In [223]: del mmap
```

Whenever a memory map falls out of scope and is garbage collected, any changes will be flushed to disk also. When *opening an existing memory map*, you still have to specify the data type and shape, as the file is only a block of binary data without any data type information, shape, or strides:

```
In [224]: mmap = np.memmap('mymmap', dtype='float64', shape=(10000, 10000))
```

```
In [225]: mmap
Out[225]:
memmap([[-0.9074, -1.0954,  0.0071, ...,  0.2753, -1.1641,  0.8521],
        [-0.0103, -0.0646, -1.0615, ..., -1.1003,  0.2505,  0.5832],
        [ 0.4583,  1.2992,  1.7137, ...,  0.8691, -0.7889, -0.2431],
        ...,
        [ 0.    ,  0.    ,  0.    , ...,  0.    ,  0.    ,  0.    ],
        [ 0.    ,  0.    ,  0.    , ...,  0.    ,  0.    ,  0.    ],
        [ 0.    ,  0.    ,  0.    , ...,  0.    ,  0.    ,  0.    ]])
```

Memory maps also work with structured or nested data types, as described in Section A.5, "Structured and Record Arrays," on page 493.

If you ran this example on your computer, you may want to delete the large file that we created above:

```
In [226]: %xdel mmap
```

```
In [227]: !rm mymmap
```

HDF5 and Other Array Storage Options

PyTables and h5py are two Python projects providing NumPy-friendly interfaces for storing array data in the efficient and compressible HDF5 format (HDF stands for *hierarchical data format*). You can safely store hundreds of gigabytes or even terabytes of data in HDF5 format. To learn more about using HDF5 with Python, I recommend reading the pandas online documentation (*http://pandas.pydata.org*).

A.9 Performance Tips

Adapting data processing code to use NumPy generally makes things much faster, as array operations typically replace otherwise comparatively extremely slow pure Python loops. Here are some tips to help get the best performance out of the library:

- Convert Python loops and conditional logic to array operations and Boolean array operations.
- Use broadcasting whenever possible.
- Use arrays views (slicing) to avoid copying data.
- Utilize ufuncs and ufunc methods.

If you can't get the performance you require after exhausting the capabilities provided by NumPy alone, consider writing code in C, FORTRAN, or Cython. I use Cython (*http://cython.org*) frequently in my own work as a way to get C-like performance, often with much less development time.

The Importance of Contiguous Memory

While the full extent of this topic is a bit outside the scope of this book, in some applications the memory layout of an array can significantly affect the speed of computations. This is based partly on performance differences having to do with the cache hierarchy of the CPU; operations accessing contiguous blocks of memory (e.g., summing the rows of a C order array) will generally be the fastest because the memory subsystem will buffer the appropriate blocks of memory into the low latency L1 or L2 CPU caches. Also, certain code paths inside NumPy's C codebase have been optimized for the contiguous case in which generic strided memory access can be avoided.

To say that an array's memory layout is *contiguous* means that the elements are stored in memory in the order that they appear in the array with respect to FORTRAN (column major) or C (row major) ordering. By default, NumPy arrays are created as C contiguous or just simply contiguous. A column major array, such as the transpose of a C-contiguous array, is thus said to be FORTRAN contiguous. These properties can be explicitly checked via the `flags` attribute on the ndarray:

```
In [228]: arr_c = np.ones((100, 10000), order='C')

In [229]: arr_f = np.ones((100, 10000), order='F')

In [230]: arr_c.flags
```

```
Out[230]:
  C_CONTIGUOUS : True
  F_CONTIGUOUS : False
  OWNDATA : True
  WRITEABLE : True
  ALIGNED : True
  WRITEBACKIFCOPY : False
  UPDATEIFCOPY : False

In [231]: arr_f.flags
Out[231]:
  C_CONTIGUOUS : False
  F_CONTIGUOUS : True
  OWNDATA : True
  WRITEABLE : True
  ALIGNED : True
  WRITEBACKIFCOPY : False
  UPDATEIFCOPY : False

In [232]: arr_f.flags.f_contiguous
Out[232]: True
```

In this example, summing the rows of these arrays should, in theory, be faster for arr_c than arr_f since the rows are contiguous in memory. Here, I check using %timeit in IPython (these results may differ on your machine):

```
In [233]: %timeit arr_c.sum(1)
444 us +- 60.5 us per loop (mean +- std. dev. of 7 runs, 1000 loops each)

In [234]: %timeit arr_f.sum(1)
581 us +- 8.16 us per loop (mean +- std. dev. of 7 runs, 1000 loops each)
```

When you're looking to squeeze more performance out of NumPy, this is often a place to invest some effort. If you have an array that does not have the desired memory order, you can use copy and pass either 'C' or 'F':

```
In [235]: arr_f.copy('C').flags
Out[235]:
  C_CONTIGUOUS : True
  F_CONTIGUOUS : False
  OWNDATA : True
  WRITEABLE : True
  ALIGNED : True
  WRITEBACKIFCOPY : False
  UPDATEIFCOPY : False
```

When constructing a view on an array, keep in mind that the result is not guaranteed to be contiguous:

```
In [236]: arr_c[:50].flags.contiguous
Out[236]: True

In [237]: arr_c[:, :50].flags
Out[237]:
  C_CONTIGUOUS : False
  F_CONTIGUOUS : False
  OWNDATA : False
  WRITEABLE : True
  ALIGNED : True
  WRITEBACKIFCOPY : False
  UPDATEIFCOPY : False
```

More on the IPython System

In Chapter 2 we looked at the basics of using the IPython shell and Jupyter notebook. In this appendix, we explore some deeper functionality in the IPython system that can either be used from the console or within Jupyter.

B.1 Terminal Keyboard Shortcuts

IPython has many keyboard shortcuts for navigating the prompt (which will be familiar to users of the Emacs text editor or the Unix bash shell) and interacting with the shell's command history. Table B-1 summarizes some of the most commonly used shortcuts. See Figure B-1 for an illustration of a few of these, such as cursor movement.

Table B-1. Standard IPython keyboard shortcuts

Keyboard shortcut	Description
Ctrl-P or up-arrow	Search backward in command history for commands starting with currently entered text
Ctrl-N or down-arrow	Search forward in command history for commands starting with currently entered text
Ctrl-R	Readline-style reverse history search (partial matching)
Ctrl-Shift-V	Paste text from clipboard
Ctrl-C	Interrupt currently executing code
Ctrl-A	Move cursor to beginning of line
Ctrl-E	Move cursor to end of line
Ctrl-K	Delete text from cursor until end of line
Ctrl-U	Discard all text on current line
Ctrl-F	Move cursor forward one character
Ctrl-B	Move cursor back one character
Ctrl-L	Clear screen

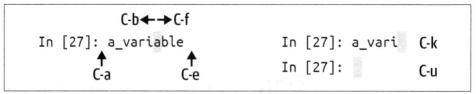

Figure B-1. Illustration of some keyboard shortcuts in the IPython shell

Note that Jupyter notebooks have a largely separate set of keyboard shortcuts for navigation and editing. Since these shortcuts have evolved more rapidly than the ones in IPython, I encourage you to explore the integrated help system in the Jupyter notebook menus.

B.2 About Magic Commands

Special commands in IPython (which are not built into Python itself) are known as *magic* commands. These are designed to facilitate common tasks and enable you to easily control the behavior of the IPython system. A magic command is any command prefixed by the percent symbol %. For example, you can check the execution time of any Python statement, such as a matrix multiplication, using the %timeit magic function:

```
In [20]: a = np.random.standard_normal((100, 100))

In [20]: %timeit np.dot(a, a)
92.5 µs ± 3.43 µs per loop (mean ± std. dev. of 7 runs, 10000 loops each)
```

Magic commands can be viewed as command-line programs to be run within the IPython system. Many of them have additional "command-line" options, which can all be viewed (as you might expect) using ?:

```
In [21]: %debug?
Docstring:
::

%debug [--breakpoint FILE:LINE] [statement [statement ...]]

Activate the interactive debugger.

This magic command support two ways of activating debugger.
One is to activate debugger before executing code.  This way, you
can set a break point, to step through the code from the point.
You can use this mode by giving statements to execute and optionally
a breakpoint.

The other one is to activate debugger in post-mortem mode.  You can
activate this mode simply running %debug without any argument.
If an exception has just occurred, this lets you inspect its stack
frames interactively.  Note that this will always work only on the last
```

```
traceback that occurred, so you must call this quickly after an
exception that you wish to inspect has fired, because if another one
occurs, it clobbers the previous one.

If you want IPython to automatically do this on every exception, see
the %pdb magic for more details.

.. versionchanged:: 7.3
When running code, user variables are no longer expanded,
the magic line is always left unmodified.

positional arguments:
statement            Code to run in debugger. You can omit this in cell
magic mode.

optional arguments:
--breakpoint <FILE:LINE>, -b <FILE:LINE>
Set break point at LINE in FILE.
```

Magic functions can be used by default without the percent sign, as long as no variable is defined with the same name as the magic function in question. This feature is called *automagic* and can be enabled or disabled with %automagic.

Some magic functions behave like Python functions, and their output can be assigned to a variable:

```
In [22]: %pwd
Out[22]: '/home/wesm/code/pydata-book'

In [23]: foo = %pwd

In [24]: foo
Out[24]: '/home/wesm/code/pydata-book'
```

Since IPython's documentation is accessible from within the system, I encourage you to explore all of the special commands available by using %quickref or %magic. This information is shown in a console pager, so you will need to press q to exit from the pager. Table B-2 highlights some of the most critical commands for being productive in interactive computing and Python development in IPython.

Table B-2. Some frequently used IPython magic commands

Command	Description
%quickref	Display the IPython Quick Reference Card
%magic	Display detailed documentation for all of the available magic commands
%debug	Enter the interactive debugger at the bottom of the last exception traceback
%hist	Print command input (and optionally output) history
%pdb	Automatically enter debugger after any exception
%paste	Execute preformatted Python code from clipboard

Command	Description
%cpaste	Open a special prompt for manually pasting Python code to be executed
%reset	Delete all variables/names defined in an interactive namespace
%page *OBJECT*	Pretty-print the object and display it through a pager
%run *script.py*	Run a Python script inside IPython
%prun *statement*	Execute *statement* with cProfile and report the profiler output
%time *statement*	Report the execution time of a single statement
%timeit *statement*	Run a statement multiple times to compute an ensemble average execution time; useful for timing code with very short execution time
%who, %who_ls, %whos	Display variables defined in interactive namespace, with varying levels of information/verbosity
%xdel *variable*	Delete a variable and attempt to clear any references to the object in the IPython internals

The %run Command

You can run any file as a Python program inside the environment of your IPython session using the %run command. Suppose you had the following simple script stored in *script.py*:

```python
def f(x, y, z):
    return (x + y) / z

a = 5
b = 6
c = 7.5

result = f(a, b, c)
```

You can execute this by passing the filename to %run:

```
In [14]: %run script.py
```

The script is run in an *empty namespace* (with no imports or other variables defined), so that the behavior should be identical to running the program on the command line using python script.py. All of the variables (imports, functions, and globals) defined in the file (up until an exception, if any, is raised) will then be accessible in the IPython shell:

```
In [15]: c
Out [15]: 7.5

In [16]: result
Out[16]: 1.4666666666666666
```

If a Python script expects command-line arguments (to be found in sys.argv), these can be passed after the file path as though run on the command line.

If you want to give a script access to variables already defined in the interactive IPython namespace, use `%run -i` instead of plain `%run`.

In the Jupyter notebook, you can also use the related `%load` magic function, which imports a script into a code cell:

```
In [16]: %load script.py

    def f(x, y, z):
        return (x + y) / z

    a = 5
    b = 6
    c = 7.5

    result = f(a, b, c)
```

Interrupting running code

Pressing Ctrl-C while any code is running, whether a script through `%run` or a long-running command, will raise a `KeyboardInterrupt`. This will cause nearly all Python programs to stop immediately except in certain unusual cases.

When a piece of Python code has called into some compiled extension modules, pressing Ctrl-C will not always cause the program execution to stop immediately. In such cases, you will have to either wait until control is returned to the Python interpreter, or in more dire circumstances, forcibly terminate the Python process in your operating system (such as using Task Manager on Windows or the `kill` command on Linux).

Executing Code from the Clipboard

If you are using the Jupyter notebook, you can copy and paste code into any code cell and execute it. It is also possible to run code from the clipboard in the IPython shell. Suppose you had the following code in some other application:

```
x = 5
y = 7
if x > 5:
    x += 1
    y = 8
```

The most foolproof methods are the `%paste` and `%cpaste` magic functions (note that these do not work in Jupyter since you can copy and paste into a Jupyter code cell).

`%paste` takes whatever text is in the clipboard and executes it as a single block in the shell:

```
In [17]: %paste
x = 5
y = 7
if x > 5:
    x += 1

    y = 8
## -- End pasted text --
```

`%cpaste` is similar, except that it gives you a special prompt for pasting code into:

```
In [18]: %cpaste
Pasting code; enter '--' alone on the line to stop or use Ctrl-D.
:x = 5
:y = 7
:if x > 5:
:    x += 1
:
:    y = 8
:--
```

With the `%cpaste` block, you have the freedom to paste as much code as you like before executing it. You might decide to use `%cpaste` to look at the pasted code before executing it. If you accidentally paste the wrong code, you can break out of the `%cpaste` prompt by pressing Ctrl-C.

B.3 Using the Command History

IPython maintains a small on-disk database containing the text of each command that you execute. This serves various purposes:

- Searching, completing, and executing previously executed commands with minimal typing
- Persisting the command history between sessions
- Logging the input/output history to a file

These features are more useful in the shell than in the notebook, since the notebook by design keeps a log of the input and output in each code cell.

Searching and Reusing the Command History

The IPython shell lets you search and execute previous code or other commands. This is useful, as you may often find yourself repeating the same commands, such as a `%run` command or some other code snippet. Suppose you had run:

```
In[7]: %run first/second/third/data_script.py
```

and then explored the results of the script (assuming it ran successfully), only to find that you made an incorrect calculation. After figuring out the problem and modifying *data_script.py*, you can start typing a few letters of the %run command and then press either the Ctrl-P key combination or the up arrow key. This will search the command history for the first prior command matching the letters you typed. Pressing either Ctrl-P or the up arrow key multiple times will continue to search through the history. If you pass over the command you wish to execute, fear not. You can move *forward* through the command history by pressing either Ctrl-N or the down arrow key. After doing this a few times, you may start pressing these keys without thinking!

Using Ctrl-R gives you the same partial incremental searching capability provided by the readline used in Unix-style shells, such as the bash shell. On Windows, readline functionality is emulated by IPython. To use this, press Ctrl-R and then type a few characters contained in the input line you want to search for:

```
In [1]: a_command = foo(x, y, z)

(reverse-i-search)`com': a_command = foo(x, y, z)
```

Pressing Ctrl-R will cycle through the history for each line, matching the characters you've typed.

Input and Output Variables

Forgetting to assign the result of a function call to a variable can be very annoying. An IPython session stores references to *both* the input commands and output Python objects in special variables. The previous two outputs are stored in the _ (one under-score) and __ (two underscores) variables, respectively:

```
In [18]: 'input1'
Out[18]: 'input1'

In [19]: 'input2'
Out[19]: 'input2'

In [20]: __
Out[20]: 'input1'

In [21]: 'input3'
Out[21]: 'input3'

In [22]: _
Out[22]: 'input3'
```

Input variables are stored in variables named _iX, where X is the input line number.

For each input variable there is a corresponding output variable _X. So after input line 27, say, there will be two new variables, _27 (for the output) and _i27 for the input:

```
In [26]: foo = 'bar'

In [27]: foo
Out[27]: 'bar'

In [28]: _i27
Out[28]: u'foo'

In [29]: _27
Out[29]: 'bar'
```

Since the input variables are strings, they can be executed again with the Python `eval` keyword:

```
In [30]: eval(_i27)
Out[30]: 'bar'
```

Here, `_i27` refers to the code input in `In [27]`.

Several magic functions allow you to work with the input and output history. `%hist` prints all or part of the input history, with or without line numbers. `%reset` clears the interactive namespace and optionally the input and output caches. The `%xdel` magic function removes all references to a *particular* object from the IPython machinery. See the documentation for these magics for more details.

 When working with very large datasets, keep in mind that IPython's input and output history may cause objects referenced there to not be garbage collected (freeing up the memory), even if you delete the variables from the interactive namespace using the `del` keyword. In such cases, careful usage of `%xdel` and `%reset` can help you avoid running into memory problems.

B.4 Interacting with the Operating System

Another feature of IPython is that it allows you to access the filesystem and operating system shell. This means, among other things, that you can perform most standard command-line actions as you would in the Windows or Unix (Linux, macOS) shell without having to exit IPython. This includes shell commands, changing directories, and storing the results of a command in a Python object (list or string). There are also command aliasing and directory bookmarking features.

See Table B-3 for a summary of magic functions and syntax for calling shell commands. I'll briefly visit these features in the next few sections.

Table B-3. IPython system-related commands

Command	Description
`!cmd`	Execute cmd in the system shell
`output = !cmd args`	Run cmd and store the stdout in output
`%alias alias_name cmd`	Define an alias for a system (shell) command
`%bookmark`	Utilize IPython's directory bookmarking system
`%cd directory`	Change system working directory to passed directory
`%pwd`	Return to the current system working directory
`%pushd directory`	Place current directory on stack and change to target directory
`%popd`	Change to directory popped off the top of the stack
`%dirs`	Return a list containing the current directory stack
`%dhist`	Print the history of visited directories
`%env`	Return the system environment variables as a dictionary
`%matplotlib`	Configure matplotlib integration options

Shell Commands and Aliases

Starting a line in IPython with an exclamation point !, or bang, tells IPython to execute everything after the bang in the system shell. This means that you can delete files (using rm or del, depending on your OS), change directories, or execute any other process.

You can store the console output of a shell command in a variable by assigning the expression escaped with ! to a variable. For example, on my Linux-based machine connected to the internet via Ethernet, I can get my IP address as a Python variable:

```
In [1]: ip_info = !ifconfig wlan0 | grep "inet "

In [2]: ip_info[0].strip()
Out[2]: 'inet addr:10.0.0.11  Bcast:10.0.0.255  Mask:255.255.255.0'
```

The returned Python object `ip_info` is actually a custom list type containing various versions of the console output.

IPython can also substitute in Python values defined in the current environment when using !. To do this, preface the variable name with the dollar sign $:

```
In [3]: foo = 'test*'

In [4]: !ls $foo
test4.py  test.py  test.xml
```

The `%alias` magic function can define custom shortcuts for shell commands. As an example:

```
In [1]: %alias ll ls -l
```

```
In [2]: ll /usr
total 332
drwxr-xr-x   2 root root  69632 2012-01-29 20:36 bin/
drwxr-xr-x   2 root root   4096 2010-08-23 12:05 games/
drwxr-xr-x 123 root root  20480 2011-12-26 18:08 include/
drwxr-xr-x 265 root root 126976 2012-01-29 20:36 lib/
drwxr-xr-x  44 root root  69632 2011-12-26 18:08 lib32/
lrwxrwxrwx   1 root root      3 2010-08-23 16:02 lib64 -> lib/
drwxr-xr-x  15 root root   4096 2011-10-13 19:03 local/
drwxr-xr-x   2 root root  12288 2012-01-12 09:32 sbin/
drwxr-xr-x 387 root root  12288 2011-11-04 22:53 share/
drwxrwsr-x  24 root src    4096 2011-07-17 18:38 src/
```

You can execute multiple commands just as on the command line by separating them with semicolons:

```
In [558]: %alias test_alias (cd examples; ls; cd ..)
```

```
In [559]: test_alias
macrodata.csv  spx.csv  tips.csv
```

You'll notice that IPython "forgets" any aliases you define interactively as soon as the session is closed. To create permanent aliases, you will need to use the configuration system.

Directory Bookmark System

IPython has a directory bookmarking system to enable you to save aliases for common directories so that you can jump around easily. For example, suppose you wanted to create a bookmark that points to the supplementary materials for this book:

```
In [6]: %bookmark py4da /home/wesm/code/pydata-book
```

Once you've done this, when you use the %cd magic, you can use any bookmarks you've defined:

```
In [7]: cd py4da
(bookmark:py4da) -> /home/wesm/code/pydata-book
/home/wesm/code/pydata-book
```

If a bookmark name conflicts with a directory name in your current working directory, you can use the -b flag to override and use the bookmark location. Using the -l option with %bookmark lists all of your bookmarks:

```
In [8]: %bookmark -l
Current bookmarks:
py4da -> /home/wesm/code/pydata-book-source
```

Bookmarks, unlike aliases, are automatically persisted between IPython sessions.

B.5 Software Development Tools

In addition to being a comfortable environment for interactive computing and data exploration, IPython can also be a useful companion for general Python software development. In data analysis applications, it's important first to have *correct* code. Fortunately, IPython has closely integrated and enhanced the built-in Python pdb debugger. Secondly, you want your code to be *fast*. For this, IPython has convenient integrated code timing and profiling tools. I will give an overview of these tools in detail here.

Interactive Debugger

IPython's debugger enhances pdb with tab completion, syntax highlighting, and context for each line in exception tracebacks. One of the best times to debug code is right after an error has occurred. The %debug command, when entered immediately after an exception, invokes the "postmortem" debugger and drops you into the stack frame where the exception was raised:

```
In [2]: run examples/ipython_bug.py
---------------------------------------------------------------
AssertionError                        Traceback (most recent call last)
/home/wesm/code/pydata-book/examples/ipython_bug.py in <module>()
     13     throws_an_exception()
     14
---> 15 calling_things()

/home/wesm/code/pydata-book/examples/ipython_bug.py in calling_things()
     11 def calling_things():
     12     works_fine()
---> 13     throws_an_exception()
     14
     15 calling_things()

/home/wesm/code/pydata-book/examples/ipython_bug.py in throws_an_exception()
      7     a = 5
      8     b = 6
----> 9     assert(a + b == 10)
     10
     11 def calling_things():

AssertionError:

In [3]: %debug
> /home/wesm/code/pydata-book/examples/ipython_bug.py(9)throws_an_exception()
      8     b = 6
----> 9     assert(a + b == 10)
     10

ipdb>
```

Once inside the debugger, you can execute arbitrary Python code and explore all of the objects and data (which have been "kept alive" by the interpreter) inside each stack frame. By default you start in the lowest level, where the error occurred. By typing **u** (up) and **d** (down), you can switch between the levels of the stack trace:

```
ipdb> u
> /home/wesm/code/pydata-book/examples/ipython_bug.py(13)calling_things()
     12         works_fine()
---> 13         throws_an_exception()
     14
```

Executing the %pdb command makes IPython automatically invoke the debugger after any exception, a mode that many users will find useful.

It's also helpful to use the debugger when developing code, especially when you need to set a breakpoint or step through the execution of a function or script to examine its behavior at each step. There are several ways to accomplish this. The first is by using %run with the -d flag, which invokes the debugger before executing any code in the passed script. You must immediately type **s** (step) to enter the script:

```
In [5]: run -d examples/ipython_bug.py
Breakpoint 1 at /home/wesm/code/pydata-book/examples/ipython_bug.py:1
NOTE: Enter 'c' at the ipdb>  prompt to start your script.
> <string>(1)<module>()

ipdb> s
--Call--
> /home/wesm/code/pydata-book/examples/ipython_bug.py(1)<module>()
1---> 1 def works_fine():
     2         a = 5
     3         b = 6
```

After this point, it's up to you how you want to work your way through the file. For example, in the preceding exception, we could set a breakpoint right before calling the works_fine function, and run the script until we reach the breakpoint by typing **c** (continue):

```
ipdb> b 12
ipdb> c
> /home/wesm/code/pydata-book/examples/ipython_bug.py(12)calling_things()
     11 def calling_things():
2--> 12         works_fine()
     13         throws_an_exception()
```

At this point, you can step into works_fine() or execute works_fine() by typing **n** (next) to advance to the next line:

```
ipdb> n
> /home/wesm/code/pydata-book/examples/ipython_bug.py(13)calling_things()
2    12         works_fine()
```

```
---> 13     throws_an_exception()
     14
```

Then, we could step into `throws_an_exception` and advance to the line where the error occurs and look at the variables in the scope. Note that debugger commands take precedence over variable names; in such cases, preface the variables with ! to examine their contents:

```
ipdb> s
--Call--
> /home/wesm/code/pydata-book/examples/ipython_bug.py(6)throws_an_exception()
      5
----> 6 def throws_an_exception():
      7     a = 5

ipdb> n
> /home/wesm/code/pydata-book/examples/ipython_bug.py(7)throws_an_exception()
      6 def throws_an_exception():
----> 7     a = 5
      8     b = 6

ipdb> n
> /home/wesm/code/pydata-book/examples/ipython_bug.py(8)throws_an_exception()
      7     a = 5
----> 8     b = 6
      9     assert(a + b == 10)

ipdb> n
> /home/wesm/code/pydata-book/examples/ipython_bug.py(9)throws_an_exception()
      8     b = 6
----> 9     assert(a + b == 10)
     10

ipdb> !a
5
ipdb> !b
6
```

In my experience, developing proficiency with the interactive debugger takes time and practice. See Table B-4 for a full catalog of the debugger commands. If you are accustomed to using an IDE, you might find the terminal-driven debugger to be a bit unforgiving at first, but that will improve in time. Some of the Python IDEs have excellent GUI debuggers, so most users can find something that works for them.

Table B-4. Python debugger commands

Command	Action
h(elp)	Display command list
help *command*	Show documentation for *command*
c(ontinue)	Resume program execution

Command	Action
q(uit)	Exit debugger without executing any more code
b(reak) *number*	Set breakpoint at *number* in current file
b *path/to/file.py:number*	Set breakpoint at line *number* in specified file
s(tep)	Step *into* function call
n(ext)	Execute current line and advance to next line at current level
u(p)/d(own)	Move up/down in function call stack
a(rgs)	Show arguments for current function
debug *statement*	Invoke statement *statement* in new (recursive) debugger
l(ist) *statement*	Show current position and context at current level of stack
w(here)	Print full stack trace with context at current position

Other ways to use the debugger

There are a couple of other useful ways to invoke the debugger. The first is by using a special set_trace function (named after pdb.set_trace), which is basically a "poor man's breakpoint." Here are two small recipes you might want to put somewhere for your general use (potentially adding them to your IPython profile, as I do):

```
from IPython.core.debugger import Pdb

def set_trace():
    Pdb(.set_trace(sys._getframe().f_back)

def debug(f, *args, **kwargs):
    pdb = Pdb()
    return pdb.runcall(f, *args, **kwargs)
```

The first function, set_trace, provides a convenient way to put a breakpoint somewhere in your code. You can use a set_trace in any part of your code that you want to temporarily stop to examine it more closely (e.g., right before an exception occurs):

```
In [7]: run examples/ipython_bug.py
> /home/wesm/code/pydata-book/examples/ipython_bug.py(16)calling_things()
     15        set_trace()
---> 16        throws_an_exception()
     17
```

Typing **c** (continue) will cause the code to resume normally with no harm done.

The debug function we just looked at enables you to invoke the interactive debugger easily on an arbitrary function call. Suppose we had written a function like the following, and we wished to step through its logic:

```
def f(x, y, z=1):
    tmp = x + y
    return tmp / z
```

Ordinarily using f would look like f(1, 2, z=3). To instead step into f, pass f as the first argument to debug, followed by the positional and keyword arguments to be passed to f:

```
In [6]: debug(f, 1, 2, z=3)
> <ipython-input>(2)f()
      1 def f(x, y, z):
----> 2     tmp = x + y
      3     return tmp / z

ipdb>
```

These two recipes have saved me a lot of time over the years.

Lastly, the debugger can be used in conjunction with %run. By running a script with %run -d, you will be dropped directly into the debugger, ready to set any breakpoints and start the script:

```
In [1]: %run -d examples/ipython_bug.py
Breakpoint 1 at /home/wesm/code/pydata-book/examples/ipython_bug.py:1
NOTE: Enter 'c' at the ipdb>  prompt to start your script.
> <string>(1)<module>()

ipdb>
```

Adding -b with a line number starts the debugger with a breakpoint set already:

```
In [2]: %run -d -b2 examples/ipython_bug.py
Breakpoint 1 at /home/wesm/code/pydata-book/examples/ipython_bug.py:2
NOTE: Enter 'c' at the ipdb>  prompt to start your script.
> <string>(1)<module>()

ipdb> c
> /home/wesm/code/pydata-book/examples/ipython_bug.py(2)works_fine()
      1 def works_fine():
1---> 2     a = 5
      3     b = 6

ipdb>
```

Timing Code: %time and %timeit

For larger-scale or longer-running data analysis applications, you may wish to measure the execution time of various components or of individual statements or function calls. You may want a report of which functions are taking up the most time in a complex process. Fortunately, IPython enables you to get this information conveniently while you are developing and testing your code.

Timing code by hand using the built-in time module and its functions, time.clock and time.time, is often tedious and repetitive, as you must write the same uninteresting boilerplate code:

```
import time
start = time.time()
for i in range(iterations):
    # some code to run here
elapsed_per = (time.time() - start) / iterations
```

Since this is such a common operation, IPython has two magic functions, %time and %timeit, to automate this process for you.

%time runs a statement once, reporting the total execution time. Suppose we had a large list of strings, and we wanted to compare different methods of selecting all strings starting with a particular prefix. Here is a list of 600,000 strings and two identical methods of selecting only the ones that start with 'foo':

```
# a very large list of strings
In [11]: strings = ['foo', 'foobar', 'baz', 'qux',
   ....:            'python', 'Guido Van Rossum'] * 100000

In [12]: method1 = [x for x in strings if x.startswith('foo')]

In [13]: method2 = [x for x in strings if x[:3] == 'foo']
```

It looks like they should be about the same performance-wise, right? We can check for sure using %time:

```
In [14]: %time method1 = [x for x in strings if x.startswith('foo')]
CPU times: user 52.5 ms, sys: 0 ns, total: 52.5 ms
Wall time: 52.1 ms

In [15]: %time method2 = [x for x in strings if x[:3] == 'foo']
CPU times: user 65.3 ms, sys: 0 ns, total: 65.3 ms
Wall time: 64.8 ms
```

The Wall time (short for "wall-clock time") is the main number of interest. From these timings, we can infer that there is some performance difference, but it's not a very precise measurement. If you try %time-ing those statements multiple times yourself, you'll find that the results are somewhat variable. To get a more precise measurement, use the %timeit magic function. Given an arbitrary statement, it has a heuristic to run a statement multiple times to produce a more accurate average runtime (these results may be different on your system):

```
In [563]: %timeit [x for x in strings if x.startswith('foo')]
10 loops, best of 3: 159 ms per loop

In [564]: %timeit [x for x in strings if x[:3] == 'foo']
10 loops, best of 3: 59.3 ms per loop
```

This seemingly innocuous example illustrates that it is worth understanding the performance characteristics of the Python standard library, NumPy, pandas, and other libraries used in this book. In larger-scale data analysis applications, those milliseconds will start to add up!

%timeit is especially useful for analyzing statements and functions with very short execution times, even at the level of microseconds (millionths of a second) or nanoseconds (billionths of a second). These may seem like insignificant amounts of time, but of course a 20-microsecond function invoked 1 million times takes 15 seconds longer than a 5-microsecond function. In the preceding example, we could very directly compare the two string operations to understand their performance characteristics:

```
In [565]: x = 'foobar'

In [566]: y = 'foo'

In [567]: %timeit x.startswith(y)
1000000 loops, best of 3: 267 ns per loop

In [568]: %timeit x[:3] == y
10000000 loops, best of 3: 147 ns per loop
```

Basic Profiling: %prun and %run -p

Profiling code is closely related to timing code, except it is concerned with determining *where* time is spent. The main Python profiling tool is the cProfile module, which is not specific to IPython at all. cProfile executes a program or any arbitrary block of code while keeping track of how much time is spent in each function.

A common way to use cProfile is on the command line, running an entire program and outputting the aggregated time per function. Suppose we had a script that does some linear algebra in a loop (computing the maximum absolute eigenvalues of a series of 100×100 matrices):

```
import numpy as np
from numpy.linalg import eigvals

def run_experiment(niter=100):
    K = 100
    results = []
    for _ in range(niter):
        mat = np.random.standard_normal((K, K))
        max_eigenvalue = np.abs(eigvals(mat)).max()
        results.append(max_eigenvalue)
    return results
some_results = run_experiment()
print('Largest one we saw: {0}'.format(np.max(some_results)))
```

You can run this script through cProfile using the following in the command line:

```
python -m cProfile cprof_example.py
```

If you try that, you'll find that the output is sorted by function name. This makes it a bit hard to get an idea of where the most time is spent, so it's useful to specify a *sort order* using the -s flag:

```
$ python -m cProfile -s cumulative cprof_example.py
Largest one we saw: 11.923204422
    15116 function calls (14927 primitive calls) in 0.720 seconds

Ordered by: cumulative time

ncalls  tottime  percall  cumtime  percall filename:lineno(function)
     1    0.001    0.001   0.721    0.721 cprof_example.py:1(<module>)
   100    0.003    0.000   0.586    0.006 linalg.py:702(eigvals)
   200    0.572    0.003   0.572    0.003 {numpy.linalg.lapack_lite.dgeev}
     1    0.002    0.002   0.075    0.075 __init__.py:106(<module>)
   100    0.059    0.001   0.059    0.001 {method 'randn')
     1    0.000    0.000   0.044    0.044 add_newdocs.py:9(<module>)
     2    0.001    0.001   0.037    0.019 __init__.py:1(<module>)
     2    0.003    0.002   0.030    0.015 __init__.py:2(<module>)
     1    0.000    0.000   0.030    0.030 type_check.py:3(<module>)
     1    0.001    0.001   0.021    0.021 __init__.py:15(<module>)
     1    0.013    0.013   0.013    0.013 numeric.py:1(<module>)
     1    0.000    0.000   0.009    0.009 __init__.py:6(<module>)
     1    0.001    0.001   0.008    0.008 __init__.py:45(<module>)
   262    0.005    0.000   0.007    0.000 function_base.py:3178(add_newdoc)
   100    0.003    0.000   0.005    0.000 linalg.py:162(_assertFinite)
   ...
```

Only the first 15 rows of the output are shown. It's easiest to read by scanning down the cumtime column to see how much total time was spent *inside* each function. Note that if a function calls some other function, *the clock does not stop running*. cProfile records the start and end time of each function call and uses that to produce the timing.

In addition to the command-line usage, cProfile can also be used programmatically to profile arbitrary blocks of code without having to run a new process. IPython has a convenient interface to this capability using the %prun command and the -p option to %run. %prun takes the same "command-line options" as cProfile but will profile an arbitrary Python statement instead of a whole *.py* file:

```
In [4]: %prun -l 7 -s cumulative run_experiment()
        4203 function calls in 0.643 seconds

Ordered by: cumulative time
List reduced from 32 to 7 due to restriction <7>

ncalls  tottime  percall  cumtime  percall filename:lineno(function)
     1    0.000    0.000   0.643    0.643 <string>:1(<module>)
     1    0.001    0.001   0.643    0.643 cprof_example.py:4(run_experiment)
   100    0.003    0.000   0.583    0.006 linalg.py:702(eigvals)
   200    0.569    0.003   0.569    0.003 {numpy.linalg.lapack_lite.dgeev}
```

```
  100    0.058    0.001    0.058    0.001 {method 'randn'}
  100    0.003    0.000    0.005    0.000 linalg.py:162(_assertFinite)
  200    0.002    0.000    0.002    0.000 {method 'all' of 'numpy.ndarray'}
```

Similarly, calling %run -p -s cumulative cprof_example.py has the same effect as the command-line approach, except you never have to leave IPython.

In the Jupyter notebook, you can use the %%prun magic (two % signs) to profile an entire code block. This pops up a separate window with the profile output. This can be useful in getting possibly quick answers to questions like, "Why did that code block take so long to run?"

There are other tools available that help make profiles easier to understand when you are using IPython or Jupyter. One of these is SnakeViz (*https://github.com/jiffy club/snakeviz/*), which produces an interactive visualization of the profile results using D3.js.

Profiling a Function Line by Line

In some cases, the information you obtain from %prun (or another cProfile-based profile method) may not tell the whole story about a function's execution time, or it may be so complex that the results, aggregated by function name, are hard to interpret. For this case, there is a small library called line_profiler (obtainable via PyPI or one of the package management tools). It contains an IPython extension enabling a new magic function %lprun that computes a line-by-line-profiling of one or more functions. You can enable this extension by modifying your IPython configuration (see the IPython documentation or the section on configuration later in this appendix) to include the following line:

```
# A list of dotted module names of IPython extensions to load.
c.InteractiveShellApp.extensions = ['line_profiler']
```

You can also run the command:

```
%load_ext line_profiler
```

line_profiler can be used programmatically (see the full documentation), but it is perhaps most powerful when used interactively in IPython. Suppose you had a module prof_mod with the following code doing some NumPy array operations (if you want to reproduce this example, put this code into a new file *prof_mod.py*):

```
from numpy.random import randn

def add_and_sum(x, y):
    added = x + y
    summed = added.sum(axis=1)
    return summed

def call_function():
```

```
    x = randn(1000, 1000)
    y = randn(1000, 1000)
    return add_and_sum(x, y)
```

If we wanted to understand the performance of the add_and_sum function, %prun gives us the following:

```
In [569]: %run prof_mod

In [570]: x = randn(3000, 3000)

In [571]: y = randn(3000, 3000)

In [572]: %prun add_and_sum(x, y)
        4 function calls in 0.049 seconds
   Ordered by: internal time
   ncalls  tottime  percall  cumtime  percall filename:lineno(function)
        1    0.036    0.036    0.046    0.046 prof_mod.py:3(add_and_sum)
        1    0.009    0.009    0.009    0.009 {method 'sum' of 'numpy.ndarray'}
        1    0.003    0.003    0.049    0.049 <string>:1(<module>)
```

This is not especially enlightening. With the line_profiler IPython extension activated, a new command %lprun is available. The only difference in usage is that we must instruct %lprun which function or functions we wish to profile. The general syntax is:

```
%lprun -f func1 -f func2 statement_to_profile
```

In this case, we want to profile add_and_sum, so we run:

```
In [573]: %lprun -f add_and_sum add_and_sum(x, y)
Timer unit: 1e-06 s
File: prof_mod.py
Function: add_and_sum at line 3
Total time: 0.045936 s
Line #      Hits         Time  Per Hit   % Time  Line Contents
==============================================================
     3                                           def add_and_sum(x, y):
     4         1        36510  36510.0     79.5      added = x + y
     5         1         9425   9425.0     20.5      summed = added.sum(axis=1)
     6         1            1      1.0      0.0      return summed
```

This can be much easier to interpret. In this case, we profiled the same function we used in the statement. Looking at the preceding module code, we could call call_function and profile that as well as add_and_sum, thus getting a full picture of the performance of the code:

```
In [574]: %lprun -f add_and_sum -f call_function call_function()
Timer unit: 1e-06 s
File: prof_mod.py
Function: add_and_sum at line 3
Total time: 0.005526 s
Line #      Hits         Time  Per Hit   % Time  Line Contents
```

```
================================================================
   3                                           def add_and_sum(x, y):
   4         1       4375    4375.0     79.2        added = x + y
   5         1       1149    1149.0     20.8        summed = added.sum(axis=1)
   6         1          2       2.0      0.0        return summed
File: prof_mod.py
Function: call_function at line 8
Total time: 0.121016 s
Line #      Hits        Time  Per Hit   % Time  Line Contents
================================================================
   8                                           def call_function():
   9         1      57169   57169.0     47.2        x = randn(1000, 1000)
  10         1      58304   58304.0     48.2        y = randn(1000, 1000)
  11         1       5543    5543.0      4.6        return add_and_sum(x, y)
```

As a general rule of thumb, I tend to prefer %prun (cProfile) for "macro" profiling, and %lprun (line_profiler) for "micro" profiling. It's worthwhile to have a good understanding of both tools.

 The reason that you must explicitly specify the names of the functions you want to profile with %lprun is that the overhead of "tracing" the execution time of each line is substantial. Tracing functions that are not of interest has the potential to significantly alter the profile results.

B.6 Tips for Productive Code Development Using IPython

Writing code in a way that makes it convenient to develop, debug, and ultimately *use* interactively may be a paradigm shift for many users. There are procedural details like code reloading that may require some adjustment, as well as coding style concerns.

Therefore, implementing most of the strategies described in this section is more of an art than a science and will require some experimentation on your part to determine a way to write your Python code that is effective for you. Ultimately you want to structure your code in a way that makes it convenient to use iteratively and be able to explore the results of running a program or function as effortlessly as possible. I have found software designed with IPython in mind to be easier to work with than code intended only to be run as as standalone command-line application. This becomes especially important when something goes wrong and you have to diagnose an error in code that you or someone else might have written months or years beforehand.

Reloading Module Dependencies

In Python, when you type import some_lib, the code in some_lib is executed, and all the variables, functions, and imports defined within are stored in the newly created `some_lib` module namespace. The next time you use `import some_lib`, you will get a reference to the existing module namespace. The potential difficulty in interactive IPython code development comes when you, say, `%run` a script that depends on some other module where you may have made changes. Suppose I had the following code in *test_script.py*:

```
import some_lib

x = 5
y = [1, 2, 3, 4]
result = some_lib.get_answer(x, y)
```

If you were to execute `%run test_script.py` then modify *some_lib.py*, the next time you execute `%run test_script.py` you will still get the *old version* of *some_lib.py* because of Python's "load-once" module system. This behavior differs from some other data analysis environments, like MATLAB, which automatically propagate code changes.[1] To cope with this, you have a couple of options. The first way is to use the `reload` function in the `importlib` module in the standard library:

```
import some_lib
import importlib

importlib.reload(some_lib)
```

This attempts to give you a fresh copy of *some_lib.py* every time you run *test_script.py* (but there are some scenarios where it will not). Obviously, if the dependencies go deeper, it might be a bit tricky to be inserting usages of `reload` all over the place. For this problem, IPython has a special `dreload` function (*not* a magic function) for "deep" (recursive) reloading of modules. If I were to run *some_lib.py* then use `dreload(some_lib)`, it will attempt to reload `some_lib` as well as all of its dependencies. This will not work in all cases, unfortunately, but when it does, it beats having to restart IPython.

Code Design Tips

There's no simple recipe for this, but here are some high-level principles I have found effective in my own work.

Keep relevant objects and data alive

It's not unusual to see a program written for the command line with a structure somewhat like the following:

---

1 Since a module or package may be imported in many different places in a particular program, Python caches a module's code the first time it is imported rather than executing the code in the module every time. Otherwise, modularity and good code organization could potentially cause inefficiency in an application.

```
from my_functions import g

def f(x, y):
    return g(x + y)

def main():
    x = 6
    y = 7.5
    result = x + y

if __name__ == '__main__':
    main()
```

Do you see what might go wrong if we were to run this program in IPython? After it's done, none of the results or objects defined in the main function will be accessible in the IPython shell. A better way is to have whatever code is in main execute directly in the module's global namespace (or in the if __name__ == '__main__': block, if you want the module to also be importable). That way, when you %run the code, you'll be able to look at all of the variables defined in main. This is equivalent to defining top-level variables in cells in the Jupyter notebook.

Flat is better than nested

Deeply nested code makes me think about the many layers of an onion. When testing or debugging a function, how many layers of the onion must you peel back in order to reach the code of interest? The idea that "flat is better than nested" is a part of the Zen of Python, and it applies generally to developing code for interactive use as well. Making functions and classes as decoupled and modular as possible makes them easier to test (if you are writing unit tests), debug, and use interactively.

Overcome a fear of longer files

If you come from a Java (or another such language) background, you may have been told to keep files short. In many languages, this is sound advice; long length is usually a bad "code smell," indicating refactoring or reorganization may be necessary. However, while developing code using IPython, working with 10 small but interconnected files (under, say, 100 lines each) is likely to cause you more headaches in general than 2 or 3 longer files. Fewer files means fewer modules to reload and less jumping between files while editing, too. I have found maintaining larger modules, each with high *internal* cohesion (the code all relates to solving the same kinds of problems), to be much more useful and Pythonic. After iterating toward a solution, of course it sometimes will make sense to refactor larger files into smaller ones.

Obviously, I don't support taking this argument to the extreme, which would to be to put all of your code in a single monstrous file. Finding a sensible and intuitive module and package structure for a large codebase often takes a bit of work, but it is especially important to get right in teams. Each module should be internally cohesive, and it should be as obvious as possible where to find functions and classes responsible for each area of functionality.

B.7 Advanced IPython Features

Making full use of the IPython system may lead you to write your code in a slightly different way, or to dig into the configuration.

Profiles and Configuration

Most aspects of the appearance (colors, prompt, spacing between lines, etc.) and behavior of the IPython and Jupyter environments are configurable through an extensive configuration system. Here are some things you can do via configuration:

- Change the color scheme
- Change how the input and output prompts look, or remove the blank line after Out and before the next In prompt
- Execute an arbitrary list of Python statements (e.g., imports that you use all the time or anything else you want to happen each time you launch IPython)
- Enable always-on IPython extensions, like the %lprun magic in line_profiler
- Enable Jupyter extensions
- Define your own magics or system aliases

Configurations for the IPython shell are specified in special *ipython_config.py* files, which are usually found in the *.ipython/* directory in your user home directory. Configuration is performed based on a particular *profile*. When you start IPython normally, you load up, by default, the *default profile*, stored in the *profile_default* directory. Thus, on my Linux OS, the full path to my default IPython configuration file is:

```
/home/wesm/.ipython/profile_default/ipython_config.py
```

To initialize this file on your system, run this in the terminal:

```
ipython profile create default
```

I'll spare you the complete details of what's in this file. Fortunately, it has comments describing what each configuration option is for, so I will leave it to the reader to tinker and customize. One additional useful feature is that it's possible to have *multiple profiles*. Suppose you wanted to have an alternative IPython configuration tailored for a particular application or project. Creating a new profile involves typing the following:

```
ipython profile create secret_project
```

Once you've done this, edit the config files in the newly created *profile_secret_project* directory and then launch IPython, like so:

```
$ ipython --profile=secret_project
Python 3.8.0 | packaged by conda-forge | (default, Nov 22 2019, 19:11:19)
Type 'copyright', 'credits' or 'license' for more information
IPython 7.22.0 -- An enhanced Interactive Python. Type '?' for help.

IPython profile: secret_project
```

As always, the online IPython documentation is an excellent resource for more on profiles and configuration.

Configuration for Jupyter works a little differently because you can use its notebooks with languages other than Python. To create an analogous Jupyter config file, run:

```
jupyter notebook --generate-config
```

This writes a default config file to the *.jupyter/jupyter_notebook_config.py* directory in your home directory. After editing this to suit your needs, you may rename it to a different file, like:

```
$ mv ~/.jupyter/jupyter_notebook_config.py ~/.jupyter/my_custom_config.py
```

When launching Jupyter, you can then add the --config argument:

```
jupyter notebook --config=~/.jupyter/my_custom_config.py
```

B.8 Conclusion

As you work through the code examples in this book and grow your skills as a Python programmer, I encourage you to keep learning about the IPython and Jupyter ecosystems. Since these projects have been designed to assist user productivity, you may discover tools that enable you to do your work more easily than using the Python language and its computational libraries by themselves.

You can also find a wealth of interesting Jupyter notebooks on the nbviewer website (*https://nbviewer.jupyter.org*).

Index

---

writelines() to a file, 79
writing CSV files, 184
writing data to a file
    binary data
        Excel format, 195
        HDF5 format, 504
        memory-mapped files, 503
        ndarrays saved, 116
        pickle format, 193
        pickle format caution, 193
        plots saved to files, 296
    text data
        CSV files, 184
        JSON data, 189
        missing data, 184

    other delimited format, 187
    subset of columns, 185

X

xlim() (matplotlib), 290
XML file format, 189
    reading, 190

Y

yield in a function, 71

Z

zip files of datasets on GitHub, 15
zip() for list of tuples, 62

About the Author

Wes McKinney is a Nashville-based software developer and entrepreneur. After finishing his undergraduate degree in mathematics at MIT in 2007, he went on to do quantitative finance work at AQR Capital Management in Greenwich, CT. Frustrated by cumbersome data analysis tools, he learned Python and started building what would later become the pandas project. He's now an active member of the Python data community and is an advocate for the use of Python in data analysis, finance, and statistical computing applications.

Wes was later the cofounder and CEO of DataPad, whose technology assets and team were acquired by Cloudera in 2014. He has since become involved in big data technology, joining the Project Management Committees for the Apache Arrow and Apache Parquet projects in the Apache Software Foundation. In 2018, he founded Ursa Labs, a not-for-profit organization focused on Apache Arrow development, in partnership with RStudio and Two Sigma Investments. In 2021, he cofounded technology startup Voltron Data, where he currently works as the Chief Technology Officer.

Colophon

The animal on the cover of *Python for Data Analysis* is a golden-tailed, or pen-tailed, tree shrew (*Ptilocercus lowii*). The golden-tailed tree shrew is the only one of its species in the genus *Ptilocercus* and family *Ptilocercidae*; all the other tree shrews are of the family *Tupaiidae*. Tree shrews are identified by their long tails and soft red-brown fur. As nicknamed, the golden-tailed tree shrew has a tail that resembles the feather on a quill pen. Tree shrews are omnivores, feeding primarily on insects, fruit, seeds, and small vertebrates.

Found predominantly in Indonesia, Malaysia, and Thailand, these wild mammals are known for their chronic consumption of alcohol. Malaysian tree shrews were found to spend several hours consuming the naturally fermented nectar of the bertam palm, equalling about 10 to 12 glasses of wine with 3.8% alcohol content. Despite this, no golden-tailed tree shrew has ever been intoxicated, thanks largely to their impressive ability to break down ethanol, which includes metabolizing the alcohol in a way not used by humans. Also more impressive than any of their mammal counterparts, including humans, is their brain-to-body mass ratio.

Despite its name, the golden-tailed shrew is not a true shrew; instead it is more closely related to primates. Because of their close relation, tree shrews have become an alternative to primates in medical experimentation for myopia, psychosocial stress, and hepatitis.

The cover image is from *Cassell's Natural History*. The cover fonts are URW Typewriter and Guardian Sans. The text font is Adobe Minion Pro; the heading font is Adobe Myriad Condensed; and the code font is Dalton Maag's Ubuntu Mono.

Printed in the USA
CPSIA information can be obtained
at www.ICGtesting.com
JSHW052349100624
64547JS00024B/141